Traveller's Language Guide German

NEW 2003

by
Rupert Livesey

Ernst Klett Sprachen
Barcelona · Budapest · London · Posen · Sofia · Stuttgart

Bildquellen
Bundesverband Selbsthilfe Körperbehinderter, Krautheim: 77;
Cycleurope, Bergisch-Gladbach: 60; Deutsche Telekom AG, Bonn:
181; Fordwerke AG: 58; H. Geißel, Stuttgart: 9, 15, 49, 83, 121,
139, 145; Ifa, Stuttgart: 19, 129; U. Messelhäuser, Salem: 73;
Österreich Werbung, Frankfurt/M. (L. Hirnsl): 93; G. Reinboth, Stutt-
gart: 31; Wolpert Fotodesign, Stuttgart: 41, 104–110, 165, 167
Umschlag: Getty Images/Imagebank (Werner Bokelberg; Werner
Dietrich); Getty Images/Stone (Rohan)

PONS Traveller's Language Guide German

by Rupert Livesey, London

Based on PONS Traveller's Language Guide German, 2000
by William Parks
Phonetic transcriptions: Michael Thiergart, Leverkusen

second edition, 2003 (1,01)
© Ernst Klett Sprachen GmbH, Stuttgart 2003
All rights reserved

Internet: www.pons.de
E-Mail: info@pons.de

Editor: Barbara Pflüger, Stuttgart
Project manager: Andrea Ender, Stuttgart
Cover: Ira Häußler, Stuttgart; Erwin Poell, Heidelberg
Layout and composition: Fotosatz Kaufmann, Stuttgart
Repro: Günther Piltz, Stuttgart
Printed in Italy at Legoprint S. a. P., Lavis (TN)

ISBN 3-12-518282-4

Vowels		
phonetic	sound in English	in German
[a]	short 'a' – somewhere between 'fan' and 'fun'	danke, Land
[aː]	'ar'/'ah' - as in 'hard', 'calm'	Abend
[ɐ]	somewhere between 'er' and 'air'	Vater
[ɛ]	'e' – as in 'net'	wenn
[ɛː]	somewhere between the vowel sound in 'fay' and 'fair'	fährt, spät
[eː]	close to the long 'a' in 'bathe'	geht
[ə]	like first syllable of 'alive'	bitte, viele
[ɪ]	'i' – as in 'fit'	mit
[iː]	'ee' – as in 'seen', 'deal'	Ziel
[ɔ]	short 'o' – as in 'hot'	Gott
[oː]	somewhere between 'loan' and 'lawn'	Lohn
[ʊ]	as in 'put', 'look'	Mutter
[uː]	as in 'fool', 'rule'	Stuhl, Fuß

Special German vowels		
[œ]	as in 'Kent', but with rounded "kissing" lips	könnte
[øː]	almost as in 'bird', 'learn'	schön
[y]	as in 'fill', with "kissing" lips	füllen
[yː]	as in 'feel', with "kissing" lips	fühlen

Diphthongs		
[aɪ]	as in 'by'	bei
[aʊ]	as in 'house'	Haus
[ɔɪ]	as in 'boy'	neu

Consonants		
[b]	as in 'ball'	Ball
[ç]	the 'h' sound at the beginning of 'hymn' or 'humour'	mich, zwanzig, Honig
[d]	as in 'down'	danke
[f]	as in 'fine'	fein
[g]	as in 'give' (never as in 'George')	geben
[h]	as in 'house'	Haus
[j]	the 'y' sound at the beginning of 'yes'	ja
[k]	as in 'kindly'	Kind

[l]	as in 'love'	Liebe
[m]	as in 'mister'	Mädchen
[n]	as in 'no'	nein
[ŋ]	the 'ng' sound as in 'longing'	lang
[p]	as in 'pair'	Paar
[ʀ]	as in French or Scottish English	warum
[s]	as in 'missing'	missen, Maß
[ʃ]	'sh' - as in 'show'	schon, Stein
[t]	as in 'table'	Tisch
[v]	as in 'very'	wo
[x]	as in 'Loch (Ness)'	Loch
[z]	as in 'zero'	sehr
[ʒ]	'zh' - as in 'massage', 'treasure', 'Zhivago'	Massage
[ts]	as in 'cats', 'its'	Zeit, Blitz
[tʃ]	'ch' – as in 'check'	deutsch
	Other symbols:	
[']	main stress	
[‚]	secondary stress	
[ː]	long vowel	
[ʔ]	glottal stop	

More detailed information about German pronunciation may be found at "A short guide to German pronunciation" on page 202.

The alphabet

A	a	[aː]	J	j	[jot]	S	s	[ɛs]
B	b	[beː]	K	k	[kaː]	T	t	[teː]
C	c	[tseː]	L	l	[ɛl]	U	u	[uː]
D	d	[deː]	M	m	[ɛm]	V	v	[fau]
E	e	[eː]	N	n	[ɛn]	W	w	[veː]
F	f	[ɛf]	O	o	[oː]	X	x	[iks]
G	g	[geː]	P	p	[peː]	Y	y	[ʔˈʏpzilɔn]
H	h	[haː]	Q	q	[kuː]	Z	z	[tsɛt]
I	i	[iː]	R	r	[ɛr]			

Abbreviations

adj	Adjektiv, Eigenschaftswort	adjective
adv	Adverb, Umstandswort	adverb
conj	Konjunktion, Bindewort	conjunction
el	Elektrotechnik, Elektrizität	electricity
f	Femininum, weiblich	feminine gender

fam	Umgangssprache, familiär	familiar, colloquial
fig	bildlich, übertragen	figurative
m	Maskulinum, männlich	masculine gender
n	Neutrum, sächlich	neuter gender
pl	Plural, Mehrzahl	plural
poss prn	Possessivpronomen, besitzanzeigendes Fürwort	possessive pronoun
prp	Präposition, Verhältniswort	preposition
rel	kirchlich, geistlich	religious
sing	Singular, Einzahl	singular
s.o.	jemand	someone
s.th.	etwas	something
tele	Telekommunikation	telecommunications
vb	Verb, Zeitwort	verb

Common abbreviations

A	Österreich	Austria
ADAC	Allgemeiner deutscher Automobilclub	German motoring association
BRD	Bundesrepublik Deutschland	Federal Republic of Germany
bzw.	beziehungsweise	or, respectively
°C	(Grad) Celsius	(degrees) Celsius/Centigrade
CH	Schweiz (Helvetia)	Switzerland
CHF	Schweizer Franken	Swiss francs
D	Deutschland	Germany
DB	Deutsche Bahn	German railways
etw.	etwas	something
EU	Europäische Union	European Union
H	Haltestelle	bus or tram stop
jdm.	jemandem	for, to someone
jdn.	jemand	someone
Jh.	Jahrhundert	century
JH	Jugendherberge	youth hostel
n. Chr.	nach Christus	AD
ÖBB	Österreichische Bundesbahnen	Austrian railways
PKW	Personenkraftwagen	car/auto
PS	Pferdestärke	horsepower
s.	siehe	see
SB	Selbstbedienung	self-service
SBB	Schweizerische Bundesbahnen	Swiss railways
Std.	Stunde	hour
Str.	Straße	street
StVO	Straßenverkehrsordnung	traffic regulations
tgl.	täglich	daily
v. Chr.	vor Christus	BC
z. B.	zum Beispiel	e.g.

Different countries,
different customs

Intercultural Tips

General

German is spoken not only in Germany but also in Austria and Switzerland. There are, however, numerous differences. In general, people in Austria and Switzerland speak more slowly than they do in Germany; their intonation is softer, so that it is sometimes difficult to differentiate between a 'b' and a 'p'. Only the context would show whether an Austrian was talking about a cake or a case when (s)he said 'Gepäck'.

In contrast to German and Austrian regional dialects, Swiss German is treated as a separate language and is spoken on TV and radio, and at school. Some words are derived from French, although stress is often placed on the first syllable of a word. Like the Germans, the Swiss also use a lot of English words, especially those for sport, e.g. 'goal' instead of 'Tor', or 'corner' instead of 'Eckball'.

There is no 'ß' in Swiss German; all words that are written with 'ß' in German – even after the recent spelling reforms – are written with 'ss' in Swiss German: e.g. 'Grüsse' instead of 'Grüße', or 'Füsse' instead of 'Füße'.

Some nouns in Swiss German are also a different gender to their counterparts in German: thus the Swiss say 'der Butter' and 'das Tram'.

Forms of address

Until you become closely acquainted, you should use the formal 'Sie' when speaking to an adult. On meeting someone for the first time, it is usual to shake hands and say your surname; only when you have got to know each other well and have exchanged first names, should you use the informal 'du'. Between children and young people it is normal to use 'du'. A short handshake is also common when meeting up with someone, and young people often give each other a kiss on the cheek.

In Austria it is normal for work colleagues and people of the same age to use 'du' to each other and, especially in country areas, 'du' is sometimes even used between strangers.

Although 'Fräulein' ('Miss') is no longer used as a form of address in Germany, it is still fairly common in Austria. In Vienna, women can expect to be addressed as 'Gnädige Frau', usually shortened to 'Gnä Frau', meaning 'madam'.

Titles are important in Germany and Austria. For example, someone with a doctorate (PhD) would be addressed as 'Frau/Herr Doktor'. Titles are less important in Switzerland.

Greetings

The most general form of greeting in German-speaking countries is **'Guten Tag'** or the more informal **'Hallo'**; in the morning you could say **'Guten Morgen'**, in the afternoon **'Guten Tag'** (**not** *'Guten Nachmittag'*) and in the evening **'Guten Abend'**. In southern Germany and Austria it is common to hear **'Grüß Gott'**, and in northern Germany **'Moin, Moin!'**, both of which just mean *'Hello!'*
If you know someone well, you could say **'Grüß dich!'** and then **'Wie geht's?'**, meaning *'How are things?'* or *'How are you doing?'*; more formally, you would use **'Wie geht es Ihnen/dir?'**, meaning *'How are you?'* In reply, you could say **'Danke, gut. Und Ihnen/dir?'** = *'Fine, thanks. And you?'*
The Swiss greet each other with **'Grüezi'**, or more informally **'Hoi'** or **'Sali'**. In Austria they say **'Servus'** or more rarely **'Habe die Ehre'**.

Farewells

The most common way of saying goodbye is **'Auf Wiedersehen!'** or informally **'Tschüs(s)'** or **'Mach's gut!'** = *'See you!'*, or **'Bis morgen'** = *'See you tomorrow'*. Among friends you could hear the Italian **'Ciao'**, and on parting late at night, you might also say **'Gute Nacht!'**
In Austria and parts of Bavaria, rather than **'Tschüs(s)'**, you are likely to hear **'Pfiat' di'** (which roughly means *'May God be with you'*). In Switzerland they say **'Auf Wiederluege'** or **'Adieu'**.

Please and Thank You

In Germany it is not nearly as common as in the UK and the US to use *'please'* and *'thank you'*, so do not take it as a sign of impoliteness or curtness if you do not hear a **'bitte'** or **'danke'** where you might expect to hear one in English. It is common in Germany, however, to reply to someone who says *'thank you'* to you. So if someone says **'Vielen Dank'** or **'Danke schön'**, you could reply **'Bitte schön'** or **'Bitte sehr'** or **'Gern geschehen'** = *'Not at all'* or *'You're welcome'* or *'It's a pleasure/My pleasure'*. In Austria you reply **'Gerne'**. A Swiss person is more likely to say **'Merci'** or **'Merci vielmals'** rather than **'Danke'**.

Mealtimes

At mealtimes it is common to say **'Guten Appetit!'** or **'Mahlzeit!'** and to reply **'Danke, gleichfalls!'** = *'Thank you, and the same to you!'* As in the UK, there are numerous expressions for *'Cheers!'* when having a drink with someone, but the most common is **'Prost!'** or more formally **'Zum Wohl!'**

In Switzerland, you wish each other '**Guten Appetit!**' or '**En Guete**'. Breakfast is called '**Morgenessen**' or '**Zmorge**', lunch is '**Zmittag**' and dinner/supper is '**Nachtessen**' or '**Znacht**'.

Telephone

When answering the telephone in Germany it is usual to give your surname or to say '**Hallo**' or '**Ja, bitte?**' if you prefer to stay anonymous – rather than to state your phone number. When saying goodbye on the phone, you say '**(Auf) Wiederhören**' rather than '**(Auf) Wiedersehen**'.

Numbers

To make a clear distinction between 1 and 7, Germans put a short horizontal line through the stem of the seven. One billion (1.000.000.000: a thousand million) = '**eine Milliarde**' in German; '**eine Billion**' in German = '*one trillion*' in English (= a million million). Decimal points are written with a comma in German: '**3,14**' and you should say: '**drei Komma eins vier**' although it is also common to hear '**drei Komma vierzehn**'.

Time

Use of the 24-hour clock is widespread, but beware! – '**halb zwei**' does <u>NOT</u> mean '*half two*' but '*half past one*'. In southern Germany you could also hear '**viertel zwei**' = '*(a) quarter past one*' or '**drei viertel zwei**' = '*(a) quarter to two*'.

Speed limits

The speed limit on motorways ('**Autobahnen**') in Switzerland is 120 km/h (75 mph) and in Austria 130 km/h. Although there is no official speed limit on German motorways, there are numerous places (such as exits and interchanges) where speed <u>is</u> restricted and these are often quite strictly controlled. In built-up areas the speed limit is 50 km/h (c. 30 mph) and in residential 'housing zones' actual walking speed.
Interspersed with the motorway service stations ('**Raststätte**'), you will also find numerous places to pull off and take a break ('**Rastplatz**').

Stamps

In Germany, the basic price of a stamp for a letter or postcard to anywhere in the EU is the same as the price within Germany.

School

Most schoolchildren wear a satchel or rucksack (for older children) to school; pupils do not wear a school uniform and there are usually no lessons in the afternoons. Those pupils who perform extremely poorly and do not achieve the required marks at the end of the year have to stay down a year.

Military Service

A system of compulsory military service operates in Germany. Every young man must do either 9 months' military service or, if they object on conscientious grounds, 10 months' community service, '**der Zivildienst**'.

Bars/Restaurants

Buying a round of drinks is not common practice in Germany. Drinks are brought directly to your table and a mark made on your coaster or beer mat. At the end of the evening these marks are counted up and you are asked if you want to pay '**zusammen**' (all together) or '**getrennt**' (individually). Tipping is normal, but in smaller amounts than in the UK; more than 10% of the bill would be considered excessive unless the service had been absolutely wonderful.

In the wine-growing regions of Austria you are likely to find a '**Heurige**', an inn selling new local wine, accompanied by a '**Jause**' (snack) or '**Hausmannskost**' (pub grub). In Switzerland, a pub is called a '**Beiz**'; the waitress is called a '**Serviertochter**' and you can order such things as a '**Panaschee**' (shandy), a '**Stange**' (small beer) or a '**Jus**' (fruit juice). The phrase '**à discrétion**' on a menu means that you can help yourself to as much as you like for a set price.

Tea

Tea in Germany is invariably made with a teabag and is very weak for most English tastes. It is also served without milk but occasionally with lemon. It is far more common to have '**Kaffee und Kuchen**' (*coffee and cake*) at teatime rather than tea.

Domestic Matters

Expect to pay for plastic bags in supermarkets and in Germany to pay a refundable deposit ('**Pfand**') on all bottles and cans of mineral water, soft drinks and beer. Household rubbish is sorted into sometimes 5 different containers: one for glass, one for paper, one for plastic, foil, cartons and tins, one for organic waste, and one for everything else.

There is a collection for bulky household waste on demand, called 'Sperrmüll', which is simply placed in piles by the roadside. It is quite acceptable to take anything from these piles that takes your fancy – thus are many items recycled rather than just thrown away.

Christmas, New Year & Easter

In German-speaking countries the most important day over Christmas is Christmas Eve ('Heiliger Abend'), during the evening of which most children are allowed to unwrap their presents.
The biggest excuse for a big fireworks party is New Year's Eve ('Silvester[abend]').
The Easter bunny ('Osterhase') comes at Easter and hides brightly decorated hard-boiled eggs (in their shells), chocolate Easter eggs and chocolate bunnies, and other presents round the house and garden for the children to find.

And Finally ...

There are many more dedicated bicycle lanes than in the UK, and some are integrated into the normal pavement – so watch out where you walk, and remember to drive on the right!

Travel preparations

Preparing for a trip ...
Click on www.marcopolo.de to find out more about your destination. In addition to the information contained in the Marco Polo travel guides you'll find the following:
- up to the minute travel information and interesting articles
- regular specials and prize competitions
- miniguides to print out and take with you

Booking a Hotel by Email

Dear Sir or Madam,

I would like to book a single/double/twin-bedded room for 2 nights on the 24 and 25 June. Please let me know if you have any vacancies and the total cost per night (plus dinner).

Yours faithfully,

Sehr geehrte Damen und Herren,

am 24. und 25. Juni benötige ich für zwei Nächte ein Einzel-/ Doppel-/Zweibettzimmer. Bitte teilen mir mit, ob Sie ein Zimmer frei haben und was es pro Nacht (einschließlich Abendessen) kostet.

Mit freundlichen Grüßen

Hiring a Car by Email

Dear Sir / Madam,

I would like to hire a small / mid-range / luxury saloon car / 7-seater people carrier from July 20–25 from Munich Airport. I depart from Frankfurt Airport so wish to leave the car there. Please inform me of your rates and what documents I shall require.

Yours faithfully,

Sehr geehrte Damen und Herren,

für den Zeitraum vom 20.–25. Juli möchte ich am Flughafen München einen Kleinwagen / Mittelklassewagen / eine Luxus-limousine / eine 7-sitzige Großraumlimousine mieten. Ich fliege von Frankfurt ab und möchte deshalb dort den Leihwagen abgeben. Bitte teilen Sie mir Ihre Tarife mit und welche Unter-lagen ich benötige.

Mit freundlichen Grüßen

General enquiries

I am planning to spend my holiday in … . Can you give me details of accommodation in the area?
Ich habe vor, meinen Urlaub in … zu verbringen. Können Sie mir bitte Informationen über Unterkünfte in der Gegend geben? [ˈɪç haːbə ˈfoɐ maɪnn ˈʔuɐlaʊp ʔɪn … tsʊ fɛˈbrɪŋŋ kœnn zi miɐ ˈbɪtə ʔɪnfɔɛmaˈtsjoːnn ˈyːbɐ ˈʔʊntɐkʏnftə ʔɪn dɐ geːgŋt geːbm]

Where is the best place to go on a boating holiday?
Welche Gegend empfiehlt sich für Ferien auf einem Boot? [ˈvɛlçə geːgŋt ʔɛmpˈfiːlt zɪç fyɐ ˈfeːʁɪən ʔaʊf ˌʔaɪnəm ˈboːt]

What sort of accommodation are you looking for?
An welche Art von Unterkunft haben Sie gedacht? [ʔan ˈvɛlçə ʔaːt fɔn ˈʔʊntɐkʊnft haːbm zi gəˈdaxt]

a hotel
ein Hotel [ʔaɪn hoˈtɛl]
guest house
eine Pension [ˌʔaɪnə paŋˈzjoːn]
bed and breakfast
ein Fremdenzimmer [ʔaɪn ˈfʁɛmdntsɪmɐ]
self-catering accommodation
eine Ferienwohnung [ˌʔaɪnə ˈfeːʁɪənˌvoːnʊŋ]

Accommodation enquiries

Hotel – Guest house – Bed & Breakfast

I'd like to stay in a hotel, but nothing too expensive – something in the mid-price range.
Ich suche ein Hotel, jedoch nicht zu teuer – etwas in der mittleren Preislage. [ˈɪç ˈzuːxə ʔaɪn hoˈtɛl jeˈdɔx nɪçt tsʊ ˈtɔje ˈʔɛtvas ʔɪn dɐ ˈmɪtlərən ˈpʁaɪslaːgə]

I'd like to stay in a hotel with a swimming pool / a golf course / tennis courts.
Ich suche ein Hotel mit Hallenbad / Golfplatz / Tennisplätzen. [ˈɪç ˈzuːxə ʔaɪn hoˈtɛl mɪt ˈhalnbaːt / ˈgɔlfplats / ˈtɛnɪsplɛtsn]

Can you recommend a good bed-and-breakfast?
Können Sie mir ein schönes Fremdenzimmer mit Frühstück empfehlen?
[kœnn zi miɐ ʔaɪn ˈʃøːnəs ˈfʁɛmdntsɪmɐ mɪt ˈfʁyːʃtʏk ˈʔɛmpfeːln]

How many people does it sleep?
Für wie viele Leute soll es sein? [fyɐ ˈviː‿fiːlə ˈlɔɪtə zɔl əs ˈzaɪn]

Are dogs allowed?
Sind dort Hunde erlaubt? [zɪnt dɔɐt ˈhʊndə ˈʔeˈlaʊpt]

Self-catering accommodation

I'm looking for a self-catering flat or bungalow.
Ich suche eine Ferienwohnung oder einen Bungalow.
[ˈʔɪç ˈzuːxə ˌʔaɪnə ˈfeːʁɪənˌvoːnʊŋ ˌʔoːdɐ ˌʔaɪnn ˈbʊŋgalo]

Can you recommend a farmhouse, suitable for children?
Können Sie mir einen kinderfreundlichen Ferienbauernhof empfehlen?
[kœnn zi miɐ ˌʔaɪnn ˈkɪndɐˌfʁɔɪntlɪçn ˈfeːʁɪənˌbaʊənhoːf ʔɛmpˈfeːln]

Is there ...?
Gibt es ...? [gɪpt əs]

a baby's cot
ein Kinderbett [ʔaɪn ˈkɪndɐbɛt]

high chair
einen Hochstuhl [ʔaɪnn ˈhoːxʃtuːl]

TV
einen Fernseher [ʔaɪnn ˈfɛɐnzeːɐ]

telephone
ein Telefon [ʔaɪn ˈteːləfoːn]

washing machine
eine Waschmaschine [ˌʔaɪnə ˈvaʃmaˌʃiːnə]

dishwasher
eine Spülmaschine [ˌʔaɪnə ˈʃpyːlmaˌʃiːnə]

microwave
eine Mikrowelle [ˌʔaɪnə ˈmɪkʁoˌvɛlə]

Is electricity included in the price?
Sind die Stromkosten im Preis eingeschlossen?
[zɪnt di ˈʃtʁoːmkɔstn ʔɪm pʁaɪs ˈʔaɪngəʃlɔsn]

Are bed linen and towels provided?
Werden Bettwäsche und Handtücher gestellt?
[veɐdn ˈbɛtvɛʃə ʔʊnt ˈhantyːçɐ gəˈʃtɛlt]

How much deposit do you require and how long in advance?
Wie viel muss ich anzahlen und wann ist die Anzahlung fällig?
[ˈviːˌfiːl mʊs ɪç ˈʔantsaːln ʔʊnt ˈvan ʔɪst di ˈʔantsaːlʊŋ ˈfɛlɪç]

Where and when should I pick up the keys?
Wo und wann kann ich die Schlüssel abholen?
[ˈvoː ʔʊnt ˈvan kan ɪç di ʃlʏsl ˈʔaphoːln]

Camping

I'm looking for a smallish camping site in .... Do you have anywhere you can recommend?
Ich suche einen kleinen Campingplatz in ... Können Sie mir irgend etwas empfehlen? [ˈʔɪç ˈzuːxə ˌʔaɪnn ˈklaɪnn ˈkɛmpɪŋplats ˌʔɪn ... kœnn zi miɐ ˈʔɪʁgn̩t ˌʔɛtvas ʔɛmpˈfeːln]

General

A regular language

For the most part German is very regular in pronunciation. Most words are spoken with stress on the first syllable: *danke, Deutschland.* Important exceptions are words beginning with *ge-, ver-, ent-* (*gegessen, verboten, Entschuldigung* – these are stressed on the second syllable) – and words borrowed from other languages. In general, words borrowed from French and English retain their original pronunciation – to the extent that German speakers can imitate this. Borrowings from English have been increasing explosively for the last half century, particularly in "modern" areas such as computer technology, high-tech, business and entertainment. You will run into countless English words in German; your best bet is simply to rely on your own familiar way of saying these.

Basic phrases

Yes.
Ja. [ja:]

No.
Nein. [naɪn]

Please.
Bitte. ['bɪtə]

Thank you.
Danke! ['daŋkə]

Many thanks! / Thanks a lot!
Vielen Dank! [fiːln daŋk]

Thanks, (and) the same to you!
Danke, gleichfalls! ['daŋkə 'glaɪçfals]

You're welcome! / Not at all!
Bitte! / Gern geschehen! ['bɪtə / 'gɛɐn gə'ʃeːn]

Not at all! / Don't mention it!
Nichts zu danken! ['nɪçts tsʊ 'daŋkn]

Pardon? / Excuse me?
Wie bitte? ['viː bɪtə]

Of course.
Selbstverständlich! [zɛlpstfɐ'ʃtɛntlɪç]

Agreed!
Einverstanden! [ˈʔaɪnfɛʃtandn]

OK!
Okay! [ʔoˈkeː], In Ordnung! [ʔɪn ˈʔɔɐtnʊŋ]

Excuse me.
Verzeihung! [fɐˈtsaɪʊŋ]

Just a minute, please.
Einen Augenblick, bitte. [ˈʔaɪnn ˈʔaʊɡn̩ˈblɪk ˈbɪtə]

Right, that's enough!
Das reicht jetzt! [das ˈʀaɪçt jɛtst]

Help!
Hilfe! [ˈhɪlfə]

Who?
Wer? [veɐ]

What?
Was? [vas]

Which?
Welcher?/Welche?/Welches? [ˈvɛlçɐ/ˈvɛlçə/ˈvɛlçəs]

Where?
Wo? [vo:]

Where is ...? / Where are ...?
Wo ist ...? / Wo sind ...? [vo: ʔɪst .../vo: zɪnt ...]

Why?
Warum? [vaˈʀʊm] / Weshalb? [vɛsˈhalp] / Wozu? [voˈtsu:]

How much? / How many?
Wie viel? / Wie viele?
[vi‿ˈfiːl / vi‿ˈfiːlə]

How long?
Wie lange? [vi‿ˈlaŋə]

When?
Wann? [van]

When? / (At) what time?
Um wie viel Uhr? [ʔʊm ˈviː‿fiːl ˈʔuɐ]

I'd like ...
Ich möchte ... [ʔɪç ˈmœçtə ...]

Is there ...?/Are there ...?
Gibt es ...? [ɡɪpt əs]

0	null	[nʊl]
1	eins	[ʔaɪns]
2	zwei	[tsvaɪ]

> "Zwo" [tsvoː] is sometimes used when speaking to distinguish "zwei" from "drei".

3	drei	[dʀaɪ]
4	vier	[fiɐ]
5	fünf	[fʏnf]
6	sechs	[zɛks]
7	sieben	['ziːbm̩]
8	acht	[axt]
9	neun	[nɔɪn]
10	zehn	[tseːn]
11	elf	[ɛlf]
12	zwölf	[tsvœlf]
13	dreizehn	['dʀaɪtseːn]
14	vierzehn	['fɪrtseːn]
15	fünfzehn	['fʏnftseːn]
16	sechzehn	['zɛçtseːn]
17	siebzehn	['ziːptseːn]
18	achtzehn	['axtseːn]
19	neunzehn	['nɔɪntseːn]
20	zwanzig	['tsvantsɪç]
21	einundzwanzig	['aɪnʊn,tsvantsɪç]
22	zweiundzwanzig	['tsvaɪʊn,tsvantsɪç]
23	dreiundzwanzig	['dʀaɪʊn,tsvantsɪç]
24	vierundzwanzig	['fiɐʊn,tsvantsɪç]
30	dreißig	['dʀaɪsɪç]
40	vierzig	['fɪrtsɪç]
50	fünfzig	['fʏnftsɪç]
60	sechzig	['zɛçtsɪç]
70	siebzig	['ziːptsɪç]
80	achtzig	['axtsɪç]
90	neunzig	['nɔɪntsɪç]
100	(ein)hundert	['(aɪn)hʊndɐt]
101	hundert(und)eins	[,hʊndɐt(ʔʊnt)ˈʔaɪns]
200	zweihundert	['tsvaɪhʊndɐt]
300	dreihundert	['dʀaɪhʊndɐt]
1000	(ein)tausend	[(,aɪn)'taʊznt]
2000	zweitausend	['tsvaɪtaʊznt]
10,000	zehntausend (10.000)	['tseːntaʊznt]

22

100,000	hunderttausend (100.000) ['hʊndɐttaʊznt]
1,000,000	eine Million (1.000.000) [aɪnə mɪ'ljoːn]
first	erster ['eːstɐ]
second	zweiter ['tsvaɪtɐ]
third	dritter ['drɪtɐ]
fourth	vierter ['fiɐtɐ]
fifth	fünfter ['fʏnftɐ]
sixth	sechster ['zɛkstɐ]
seventh	siebter ['ziːptɐ]
eighth	achter ['ʔaxtɐ]
ninth	neunter ['nɔɪntɐ]
tenth	zehnter ['tseːntɐ]
1/2	einhalb [aɪnhalp]
1/3	ein Drittel [aɪn 'drɪtl]
1/4	ein Viertel [aɪn 'fɪrtl]
3/4	drei Viertel ['draɪ 'fɪrtl]
3.5 %	drei Komma fünf Prozent (3,5 %) ['draɪ 'kɔma 'fʏnf pro'tsɛnt]

> Note that for numbers use of comma and point are reversed: "1,200,500 people" becomes "1.200.500 Menschen" and "3.5 percent" becomes "3,5 Prozent".

27 °C	siebenundzwanzig Grad Celsius ['ziːbmʊn,tsvantsɪç graːt 'tsɛlzɪʊs]
–5 °C	minus 5 Grad ['miːnʊs fʏnf graːt]
1999	neunzehnhundertneunundneunzig ['nɔɪnts(e)n,hʊndɐt,nɔɪn(ʊ)n'nɔɪntsɪç]
2003	zweitausenddrei ['tsvaɪtaʊznt'draɪ]
millimetre	der Millimeter [dɐ 'mɪli,meːtɐ]
centimetre	der Zentimeter [dɐ ,tsɛnti'meːtɐ]
metre	der Meter [dɐ 'meːtɐ]
kilometre	der Kilometer [dɐ ,kilo'meːtɐ]
litre	der Liter [dɐ 'liːtɐ]
gram(s)	das Gramm [das gram]
kilogram(s)	das Kilo [das 'kiːlo]
pound(s)	das Pfund [das (p)fʊnt]

23

Weights and measures

All German-speaking countries use the metric system. An inch is about 2.5 centimetres, a metre is a bit more than a yard, a mile is about 1.6 kilometres, and a litre is roughly a quart.

1 Zentimeter (cm)	≅ 0.39 inches
1 Meter (m) = 100 cm	≅ 3.28 feet / 39.3 inches
1 Kilometer (km) = 1000 m	≅ 0.62 miles
1 Liter (l) ['li:tɐ]	≅ 1.75 pints (*UK*)/ 2.11 pints (*US*)/ 0.87 quarts (*UK*)/ 1.05 quarts (*US*)/ 0.22 gallons (*UK*)/ 0.26 gallons (*US*)
1 Gramm (g) ['gʀam]	≅ 0.03 ounces
1 Kilogramm (kg) = 1000 g	≅ 30 ounces / 2 pounds/0.15 stone
1 Zentner = 50 kg ['tsɛntnɐ]	≅ 7.5 stone/ 0.98 hundredweight (*UK*)/ 110 lb. (*US*)

Telling the time

Time

What time is it, please?

Wie viel Uhr ist es bitte? ['vi:_fil ꞌʔuɐ ꞌʔɪst əs 'bɪtə]

It's (exactly/about) ...

Es ist (genau/ungefähr) ... [ꞌʔəs ɪst gəꞌnaʊ/ꞌʔʊngəꞌfɛɐ]

three o'clock.

drei Uhr. [dʀaɪ ꞌʔuɐ]

five past three.

fünf nach drei. [fʏnf nax 'dʀaɪ]

ten past three.

drei Uhr zehn. [dʀaɪ ꞌʔuɐ tseːn]

quarter past three.

Viertel nach drei. ['fɪʀtl nax dʀaɪ]

half past three.

halb vier. [halp fiɐ]

quarter to four.

Viertel vor vier. ['fɪʀtl foɐ fiɐ]

five to four.
fünf vor Vier. [fʏnf fɔɐ fiɐ]
twelve noon.
zwölf Uhr Mittag. [tsvœlf ˀuɐ ˈmɪta:k]
midnight.
Mitternacht. [ˈmɪtɐnaxt]

What time?/When?
Um wie viel Uhr?/Wann? [ˀʊm ˈvi:_fi:l ˀuɐ / van]

At one o'clock.
Um ein Uhr. [ˀʊm ˀaɪn ˀuɐ]

At two o'clock.
Um zwei Uhr. [ˀʊm tsvaɪ ˀuɐ]

At about four o'clock.
Gegen vier Uhr. [ˈge:gn fiɐ ˀuɐ]

In an hour's time
In einer Stunde. [ˀɪn ˀaɪnɐ ˈʃtʊndə]

In two hours' time.
In zwei Stunden. [ˀɪn tsvaɪ ʃtʊndn]

Not before nine a.m.
Nicht vor neun Uhr morgens. [nɪçt foɐ ˈnɔɪn uɐ ˈmɔɐgn̩s]

Between three and four.
Zwischen drei und vier. [ˈtsvɪʃn draɪ ˀʊnt fiɐ]

After eight p.m.
Nach acht Uhr abends/zwanzig Uhr.
[nax ˀaxt uɐ ˀa:bms/ˈtsvantsɪç ˀuɐ]

> Germans like to use the 24 hour time system. 10 a.m. is *zehn Uhr* and 10 p.m. is *zweiundzwanzig Uhr*.

How long?
Wie lange? [vi_ˈlaŋə]

For two hours.
Zwei Stunden (lang). [tsvaɪ ʃtʊndn laŋ]

From ten to eleven.
Von zehn bis elf. [fɔn tse:n bɪs ˀɛlf]

Till five o'clock.
Bis fünf/siebzehn Uhr. [bɪs fʏnf/ˈzi:ptse:n ˀuɐ]

Since when?
Seit wann? [zaɪt ˈvan]

Since eight a.m.
Seit acht Uhr morgens. [zaɪt ˀaxt uɐ ˈmɔɐgn̩s]

For half an hour.
Seit einer halben Stunde. [zaɪt ˈʔaɪnɐ ˈhalbm̩ ˈʃtʊndə]

For a week.
Seit acht Tagen. [zaɪt ʔaxt ˈtaːgn̩]

about noon	gegen Mittag [ˈgeːgn̩ ˈmɪtaːk]
in the afternoon	nachmittags [ˈnaxmɪtaːks]
daily	täglich [ˈtɛːklɪç]
during the day	tagsüber [ˈtaːksʔyːbɐ]
during the morning	vormittags [ˈfoːɐmɪtaːks]
in the evening	abends [ˈʔaːbm̩s]
every day	jeden Tag [ˈjeːdn̩ taːk]
every hour, hourly	stündlich [ˈʃtʏntlɪç]
now and then	ab und zu [ˈʔap ʊn ˈtsuː]
in a fortnight	in 14 (vierzehn) Tagen [ˈʔɪn ˈfɪɐtseːn ˈtaːgn̩]
at lunch time	mittags [ˈmɪtaːks]
last Monday morning	letzten Montagmorgen [ˈlɛtstn̩ moːntaːkˈmɔɐgn̩]
ten minutes ago	vor zehn Minuten [foːɐ tseːn mɪˈnuːtn̩]
in the morning	morgens [ˈmɔɐgn̩s]
never	nie [niː]
next year	nächstes Jahr [ˈnɛːçstəs ˈjaː]
at night	nachts [naxts]
now	jetzt [jɛtst]
on Sunday	am Sonntag [ˈʔam ˈzɔntaːk]
recently	kürzlich [ˈkʏɐtslɪç]
sometimes	manchmal [ˈmançmaːl]
soon	bald [balt]
the day before yesterday	vorgestern [ˈfoːɐgɛstɐn]
the day after tomorrow	übermorgen [ˈʔyːbɐmɔɐgn̩]
this morning/this evening	heute Morgen/heute Abend [ˈhɔɪtə ˈmɔɐgn̩/hɔɪtə ˈʔaːbmt]
this week	diese Woche [ˈdiːzə ˈvɔxə]
today	heute [ˈhɔɪtə]
tomorrow	morgen [ˈmɔɐgn̩]
tomorrow morning/	morgen früh/morgen Abend
tomorrow evening	[ˈmɔɐgn̩ ˈfʁyː/mɔɐgn̩ ˈʔaːbmt]
at the weekend	am Wochenende [ˈʔam ˈvɔxn̩ʔɛndə]
yesterday	gestern [ˈgɛstɐn]

The Days of the Week

Monday	Montag	['moːntaːk]
Tuesday	Dienstag	['diːnstaːk]
Wednesday	Mittwoch	['mɪtvɔx]
Thursday	Donnerstag	['dɔnestaːk]
Friday	Freitag	['fʀaɪtaːk]
Saturday	*(southern Germany)* Samstag	['zamstaːk]
	(northern Germany) Sonnabend	
	['zɔnaːbmt]	
Sunday	Sonntag	['zɔntaːk]

The Months of the Year

January	Januar ['janʊaː], *(Austria)* Jänner	['jɛnɐ]
February	Februar	['feːbʀʊaː]
March	März	[mɛɛts]
April	April	[ʔaˈpʀɪl]
May	Mai	[maɪ]
June	Juni	['juːni]
July	Juli	['juːli]
August	August	[ʔaʊˈɡʊst]
September	September	[zɛpˈtɛmbɐ]
October	Oktober	[ʔɔkˈtoːbɐ]
November	November	[noˈvɛmbɐ]
December	Dezember	[deˈtsɛmbɐ]

The Seasons

spring	der Frühling	[dɐ ˈfʀyːlɪŋ]
summer	der Sommer	[dɐ ˈzɔmɐ]
autumn (*Am* fall)	der Herbst	[dɐ ˈhɛɐpst]
winter	der Winter	[dɐ ˈvɪntɐ]

Holidays

In addition to the holidays mentioned below there are various local religious holidays.

New Year's Day	Neujahr	[nɔɪˈjaː]
Swiss Holiday (2.1.)	Berchtoldstag	['bɛɛçtɔldstaːk]
Epiphany (6.1.)	Erscheinungsfest	[ʔeˈʃaɪnʊŋsfɛst]
Monday before Shrove Tuesday	Rosenmontag [ʀoːznˈmoːntaːk], *(Switzerland)* Fastnachtmontag [ˌfasnaxtˈmoːntaːk]	
Shrove Tuesday	Faschingsdienstag [ˌfaʃɪŋsˈdiːns taːk], Fas(t)nachtdienstag [ˌfasnaxtˈdiːns taːk]	

27

Good Friday	Karfreitag [kaˈfraɪtaːk]
Easter Sunday	Ostersonntag [ˌʔoːsteˈzɔntaːk]
Easter Monday	Ostermontag [ˌʔoːsteˈmoːntaːk]
Labour Day (GB)	Tag der Arbeit (Erster Mai) [taːk de ˈʔaʀbaɪt (ˈʔeeste ˈmaɪ)]
Whit Sunday/Pentecost	Pfingstsonntag [ˌpfɪŋstˈzɔntaːk]
Whit Monday	Pfingstmontag [ˌpfɪŋstˈmoːntaːk]
Ascension Day	Christi Himmelfahrt [ˌkʀɪsti ˈhɪmlˌfaːt]
Corpus Christi	Fronleichnam [fʀɔnˈlaɪçnaːm]
German Unification Day . . (October 3rd)	Tag der deutschen Einheit [taːk de dɔɪtʃn ˈaɪnhaɪt]
Austrian National Day	26. (Sechsundzwanzigster) Oktober [ˈzɛksʊnˌtsvantsɪçste ˈɔkˈtoːbe]
Swiss National Day	Erster August [ˈʔeeste ˈʔaʊˈɡʊst]
All Saints (Nov. 1st)	Allerheiligen [ˈʔaleˈhaɪlɪɡn]
Christmas Eve	Heiliger Abend [ˈhaɪlɪɡe ˈʔaːbmt], Heiligabend [ˌhaɪlɪç ˈʔaːbmt]
Christmas	Weihnachten [ˈvaɪnaxtn]
Christmas Day	Erster Weihnachts(feier)tag [ˈʔeeste ˈvaɪnaxtsˌ(faɪe)taːk]
Boxing Day	Zweiter Weihnachts(feier)tag [ˈtsvaɪte ˈvaɪnaxtsˌ(faɪe)taːk]
New Year's Eve	Silvester [sɪlˈvɛste]

The date

Can you tell me what the date today is, please?
Können Sie mir bitte sagen, den Wievielten wir heute haben?
·[kœnn zi mie ˈbɪtə zaːɡn den ˈviːfiːltn vie ˌhɔɪtə ˈhaːbm]

Today's the fourth of August.
Heute ist der vierte August. [ˈhɔɪtə ˈʔɪst de ˈfiɐtə ˈʔaʊˈɡʊst]

The weather

What wonderful/dreadful weather!
Was für ein herrliches/schreckliches Wetter!
[ˈvas fye ˈʔaɪn ˈhɛelɪçəs/ˈʃʀɛklɪçəs vɛtə]

It's very cold/hot/humid.
Es ist sehr kalt/heiß/schwül. [ˈʔəs ɪst zee kalt/haɪs/ʃvyːl]

It's foggy/windy..
Es ist neblig/windig. [ˈʔəs ɪst ˈneːblɪç/ˈvɪndɪç]

It's going to stay fine.
Es bleibt schön. [ˈʔəs blaɪpt ʃøːn]

It's going to get warmer/colder.
Es wird wärmer/kälter. [ˀəs vɪʁt 'vɛːmɐ/'kɛltɐ]

It's going to rain/snow.
Es wird regnen/schneien. [ˀəs vɪʁt 'ʁeːknən/'ʃnaɪən]

It's blowing a gale.
Ein Sturm tobt. [ˀaɪn ʃtʊɐm toːpt]

The roads are icy.
Die Straßen sind glatt. [di 'ʃtʁaːsn zɪnt 'glat]

Visibility is only 20 metres.
Die Sicht beträgt nur zwanzig Meter.
[di 'zɪçt bəˈtʁɛkt nuɐ 'tsvantsɪç 'meːtɐ]

You need snow chains.
Schneeketten sind erforderlich. ['ʃneːkɛtn zɪnt ˀɛ'fˀɔɐdelɪç]

air	die Luft [di lʊft]
black ice	das Glatteis [das 'glataɪs]
changeable	wechselhaft ['vɛkslhaft]
cloud	die Wolke [di 'vɔlkə]
cloudy	bewölkt [bə'vœlkt]
cold	kalt [kalt]
fog	der Nebel [dɐ 'neːbl]
frost	der Frost [dɐ fʁɔst]
gale	der Sturm [dɐ ʃtʊɐm]
gust of wind	die Bö [di bøː]
hail(stones)	der Hagel [dɐ 'haːgl]
heat	die Hitze [di 'hɪtsə]
high tide	die Flut [di fluːt]
hot	heiß [haɪs]
humid	schwül [ʃvyːl]
ice	das Eis [das ˀaɪs]
lightning	der Blitz [dɐ blɪts]
low tide	die Ebbe [di ˀɛbə]
rain	der Regen [dɐ 'ʁeːgn]
rainy	regnerisch ['ʁeːknəʁɪʃ]
shower	der Regenschauer [dɐ 'ʁeːgnʃaʊɐ]
snow	der Schnee [dɐ ʃneː]
storm	der Sturm [dɐ ʃtʊɐm]
sun	die Sonne [di 'zɔnə]
sunny	sonnig ['zɔnɪç]
temperature	die Temperatur [di ˌtɛmpəʁa'tuɐ]
thunder	der Donner [dɐ 'dɔnɐ]
warm	warm [vaːm]
weather forecast	die Wettervorhersage [di 'vɛtɐfoˌheːzaːgə]
weather report	der Wetterbericht [dɐ 'vɛtɐbəʁɪçt]

wet	nass [nas]
wind	der Wind [dɐ vɪnt]
wind-force	die Windstärke [di ˈvɪntʃtɛɐkə]

Colours

beige	beige [beːʃ]
black	schwarz [ʃvaːts]
blue	blau [blaʊ]
brown	braun [bʀaʊn]
coloured	farbig [ˈfaʀbɪç]
green	grün [gʀyːn]
grey	grau [gʀaʊ]
pink	rosa [ˈʀoːza]
plain	einfarbig [ˈʔaɪnfaʀbɪç]
purple	lila [ˈliːla]
red	rot [ʀoːt]
turquoise	türkisfarben [tʏɐˈkiːsfaːbm̩]
white	weiß [vaɪs]
yellow	gelb [gɛlp]

dark blue/dark green	dunkelblau [dʊŋklˈblaʊ]/ dunkelgrün [dʊŋklˈgʀyːn]
light blue/light green	hellblau [hɛlˈblaʊ]/hellgrün [hɛlˈgʀyːn]

Personal contact

> **Two "yous"**
> Germans have two ways of saying "you", depending on their
> relationship to the person they are talking to. With some people
> – members of the family, children and good friends – they are
> on familiar terms, use first names and the word *du* [duː]. Other
> people they address using last names (surnames); with these
> people they have a formal relationship and use the word *Sie* [ziː].

Greetings and farewells

Saying hello

Good morning!
Guten Morgen! [ˈguːtn̩ ˈmɔɐɡn̩]

Good afternoon!
Guten Tag! [ˈguːtn̩ taːk]

Good evening!
Guten Abend! [ˈguːtn̩ ˈaːbm̩t]

Hello!/Hi!
Hallo!/Grüß dich! [ˈhalo:/ˈɡʀyːs dɪç]

What's your name? (*formal*) / (*familiar*)
Wie ist Ihr Name? [viː ʔɪst ʔiɐ ˈnaːmə] / **Wie heißt du?** [viː ˈhaist du]

My name's ...
Mein Name ist ... [main ˈnaːmə ʔɪst]

I'm called ...
Ich heiße ... [ʔɪç ˈhaisə]

How are you? (*formal*) / (*familiar*)
Wie geht es Ihnen? [viː ˈɡeːt əs ʔiːnn] / **Wie geht's?** [viː ˈɡeːts]

Fine thanks. And you? (*formal*) / (*familiar*)
Danke. Und Ihnen/dir? [ˈdaŋkə. ʔʊnt ˈdiɐ]

Introductions

May I introduce you?
Darf ich bekannt machen? [ˈdaːf ɪç bəˈkant maxn̩]

This is ...
Das ist ... [das ʔɪst]

  Mrs/Ms ...
  Frau ... [fʀaʊ ...]

  Mr ...
  Herr ... [hɛɐ ...]

my husband.
mein Mann. [maɪn 'man]

my wife.
meine Frau. [ˌmaɪnə 'fʀaʊ]

my son.
mein Sohn. [maɪn 'zoːn]

my daughter.
meine Tochter. [ˌmaɪnə 'tɔxtɐ]

my girlfriend.
meine Freundin. [ˌmaɪnə 'fʀɔɪndɪn]

my boyfriend.
mein Freund. [maɪn 'fʀɔɪnt]

Nice to meet you.
Es freut mich, Sie kennen zu lernen.
[ʔəs 'fʀɔɪt mɪç zi 'kɛnn tsʊ lɛʀnn]

Saying goodbye

Auf Wiedersehen is the German way of saying "goodbye". But you will often hear it shortened to *Wiederseh'n* ['viːdezeːn]. Less formal variations are *Ciao* [tʃaʊ] (from Italian) or *Tschüs* [tʃy(ː)s]. Use *bis dann* [bɪs 'dan] to say "see you later".

Goodbye!
Auf Wiedersehen! [ʔaʊf 'viːdezeːn]

See you soon!
Bis bald! [bɪs 'balt]

See you later!
Bis später! [bɪ‿'ʃpɛːtɐ]

See you tomorrow!
Bis morgen! [bɪs 'mɔɐgn]

All the best!
Mach's gut! [maxs 'guːt]

See you soon!
Bis bald! [bɪs 'balt]

Good night!
Gute Nacht! [ˌguːtə 'naxt]

Cheerio! Bye-bye!
Tschüs! [tʃyːs]

Have a good trip!
Gute Reise! [ˌguːtə 'ʀaɪzə]

Requesting and thanking

Please.
Bitte. ['bɪtə]

Yes, please.
Ja, bitte. [ja: 'bɪtə]

Thank you.
Danke. ['daŋkə]

Thank you very much.
Vielen Dank. [fi:ln 'daŋk]

You're welcome.
Bitte sehr. ['bɪtə zeɐ]

No, thank you.
Nein, danke. [naɪn 'daŋkə]

Yes, thank you.
Danke, sehr gern. ['daŋkə zeɐ 'gɛɐn]

That's very kind, thank you.
Das ist nett, danke. [das ɪst 'nɛt 'daŋkə]

Don't mention it.
Gern geschehen. ['gɛɐn gə'ʃe:n]

Do you mind?
Gestatten Sie? [gə'ʃtatn zi]

Please forgive the interruption.
Entschuldigen Sie bitte die Störung.
[ʔɛnt'ʃʊldɪgn zi 'bɪtə di 'ʃtø:ʀʊŋ]

Excuse me, may I ask you something?
Entschuldigen Sie bitte, dürfte ich Sie etwas fragen?
[ʔɛnt'ʃʊldɪgn zi 'bɪtə 'dʏɐftə ʔɪç zi ˌʔɛtvas 'fʀa:gn]

Can /Could I ask you a favour?
Darf /Dürfte ich Sie um einen Gefallen bitten?
[da:f/'dʏɐftə ʔɪç zi ʊm ʔaɪnn gə'faln bɪtn]

Would you be so kind as to ...?
Würden Sie bitte so freundlich sein und ...?
['vʏɐdn zi 'bɪtə zo 'fʀɔɪntlɪç zaɪn ʔunt ...]

Thank you very much /Thanks a million, you've been a great help.
Vielen /Tausend Dank, Sie haben mir sehr geholfen. [fi:ln/'taʊznt 'daŋk zi ha:bm miɐ 'zeɐ gə'hɔlfn]

That was very kind of you.
Das war sehr lieb von Ihnen. [das va: zeɐ li:p fɔn ʔi:nn]

Can you tell me..., please?
Können Sie mir bitte sagen, ...? [kœnn zi miɐ 'bɪtə za:gn]

Can you recommend ...?
Können Sie mir bitte ... empfehlen?
[kœnn zi miɐ 'bɪtə ... ʔɛmp'fe:ln]

Could you help me, please?
Können Sie mir bitte helfen? ['kœnn zi miɐ 'bɪtə 'hɛlfn]

> Every *danke* should be followed up by the response *bitte* or
> *gerne* in Austria. This may seem almost like a ritual, but it's a
> sign of elementary politeness. *Bitte* has basically two meanings:
> (1) "You're welcome" when used after *danke*; (2) "please"
> when added to requests such as above, *Können Sie mir bitte
> helfen?* But be careful: if someone offers you something and
> you reply with *danke*, this will be interpreted as meaning "no,
> thank you". If you want to accept something, say *ja, bitte*.

Apologies

I'm sorry!
Entschuldigung! [ʔɛnt'ʃʊldɪgʊŋ]

I'm very sorry!
Das tut mir sehr Leid! [das tu:t miɐ zeɐ 'laɪt]

I didn't mean it.
Es war nicht so gemeint. [ʔəs va: nɪçt zo gə'maɪnt]

That's all right! / It doesn't matter!
Keine Ursache! / Macht nichts! ['kaɪnə ʔuɐzaxə / maxt nɪçts]

Congratulations/Best wishes

Congratulations!
Herzlichen Glückwunsch! [ˌhɛɐtslɪçn 'glʏkvʊnʃ]

All the best!
Alles Gute! [ˌʔaləs 'gu:tə]

Good luck!
Viel Glück! [fi:l glʏk] / Viel Erfolg! [fi:l ʔe'fɔlk]

I'll keep my fingers crossed for you.
Ich drück' Ihnen die Daumen. [ʔɪç 'dʀʏk ʔi:nn di 'daʊmm]

Bless you! *(after sneezing)*
Gesundheit! [gə'zʊnthaɪt]

Get well soon!
Gute Besserung! [ˌgu:tə 'bɛsəʀʊŋ]

Agreement

Good.
Gut. [guːt]

Right.
Richtig. [ˈʀɪçtɪç]

Agreed! / It's a deal!
Einverstanden! / Abgemacht! [ˈʔaɪnfɛʃtandn / ˈʔapɡəmaxt]

That's all right!
Geht in Ordnung! [geːt ɪn ˈʔɔɛtnʊŋ]

Okay! / O.K.! / OK
Okay! / o.k.! / O.K.! [ˈʔoˈkeː]

Exactly!
Genau! [ɡəˈnaʊ]

Oh!
Ach! [ʔax]

Oh, I see!
Ach, so! [ʔax ˈzoː]

Really?
Wirklich? [ˈvɪʁklɪç]

How interesting!
Interessant! [ˈʔɪntʀəˈsant]

How nice!
Wie schön! [vi ˈʃøːn]

I understand.
Ich verstehe. [ˈʔɪç fɛˈʃteː(ə)]

That's how it is.
So ist es eben. [zoː ˈʔɪst əs ˈʔeːbm]

I entirely agree with you.
Ganz Ihrer Meinung. [ˈɡants ˌʔiːʀɐ ˈmaɪnʊŋ]

That's right.
Das stimmt. [das ʃtɪmt]

I think that's a good idea.
Das finde ich gut. [das fɪndə ˈʔɪç guːt]

With pleasure.
Mit Vergnügen! [mɪt fɛˈɡnyːɡn]

That sounds good to me.
Das hört sich gut an. [das høɛt zɪç ˈguːt an]

Refusal

I don't want to.
Ich will nicht. [ˀɪç ˈvɪl nɪçt]

I don't feel like it.
Dazu habe ich keine Lust. [ˈdaːtsu habə ɪç ˈkaɪnə lʊst]

I can't agree to that.
Damit bin ich nicht einverstanden.
[ˈdaːmɪt bɪn ɪç nɪçt ˀaɪnfɛʃtandn]

That's out of the question.
Das kommt nicht in Frage. [das kɔmt ˈnɪçt ˀɪn ˈfʀaːgə]

Certainly not!/No way!
Auf gar keinen Fall! [ˀaʊf ˈgaː kaɪnn fal]

Count me out!
Ohne mich! [ˌˀoːnə ˈmɪç]

I don't like this at all.
Das gefällt mir gar nicht. [das gəˈfɛlt miɐ ˈgaː nɪçt]

Preferences

I like it.
Das gefällt mir. [das gəˈfɛlt miɐ]

I don't like it.
Das gefällt mir nicht. [das gəˈfɛlt miɐ nɪçt]

I'd rather ...
Ich möchte lieber ... [ˀɪç ˈmœçtə ˈliːbɐ]

I'd really like ...
Am liebsten wäre mir ... [ˀam ˈliːpstn ˈvɛːʀə miɐ]

I'd like to find out more about it.
Darüber würde ich gerne mehr erfahren.
[ˈdaːʀyːbɐ ˈvyɐdə ˀɪç ˌgɛɐnə ˈmeɐ ˀɐˈfaːʀən]

Ignorance

I don't know (that).
Das weiß ich nicht. [das ˈvaɪs ɪç nɪçt]

No idea!
Keine Ahnung! [ˈkaɪnə ˀaːnʊŋ]

Indecision

I don't care.
Das ist mir egal. [das ɪst miɐ eˈgal]

I don't know yet.
Ich weiß noch nicht. [ˀɪç ˈvaɪs nɔx nɪçt]

Perhaps./Maybe.
Vielleicht. [fɪˈlaɪçt]

Probably.
Wahrscheinlich. [vaˈʃaɪnlɪç]

Delight

Great!
Großartig! [ˈgʁoːsaːtɪç]

Fine!
Prima! [ˈpʁiːma]

Fantastic!
Toll! [tɔl]

Contentment

I am completely satisfied.
Ich bin voll und ganz zufrieden. [ʔɪç bɪn ˈfɔl ʊnt gants tsʊˈfʁiːdn]

I can't complain.
Ich kann mich nicht beklagen. [ʔɪç kan mɪç nɪçt bəˈklaːgŋ]

That worked out extremely well.
Das hat hervorragend geklappt. [das hat heˈfoːʁaːgŋt gəˈklapt]

Boredom

How boring! / What a bore!
Wie langweilig! / So was von langweilig!
[vi ˈlaŋvaɪlɪç / ˈzoːvas fɔn ˈlaŋvaɪlɪç]

... is dead boring.
... ist total öde. [ʔɪst toˈtaːl ˈʔøːdə]

Astonishment – Surprise

Oh, I see!
Ach so! [ʔax ˈzoː]

You don't say!
Ach nein! [ʔax ˈnaɪn]

Really?
Wirklich? [ˈvɪʁklɪç]

Incredible!
Unglaublich! [ʔʊnˈglaʊplɪç]

Relief

It's lucky ...!
Ein Glück, dass ...! [ʔaɪn ˈglʏk das]

Thank God!
Gott sei Dank! [ˌɡɔt zaɪ ˈdaŋk]

At last!
Endlich! [ˈʔɛntlɪç]

Composure

Don't panic!
Nur keine Panik! [ˈnuɐ ˌkaɪnə ˈpaːnɪk]

Don't get excited!
Nur keine Aufregung! [ˈnuɐ ˌkaɪnə ˈʔaʊfʀeːɡʊŋ]

Don't you worry about a thing.
Machen Sie sich keine Sorgen. [maxn ziː zɪç ˈkaɪnə ˈzɔɐɡn]

Annoyance

How annoying!
Das ist aber ärgerlich! [das ʔɪst ˈʔaːbɐ ˈʔɛɐɡəlɪç]

Blast!
Verflixt! [fɛˈflɪkst]

What a nuisance!
So ein Mist! [zo ʔaɪn mɪst]

Enough of this!
Jetzt reicht's! [jɛtst ˈraɪçts]

… is getting on my nerves / wick.
… geht mir auf den Geist / Wecker / Keks.
[ɡeːt miɐ ʔaʊf den ˈɡaɪst / ˈvɛkɐ / ˈkeːks]

That's outrageous! / What a cheek!
Eine Unverschämtheit ist das! / So eine Frechheit!
[ˌʔaɪnə ˈʔʊnfɛʃɛːmthaɪt ʔɪst das / ˈzoː ˌʔaɪnə ˈfʀɛçhaɪt]

That can't be true!
Das darf doch wohl nicht wahr sein!
[das daːf dɔx voːl nɪçt ˈvaː zaɪn]

Rebuking

What do you think you're doing!
Was fällt Ihnen ein! [vas ˈfɛlt ˈʔiːnn ˈʔaɪn]

Don't come anywhere near me!
Kommen Sie mir bloß nicht zu nahe!
[kɔmm ziː miɐ ˈbloːs nɪçt tsʊ ˈnaː]

That's completely out of the question.
Das kommt gar nicht in Frage. [das kɔmt ˈɡaː nɪçt ɪn ˈfʀaːɡə]

I'm (so) sorry!
Es tut mir Leid! [ˀɛs tuːt miɐ laɪt]

I feel really sorry for ...
Es tut mir richtig Leid für ... [ˀɛs tuːt miɐ ˈʁɪçtɪç ˈlaɪt fyɐ]

Oh dear!
Oh je! [ˀoˈjeː]

What a pity!
Schade! [ˈʃaːdə]

German gestures

Most German gestures can be easily understood by English-speaking people as they differ only marginally from ones we use ourselves. There are however, one or two that may need further explanation.

- The German expression for good luck is not "I'll keep my fingers crossed", but "I'll press my thumbs for you – Ich drück' dir die Daumen", thus the corresponding gesture involves wrapping the four fingers of one hand around the thumb of the same hand and pressing firmly.
- Tapping one's index finger against one's temple does **not** indicate that you think someone has been rather clever – on the contrary, in Germany it indicates that you think they're mad.
- If people start rapping loudly on the table with their knuckles in Germany it means that they either agree with what you have said or are expressing their thanks. If this happens in a pub, it's a form of welcome.

Good luck!

Excellent!

Maybe?

Can't help it!

Idiot!

No idea!/Don't know!

How nice! / That's lovely!
Wie schön! [vi: ˈʃøːn]

That is very kind / nice of you.
Das ist sehr nett von Ihnen/dir. [das ʔɪst zeɐ ˈnɛt fɔn ˈʔiːnn/diɐ]

I think you're very nice.
Ich finde Sie sehr sympathisch /nett.
[ˈʔɪç ˈfɪndə zi zeɐ zɪmˈpaːtɪʃ / nɛt]

That meal was really excellent!
Das Essen war ausgezeichnet! [das ˈʔɛsn va ˈʔaʊsɡəˈtsaɪçnət]

We've seldom had such a good meal.
Wir haben selten so gut gegessen wie bei Ihnen.
[viɐ ˈhaːbm ˈzɛltn soː ɡuːt ɡəˈɡɛsn vi: baɪ ˈʔiːnn]

It really is lovely here!
Es ist wirklich traumhaft hier! [ʔəs ɪst ˈvɪʁklɪç ˈtʁaʊmhaft hiɐ]

Well, you speak very good English.
Sie sprechen aber sehr gut Englisch.
[zi ˈʃpʁɛçn ˌʔaːbɐ ˈzeɐ ɡuːt ˈʔɛŋlɪʃ]

We felt very welcome here.
Wir haben uns bei Ihnen sehr wohl gefühlt.
[viɐ ˈhaːbm ʊns baɪ ˈʔiːnn zeɐ voːl ɡəˈfyːlt]

That looks good!
Das sieht gut aus! [das ziːt ˈɡuːt ʔaʊs]

The dress suits you.
Das Kleid steht Ihnen/dir gut. [das klaɪt ʃteːt ˈʔiːnn/diɐ ˈɡuːt]

cosy	. . . .	gemütlich [ɡəˈmyːtlɪç]
delicious	. . . .	köstlich [ˈkœstlɪç]
friendly	. . . .	freundlich [ˈfʁɔɪntlɪç]
gorgeous	. . . .	hinreißend [ˈhɪnʁaɪsnt]
impressive	. . . .	beeindruckend [bəˈʔaɪndʁʊknt]
kind	. . . .	liebenswürdig [ˈliːbmsvʏɐdɪç]
lovely	. . . .	schön [ʃøːn]
pleasant	. . . .	angenehm [ˈʔanɡəneːm]
pretty	. . . .	hübsch [hʏpʃ]
tasty	. . . .	lecker [ˈlɛkɐ]
excellent	. . . .	ausgezeichnet [ˈʔaʊsɡəˈtsaɪçnət]
glorious, splendid	. . . .	herrlich [ˈhɛɐlɪç]

Personal information

Where are you from?
Woher kommen Sie? [ˌvoheɐ ˈkɔmm ziː]

I'm from ...
Ich bin aus ... [ˀɪç bɪn aʊs ...]

Have you been here long?
Sind Sie schon lange hier? [ˈzɪnt zi ʃon ˈlaŋə hiɐ]

I've been here since ...
Ich bin seit ... hier. [ˀɪç bɪn zaɪt ... hiɐ]

How long are you staying?
Wie lange bleiben Sie? [vi ˈlaŋə ˈblaɪbm ziː]

Is this your first time here?
Sind Sie zum ersten Mal hier? [ˈzɪnt zi tsʊm ˈɛɐstn maːl hiɐ]

Do you like it here?
Gefällt es Ihnen hier? [gəˈfɛlt əs ˀiːnn hiɐ]

How old are you?
Wie alt sind Sie? [vi ˀalt zɪnt ziː]

I'm thirty-nine.
Ich bin neununddreißig. [ˀɪç bɪn ˌnɔɪnʊnˈdraɪsɪç]

What do you do for a living?
Was machen Sie beruflich? [vas maxn zi bəˈruːflɪç]

I'm a ...
Ich bin ... [ˀɪç bɪn]

I work for ...
Ich arbeite bei ... [ˀɪç ˀaːbaɪtə baɪ]

I'm retired.
Ich bin Rentner/Rentnerin. [ˀɪç bɪn ˈrɛntnɐ/ ˈrɛntnərɪn]

I'm still at school.
Ich gehe noch zur Schule. [ˀɪç geː nɔx tsʊɐ ˈʃuːlə]

I'm a student.
Ich bin Student/Studentin. [ˀɪç bɪn ʃtʊˈdɛnt/ ʃtʊˈdɛntɪn]

43

Family

Are you married?
Sind Sie verheiratet? ['zɪnt zi fɛ'haɪʁaːtət]

Do you have any children?
Haben Sie Kinder? ['haːbm̩ zi 'kɪndɐ]

Yes, but they're all grown up.
Ja, aber sie sind schon erwachsen. [jaː ˀabɐ zi zɪnt ʃoːn ˀɛ'vaksn̩]

How old are your children?
Wie alt sind Ihre Kinder? [viː ˀalt zɪnt ˀiːʁə 'kɪndɐ]

My daughter is 8 (years old) and my son is 5.
Meine Tochter ist acht (Jahre alt) und mein Sohn ist fünf.
[maɪnə 'tɔxtɐ ˀɪst ˀaxt ('jaːʁə ˀalt) ˀʊnt maɪn 'zoːn ˀɪst fʏnf]

Hobbies

> ➤ also "Other sporting activities" and "Creative holidays"

Do you have a hobby?
Haben Sie / Hast du ein Hobby? [haːbm̩ zi/hast du ˀaɪn 'hɔbi]

I spend a lot of time with my children.
Ich verbringe viel Zeit mit meinen Kindern.
[ˀɪç fɛ'bʁɪŋə fiːl tsaɪt mɪt maɪnn̩ 'kɪndɐn]

I surf the Internet a lot.
Ich surfe viel im Internet. [ˀɪç 'səːfə fiːl ɪm ˀɪntɛnɛt]

I do a little painting.
Ich male ein wenig. [ˀɪç 'maːlə ˀaɪn 'veːnɪç]

I collect antiques/stamps.
Ich sammle Antiquitäten/Briefmarken.
[ˀɪç 'zamlə ˀantɪkvi:'tɛːtn̩/'bʁiːfmaːkŋ̍]

What are you interested in?
Wofür interessieren Sie sich so? ['voːfyɐ ˀɪntʁə'siːʁən zi zɪç zoː]

I'm interested in ...
Ich interessiere mich für ... [ˀɪç ˀɪntʁə'siːʁə mɪç fyɐ ...]

I'm active in ...
Ich bin bei ... aktiv. [ˀɪç bɪn baɪ ... ak'tiːf]

... is one of my favourite pastimes.
... ist eine meiner Lieblingsbeschäftigungen.
[ˀɪst ˀaɪnə ˌmaɪnɐ 'liːplɪŋsbəʃɛftɪgʊŋŋ̍]

cooking	kochen ['kɔxn]
drawing	zeichnen ['tsaɪçnn]
handicrafts	basteln [bastln]
learning languages	Sprachen lernen ['ʃpraːxn lɛɐnn]
listening to music	Musik hören [muˈziːk ˈhøːɐən]
making music	musizieren [muziˈtsiːɐən]
playing cards/chess	Karten/Schach spielen [ˈkaːtn/ʃax ʃpiːln]
pottery	töpfern ['tœpfɐn]
reading	lesen [leːzn]
surfing the Internet	im Internet surfen [ˈʔɪntɐnɛt səːfn]
travelling	reisen [ʀaɪn]
watching television	fernsehen [ˈfɛɐnzeːn]
writing	schreiben [ʃʀaɪbm]

You can also say, *ich koche gern* - *I like cooking* (literally: "I cook gladly") or *ich arbeite gern im Garten* – *I like gardening* etc.

Fitness

➤ also Other sporting activities

How do you keep fit?
Wie halten Sie sich fit? [viː haltn ziː zɪç fɪt]

I go jogging/swimming/cycling.
Ich jogge/schwimme/fahre Rad. [ʔɪç ˈdʒɔgə/ˈʃvɪmə/ˈfaːʀə ʀaːt]

I play squash/tennis/golf once a week.
Ich spiele einmal die Woche Squash/Tennis/Golf. [ʔɪç ʃpiːlə ʔaɪnmaːl diː ˈvɔxə skvɔʃ/ˈtɛnɪs/gɔlf]

I go to a fitness centre regularly.
Ich gehe regelmäßig ins Fitnesscenter. [ʔɪç geːə ˈʀeːglmɛːsɪç ʔɪns ˈfɪtnəsˌtsɛntɐ]

I work out twice a week.
Ich trainiere zweimal die Woche. [ʔɪç treˈniːʀə ˈtsvaɪmaːl diː ˈvɔxə]

I live a healthy life.
Ich lebe gesund. [ʔɪç leːbə gəˈzʊnt]

What sport do you go in for?
Welchen Sport treiben Sie? [vɛlçn ʃpɔet tʀaɪbm ziː]

I play ...
Ich spiele ... [ʔɪç ˈʃpiːlə]

I'm a ... fan.
Ich bin ein Fan von ... [ʔɪç bɪn ʔaɪn fɛːn fɔn ...]

45

I like to go to ...
Ich gehe gern ... [ʔɪç 'geː 'gɛɐn]

Can I play too?
Kann ich mitspielen? [kan ɪç 'mɪtʃpiːln]

Making a date

Have you got any plans for tomorrow evening?
Haben Sie/Hast du morgen Abend schon etwas vor?
['haːbm ziː/hast dʊ 'mɔɐgn ʔaːbmt ʃon ˌʔɛtvas 'foɐ]

Shall we go together?
Wollen wir zusammen hingehen? ['vɔln viɐ tsʊ'zamm 'hɪngeːn]

Shall we go out together this evening?
Wollen wir heute Abend miteinander ausgehen?
['vɔlən viɐ 'hɔɪtə 'abɛnt 'mɪtaɪn'andɐ 'aʊsgeːn]

Can I take you out for dinner tomorrow evening?
Darf ich Sie/dich morgen Abend zum Essen einladen?
['daːf ɪç ziː/dɪç mɔɐgn ʔaːbmt tsʊm ʔɛsn ʔaɪnlaːdn]

When shall we meet?
Wann treffen wir uns? [van 'tʀɛfn viɐ ʔʊns]

Let's meet at 9 o'clock in front of ...
Treffen wir uns um neun Uhr vor ...
['tʀɛfn viɐ ʔʊns ʔʊm nɔɪn uɐ foɐ ...]

I'll pick you up.
Ich hole Sie/dich ab. [ʔɪç hoːlə ziː/dɪç ʔap]

Can I see you again?
Kann ich dich wieder sehen? ['kan ɪç dɪç 'viːdeːzeːn]

That was a really nice evening!
Das war wirklich ein netter Abend! [das va 'vɪʁklɪç ʔaɪn 'nɛtɐ ʔaːbmt]

Flirting

You have lovely eyes.
Du hast wunderschöne Augen. [du hast 'vʊndɐʃøːnə ʔaʊgn]

I like the way you laugh.
Mir gefällt, wie du lachst. [mɪɐ gəˈfɛlt vi du laxst]

I like you.
Du gefällst mir. [du gəˈfɛlst mɪɐ]

I like you a lot.
Ich mag dich. [ˀɪç maːk dɪç]

I think you're great.
Ich finde dich ganz toll! [ˀɪç ˈfɪndə dɪç gants tɔl]

I'm crazy about you.
Ich bin verrückt nach dir. [ˀɪç bɪn fɛˈʀʏkt nax diɐ]

I'm in love with you.
Ich bin in dich verliebt. [ˀɪç bɪn ɪn dɪç fɛˈliːpt]

I love you.
Ich liebe dich. [ˀɪç ˈliːbə dɪç]

Do you have a steady boyfriend / a steady girlfriend?
Hast du einen festen Freund / eine feste Freundin?
[hast duː ˀaɪnn ˈfɛstn fʀɔɪnt / ˀaɪnə ˈfɛstə ˈfʀɔɪndɪn]

Do you live with someone?
Lebst du mit jemandem zusammen?
[ˈleːpst du mɪt ˈjeːmandəm tsʊˈzamm]

I'm divorced.
Ich bin geschieden. [ˀɪç bɪn gəˈʃiːdn]

We're separated.
Wir leben getrennt. [viɐ leːbm gəˈtʀɛnt]

Let's have a cuddle.
Wir können kuscheln. [viɐ kœnn ˈkʊʃln]

Please go now.
Bitte geh jetzt! [ˈbɪtə geː jɛtst]

Please leave me alone.
Lassen Sie mich bitte in Ruhe! [lasn zi mɪç ɪn ˈʀuə]

Stop that right now!
Hören Sie sofort damit auf! [høːɐn zi zoˈfɔɐt ˌdamɪt ˀaʊf]

Language difficulties

Pardon? / Excuse me?
Wie bitte? [ˈviː bɪtə]

I don't understand.
Ich verstehe Sie nicht. [ˀɪç fɛˈʃteː zi nɪçt]

Would you repeat that, please?
Könnten Sie das bitte wiederholen? [kœntn zi das ˈbɪtə viːdɐˈhoːln]

Would you speak more slowly, please?
Könnten Sie bitte etwas langsamer sprechen?
[kœntn zi ˈbɪtə ˌˀɛtvas ˈlaŋzamɐ ʃpʀɛçn]

Yes, I understand/see.
Ja, ich verstehe. [ja: ˀɪç fɐˈʃteː]

Do you speak ...
Sprechen Sie ... [ˈʃpʀɛçn̩ zi]

German?
Deutsch? [ˈdɔɪtʃ]

English?
Englisch? [ˈˀɛŋlɪʃ]

French?
Französisch? [fʀanˈtsøːzɪʃ]

I only speak a little German.
Ich spreche nur wenig Deutsch. [ˀɪç ˈʃpʀɛçə nuɐ ˈveːnɪç ˈdɔɪtʃ]

KARLSPLATZ

Getting around

First-class roads and public transportation

Travellers in the German-speaking countries profit from excellent road systems and reliable public transportation. IC and ICE trains provide the fastest and most convenient connections between city centres. Reservations on trains are easy to make and will make your trip more pleasant. If you prefer to go by car, you will have the advantage of flexibility in getting to destinations outside city centres. Be ready, however, for rather aggressive driving behaviour by Anglo-Saxon standards. Tailgating is a national sport, and many drivers seem oblivious to speed limits. These are well-posted on freeways/motorways and highways. Be advised that there are radar checks and police who may stop speeders. This can be quite expensive.

Asking for directions

Useful words

left	links [lɪŋks]
right	rechts [rɛçts]
straight on/straight ahead	geradeaus [gʀaːdəˈʔaʊs]
in front of	vor [foɐ]
behind	hinter [ˈhɪntɐ]
next to	neben [ˈneːbm̩]
in the vicinity (of)	in der Nähe (von) [ɪn dɐ ˈnɛːə fɔn]
opposite	gegenüber [geːgŋˈʔyːbɐ]
here	hier [hiɐ]
there	dort [dɔɐt]
near	nah [naː]
far	weit [vaɪt]
after	nach [naːx]
street/road	die Straße [di ˈʃtʀaːsə]
curve/bend	die Kurve [di ˈkʊɐvə]
intersection/junction	die Kreuzung [di ˈkʀɔɪtsʊŋ]
traffic light	die Ampel [di ˈʔampl̩]
the street corner	die Straßenecke [di ˈʃtʀaːsn̩ˈʔɛkə]

Directions

Excuse me, how do you get to ...?
Entschuldigen Sie bitte, wie komme ich nach ...?
[ˈʔɛntʃʊldɪgn̩ zi ˈbɪtə viː ˈkɔmə ɪç naːx]

Straight on until you get to ...
Immer geradeaus bis ... [ˈʔɪmɐ gʀaːdəˈʔaʊs bɪs ...]

Then turn left/right at the traffic lights.
Dann bei der Ampel links/rechts abbiegen.
[dan baɪ dɐ ʔampl lɪŋks/ʀɛçts 'apbiːgn̩]

Follow the signs.
Folgen Sie den Schildern. ['fɔlgn̩ zi den 'ʃɪldɐn]

How far is it?
Wie weit ist das? [viː vaɪt ʔɪst das]

It's very near here.
Es ist ganz in der Nähe. [ʔəs ʔɪst gants ɪn dɐ 'nɛːə]

Excuse me, is this the road to ...?
Bitte, ist das die Straße nach ...? ['bɪtə ʔɪst 'das di 'ʃtʀaːsə nax]

Excuse me, where's ..., please?
Bitte, wo ist ...? [bɪtə voː ʔɪst ...]

I'm sorry, I don't know.
Tut mir Leid, das weiß ich nicht. [tut miɐ laɪt das 'vaɪs ɪç nɪçt]

I'm not from round here.
Ich bin nicht von hier. [ʔɪç 'bɪn nɪçt fɔn hiɐ]

Go straight on.
Gehen Sie geradeaus. [geːn zi gʀaːdəʔaʊs]

Turn left/right.
Gehen Sie nach links/nach rechts. [geːn zi nax lɪŋks/nax ʀɛçts]

The first street on the left.
Erste Straße links. [ʔeɐstə 'ʃtʀaːsə lɪŋks]

The second street on the right.
Zweite Straße rechts. ['tsvaɪtə 'ʃtʀaːsə ʀɛçts]

Cross ...
Überqueren Sie ... [ʔyːbɐ'kveɐn zi ...]

  the bridge.
  die Brücke. [di 'bʀʏkə]

  the square.
  den Platz. [den 'plats]

  the street.
  die Straße. [di 'ʃtʀaːsə]

The best thing would be to take the number ... bus.
Sie nehmen am besten den Bus Nummer ...
[zi 'neːmm̩ am 'bɛstn̩ den bʊs 'nʊmɐ ...]

Passport control

Your passport, please.
Ihren Pass, bitte! [ˀiɐn pas ˈbɪtə]

Have you got a visa?
Haben Sie ein Visum? [haːbm̩ zi ˀaɪn ˈviːzʊm]

Can I get a visa here?
Kann ich das Visum hier bekommen?
[ˈkan ɪç das ˈviːzʊm ˈhiɐ bəˈkɔmm̩]

Customs

Have you got anything to declare?
Haben Sie etwas zu verzollen? [ˈhaːbm̩ zi ˀɛtvas tsʊ fɐˈtsɔln]

Pull over to the right/the left, please.
Fahren Sie bitte rechts/links heran!
[ˈfaːʁən zi ˈbɪtə ʁɛçts/lɪŋks həˈʁan]

Open the boot/trunk, please.
Öffnen Sie bitte den Kofferraum! [ˀœfnən zi ˈbɪtə den ˈkɔfɐʁaʊm]

Open this case, please.
Öffnen Sie bitte diesen Koffer! [ˀœfnən zi ˈbɪtə diːzn̩ ˈkɔfɐ]

Do I have to pay duty on this?
Muss ich das verzollen? [ˈmʊs ɪç das fɐˈtsɔln]

Particulars/Personal statistics

Christian name/first name	der Vorname [dɐ ˈfoɐnaːmə]
date of birth	das Geburtsdatum [das gəˈbʊɐtsdaːtʊm]
maiden name	der Geburtsname [dɐ gəˈbʊɐtsnaːmə]
marital status	der Familienstand [dɐ faˈmiːljənʃtant]
married	verheiratet [fɐˈhaɪʁaːtət]
single	ledig [ˈleːdɪç]
widow, widower	verwitwet [fɐˈvɪtvət]
nationality	die Staatsangehörigkeit [di ˈʃtaːtsˀangəhøːʁɪçkaɪt]
place of birth	der Geburtsort [dɐ gəˈbʊɐtsˀɔɐt]
place of residence	der Wohnort [dɐ ˈvoːnˀɔɐt]
surname/last name	der Familienname [dɐ faˈmiːljənnaːmə]

At the border

border crossing	der Grenzübergang [dɐ ˈgʁɛntsˀyːbɐgaŋ]

52

customs	der Zoll [dɐ 'tsɔl]
driving licence	der Führerschein [dɐ 'fy:ʀɐʃaɪn]
duties	die Zollgebühren *f pl* [di 'tsɔlgəby:ʀən]
duty-free	zollfrei ['tsɔlfʀaɪ]
entering (a country)	die Einreise [di ˈʔaɪnʀaɪzə]
EU citizen	EU-Bürger/EU-Bürgerin [ʔeˈʔu: bʏɐgɐ/ʔeˈʔu: bʏɐgəʀɪn]
green card	die grüne Versicherungskarte [di 'gry:nə fɛ'zɪçəʀʊŋska:tə]
identity card	der Personalausweis [dɐ p(ɛ)ezoˈna:lˌʔaʊsvaɪs]
international car index mark	das Nationalitätskennzeichen [das natsjonalɪ'tɛ:tskɛntsaɪçn̩]
international vaccination certificate	der internationale Impfpass [dɐ ˈʔɪntɐnatsjonaːlə ˈʔɪmpfpas]
leaving (a country)	die Ausreise [di 'aʊsraɪzə]
liable to duty	zollpflichtig ['tsɔl(p)flɪçtɪç]
number plate/license plate	das Nummernschild [das 'nʊmɐnʃɪlt]
passport	der Reisepass [dɐ 'ʀaɪzəpas]
passport check	die Passkontrolle [di 'paskɔntʀɔlə]
valid	gültig ['gʏltɪç]
visa	das Visum [das 'vi:zʊm]

Cars and motorcycles

In German-speaking countries people drive on the right side of the road and overtake on the left. There are three main categories of roads: *Landstraßen* (ordinary roads), *Bundesstraßen* (highways) and *Autobahnen* (motorways/freeways).
On Swiss and Austrian motorways motorists have to pay a toll. Safety belts (*Sicherheitsgurte*) and special child seats for small children are mandatory.

country road	die Landstraße [di 'lantʃtʀa:sə]
dual carriageway/ divided highway	die Schnellstraße [di 'ʃnɛlʃtʀa:sə]
fine	das Bußgeld [das 'bu:sgɛlt]
to hitchhike	trampen [tʀɛmpm̩]
hitchhiker	der Anhalter [der ˈʔanhaltɐ]
legal alcohol limit	die Promillegrenze [di pʀoˈmɪləˌgʀɛntsə]
main street	die Hauptstraße [di 'haʊptʃtʀa:sə]
motorway/freeway	die Autobahn [di ˈʔaʊtoba:n]
motorway toll	die Autobahngebühren [di ˈʔaʊtoba:ngəˌby:ʀən]

radar check	die Radarkontrolle [di ʀaˈdaːkɔnˌtʀɔlə]
(motorway) service area ...	die Raststätte [di ˈʀastʃtɛtə]
side-street	die Nebenstraße [di ˈneːbmʃtʀaːsə]
sign (directions)	der Wegweiser [dɐ ˈveːkvaɪzɐ]
street/road	die Straße [di ˈʃtʀaːsə]
traffic jam	der Stau [dɐ ʃtaʊ]

At the gas/petrol station
➤ also At the garage

Where's the nearest gas/petrol station, please?
Wo ist bitte die nächste Tankstelle?
[voː ʔɪst ˈbɪtə di ˈnɛːçstə ˈtaŋkʃtɛlə]

I'd like ... litres of ...
Ich möchte ... Liter ... [ʔɪç ˈmœçtə ... ˈliːtɐ]
  regular (petrol)/normal gasoline.
  Normalbenzin. [nɔ'maːlbɛntsiːn]
  super/premium.
  Super. [ˈzuːpɐ]
  diesel.
  Diesel. [ˈdiːzl]
  leaded.
  verbleit. [fɐˈblaɪt]
  unleaded.
  bleifrei. [ˈblaɪfʀaɪ]

Super/premium, please. For 50 euros.
Super bitte, für fünfzig Euro. [ˈzuːpɐ ˈbɪtə fyɐ ˈfʏnftsɪç ˈʔɔɪro]

Fill her up, please.
Volltanken, bitte. [ˈfɔltaŋkn̩ ˈbɪtə]

Would you mind checking the oil?
Würden Sie bitte den Ölstand prüfen?
[vvɐdn zi ˈbɪtə den ˈʔøːlʃtant pʀyːfn]

I'd like a road map of this area, please.
Ich hätte gern eine Straßenkarte dieser Gegend.
[ˈʔɪç ˈhɛtə gɛɐn ʔaɪnə ˈʃtʀaːsŋkaːtə dizɐ ˈgeːgn̩t]

Parking

Parking can be a problem in inner cities. As elsewhere, you'll
have to live with parking meters (Parkuhren), or you'll need a
parking disc (Parkscheibe) for restricted zones. Find a car
park/garage (Parkhaus – look for a sign with a large "P" on it),
or park on the outskirts of town and take the bus. In either
case, make sure you have enough small change.

Excuse me, is there a place to park near here?

Entschuldigen Sie bitte, gibt es hier in der Nähe eine Parkmöglichkeit? [ʔɛntˈʃʊldɪgŋ zi ˈbɪtə gɪpt əs hiɐ ʔɪn dɐ ˈnɛːə ʔaɪnə ˈpaːkmøːklɪçkaɪt]

Can I park my car here?

Kann ich den Wagen hier abstellen? [ˈkan ɪç den ˈvaːgŋ hiɐ ˈʔapʃtɛln]

Is there an attendant?

Ist der Parkplatz bewacht? [ʔɪst dɐ ˈpaːkplats bəˈvaxt]

How much is it by the hour?

Wie hoch ist die Parkgebühr pro Stunde?
[viː hoːx ʔɪst di ˈpaːkgəbyɐ pʀo ˈʃtʊndə]

Is the car park/garage open all night?

Ist das Parkhaus die ganze Nacht geöffnet?
[ʔɪst das ˈpaːkhaʊs di ˈgantsə naxt gəˈʔœfnət]

A breakdown

My car's broken down.

Ich habe eine Panne. [ʔɪç ˈhaːbə ʔaɪnə ˈpanə]

Is there a garage near here?

Ist hier in der Nähe eine Werkstatt?
[ʔɪst hiɐ ʔɪn dɐ ˈnɛːə ʔaɪnə ˈvɛɐkʃtat]

Would you call the breakdown service, please?

Würden Sie bitte den Pannendienst anrufen?
[vvɐdn zi ˈbɪtə den ˈpanndiːnst ʔanʀuːfn]

Could you help me out with some petrol?

Könnten Sie mir mit Benzin aushelfen?
[ˈkœntn zi miɐ mɪt bɛnˈtsiːn ʔaʊshɛlfn]

Could you help me change the tyre?

Könnten Sie mir beim Reifenwechsel helfen?
[ˈkœntn zi miɐ baɪm ˈʀaɪfnvɛksl ˈhɛlfn]

Could you help me jump-start my car?

Könnten Sie mir Starthilfe geben? [ˈkœntn zi miɐ ˈʃtaːthɪlfə geːbm]

Could you give me a lift to the nearest garage?

Würden Sie mich bis zur nächsten Werkstatt mitnehmen?
[vvɐdn zi mɪç bɪs tsʊɐ nɛːçstn ˈvɛɐkʃtat ˈmɪtneːmm]

55

Three main motoring associations, the *ADAC* in Germany, the *ÖAMTC* in Austria and the *TCS* in Switzerland will assist you if your car breaks down. You can call from emergency telephones on all motorways and on many main roads. Simple repair jobs are free, but you'll have to pay for towing service. There may also be reciprocal agreements if you're a member of an automobile association in your own country.

breakdown	die Panne [di ˈpanə]
breakdown service	der Pannendienst [dɐ ˈpanndiːnst]
breakdown vehicle	der Abschleppwagen [dɐ ˈʔapʃlɛpvaːgn]
emergency telephone	die Notrufsäule [di ˈnoːtʁufzɔɪlə]
flat (tyre)	die (Reifen)Panne [di ˈ(ʁaɪfn)panə]
gasoline can	der Benzinkanister [dɐ bɛnˈtsiːnkaˌnɪstɐ]
hazard warning lights	die Warnblinkanlage [di ˈvaːnblɪŋkʔanlaːgə]
jack	der Wagenheber [dɐ ˈvaːgnheːbɐ]
jump leads	das Starthilfekabel [das ˈʃtaːthɪlfəkaːbl]
petrol can	der Benzinkanister [dɐ bɛnˈtsiːnkaˌnɪstɐ]
puncture	die Panne [di ˈpanə]
spare tyre	der Ersatzreifen [dɐ ʔeˈzatsʁaɪfn]
to tow (away)	abschleppen [ˈʔapʃlɛpm]
tools	das Werkzeug [das ˈvɛɐktsɔɪk]
tow truck	der Abschleppwagen [dɐ ˈʔapʃlɛpvaːgn]
towing service	der Abschleppdienst [dɐ ˈʔapʃlɛpdiːnst]
towrope	das Abschleppseil [das ˈʔapʃlɛpzaɪl]
warning triangle	das Warndreieck [das ˈvaːndʁaɪɛk]

At the garage

The car won't start.
Der Motor springt nicht an. [dɐ ˈmoːtoɐ ʃpʁɪŋt nɪçt ˈʔan]

There's something wrong with the engine.
Mit dem Motor stimmt was nicht. [mɪt dem ˈmoːtoɐ ʃtɪmt vas nɪçt]

The brakes don't work.
Die Bremsen funktionieren nicht. [di ˈbʁɛmzn fuŋktsjoˈniːən nɪçt]

I'm losing oil.
Der Wagen verliert Öl. [dɐ ˈvaːgn fɐˈliːɐt ˈʔøːl]

When will the car be ready?
Wann ist der Wagen fertig? [ˈvan ʔɪst dɐ ˈvaːgn ˈfɛɐtɪç]

Roughly how much will it cost?
Was wird es ungefähr kosten? [vas vɪɐt əs ˈʔʊngəfɛɐ ˈkɔstn]

alarm system	die Alarmanlage [di ʔa'la:manla:gə]
anti-freeze	das Frostschutzmittel [das 'frɔstʃʊtsmɪtl]
accelerator/gas pedal	das Gaspedal [das 'ga:speda:l]
air filter	der Luftfilter [dɐ 'lʊftfɪltɐ]
automatic (transmission)	das Automatikgetriebe [das ʔaʊto'ma:tɪkgə,tri:bə]
bonnet/hood	die Motorhaube [di 'mo:tɔ,haʊbə]
brake fluid	die Bremsflüssigkeit [di 'brɛmsflʏsɪçkaɪt]
brake lights	die Bremslichter [di 'brɛmslɪçtɐ]
clutch	die Kupplung [di 'kʊplʊŋ]
cooling water	das Kühlwasser [das 'ky:lvasɐ]
dipped/dimmed headlights	das Abblendlicht [das 'ʔapblɛntlɪçt]
dynamo/generator	die Lichtmaschine [di 'lɪçtmaʃi:nə]
engine/motor	der Motor [dɐ 'mo:tɔɐ]
fault	der Defekt [dɐ de'fɛkt]
full beam/high beams	das Fernlicht [das 'fɛɐnlɪçt]
garage	die Werkstatt [di 'vɛɐkʃtat]
gear	der Gang [dɐ gaŋ]
first/bottom/low gear	erster Gang ['ʔeɐstɐ gaŋ]
neutral	der Leerlauf [dɐ 'leɐlaʊf]
reverse gear	der Rückwärtsgang [dɐ 'rʏkvɛɐtsgaŋ]
gearbox/transmission	das Getriebe [das gə'tri:bə]
hand brake/emergency brake	die Handbremse [di 'hantbrɛmzə]
horn	die Hupe [di 'hu:pə]
ignition	die Zündung [di 'tsʏndʊŋ]
left-hand-drive car	der Linkslenker [dɐ 'lɪŋkslɛŋkɐ]
motorbike/motorcycle	das Motorrad [das mo'to:rat]
oil	das Öl [das 'ʔø:l]
oil change	der Ölwechsel [dɐ 'ʔø:lvɛksl]
petrol/gas pump	die Benzinpumpe [di bɛn'tsi:npʊmpə]
petrol/gas tank	der Tank [dɐ taŋk]
rear/tail light	das Rücklicht [das 'rʏklɪçt]
right-hand-drive car	der Rechtslenker [dɐ 'rɛçtslɛŋkɐ]
screw	die Schraube [di 'ʃraʊbə]
short-circuit	der Kurzschluss [dɐ 'kʊɐtʃlʊs]
sidelights	das Standlicht [das 'ʃtantlɪçt]
spark plug	die Zündkerze [di 'tsʏntkɛɐtsə]
speedometer	der Tacho(meter) [dɐ ,taxo('me:tɐ)]
starter	der Anlasser [dɐ 'ʔanlasɐ]
transmission/ gearbox	das Getriebe [das gə'tri:bə]
wheel	das Rad [das ra:t]
winter tyre	der Winterreifen [dɐ 'vɪntɐraɪfn]

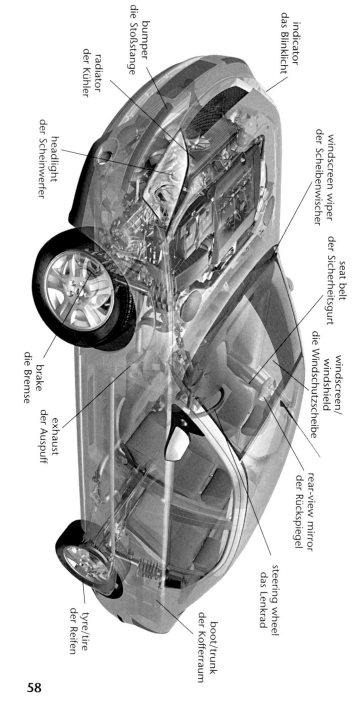

indicator
das Blinklicht

bumper
die Stoßstange

radiator
der Kühler

headlight
der Scheinwerfer

windscreen wiper
der Scheibenwischer

seat belt
der Sicherheitsgurt

windscreen/
windshield
die Windschutzscheibe

rear-view mirror
der Rückspiegel

brake
die Bremse

exhaust
der Auspuff

steering wheel
das Lenkrad

tyre/tire
der Reifen

boot/trunk
der Kofferraum

58

Accident

There's been an accident.
Es ist ein Unfall passiert. [ˈʔɛs ˈʔɪst aɪn ˈʔʊnfal paˈsiet]

Quick! Please call ...
Rufen Sie bitte schnell ... [ˈʀuːfn̩ zi ˈbɪtə ʃnɛl ...]
  an ambulance.
  einen Krankenwagen. [ˈʔaɪnn̩ ˈkʀaŋkn̩vaːgn̩]
  the police.
  die Polizei. [di pɔliˈtsaɪ]
  the fire brigade/department.
  die Feuerwehr. [di ˈfɔjeveɐ]

Have you got a first-aid kit?
Haben Sie Verbandszeug? [haːbm̩ zi fɛˈbantstsɔɪk]

> It is mandatory in Germany, Austria and Switzerland to carry a
> first-aid kit and a warning triangle in your vehicle. If you're in-
> volved in an accident, do not move your car nor allow the
> other party to leave until the police come.

You ...
Sie haben ... [zi ˈhaːbm̩]
  didn't yield (observe the right of way).
  die Vorfahrt nicht beachtet. [di ˈfoɐfaːt nɪçt bəˈʔaxtət]
  didn't signal/indicate.
  nicht geblinkt. [nɪçt gəˈblɪŋkt]

You ...
Sie sind ... [zi zɪnt]
  were speeding (driving too fast).
  zu schnell gefahren. [tsʊ ˈʃnɛl gəˈfaːʀən]
  were too close behind/tailgating.
  zu dicht aufgefahren. [tsʊ dɪçt ˈʔaʊfgəfaːʀən]
  went through a red light.
  bei Rot über die Kreuzung gefahren.
  [baɪ ʀoːt ˈʔyːbɐ di ˈkʀɔɪtsʊŋ gəˈfaːʀən]

Please give me your name and address.
Geben Sie mir bitte Ihren Namen und Ihre Anschrift.
[geːbm̩ zɪ miɐ ˈbɪtə ˈʔien ˈnaːmm̩ ʊnt ˌiʀə ˈʔanʃʀɪft]

We should call the police.
Wir sollten die Polizei holen. [viɐ zɔltn̩ di pɔliˈtsaɪ hoːln̩]

Can we settle this ourselves, without the police?
Können wir uns so einigen, ohne die Polizei?
[kœnn viɐ ˈʔʊns ˈzoː ˈʔaɪnɪgŋ oːnə di pɔliˈtsaɪ]

Thank you very much for your help.
Vielen Dank für Ihre Hilfe! [fiːln̩ ˈdaŋk fyɐ ˈʔiːʀə ˈhɪlfə]

Car/Motorbike/Bicycle rental

pump
die Luftpumpe

saddle
der Sattel

gears
die Gangschaltung

handlebars
der Lenker

front light
das Vorderlicht

rear light,
tail light
das Rücklicht

brake
die Bremse

(inner) tube
der Schlauch
(Reifen)

tyre, tire
der Mantel
(Reifen)

chain
die Kette

pedal
das Pedal

wheel
das Rad

spoke
die Speiche

hub
die Nabe

I'd like to hire/rent ... for two days/for a week.
Ich möchte für zwei Tage / für eine Woche ... mieten.
[ʔɪç ˈmœçtə fʁe tsvaɪ ˈtaːgə / fʏe ˈʔaɪnə ˈvɔxə ... miːtn]

a car
einen Wagen / ein Auto [ʔaɪnn ˈvaːgn / ʔaɪn ˈʔaʊto]

a jeep
einen Geländewagen [ʔaɪnn gəˈlɛndəvaːgn]

a motorbike/motorcycle
ein Motorrad [ʔaɪn moˈtoːʁat]

a scooter
einen Roller [ʔaɪnn ˈʁɔlə]

a bike/bicycle
ein Fahrrad [ʔaɪn ˈfaːʁat]

How much does it cost per week?
Wie hoch ist die Wochenpauschale? [vi hoːx ʔɪst di ˈvɔxnpaʊʃaːlə]

Does that include unlimited mileage?
Ist das einschließlich unbegrenzter Kilometerzahl?
[ʔɪst das ˈʔaɪnʃliːslɪç ˈʔʊnbəgʁɛntstə kɪloˈmeːtetsaːl]

What do you charge per kilometre?
Wie viel verlangen Sie pro gefahrenen Kilometer?
[ˈviː_fiːl fɛˈlaŋŋ zi pʁo gəˈfaːʁ(ʁə)nn kɪloˈmeːtɐ]

> Conversion factor for kilometres: 1 mile = 1.6 km; 1 km = 0.6 mile. Cut the kilometres in half, add 10 percent of the original, and you'll have it in miles. 40 km = 20 + 4 = 24 miles.

How much is the deposit?
Wie hoch ist die Kaution? [vi 'hoːx ʔɪst di kaʊ'tsjoːn]

Does the vehicle have comprehensive insurance/full coverage?
Ist das Fahrzeug vollkaskoversichert?
[ʔɪst das 'faːtsɔɪk 'fɔlkaskofɐˌzɪçɐt]

Is it possible to leave the car in ...?
Ist es möglich, das Fahrzeug in ... abzugeben?
[ʔɪst əs 'møːklɪç das 'faːtsɔɪk ʔɪn ... ʔaptsʊgeːbm]

child seat	der Kindersitz [dɐ 'kɪndɐzɪts]
crash helmet	der Sturzhelm [dɐ 'ʃtʊɐtshɛlm]
to deposit *(money)*	Geld hinterlegen [gɛlt hɪntɐ'leːgn]
deposit	die Kaution [di kaʊ'tsjoːn]
driving licence	der Führerschein [dɐ 'fyːʀɐʃaɪn]
fully comprehensive insurance	die Vollkasko [di 'fɔlkasko]
green card	die grüne Versicherungskarte [di 'gʀyːnə fɐ'zɪçɐʀʊŋskaːtə]
ignition key	der Zündschlüssel [dɐ 'tsʏntʃlʏsl]
safety belt	der Sicherheitsgurt [dɐ 'zɪçɐhaɪtsgurt]
papers	die Papiere *n pl* [di pa'piːʀə]
sunroof	das Schiebedach [das 'ʃiːbədax]
third party, fire and theft	die Teilkasko [di 'taɪlkasko]
weekend rate	die Wochenendpauschale [di 'vɔxn̩ʔɛntpaʊʃaːlə]

Signs and Notices

Achtung	look out, danger
Anlieger frei	residents only
Anfänger	learner, beginner
Ausfahrt	exit
Ausfahrt freihalten	keep exit clear
... ausgenommen	except for ...
Autofähre	car-ferry
Behelfsausfahrt	temporary exit
Bis zur Haltelinie vorfahren	drive up to line
Bitte einordnen	get in lane
Bushaltestelle	bus stop
Einbahnstraße	one-way street
Einfahrt	entrance
Fahrbahn wechseln	change lane
Fahrbahnverengung	road narrows

Feuerwehrzufahrt	fire brigade/department access
Frauenparkplätze	parking spaces for women only
Fußgängerzone	pedestrian precinct/zone
Gefahr	danger
Gefährliche Kurve	dangerous bend/curve
Gegenverkehr	two-way traffic
Geschwindigkeitsbegrenzung	speed limit
Gesperrt (für Fahrzeuge aller Art)	closed (to all vehicles)
Gewichtsgrenze	weight limit
Glatteis	black ice
Haarnadelkurve	hairpin bend/curve
Hochwasser	flooding
Industriegebiet	industrial area
Innenstadt	city centre, downtown
Keine Einfahrt	no entry
Krankenhaus	hospital
Kreisverkehr	roundabout/traffic circle
Kreuzung	cross-road/intersection
Kurzparkzone	limited parking zone
Ladezone	loading zone
Langsam fahren	reduce speed
Licht	headlights
Nebel	fog
Notruf	emergency phone
Ölspur	oil slick
Parken verboten	no parking
Parkhaus	parking building/garage
Parkplatz	parking lot, car park
Parkscheinautomat	ticket machine
Rechts (Links) fahren	keep right (left)
Rechtsabbiegen verboten	no right turn
Rutschgefahr	slippery road
Sackgasse	dead end
Schritt fahren	drive at walking speed
Schule	school
Schulkinder überqueren	children crossing
Seitenwind	side-wind
Spielstraße	children playing
Starkes Gefälle	steep hill
Stau	traffic jam
Steinschlag	falling rocks
Straßenarbeiten	construction, road works
Tunnel	tunnel
Überholverbot	no overtaking/passing
Umleitung	detour/diversion
Unbeschrankter Bahnübergang	crossing – no gates/unprotected crossing
Unfall	accident
Verschmutzte Fahrbahn	muddy road surface
Vorfahrt beachten	give way/yield
Vorsicht	caution
Wenden verboten	no U-turn
Wildwechsel	deer crossing
Zebrastreifen	zebra crossing
Zentrum	city centre, downtown

Booking a flight

Can you tell me when the next flight to ... is, please?
Können Sie mir bitte sagen, wann die nächste Maschine nach ...
fliegt? [k'ɛnn zi miɐ 'bɪtə za:gŋ van di 'nɛːçstə ma'ʃiːnə nax ... fliːkt]

Are there any seats left?
Sind noch Plätze frei? [zɪnt nɔx 'plɛtsə fʀaɪ]

I'd like to book a single/one-way flight to ...
Ich möchte einen einfachen Flug nach ... buchen.
[ʔɪç 'mœçtə ʔaɪnn ʔ'aɪnfaxn fluːk nax ... buːxn]

I'd like to book a return flight to ...
Ich möchte einen Hin- und Rückflug nach ... buchen.
[ʔɪç 'mœçtə ʔaɪnn hɪn ʊnt 'ʀʏkfluːk nax ... buːxn]

How much is an economy class/a first class ticket?
Was kostet bitte der Flug Touristenklasse/ erste Klasse?
[vas 'kɔstət bɪtə de 'fluːk tʊ'ʀɪstnklasə/'ʔeɐstə 'klasə]

Smoking or non-smoking?
Raucher oder Nichtraucher? ['ʀaʊxɐ ʔ'oːdɐ 'nɪçtʀaʊxɐ]

I'd like ...
Ich möchte ... [ʔɪç 'mœçtə ...]

  a window seat.
  einen Fensterplatz. [ʔaɪnn 'fɛnstɐplats]

  an aisle seat.
  einen Platz am Gang. [ʔaɪnn plats am gaŋ]

I'd like to cancel my flight.
Ich möchte diesen Flug stornieren. [ʔɪç 'mœçtə 'diːzn fluːk ʃtɔ'niɐn]

I'd like to change the booking.
Ich möchte diesen Flug umbuchen.
[ʔɪç 'mœçtə 'diːzn fluːk ʔ'ʊmbuːxn]

At the airport

Where's the ... counter, please?
Wo ist bitte der Schalter der ...-Fluggesellschaft?
[voː ʔɪst bɪtə de 'ʃaltɐ de ...'fluːkgə‚zɛlʃaft]

Could I see your ticket, please?
Könnte ich bitte Ihren Flugschein sehen?
['kœntə ɪç 'bɪtə ʔ'iːʀən 'fluːkʃaɪn zeːn]

Can I take this as hand luggage?
Kann ich das als Handgepäck mitnehmen?
[kan ɪç das ʔals 'hantgəpɛk 'mɪtneːmm]

On board

Could you bring me a glass of water, please?
Könnten Sie mir bitte ein Glas Wasser bringen?
['kœntn zi miɐ 'bɪtə ʔaɪn glaːs 'vasɐ brɪŋŋ]

Could I have another cushion/blanket, please?
Könnte ich bitte noch ein Kissen/ eine Decke haben?
['kœntə ɪç 'bɪtə nɔx ʔaɪn kɪsn/ʔaɪnə 'dɛkə haːbm]

Would it be possible for us to change seats?
Wäre es möglich, dass wir den Platz tauschen?
[vɛːʀə ʔəs 'møːklɪç das viɐ den plats taʊʃn]

Arrival ➤ also Lost-property office

My luggage is missing.
Mein Gepäck ist verloren gegangen.
[maɪn gə'pɛk ʔɪst fɛ'loɐn gə'gaŋŋ]

My suitcase has been damaged.
Mein Koffer ist beschädigt worden. [maɪn 'kɔfɐ ʔɪst bə'ʃɛːdɪkt vɔɐdn]

Where does the bus to ... leave from?
Wo fährt der Bus in Richtung ... ab?
[voː feɐt dɐ bʊs ʔɪn 'ʀɪçtʊŋ ... ʔap]

➤ also Train

accompanying adult	die Begleitperson [di bə'glaɪtpɛ(ɛ)ezoːn]
airline	die Fluggesellschaft [di 'fluːkgə,zɛlʃaft]
airport	der Flughafen [dɐ 'fluːkhaːfn]
airport bus	der Flughafenbus [dɐ 'fluːkhaːfn,bʊs]
airport tax	die Flughafengebühr [di 'fluːkhaːfngə,byɐ]
arrival	die Ankunft [di 'ʔankʊnft]
baggage	das Gepäck [das gə'pɛk]
boarding card	die Bordkarte [di 'bɔɐtkaːtə]
to cancel	stornieren [ʃtɔ'niːɐn]
to change the booking	umbuchen ['ʔʊmbuːxn]
to check in	einchecken ['ʔaɪntʃɛkŋ]
connection	der Anschluss [dɐ 'ʔanʃlʊs]
delay	die Verspätung [di fɛ'ʃpɛːtʊŋ]
departure	der Abflug [dɐ 'ʔapfluːk]
scheduled time of departure	planmäßiger Abflug ['plaːnmɛˌsɪgɐ 'ʔapfluːk]
domestic flight	der Inlandsflug [dɐ 'ʔɪnlantsfluːk]
duty-free shop	zollfreier Laden ['tsɔlfʀaɪɐ laːdn]
emergency chute	die Notrutsche [di 'noːtʀʊtʃə]
emergency exit	der Notausgang [dɐ 'noːtʔaʊsgaŋ]
emergency landing	die Notlandung [di 'noːtlandʊŋ]

excess baggage	das Übergepäck [das ˈʔyːbegəpɛk]
flight	der Flug [de fluːk]
gate	der Flugsteig [de ˈfluːkʃtaɪg]
international flight	der Auslandsflug [de ˈʔaʊslantsfluːk]
landing	die Landung [di ˈlandʊŋ]
life jacket	die Schwimmweste [di ˈʃvɪmvɛstə]
luggage	das Gepäck [das geˈpɛk]
luggage van/baggage car	der Gepäckwagen [de gəˈpɛkvaːgn̩]
luggage/baggage reclaim	die Gepäckausgabe [di gəˈpɛkʔaʊsgaːbə]
passenger	der Passagier [de pasaˈʒiɐ]
pilot	der Pilot [de piˈloːt]
security charge	die Sicherheitsgebühr [di ˈzɪçɐhaɪtsgəˌbyɐ]
security control	die Sicherheitskontrolle [di ˈzɪçɐhaɪtskɔnˌtrɔlə]
steward/stewardess	der Steward/die Stewardess [de ˈstjuaːt/di ˈstjuadɛs]
stopover	die Zwischenlandung [di ˈtsvɪʃn̩ˌlandʊŋ]
take-off	der Abflug [de ˈʔapfluːk]
terminal	das Terminal [das ˈtɐːmɪnəl]
time of arrival	die Ankunftszeit [di ʔankʊnfˌtsaɪt]

Train

Intercity trains (IC) connect most cities on an hourly basis. *EuroCity* (EC) trains connect European cities. The fastest trains are the *InterCity Express* (ICE), but they connect fewer places. In addition, there are *InterRegio* (IR) trains and *D-Zug/Schnellzug* (express) trains. For a small fee it is possible to reserve seats in advance. If you travel less than 50 km, you have to pay an extra fee for express trains.

Buying tickets

Single/One-way to Frankfurt, please.
Eine einfache Fahrt nach Frankfurt, bitte.
[ˈʔaɪnə ˈʔaɪnfaxə faːt nax ˈfrankfʊet ˈbɪtə]

Two returns to Stuttgart, please.
Zweimal Stuttgart hin und zurück, bitte.
[ˈtsvaɪmal ˈʃtʊtgaːt hɪn ʊnt tsʊˈrʏk ˈbɪtə]

first-class
erster Klasse [ˈʔeɐstɐ ˈklasə]

Is there a reduction for children/students/senior citizens?
Gibt es eine Ermäßigung für Kinder/ Studenten/Senioren?
[gɪpt əs ˀaɪnə ˀeˈmɛːsɪgʊŋ fyɐ ˈkɪndɐ/ ʃtʊˈdɛntn/zenˈjoːʀən]

I'd like to book two non-smoking seats, please,
Ich möchte gern zwei Nichtraucherplätze reservieren:
[ˀɪç ˈmœçtə gɛɐn tsvaɪ ˈnɪçtʀaʊxɐˌplɛtsə ʀezeˈviːʀən]

  for the EC to …
  für den EC nach … [fyɐ den ˀeˈtseː nax]
  on … at … (o'clock)
  am … um …Uhr [ˀam … ˀʊm … ˀuɐ]
  in the couchette car
  im Liegewagen [ˀɪm ˈliːgəvaːgŋ]
  in the sleeping car
  im Schlafwagen [ˀɪm ˈʃlaːfvaːgŋ]
  in the restaurant car
  im Speisewagen [ˀɪm ˈʃpaɪzəvaːgŋ]

Is there a motorail train to …?
Gibt es einen Autoreisezug nach …?
[gɪpt əs ˀaɪnn ˀˀaʊtoˌʀaɪzetsuːk nax]

Is there a connection to Leipzig at Fulda?
Habe ich in Fulda Anschluss nach Leipzig?
[haːb ɪç ˀɪn ˈfʊlda ˀˀanʃlʊs nax ˈlaɪptsɪç]

How many times do I have to change?
Wie oft muss ich da umsteigen? [viː ˀɔft mʊs ɪç da ˀˀʊmʃtaɪgŋ]

I'd like to register/check this suitcase.
Ich möchte diesen Koffer als Reisegepäck aufgeben.
[ˀɪç ˈmœçtə diːzn ˈkɔfɐ ˀals ˈʀaɪzəgəpɛk ˀˀaʊfgeːbm]

Where can I check in my bicycle?
Wo kann ich mein Fahrrad aufgeben?
[ˈvoː kan ɪç maɪn ˈfaːʀaːt ˀˀaʊfgeːbm]

Excuse me, which platform does the train to Heidelberg leave from?
Entschuldigen Sie bitte, von welchem Gleis fährt der Zug nach Heidelberg ab?
[ˀˀɛntʃʊldɪgŋ ziː ˈbɪtə fɔn vɛlçm glaɪs feɐt de tsuːk nax ˈhaɪdlbɛɐk ˀap]

The intercity … from Hamburg is running 10 minutes late.
Der Intercity … aus Hamburg hat voraussichtlich zehn Minuten Verspätung.
[de ˀˀɪntɐˈsɪti ˀˀaʊs ˈhambʊɐk hat foˈʀaʊsɪçtlɪç ˈtseːn mɪˈnuːtn feˈʃpɛːtʊŋ]

66

On the train

All aboard, please!
Bitte einsteigen! ['bɪtə 'ʔaɪnʃtaɪgn̩]

Is this seat taken/free?
Ist dieser Platz noch frei? [ʔɪst 'diːzɐ plats nɔx fʀaɪ]

Excuse me, I think that's my seat.
Entschuldigen Sie, ich glaube das ist mein Platz.
[ʔɛntʃʊldɪgn̩ ziː ʔɪç 'glaʊbə das ɪst 'maɪn plats]

Here is my seat reservation.
Hier ist meine Platzreservierung. [hiɐ ʔɪst ˌmaɪnə 'platsʀezɛviːʀʊŋ]

May I open/shut the window?
Darf ich bitte das Fenster aufmachen/schließen?
[daʀf ɪç 'bɪtə das 'fɛnstɐ 'ʔaʊfmaxn̩/ʃliːsn̩]

Tickets, please.
Die Fahrkarten, bitte. [diː 'faːkaːtn̩ 'bɪtə]

➢ also Plane

arrival	die Ankunft [diː 'ʔankʊnft]
baggage	das Gepäck [das gə'pɛk]
children's ticket	die Kinderfahrkarte [diː 'kɪndɐˈfaːkaːtə]
coach number	die Wagennummer [diː 'vaːgn̩nʊmɐ]
compartment	das Abteil [das ʔap'taɪl]
corridor	der Gang [dɐ gaŋ]
departure	die Abfahrt [diː 'ʔapfaːt]
to get on	einsteigen ['ʔaɪnʃtaɪgn̩]
to get off	aussteigen ['ʔaʊsʃtaɪgn̩]
guard/conductor	der Zugbegleiter/die Zugbegleiterin [dɐ 'tsuːkbəˌglaɪtɐ/diː 'tsuːkbəˌglaɪtəʀɪn]
(left-luggage) locker	das Schließfach [das 'ʃliːsfax]
left-luggage office/	die Gepäckaufbewahrung
baggage deposit	[diː gə'pɛkˌʔaʊfbəvaːʀʊŋ]
luggage	das Gepäck [das gə'pɛk]
luggage counter	der Gepäckschalter [dɐ gə'pɛkʃaltɐ]
main station	der Hauptbahnhof [dɐ 'haʊptbaːnhoːf, 'haʊpbaːnof)]
motorail train	der Autoreisezug [dɐ 'ʔaʊtoˌʀaɪzətsuːk]
no-smoking compartment .	das Nichtraucherabteil [das 'nɪçtʀaʊxɐʔaptaɪl]
open-plan carriage/	der Großraumwagen
open seating area car	[dɐ 'gʀoːsʀaʊmvaːgn̩]
platform	das Gleis [das glaɪs]
railcard	die Bahncard [diː 'baːnkaːt]
reduction	die Ermäßigung [diː ɐ'mɛːsɪgʊŋ]

reservation	die Reservierung [di ʀezɐˈviːʀʊn]
restaurant car	der Speisewagen [dɐ ˈʃpaɪzəvaːgn̩]
return ticket/round-trip	die Rückfahrkarte [di ˈʀʏkfaːˌkaːtə]
seat reservation	die Platzreservierung [di ˈplatsʀezɐˌviːʀʊn]
severely handicapped person	der/die Schwerbehinderte [dɐ/di ˈʃveːbəhɪndetə]
smoking compartment	das Raucherabteil [das ˈʀaʊxɐʔapˌtaɪl]
station	der Bahnhof [dɐ ˈbaːnhoːf]
stop	der Aufenthalt [dɐ ˈʔaʊfn̩talt]
supplementary charge	der Zuschlag [dɐ ˈtsuːʃlaːk]
ticket collector/conductor	der Schaffner/die Schaffnerin [dɐ ˈʃafnɐ/di ˈʃafnəʀɪn]
track	das Gleis [das glaɪs]
train fare	der Fahrpreis [dɐ ˈfaːpʀaɪs]
ticket	die Fahrkarte [di ˈfaːkaːtə]
ticket check/inspection	die Fahrkartenkontrolle [di ˈfaːkaːtn̩kɔnˌtʀɔlə]
ticket office	der Fahrkartenschalter [dɐ ˈfaːkaːtn̩ʃaltɐ]
timetable	der Fahrplan [dɐ ˈfaːplaːn]
train	der Zug [dɐ tsuːk]
waiting room	der Wartesaal [dɐ ˈvaːtəzaːl]
wheelchair user	der Rollstuhlfahrer/die Rollstuhlfahrerin [dɐ ˈʀɔlʃtuːlˌfaːʀɐ/di ˈʀɔlʃtuːlˌfaːʀəʀɪn]
window seat	der Fensterplatz [dɐ ˈfɛnstɐplats]

Ship

Information

Can you tell me when the next ship/ the next ferry leaves for ..., please?
Können Sie mir bitte sagen, wann das nächste Schiff/die nächste Fähre nach ... abfährt?
[kœnn zi miɐ ˈbɪtə zaːgn̩ van das ˈnɛːçstə ʃɪf/di: ˈnɛːçstə ˈfeːʀə ... ˈʔapfeːt]

How long does the crossing take?
Wie lange dauert die Überfahrt? [vi_ˈlaŋə ˈdaʊɐt di ˈʔyːbɐfaːt]

When do we land at ...?
Wann legen wir in ... an? [van ˈleːgn̩ viɐ ʔɪn ... an]

How long are we stopping at ...?
Wie lange haben wir in ... Aufenthalt?
[vi laŋə haːbm̩ viɐ ʔɪn ... ˈʔaʊfn̩talt]

I'd like ..., please.
Ich möchte bitte ... [ˀɪç ˈmœçtə ˈbɪtə]

a ticket to ...
eine Schiffskarte nach ... [ˀaɪnə ˈʃɪfskaːtə nax]

first class
erste Klasse [ˀeɐstə ˈklasə]

tourist class
Touristenklasse [tʊˈrɪstnklasə]

a single cabin
eine Einzelkabine [ˀaɪntslkabiːnə]

a double cabin
eine Zweibettkabine [ˈtsvaɪbɛtkabiːnə]

I'd like a ticket for the round trip at ... o'clock.
Ich möchte eine Karte für die Rundfahrt um ... Uhr.
[ˀɪç ˈmœçtə ˀaɪnə ˈkaːtə fyɐ diː ˈrʊntfaːt ˀʊm ... ˀuɐ]

On board

Where's the restaurant/lounge, please?
Wo ist bitte der Speisesaal/der Aufenthaltsraum?
[voː ˀɪst ˈbɪtə dɐ ˈʃpaɪzəzaːl/dɐ ˀaʊfntalts͜raʊm]

I don't feel well.
Ich fühle mich nicht wohl. [ˀɪç ˈfyːlə mɪç nɪçt voːl]

Could you call the ship's doctor, please.
Könnten Sie bitte den Schiffsarzt rufen?
[kœntn zɪ bɪtə den ˈʃɪfsˀaːtst ruːfn]

Could you give me something for seasickness, please?
Könnten Sie mir bitte ein Mittel gegen Seekrankheit geben?
[kœntn zi miɐ ˈbɪtə ˀaɪn ˈmɪtl geːgn ˈzeːkraŋkaɪt geːbm]

booking	die Buchung [di ˈbuːxʊŋ]
cabin	die Kabine [di kaˈbiːnə]
captain	der Kapitän [dɐ kapiˈtɛːn]
car ferry	die Autofähre [di ˀaʊtofɛːʀə]
coast	die Küste [di ˈkʏstə]
deck	das Deck [das dɛk]
to dock at	anlegen in [ˀanleːgŋ ˀɪn]
excursion	der Landausflug [dɐ ˈlantˀaʊsfluːk]
ferry	die Fähre [di ˈfɛːʀə]
harbo(u)r	der Hafen [dɐ ˈhaːfn]
hovercraft	das Luftkissenboot [das ˈlʊftkɪsnboːt]
to land at	anlegen in [ˀanleːgŋ ˀɪn]
life jacket	die Schwimmweste [di ʃvɪmvɛstə]
life belt/life preserver	der Rettungsring [dɐ ʀɛtʊŋsʀɪŋ]
lifeboat	das Rettungsboot [das ˈʀɛtʊŋsboːt]
port	der Hafen [dɐ ˈhaːfn]

quay	. . . .	der Kai [de kaɪ]
round trip	. . . .	die Rundfahrt [di 'ʀʊntfaːt]
seasick	. . . .	seekrank ['zeːkʀaŋk]
ticket	. . . .	die Fahrkarte [di 'faːkaːtə]

Local transportation

Take advantage of the excellent public transportation found in Germany. There will often be different providers, one for say the city area, another for the surrounding area. These providers are usually integrated into a network, and you will be able to buy tickets valid for all vehicles. Ask for help if you're not sure. A good place to start is the local tourist office. Within a municipal area, you will find buses, trams/streetcars, and even a *U-Bahn* (underground/subway). Rural areas are almost always served by buses.

Normally, you can buy a ticket from the driver, but it may be cheaper to buy one from a vending machine. Multiple tickets, family tickets (*Familienkarte*) and day passes for all routes (*Netzkarte*) are usually available. Make sure the ticket has a date and time stamped on it, otherwise you will be expected to have it stamped by a separate machine, labelled *entwerten*. There are no longer conductors on German buses or trams, but you may run into a *Kontrolleur* (inspector) who fines people without valid stamped tickets.

Excuse me, where's the next ...
Bitte, wo ist die nächste ... ['bɪtə voː ʔɪst di nɛçstə ...]
   bus stop?
   Bushaltestelle? ['bʊshaltəʃtɛlə]
   tram/streetcar stop?
   Straßenbahnhaltestelle? ['ʃtʀaːsnbaːn‚haltəʃtɛlə]
   underground station?
   U-Bahnstation? [ʔuːbaːnʃtaˌtsjoːn]

Which line goes to ... ?
Welche Linie fährt nach ...? ['vɛlçə 'liːnjə feːt nax ...]

When's the last (underground/tube) train to ...?
Wann fährt die letzte U-Bahn nach ...?
['van feːt di 'lɛtstə ʔuːbaːn nax]

Excuse me, does this bus go to ...?
Entschuldigen Sie, ist das der Bus nach ...?
[ʔɛnt'ʃʊldɪgn̩ ziː ʔɪst das de bʊs nax]

How many stops is it?
Wie viele Haltestellen sind es? ['vi:_fi:lə 'haltəʃtɛln ‚zɪnt əs]

Excuse me, where do I have to get out?
Entschuldigen Sie, wo muss ich aussteigen?
[ʔɛntˈʃʊldɪɡn̩ zi vo: mʊs ɪç ˈʔaʊstaɪɡn̩]

Excuse me, will I have to change?
Entschuldigen Sie, muss ich umsteigen?
[ʔɛntˈʃʊldɪɡn̩ zi mʊs ɪç ˈʔʊmʃtaɪɡn̩]

Could you let me know when I have to get off, please?
Könnten Sie mir bitte Bescheid geben, wann ich aussteigen
muss? [kœntn̩ zi miɐ ˈbɪtə bəˈʃaɪt geːbm̩ vɛn ɪç ˈʔaʊstaɪɡn̩ mʊs]

A ticket to ..., please.
Bitte, einen Fahrschein nach ... ['bɪtə ʔaɪnn̩ 'fa:ʃaɪn nax]

The ticket machine is bust/broken.
Der Fahrkartenautomat ist kaputt/defekt.
[dɐ ˈfaːkaːtn̩ʔaʊtoˌmaːt ʔɪst kaˈpʊt/deˈfɛkt]

The machine doesn't accept notes.
Der Automat nimmt keine Geldscheine an.
[dɐ ʔaʊtoˈmaːt nɪmt ˈkaɪnə ˈɡɛltʃaɪnə ʔan]

bus	der Bus [dɐ bʊs]
bus station	der Busbahnhof [dɐ ˈbʊsˌbaːnhoːf]
departure	die Abfahrt [di ˈʔapfaːt]
direction	die Richtung [di ˈʀɪçtʊŋ]
fare	der Fahrpreis [dɐ ˈfaːpʀaɪs]
to get on	einsteigen [ˈʔaɪnʃtaɪɡn̩]
inspector	der Kontrolleur [dɐ kɔntʀoˈløɐ]
local train	der Nahverkehrszug
	[dɐ ˈnaːfɐˌkeɐstsuːk]
day ticket (pass)	die Tageskarte [di ˈtaːɡəskaːtə]
rack-railway/cable car	die Zahnradbahn [di ˈtsaːnʀatˌbaːn]
stop	die Haltestelle [di ˈhaltəʃtɛlə]
suburban train	die S-Bahn [di ˈɛsbaːn]
terminus	die Endstation [di ˈʔɛntʃtatsjoːn]
ticket	der Fahrschein [dɐ ˈfaːʃaɪn]
conductor/ ticket collector .	der Schaffner [dɐ ˈʃafnɐ]
ticket machine	der Fahrkartenautomat
	[dɐ ˈfaːkaːtn̩ʔaʊtoˌmaːt]
timetable	der Fahrplan [dɐ ˈfaːplaːn]
tram/streetcar	die Straßenbahn [di ˈʃtʀaːsnbaːn]
underground/subway (US) .	die U-Bahn [di ˈʔuːbaːn]
weekly season ticket/	die Wochenkarte [di ˈvɔxnkaːtə]
one-week pass	

Excuse me, where's the nearest taxi rank/stand?
Entschuldigen Sie bitte, wo ist der nächste Taxistand?
[ʔɛntʃʊldɪgŋ zi ˈbɪtə ˈvoː ʔɪst de ˈnɛːçstə ˈtaksiʃtant]

To the station, please.
Zum Bahnhof, bitte. [tsʊm ˈbaːnhoːf ˈbɪtə]

To the ... Hotel, please.
Zum ... Hotel, bitte. [tsʊm ... hoˈtɛl ˈbɪtə]

To ... Street, please.
In die ...-Straße, bitte. [ʔɪn di ... ˈʃtʁaːsə ˈbɪtə]

To (name of a town)..., please.
Nach ..., bitte. [nax ... ˈbɪtə]

How much will it cost to ...?
Wie viel kostet es nach ...? [ˈviː_fil ˈkɔstət əs nax]

Could you stop here, please?
Halten Sie bitte hier. [ˈhaltn zi ˈbɪtə hiɐ]

That's for you.
Das ist für Sie. [das ʔɪst fyɐ ˈziː]

Keep the change.
Behalten Sie das Restgeld. [bəˈhaltn zi das ˈʁɛstgɛlt]

fasten one's seat belt	anschnallen [ˈʔanʃnaln]
flat rate	der Pauschalpreis [de paʊˈʃaːlpʁaɪs]
house number	die Hausnummer [di ˈhaʊsnʊmɐ]
price per kilometre	der Kilometerpreis [de kiloˈmeːtɐpʁaɪs]
receipt	die Quittung [di ˈkvɪtʊŋ]
seat belt	der Sicherheitsgurt [de ˈzɪçɐhaɪtsˌgʊɐt]
to stop	anhalten [ˈʔanhaltn]
taxi rank/stand	der Taxistand [de ˈtaksiʃtant]
taxi driver	der Taxifahrer/die Taxifahrerin [de ˈtaksifaːʁɐ/di ˈtaksifaːʁəʁɪn]
tip	das Trinkgeld [das ˈtʁɪŋk(g)ɛlt]

Adequate facilities

If you are travelling with small children, you will find adequate facilities almost everywhere. Playgrounds are easy to find, the larger department stores usually have baby-care rooms, and almost all restaurants have highchairs for the asking. If you are driving, you will find resting areas at regular intervals along the autobahn with play areas and child-friendly restaurants.

Useful phrases

Could you tell me if there is a children's playground here, please?

Könnten Sie mir bitte sagen, ob es hier einen Kinderspielplatz gibt? [kœn zi miɐ 'bɪtə za:gn ʔɔp əs hiɐ ʔaɪnn 'kɪndeʃpi:lplats gɪpt]

Is there a baby-sitting service here?

Gibt es hier eine Kinderbetreuung? [gɪpt əs hiɐ ˌʔaɪnə 'kɪndebətʀɔɪʊn]

From what age onward?

Ab welchem Alter? [ab 'vɛlçm ʔaltɐ]

Do you know anyone who could baby-sit for us?

Kennen Sie jemanden, der bei uns babysitten kann? ['kɛnn zi 'je:mandn dɐ baɪ ʔʊns 'be:bisɪtn kan]

Do you have a baby intercom?

Haben Sie ein Babyfon? ['ha:bm zi ʔaɪn 'be:bifo:n]

Is there a reduction for children?

Gibt es eine Ermäßigung für Kinder? [gɪpt əs ˌʔaɪnə ʔɐ'mɛ:sɪgʊn fyɐ 'kɪndɐ]

On the road

We're travelling with a young child.

Wir reisen mit einem Kleinkind. [viɐ 'ʀaɪzn mɪt ˌʔaɪnəm 'klaɪnkɪnt]

Can we get seats right at the front?

Können wir Plätze ganz vorn bekommen? [kœn viɐ 'plɛtsə gants 'fɔɐn bə'kɔmm]

Do you rent out child seats for the car?

Verleihen Sie Kinderautositze? [fɐ'laɪn zi 'kɪndɐˌʔautozɪtsə]

Do you possibly have any crayons and a colouring book for our child?

Haben Sie vielleicht Stifte und ein Malbuch für unser Kind? ['ha:bm zi fɪ'laɪçt ʃtɪftə ʔʊnt aɪn 'ma:lbu:x fyɐ ʔʊnsɐ 'kɪnt]

At the restaurant

Could you bring us a highchair, please?
Könnten Sie bitte noch einen Kinderstuhl bringen?
[kœntn zi 'bɪtə nɔx ?aɪnn 'kɪndəʃtu:l bʀɪŋŋ]

Do you also have children's portions?
Gibt es auch Kinderportionen? [gɪpt əs aʊx 'kɪndepɔ'tsjo:nn]

Could you warm up the baby bottle, please?
Könnten Sie mir bitte das Fläschchen warm machen?
['kœntn zi mie 'bɪtə das 'flɛʃçn va:m maxn]

Could you tell me where I can breast-feed my baby?
Könnten Sie mir bitte sagen, wo ich hier stillen kann?
[kœntn zi mie 'bɪtə za:gŋ vo: ıç hie 'ʃtɪln kan]

adventure playground	der Abenteuerspielplatz [dɐ 'a:bmtɔɪɐʃpi:lplats]
baby food	die Kindernahrung [di 'kɪndena:ʀʊŋ]
baby intercom	das Babyfon [das 'be:bifo:n]
baby seat	die Babyschale [di 'be:biʃa:lə]
baby's bottle	die Trinkflasche [di 'tʀɪŋkflaʃə]
baby's changing table	der Wickeltisch [dɐ 'vɪkltɪʃ]
baby-sitter	der Babysitter [dɐ 'be:bisɪtɐ]
baby-sitting service	die Kinderbetreuung [di 'kɪndebətʀɔjʊŋ]
baby bonnet	die Schildmütze [di 'ʃɪltmʏtsə]
baby carriage *(US)*	der Kinderwagen [dɐ 'kɪndeva:gŋ]
child reduction	die Kinderermäßigung [di 'kɪndɐʔe'mɛ:sɪgʊŋ]
child seat	der Kindersitz [dɐ 'kɪndezɪts]
child seat cushion	das Kindersitzkissen [das 'kɪndezɪtskɪsn]
children's bed	das Kinderbett [das 'kɪndebɛt]
children's clothing	die Kinderkleidung [di 'kɪndeklaɪdʊŋ]
children's club	der Miniclub [dɐ 'mɪniklʊp]
children's playground	der Kinderspielplatz [dɐ 'kɪndeʃpi:lplats]
children's pool	das Kinderbecken [das 'kɪndebɛkŋ]
colouring book	das Malbuch [das 'ma:lbu:x]
cot	das Kinderbett [das 'kɪndebɛt]
diapers *(US)*	die Windeln *f pl* [di vɪndln]
dummy	der Schnuller [dɐ 'ʃnʊlɐ]
feeding bottle	die Saugflasche [di 'zaʊkflaʃə]
highchair	der Kinderstuhl [dɐ 'kɪndeʃtu:l]
nappies	die Windeln *f pl* [di vɪndln]
pacifier *(US)*	der Schnuller [dɐ 'ʃnʊlɐ]
paddling pool	das Planschbecken [das 'planʃbɛkn]
protection against sun	der Sonnenschutz [dɐ 'zɔnnʃʊts]
rubber ring	der Schwimmring [dɐ 'ʃvɪmʀɪŋ]

75

sand-castle	die Sandburg [di 'zantbuɐk]
swimming lessons	der Schwimmkurs [dɐ 'ʃvɪmkuɐs]
teat	der Sauger [dɐ 'zaʊgɐ]
toys	die Spielsachen f pl [di 'ʃpiːl zaːxn]
water wings	die Schwimmflügel m pl [di 'ʃvɪmflyːgl]

Health

Could you tell me if there's a pediatrician here?
Könnten Sie mir bitte sagen, ob es hier einen Kinderarzt gibt?
[kœntn zi miɐ 'bɪtə zaːgn 'ɔp əs hiɐ 'ʔaɪnn 'kɪndɐʔaːtst gɪpt]

My child has ...
Mein Kind hat ... [maɪn 'kɪnt hat]

My child is allergic to ...
Mein Kind ist allergisch gegen ... [maɪn 'kɪnt ɪst ʔa'lɛɐgɪʃ geːgn ...]

He/She has been sick.
Er/Sie hat erbrochen. [ʔeɐ/zi hat ʔɛ'bʀɔxn]

He/She has (got) diarrhoea.
Er/Sie hat Durchfall. [ʔeɐ/zi hat 'dʊɐçfal]

He/She has been stung.
Er/Sie ist gestochen worden. [ʔeɐ/zi ɪst gə'ʃtɔxn vɔɐdn]

allergy	die Allergie [di ʔal(ɛ)ɐ'giː]
chickenpox	die Windpocken f pl [di 'vɪntpɔkn]
children's illness	die Kinderkrankheit [di 'kɪndɐˌkʀaŋkhaɪt]
cold	die Erkältung [di ʔe'kɛltʊŋ] , der Schnupfen [dɐ ʃnʊpfn]
fever	das Fieber [das 'fiːbɐ]
fungal infection	der Pilz [dɐ pɪlts]
German measles	die Röteln f pl [di ʀøːtln]
inflammation of the middle ear	die Mittelohrentzündung [di 'mɪtlʔoɐˌʔɛnˌtsʏndʊŋ]
insect bite	der Insektenstich [dɐ ʔɪn'zɛktnʃtɪç]
measles	die Masern f pl ['maːzen]
medicinal food	die Heilnahrung [di 'haɪlnaːʀʊŋ]
mumps	der Mumps [dɐ mʊmps]
pediatric clinic	das Kinderkrankenhaus [das 'kɪndɐˌkʀaŋknhaʊs]
rash	der Ausschlag [dɐ 'ʔaʊʃlaːk]
scarlet fever	der Scharlach [dɐ 'ʃaːlax]
temperature	das Fieber [das 'fiːbɐ]
vaccination card	der Impfpass [dɐ 'ʔɪm(p)fpas]
wind	die Blähungen f pl [di 'blɛːʊŋŋ]

Disabled travellers

Problematical buildings, helpful people

Although most German cities are trying very hard to improve conditions, disabled people will encounter a number of problems. Historical sections of towns present obvious problems such as narrow streets with cobblestones. Older buildings usually have steps, and even if you get in, there may not be a lift for going up inside. Much work has been done in larger cities to level curbs and make public transportation accessible. Large department stores are almost always accessible and have suitable toilet facilities. It is possible to travel by train, but wheelchair users should try to travel by *IC* or *ICE* (express) trains and avoid older passenger trains marked *E-Zug* or those printed in black on schedules. Larger hotels and modern restaurants are usually fully prepared for the disabled. Information will be essential, so the tourist information office should be one of your first stops. Ask if there is a *Stadtführer für Behinderte*, a guide to the city for the disabled. Most people are very willing to help if you run into trouble.

I have a disability.
Ich habe eine Behinderung. [ʔɪç ˈhaːbə ʔaɪnə bəˈhɪndəʀʊŋ]

I'm ...
Ich bin ... [ʔɪç bɪn ...]
  a paraplegic.
  querschnittsgelähmt. [ˈkveɐʃnɪtsɡəlɛːmt]
  partially sighted / visually impaired.
  sehbehindert. [ˈzeːbəhɪndɛt]

I have ...
Ich habe ... [ʔɪç ˈhaːbə]
  a physical handicap.
  eine körperliche Behinderung. [ʔaɪnə ˈkœɐpɛlɪçə bəˈhɪndəʀʊŋ]
  multiple sclerosis.
  Multiple Sklerose. [mʊlˈtiːplə skleˈʀoːzə]

Can you help me ...
Können Sie mir helfen, ... [ˈkœnn zi mɪɐ hɛlfn]
  to cross this street.
  die Straße zu überqueren. [di ˈʃtʀaːsə tsʊ ʔybɐˈkveɐn]
  to get into the bus.
  in den Bus zu kommen. [ɪn den bʊs tsʊ kɔmm]

Can you help me up these steps?
Können Sie mir helfen, die Treppen hinaufzukommen?
[ˈkœnn zi mɪɐ hɛlfn di tʀɛpm hɪnˈaʊftsʊkɔmm]

We have to go up backwards.
Wir müssen rückwärts hinauf. [viɐ mʏsn ˈʀʏkvɛɐts hɪnˈaʊf]

We'll need one more person to help.
Wir brauchen noch jemanden, der hilft.
[vie brauxn nɔx 'je:mandn dee hɪlft]

Tilt the wheelchair back first.
Zuerst den Rollstuhl kippen. [tsu'ʔeest den 'rɔlʃtu:l kɪpm]

Could you put the wheelchair in the back of the car?
Könnten Sie den Rollstuhl hinten ins Auto stellen?
['kœntn zi den 'rɔlʃtu:l 'hɪntn ɪns ʔauto 'ʃtɛln]

Do you have a bathroom/a toilet for disabled people?
Haben Sie ein Bad/eine Toilette für Behinderte?
['ha:bm zi ʔaɪn ba:t/ʔaɪnə to'lɛtə fye bə'hɪndetə]

Getting around

Can I take a folding wheelchair with me on the plane?
Kann ich einen faltbaren Rollstuhl im Flugzeug mitnehmen?
[kan ɪç ʔaɪnn 'faltbaʁən 'rɔlʃtu:l ɪm 'flu:ktsɔɪk 'mɪtne:mm]

Will a wheelchair be provided at the airport?
Wird ein Rollstuhl am Flughafen bereitgestellt?
[vɪed ʔaɪn 'rɔlʃtu:l am 'flu:kha:fn bə'ʁaɪtgəʃtɛlt]

I'd like an aisle seat.
Ich möchte einen Sitz am Gang. ['ɪç 'mœçtə ʔaɪnn zɪts am 'gaŋ]

Is there a toilet for the disabled?
Gibt es eine Behindertentoilette? [gɪpt əs ʔaɪnə bə'hɪndetnto'lɛtə]

Is there a washroom for the disabled?
Gibt es einen Behindertenwaschraum?
[gɪpt əs ʔaɪnn bə'hɪndetn,vaʃʁaum]

Could someone help me change trains?
Könnte mir jemand beim Umsteigen behilflich sein?
['kœntə mie 'je:mant baɪm 'ʔʊmʃtaɪgn bə'hɪlflɪç zaɪn]

Is the entrance to the carriage at ground level?
Ist der Einstieg in den Wagen ebenerdig?
[ʔɪst de 'ʔaɪnʃti:k ɪn den va:gn 'ʔe:bm'ʔeedɪç]

Are there low-floor buses?
Gibt es Niederflurbusse? [gɪpt əs 'ni:deflue,busə]

Are there ramps to the platforms for wheelchair users?
Gibt es Rampen zu den Bahnsteigen für Rollstuhlfahrer?
[gɪpt əs 'ʁampm tsʊ den 'ba:nʃtaɪgn fye 'rɔlʃtu:l,fa:ʁe]

Are there rental cars with hand controls for the disabled?
Gibt es für Körperbehinderte Leihwagen mit Handbetrieb?
[gɪpt əs fye 'kœepebə,hɪndetə 'laɪva:gn mɪt 'hantbətʁi:b]

Do you rent camper vans suitable for wheelchair users?
Vermieten Sie rollstuhlgerechte Wohnmobile?
[fɛˈmiːtn̩ ziː ˈʀɔlʃtuːlɡəˌʀɛçtə ˈvoːnmobiːlə]

Is it possible to rent handbikes here?
Kann man hier Handbikes leihen? [kan man hiɐ ˈhɛntbaɪks laɪn]

Accommodation

Do you have information about hotels suitable for wheelchair users?
Haben Sie Informationen über Hotels, die für Rollstuhlfahrer geeignet sind? [ˈhaːbm̩ ziː ɪnfɔmaˈtsjoːnn̩ ˀyːbɐ hoˈtɛls diː fyɐ ˈʀɔlʃtuːlˌfaːʀɐ ɡəˀʔaɪknət zɪnt]

What hotels can you recommend for disabled people?
Welche Hotels können Sie Behinderten empfehlen?
[ˈvɛlçə hoˈtɛls ˈkœnn̩ ziː bəˈhɪndɛtn̩ ˀɛmˈpfeːln]

Could you tell me which hotels and camping sites have special facilities for the disabled?
Könnten Sie mir bitte sagen, welche Hotels und Campingplätze behindertengerechte Einrichtungen haben?
[kœntn̩ ziː miɐ ˈbɪtə zaːɡn̩ ˈvɛlçə hoˈtɛls ʊnt ˈkɛmpɪŋplɛtsə bəˈhɪndetnɡəˌʀɛçtə ˀʔaɪnʀɪçtʊŋŋ haːbm̩]

Museums, sights, theatre ...

Is there a lift to the exhibition?
Gibt es einen Aufzug zu der Ausstellung?
[ɡɪpt əs ˀʔaɪnn̩ ˀʔaʊftsuːk tsʊ deː ˀʔaʊʃtɛlʊŋ]

I'm a wheelchair user. How do I get up there?
Ich bin Rollstuhlfahrer. Wie komme ich da hoch?
[ˀʔɪç bɪn ˈʀɔlʃtuːlˌfaːʀɐ viː ˈkɔmə ˀʔɪç daː ˈhoːx]

Are there guided tours (of the city) for the disabled?
Gibt es (Stadt)führungen für Behinderte?
[ɡɪpt əs (ˈʃtat)ˌfyːʀʊŋŋ fyɐ bəˈhɪndetə]

Do you have an induction loop?
Haben Sie eine Induktionsschleife?
[ˈhaːbn̩ ziː ˀʔaɪnə ˀʔɪndʊkˈtsjoːnsˌʃlaɪfə]

Are there museum tours for the blind?
Gibt es Museumsführungen für Blinde?
[ɡɪpt əs muˈzeʊmsˌfyːʀʊŋŋ fyɐ ˈblɪndə]

access . . . . der Zugang [de ˈtsuːɡaŋ]
accessible . . . . zugänglich [ˈtsuːɡɛŋlɪç]
accompanying person . . . . die Begleitperson [di bəˈɡlaɪtpɛ(ɛ)ɐˌzoːn]

80

aid to walking	die Gehhilfe [di 'ge:hɪlfə]
amputated	amputiert [ampu'tiɐt]
at ground level	ebenerdig [ˈʔeːbmˈʔeɐdɪç]
blind	blind [blɪnt]
blind person	der Blinde [dɐ 'blɪndə]
braille	die Blindenschrift [di 'blɪndnʃrɪft]
cane	der Taststock [dɐ 'tastʃtɔk]
care	die Betreuung [di bə'trɔɪʊŋ]
crutch	die Krücke [di 'krʏkə]
deaf	gehörlos [gə'høːɐloːs], taub [taʊp]
deaf person	der/die Gehörlose [dɐ/dɪ gə'høːɐloːzə]
deaf-mute	taubstumm ['taʊpʃtʊm]
deaf-mute (person)	der/die Taubstumme [dɐ/dɪ 'taʊpʃtʊmə]
disability	die Behinderung [di bə'hɪndərʊŋ]
disabled	behindert [bə'hɪndɐt]
disabled person	der/die Behinderte [dɐ/dɪ bə'hɪndɐtə]
disability identification	der Behindertenausweis [dɐ bə'hɪndɐtnˈʔaʊsvaɪs]
door opener	der Türöffner [dɐ 'tyɐʔœfnɐ]
door width	die Türbreite [di 'tyɐbraɪtə]
doorstep	die Türschwelle [di 'tyɐʃvɛlə]
elevator	der Lift [dɐ lɪft]
epilepsy	die Epilepsie [di epilɛp'si]
good clearance	unterfahrbar ['ʊntɐfaːba:]
gradient	die Steigung [di 'ʃtaɪɡʊŋ]
guide dog	der Blindenhund [dɐ 'blɪndnhʊnt]
hall width	die Flurbreite [di 'fluɐbraɪtə]
hand throttle (car)	das Handgas [das 'hantga:s]
hand-operated bike	das Handbike [das 'hɛntbaɪk]
handicap	die Behinderung [di bə'hɪndərʊŋ]
handle	der Haltegriff [dɐ 'haltəɡrɪf]
handrail	der Handlauf [dɐ 'hantlaʊf]
hard of hearing	schwerhörig ['ʃveɐhøːrɪç]
headphones	der Kopfhörer [dɐ 'kɔpfhøːʀɐ]
height	die Höhe [di høːə]
hydraulic ramp	die Hebebühne [di 'heːbəbyːnə]
induction loop	die Induktionsschleife [di ɪndʊk'tsjoːnʃlaɪfə]
in need of care	pflegebedürftig ['pfleːɡəbədʏftɪç]
keyboard telephone	das Schreibtelefon [das 'ʃraɪptələfoːn]
lift	der Lift [dɐ lɪft]
mentally handicapped	geistig behindert ['ɡaɪstɪç bə'hɪndɐt]
mute	stumm [ʃtʊm]
out-patient	ambulant [ambʊ'lant]
paraplegic, quadriplegic	querschnittsgelähmt ['kveɐʃnɪtsɡə,lɛːmt]

parking space for disabled .	der Behindertenparkplatz
	[der bə'hɪndɐtnpa:kplats]
partially sighted	sehbehindert ['se:bəhɪndɐt]
passable	befahrbar [bə'fa:ba:]
ramp	die Rampe [di 'Rampə]
seeing-eye dog (US)	der Blindenhund [dɐ 'blɪndnhʊnt]
self-opening door	die automatische Tür
	[di ʔaʊto'ma:tɪʃə ty:ɐ]
steering knob	der Lenkrad-Drehknopf
	[dɐ 'lɛŋkRat,dRe:knɔpf]
shower seat	der Duschsitz [dɐ 'du:ʃzɪts]
sign language	die Zeichensprache [di 'tsaɪçnʃpRa:xə]
step	die Stufe [di 'ʃtu:fə]
stairs	die Treppen f pl [di tRɛpm]
suitable for the disabled . . .	behindertengerecht
	[bə'hɪndɐtngə,Rɛçt]
suitable for wheelchair users	rollstuhlgerecht ['Rɔlʃtu:lgə,Rɛçt]
toilet for the disabled	die Behindertentoilette
	[di bə'hɪndɐtntoˌlɛtə]
transport service	das Fahrdienst [das 'fa:di:nst]
visually impaired	sehbehindert ['se:bəhɪndɐt]
wheelchair	der Rollstuhl [dɐ 'Rɔlʃtu:l]
battery-driven	batteriebetrieben [batə'Ri: bə'tRi:bm]
electric wheelchair	der E-Rollstuhl [dɐ ʔe:,Rɔlʃtu:l]
folding wheelchair	der Faltrollstuhl [dɐ 'falt,Rɔlʃtu:l]
wheelchair cabin (ship)	die Rollstuhlkabine [di 'Rɔlʃtu:lka,bi:nə]
wheelchair hiking	das Rollstuhlwandern
	[das 'Rɔlʃtu:l,vandɐn]
wheelchair user (man)	der Rollstuhlfahrer [dɐ 'Rɔlʃtu:l,fa:Rɐ]
wheelchair user (woman) . .	die Rollstuhlfahrerin
	[di 'Rɔlʃtu:l,fa:Rəʀɪn]
width	die Breite [di 'bRaɪtə]

Accommodation

A good night's sleep

Finding a place to stay is easy enough in Germany. If you want to save money or get more of a "German feel" to your stay, time your overnight stops so you'll be in smaller towns or even rural areas. Hotels, especially in cities, are international in character. *Gasthaus* means basically a small hotel and will be more local in character. *Gasthof* is about the same thing, but in a rural area. A *Pension* is a bed-and-breakfast place, often your best value, and usually the most personal in character. *Hotel Garni* means they only serve breakfast. *Fremdenzimmer* means accommodation in a private house. Look for the sign *Zimmer frei* (vacancies).

Information

Can you recommend ..., please?
Können Sie mir bitte ... empfehlen?
['kœnn zi miɐ 'bɪtə ... ?ɛm'pfeːln]

a good hotel
ein gutes Hotel [?aɪn 'guːtəs ho'tɛl]
a simple hotel
ein einfaches Hotel [?aɪn ?aɪnfaxəs ho'tɛl]
a bed-and-breakfast
eine Pension [?aɪnə paŋ'zjoːn]

Is it central/quiet/near the beach?
Ist es zentral/ruhig/in Strandnähe gelegen?
[?ɪst əs tsɛn'tʀaːl/ʀuːɪç/?ɪn 'ʃtʀantnɛːə gə'leːgn]

Is there ... here too?
Gibt es hier auch ... [gɪpt əs hiɐ ?aʊx]
a youth hostel
eine Jugendherberge? [?aɪnə 'juːgṇthɛɐˌbɛɐgə]
a camping site
einen Campingplatz? [?aɪnn 'kɛmpɪŋplats]

At the hotel

At the reception desk

I've reserved a room. My name's ...
Ich habe ein Zimmer reserviert. Mein Name ist ...
[?ɪç 'haːbə aɪn 'tsɪmɐ ʀeze'viɐt maɪn 'naːmə ?ɪst ...]

Have you got any vacancies?
Haben Sie noch Zimmer frei? ['haːbm zi nɔx 'tsɪmɐ fʀaɪ]
... for one night
... für eine Nacht [... fyɐ ?aɪnə naxt]

... for two days
... für zwei Tage [... fyɐ tsvaɪ 'ta:gə]

... for a week
... für eine Woche [... fyɐ 'ʔaɪnə 'vɔxə]

No, I'm afraid not.
Nein, leider nicht. [naɪn 'laɪdɐ 'nɪçt]

Yes, what sort of room would you like?
Ja, was für ein Zimmer wünschen Sie?
[ja: vas fyɐ ʔaɪn 'tsɪmɐ 'vʏnʃn zi:]

I'd like ...
Ich hätte gern ... [ʔɪç 'hɛtə gɛɐn]

  a single room
  ein Einzelzimmer [ʔaɪn 'ʔaɪntsltsɪmɐ]

  a double room
  ein Doppelzimmer [ʔaɪn 'dɔpltsɪmɐ]

  a quiet room
  ein ruhiges Zimmer [ʔaɪn 'ʀʊɪgəs 'tsɪmɐ]

  with a shower
  mit Dusche [mɪt 'du:ʃə]

  with a bath
  mit Bad [mɪt ba:t]

  with a balcony/terrace
  mit Balkon/Terrasse [mɪt bal'kɔŋ/te'ʀasə]

  with a view of the mountains
  mit Blick auf die Berge [mɪt blɪk aʊf di 'bɛɐgə]

Can I see the room?
Kann ich das Zimmer ansehen? [kan ɪç das 'tsɪmɐ 'ʔanze:n]

Can I see a different one, please.
Kann ich bitte noch ein anderes sehen?
[kan ɪç 'bɪtə nɔx aɪn 'ʔandərəs ze:n]

I'll take this room.
Dieses Zimmer nehme ich. ['di:zəs 'tsɪmɐ 'ne:mə ɪç]

Can you put a third bed/a cot in the room?
Können Sie noch ein drittes Bett/ein Kinderbett dazustellen?
['kœnn zi nɔx aɪn bɛt/aɪn 'kɪndebɛt da'tsu:ʃtɛln]

Beds usually have a duvet/comforter instead of a top sheet and blankets. There will be an extra blanket in the wardrobe/cabinet. Don't expect to find tea or coffee-making facilities in the room.

How much is the room with ...
Was kostet das Zimmer mit ..., bitte?
[vas 'kɔstət das 'tsɪmɐ mɪt ... bɪtə]

breakfast?
Frühstück ['fʀy:ʃtʏk]
half-board (breakfast and dinner)?
Halbpension ['halpaŋzjoːn]
full board (all meals)?
Vollpension ['fɔlpaŋzjoːn]

Could you fill out the registration form, please?
Wollen Sie bitte den Anmeldeschein ausfüllen?
[vɔln zi 'bɪtə den ʔanmɛldəʃaɪn ʔaʊsfʏln]

May I see your passport?
Darf ich Ihren Ausweis sehen? [daːf ɪç 'iːʀən/ʔien ʔaʊsvaɪs zeːn]

Where can I park the car?
Wo kann ich den Wagen abstellen? [voː kan ɪç den 'vaːgn ʔapʃtɛln]
In our garage.
In unserer Garage. ['ʔɪn ˌʊnzəʀe gaˈʀaːʒə]
In our car park.
Auf unserem Parkplatz. [ʔaʊf ˌʊnzem 'paːkplats]

Asking for service

➤ also Breakfast

When is breakfast served?
Ab wann gibt es Frühstück? [ʔap 'van gɪpt əs 'fʀyːʃtʏk]

When are the meals served?
Wann sind die Essenszeiten? [van zɪnt die ʔɛsnstsaɪtn]

Where's the restaurant?
Wo ist der Speisesaal? [voː ʔɪst de 'ʃpaɪzəzaːl]

Where's the breakfast room?
Wo ist der Frühstücksraum? [voː ʔɪst de 'fʀyːʃtʏksʀaʊm]

Could you wake me at seven o'clock tomorrow morning, please.
Könnten Sie mich bitte morgen früh um sieben Uhr wecken?
[kœntn zi mɪç 'bɪtə 'mɔegn fry: ʊm 'ziːbm ʔue 'vɛkn]

How does ... work?
Wie funktioniert ...? [vi: fʊŋktsjoˈniet]

Room 24 please!
Zimmernummer vierundzwanzig, bitte!
['tsɪmenʊme 'fie(ʊ)n'tsvantsɪç 'bɪtə]

Is there any post/mail for me?
Ist Post für mich da? [ʔɪst pɔst fye mɪç da:]

Where can I ...
Wo kann ich ... [voː kan ɪç]
get something to drink?
hier etwas trinken? [hie ˌʔɛtvas 'tʀɪŋkn]

hire a car?
ein Auto mieten? [ʔaɪn ʔˈaʊto miːtn]
telephone from (here)?
hier telefonieren? [hiɐ teləfoˈniːʀən/-ˈniɐn]

Can I leave my valuables in your safe?
Kann ich meine Wertsachen bei Ihnen in den Safe geben?
[kan ɪç ˌmaɪnə ˈveɐtzaxn baɪ ʔiːnn ʔɪn den ˈsɛɪf/seːf geːbm]

Can I leave my luggage here?
Kann ich mein Gepäck hier lassen? [kan ɪç maɪn gəˈpɛk ˈhiɐ_lasn]

Complaints

The room hasn't been cleaned today.
Das Zimmer ist heute nicht geputzt worden.
[das ˈtsɪmɐ ʔɪst ˈhɔɪtə nɪçt gəˈpʊtst vɔɐdn]

The air-conditioning doesn't work.
Die Klimaanlage funktioniert nicht.
[di ˈkliːmaʔanˌlaːgə fʊŋktsjoˈniɐt nɪçt]

The tap/faucet drips.
Der Wasserhahn tropft. [dɐ ˈvasɐhaːn tʀɔpft]

There's no (hot) water.
Es kommt kein (warmes) Wasser. [ʔəs kɔmt kaɪn (vaːməs) ˈvasɐ]

The toilet/washbasin is blocked up.
Die Toilette/Das Waschbecken ist verstopft.
[di tɔ(ɪ)ˈlɛtə/das ˈvaʃbɛkn ʔɪst fɐˈʃtɔpft]

I'd like to have a different room.
Ich hätte gern ein anderes Zimmer.
[ʔɪç ˈhɛtə gɛɐn ʔaɪn ʔˈandəʀəs ˈtsɪmɐ]

Departure

I'm leaving tomorrow at ... o'clock.
Ich reise morgen um ... Uhr ab. [ʔɪç ˈʀaɪzə mɔɐgn ʊm ... ʔuɐ ʔˈap]

I'd like my bill, please.
Könnten Sie bitte die Rechnung fertig machen?
[kœntn zi ˈbɪtə di ˈʀɛçnʊŋ ˈfɛɐtɪç maxn]

Can I pay by credit card?
Kann ich mit Kreditkarte bezahlen?
[ˈkan ɪç mɪt kʀeˈdiːtˌkaːtə bəˈtsaːln]

Would you call a taxi for me, please.
Könnten Sie mir bitte ein Taxi rufen?
[kœntn zi miɐ ˈbɪtə ʔaɪn ˈtaksi ʀuːfn]

Thank you very much for everything. Goodbye!
Vielen Dank für alles! Auf Wiedersehen!
[ˈfiːln daŋk fyɐ ʔˈaləs ʔaʊf_ˈviːdəzeːn]

adapter	der Zwischenstecker [dɐ ˈtsvɪʃnʃtɛkɐ]
air-conditioning	die Klimaanlage [di ˈkliːmaʔanˌlaːɡə]
ashtray	der Aschenbecher [dɐ ˈʔaʃnbɛçɐ]
balcony	der Balkon [dɐ balˈkɔn]
bath	die Badewanne [di ˈbaːdəvanə]
bathroom	das Badezimmer [das ˈbaːdətsɪmɐ]
bath towel	das Badetuch [das ˈbaːdətuːx]
bed	das Bett [das bɛt]
bed linen	die Bettwäsche [di ˈbɛtvɛʃə]
bedside table	der Nachttisch [dɐ ˈnaxttɪʃ]
bidet	das Bidet [das biˈdeː]
bin	der Abfalleimer [dɐ ˈʔapfalˌʔaɪmɐ]
blanket	die Bettdecke [di ˈbɛtdɛkə]
breakfast	das Frühstück [das ˈfryːʃtʏk]
breakfast room	der Frühstücksraum [dɐ ˈfryːʃtʏksraʊm]
buffet breakfast	das Frühstücksbüfett [das ˈfryːʃtʏksbyˌfeː]
chair	der Stuhl [dɐ ˈʃtuːl]
to clean	reinigen [ˈraɪnɪɡn]
clothes closet/cabinet	der Kleiderschrank [dɐ ˈklaɪdɐʃraŋk]
coat hanger	der Kleiderbügel [dɐ ˈklaɪdɐbyːɡl]
cover/place (for breakfast)	das Gedeck (für das Frühstück) [das ɡəˈdɛk fyɐ (da)s ˈfryːʃtʏk]
dining room	der Speisesaal [dɐ ˈʃpaɪzəzaːl]
dinner	das Abendessen [das ˈʔaːbmtˌʔɛsn]
door	die Tür [di tyɐ]
door code	der Türcode [dɐ ˈtyɐkoːt]
elevator	der Aufzug [dɐ ˈʔaʊftsuːk]
extra week	die Verlängerungswoche [di fɐˈlɛŋərʊŋsˌvɔxə]
fan	der Ventilator [dɐ vɛntiˈlaːtoɐ]
faucet	der Wasserhahn [dɐ ˈvasɐhaːn]
floor (= storey)	die Etage [di ʔeˈtaːʒə]
garage	die Garage [di ɡaˈraːʒə]
glass	das Wasserglas [das ˈvasɐɡlaːs], das Glas [das ɡlaːs]
handheld shower	die Handbrause [di ˈhantbraʊzə]
heating	die Heizung [di ˈhaɪtsʊŋ]
high season	die Hauptsaison [di ˈhaʊptzɛˌzɔŋ]
in-room telephone	das Zimmertelefon [das ˈtsɪmɐteləˌfoːn]
key	der Schlüssel [dɐ ˈʃlʏsl]
lamp	die Lampe [di ˈlampə]
lavatory	die Toilette [di toˈlɛtə]
lift	der Aufzug [dɐ ˈʔaʊftsuːk]
light	das Licht [das lɪçt]
light bulb	die Glühbirne [di ˈɡlyːbɪrnə]

lounge	der Aufenthaltsraum [de ˈʔaʊfntalts,ʁaʊm]
low season/off-season	die Vorsaison [di ˈfoɐze,zɔŋ]; die Nachsaison [di ˈnaːxze,zɔŋ]
lunch	das Mittagessen [das ˈmɪtak,ʔɛsn]
maid	das Zimmermädchen [das ˈtsɪmɐmɛːtçn]
mattress	die Matratze [di maˈtʁatsə]
motel	das Motel [das moˈtɛl]
mug	der Becher [de ˈbɛçɐ]
notepad	der Notizblock [de noˈtiːtsblɔk]
overnight stay	die Übernachtung [di ʔybɐˈnaxtʊŋ]
pillow	das Kopfkissen [das ˈkɔpfkɪsn]
plug	der Stecker [de ˈʃtɛkɐ]
porter	der Portier [de pɔɐˈtjeː]
price list (e.g. for the minibar)	die Preisliste (z.B. für die Minibar) [di ˈpʁaɪslɪstə (tsʊm ˈbaɪʃpiːl fyɐ di ˈmɪnibaː)]
radio	das Radio [das ˈʁaːdjo]
reception	die Rezeption [di ʁetsɛpˈtsjoːn]
registration	die Anmeldung [di ʔanmɛldʊŋ]
to repair	reparieren [ʁɛpaˈʁiːʁən/-ˈʁiən]
reservation	die Reservierung [di ʁezɐˈviːʁʊŋ]
restroom	die Toilette [di toˈlɛtə]
room	das Zimmer [das ˈtsɪmɐ]
room service	der Zimmerservice [de ˈtsɪmɐˌsœːsəˈviːs]
safe	der Safe [de sɛɪf/seːf]
shoe cleaning kit	das Schuhputzzeug [das ˈʃuːpʊts,tsɔɪk]
shower	die Dusche [di ˈduːʃə]
shower curtain	der Duschvorhang [de ˈduːʃfoɐhaŋ]
showerhead	der Brausekopf [de ˈbʁaʊzəkɔpf]
sliding door	die Schiebetür [di ˈʃiːbətyɐ]
socket	die Steckdose [di ˈʃtɛkdoːzə]
table	der Tisch [de tɪʃ]
tap	der Wasserhahn [de ˈvasɐhaːn]
television, TV	der Fernseher [de ˈfɛɐnzeɐ]
television lounge	der Fernsehraum [de ˈfɛɐnzeː,ʁaʊm]
terrace	die Terrasse [di teˈʁasə]
toilet	die Toilette [di toˈlɛtə]
toilet paper	das Toilettenpapier [das toˈlɛtnpaˌpiɐ]
towel	das Handtuch [das ˈhantuːx]
tumbler	das Wasserglas [das ˈvasɐglaːs]
wardrobe	der Kleiderschrank [de ˈklaɪdɐʃʁaŋk]
washbasin	das Waschbecken [das ˈvaʃbɛkn]
water	das Wasser [das ˈvasɐ]
cold water	kaltes Wasser [ˈvaːməs ˈvasɐ]

hot water	warmes Wasser ['kaltəs 'vasə]
water glass	das Wasserglas [das 'vasəgla:s]
window	das Fenster [das 'fɛnstɐ]
writing paper	das Briefpapier [das 'bʀi:fpapiɐ]

Holiday cottages and flats

Is electricity/water included in the price?
Ist der Stromverbrauch/Wasserverbrauch im Mietpreis enthalten?
['ʔɪst dɐ 'ʃtʀo:mfɐbʀaʊx /'vasɐfɐbʀaʊx ʔɪm 'mi:tpʀaɪs ʔɛnt'haltn̩]

Are pets allowed?
Sind Haustiere erlaubt? [zɪnt 'haʊsti:ʀə ʔe'laʊpt]

Clean up thoroughly before you leave.
Machen Sie gründlich sauber, bevor Sie abreisen.
[maxn̩ zi 'gʀʏntlɪç 'zaʊbɐ bə'foɐ zi ʔ'apʀaɪzn̩]

Do we have to clean the place ourselves before we leave?
Müssen wir die Endreinigung selbst übernehmen?
[mʏsn̩ viɐ di ʔ'ɛntʀaɪnɪgʊŋ 'zɛlpst ʔybɐ'ne:mm]

> Hikers and mountaineers have a large choice of mountain huts, usually run by the national alpine clubs. Many serve meals, but otherwise you can bring your own food.

➤ **also At the hotel**

additional costs	die Nebenkosten [di 'ne:bmkɔstn̩]
apartment	die Wohnung [di 'vo:nʊŋ]
bedroom	das Schlafzimmer [das 'ʃla:ftsɪmɐ]
bungalow	der Bungalow [dɐ 'bʊŋgalo:]
bunk bed	das Etagenbett [das ʔe'ta:ʒnbɛt]
coffee machine	die Kaffeemaschine [di 'kafemaʃi:nə]
cooker	der Herd [dɐ heɐt]
crockery	das Geschirr [das gə'ʃɪʀ]
day of arrival	der Anreisetag [dɐ ʔ'anʀaɪzə,ta:k]
day of departure	der Abreisetag [dɐ ʔ'apʀaɪzə,ta:k]
dishes	das Geschirr [das gə'ʃɪʀ]
dishwasher	die Geschirrspülmaschine [di gə'ʃɪʀʃpy:lmaʃɪnə]
electricity	der Strom [dɐ ʃtʀo:m]
farm	der Bauernhof [dɐ 'baʊɐnho:f]
flat	die Wohnung [di 'vo:nʊŋ]
flat rate for electricity	die Strompauschale [di 'ʃtʀo:mpaʊʃa:lə]
fridge/refrigerator	der Kühlschrank [dɐ 'ky:lʃʀaŋk]

garbage	der Müll [dɐ mʏl]
holiday camp	die Ferienanlage [di ˈfeːʁiənˈʔanlaːgə]
holiday home	das Ferienhaus [das ˈfeːʁiənhaʊs]
kitchenette	die Kochnische [di ˈkɔxniːʃə]
landlord/landlady	der Hausbesitzer/die Hausbesitzerin
	[dɐ ˈhaʊsbəzɪtsɐ/di ˈhaʊsbəzɪtsəʁɪn]
to let	vermieten [fɛˈmiːtn̩]
living room	das Wohnzimmer [das ˈvoːntsɪmɐ]
microwave	die Mikrowelle [di ˈmiːkʁovɛlə]
pets	die Haustiere n pl [di ˈhaʊstiːʁə]
range	der Herd [dɐ heːɐt]
to rent	vermieten [fɛˈmiːtn̩]
rent	die Miete [di ˈmiːtə]
rubbish	der Müll [dɐ mʏl]
stove	der Herd [dɐ heːɐt]
studio apartment	das Apartment [das ʔaˈpaːtmənt]
studio couch	die Schlafcouch [di ˈʃlaːfkaʊtʃ]
tea towel	das Geschirrtuch [das gəˈʃɪʁtuːx]
toaster	der Toaster [dɐ ˈtoːstɐ]
voltage	die Stromspannung [di ˈʃtʁoːmˌʃpanʊŋ]
water consumption	der Wasserverbrauch [dɐ ˈvasɐfɛbʁaʊx]

Camping

Could you tell me if there's a camping site nearby?
Könnten Sie mir bitte sagen, ob es in der Nähe einen Camping-platz gibt?
[kœntn̩ zi miɐ ˈbɪtə zaːgn̩ ʔɔp əs ɪn dɐ ˈnɛːə ʔaɪnn ˈkɛmpɪŋplats gɪpt]

Have you got room for another caravan/tent?
Haben Sie noch Platz für einen Wohnwagen/ein Zelt?
[ˈhaːbm̩ zi nɔx plats fyɐ ʔaɪnn ˈvoːnvaːgn̩/ʔaɪn tsɛlt]

How much does it cost per day and person?
Wie hoch ist die Gebühr pro Tag und Person?
[viː hoːx ʔɪst di gəˈbyɐ pʁo taːk ʊnt pɛˈzoːn]

What's the charge for ...
Wie hoch ist die Gebühr für ... [viː hoːx ɪst di gəˈbyɐ fyɐ ...]

the car?
das Auto? [das ˈʔaʊto]

the camper van/motor home/RV?
das Wohnmobil? [das ˈvoːnmoˌbiːl]

the caravan/trailer?
den Wohnwagen? [den ˈvoːnvaːgn̩]

the tent?
das Zelt? [das ˈtsɛlt]

We'll be staying for ... days/weeks.
Wir bleiben ... Tage/Wochen. [viɐ blaɪbm̩ ... 'taːgə/'vɔxn̩]

Where are ...
Wo sind ...? [voː zɪnt]

  the toilets?
  die Toiletten? [di toˈlɛtn̩]

  the washrooms?
  die Waschräume? [di ˈvaʃʀɔɪmə]

  the showers?
  die Duschen? [di ˈduːʃn̩]

Are there power points/outlets here?
Gibt es hier Stromanschluss? [gɪpt əs hiɐ ˈʃtʀoːmanʃlʊs]

Is the camping site guarded at night?
Ist der Campingplatz bei Nacht bewacht?
[ˈʔɪst dɐ ˈkɛmpɪŋplats baɪ ˈnaxt bəˈvaxt]

booking	die Voranmeldung [di ˈfoɐˈʔanmɛldʊŋ]
to camp	zelten [ˈtsɛltn̩]
camping	das Camping [das ˈkɛmpɪŋ]
camping guide	der Campingführer [dɐ ˈkɛmpɪŋfyːʀɐ]
camping site	der Campingplatz [dɐ ˈkɛmpɪŋplats]
cooker	der Kocher [dɐ ˈkɔxɐ]
dryer	der Wäschetrockner [dɐ ˈvɛʃətʀɔknɐ]
drinking water	das Trinkwasser [das ˈtʀɪŋkvasɐ]
electricity	der Strom [dɐ ʃtʀoːm]
gas canister	die Gasflasche [di gaˈsflaʃə]
gas cartridge	die Gaskartusche [di ˈgaːskaˌtʊʃə]
lavatory	der Waschraum [dɐ ˈvaʃʀaʊm]
paraffin lamp	die Petroleumlampe
	[di peˈtʀoːleʊmˌlampə]
plug	der Stecker [dɐ ˈʃtɛkɐ]
power point/outlet	die Steckdose [di ˈʃtɛkdoːzə]
propane (gas)	das Propangas [das pʀoˈpaːngaːs]
sink	das Geschirrspülbecken
	[das gəˈʃɪʀspyːlbɛkn̩]
tent	das Zelt [das tsɛlt]
tent peg	der Hering [dɐ ˈheːʀɪŋ]
washroom	der Waschraum [dɐ ˈvaʃʀaʊm]
water	das Wasser [das ˈvasɐ]
water canister	der Wasserkanister [dɐ ˈvasɐkanˌɪstɐ]

Eating and drinking

Good eating and drinking

In Austria, Germany and Switzerland you have a number of different kinds of eating and drinking establishments to choose from:

- **Restaurant** – as elsewhere
- **Café** – a coffee house
- **Gasthaus** – a small hotel with a restaurant
- **Gasthof** – a *Gasthaus* in a rural area
- **Biergarten** – outdoor pub/tavern
- **Gartenwirtschaft** – an outdoor restaurant, usually with a limited menu
- **Ratskeller** – a restaurant in the cellar of the *Rathaus* (town hall)
- **Bistro** – a trendy pub or small restaurant, usually with a bar
- **Kneipe** – pub
- **Imbissstube** – fast-food place
- **Konditorei** – pastry shop usually with a café

In Austria you also encounter simple restaurants called *Beisl*.

Eating out

Is there ... here?
Gibt es hier ... ? [gɪpt əs hiɐ]

a good restaurant
ein gutes Restaurant [ʔaɪn ˈguːtəs ʀɛstoˈʀaŋ]

an inexpensive restaurant
ein preiswertes Restaurant [ʔaɪn ˈpʀaɪsveɐtəs ʀɛstoˈʀaŋ]

a gourmet restaurant
ein Feinschmeckerlokal [ʔaɪn ˈfaɪnʃmɛkeloˌkaːl]

a fast-food place
einen Schnellimbiss [ʔaɪnn ˈʃnɛlɪmbɪs]

The restaurant business in Germany is rapidly falling into "exotic" hands. In cities and larger towns you'll easily find Italian, Greek, Chinese and even Indian restaurants. The Italians and Greeks are often your best bet for tasty, inexpensive food. There are numerous Turkish fast-food places as a good alternative to the international fast-food chains. If you insist on getting "typical German food", find a *Gasthof* outside town or go to a fancy hotel.

Where's a good place to eat near here?
Wo kann man hier in der Nähe gut essen?
[vo: kan man hie ʔɪn de 'nɛːə guːt ʔɛsn]

Is there a good, inexpensive restaurant here?
Gibt es hier ein preiswertes Restaurant? [gɪpt əs hie ʔaɪn 'praɪs↓
veetəs ʀɛsto'ʀaŋ]

At the restaurant

Would you reserve us a table for a party of four for this evening, please?
Reservieren Sie uns bitte für heute Abend einen Tisch für vier
Personen. [ʀɛzɛ'viːʀən zi ʔʊns 'bɪtə fye 'hɔɪtə ʔaːbmt ʔaɪnn tɪʃ fye fie
pe'zoːnn]

Is this table free?
Ist dieser Tisch noch frei? [ʔɪst 'diːzɐ tɪʃ nɔx 'fʀaɪ]

> In most restaurants you simply pick out your own table. It is
> also quite common, if the restaurant is crowded, to sit down
> with people who are strangers to you. You ask if there are
> seats "free" (not taken).

Are these seats taken?
Sind hier noch Plätze frei? [zɪnt hie 'plɛtsə nɔx 'fʀaɪ]

A table for three, please.
Einen Tisch für drei Personen, bitte.
[ʔaɪnn tɪʃ fye dʀaɪ pe'zoːnn 'bɪtə]

Where are the toilets?
Wo sind die Toiletten? [vo: zɪnt di to'lɛtn]

Is it OK if I smoke?
Darf ich rauchen? [daːf ɪç 'ʀaʊxn]

Ordering

Can we have the menu/drinks list, please?
Können wir bitte die Speisekarte/Getränkekarte haben?
[kœnn vie 'bɪtə di 'ʃpaɪzəkaːtə/gə'tʀɛŋkəkaːtə haːbm]

Are you ready to order?
Haben Sie schon gewählt? ['ha:bm zi ʃon gə've:lt]

What can you recommend?
Was können Sie mir empfehlen? [vas kœnn zi miɐ ˀɛm'fe:ln]

I'll have ... to start off with.
Als Vorspeise nehme ich ... [ˀals 'foɐʃpaɪzə 'ne:mə ˀɪç]

I'll have ... for the main course.
Als Hauptgericht nehme ich ... [ˀals 'haʊptgəʀɪçt 'ne:mə ˀɪç]

I don't want any dessert, thank you.
Ich möchte keinen Nachtisch, danke.
[ˀɪç 'mœçtə ˌkaɪnn 'na:xtɪʃ 'daŋkə]

I'm afraid we've run out of ...
Wir haben leider kein ... mehr. [viɐ ha:bm 'laɪdɐ 'kaɪn ... meɐ]

We only serve this dish if it's been pre-ordered.
Dieses Gericht servieren wir nur auf Bestellung.
['di:zəs gə'ʀɪçt zɛ'vi:ʀən viɐ nuɐ ˀaʊf bə'ʃtɛlʊŋ]

Could I have chicken instead of fish?
Könnte ich statt Fisch Huhn haben? ['kœntə ˀɪç ʃtat fɪʃ hu:n ha:bm]

I'm allergic to ...
Ich vertrage kein ... [ˀɪç fɛ'tʀa:gə kaɪn ...]

Could you make this dish without ...?
Könnten Sie das Gericht ohne ... zubereiten?
['kœntn zi das gə'ʀɪçt o:nə ... 'tsu:bəʀaɪtn]

Do you have children's portions?
Gibt es auch Kinderportionen? [gɪpt əs aʊx 'kɪndɐpɔ'tsjo:nn]

How would you like your steak?
Wie möchten Sie Ihr Steak haben? [vi mœçtn zi ˀiɐ 'ste:k ha:bm]
  well-done
  gut durch [gu:t dʊɐç]
  medium
  halb durch [halp dʊɐç]
  rare
  englisch [ˀɛŋlɪʃ]

What would you like to drink?
Was möchten Sie trinken? [vas mœçtn zi 'tʀɪŋkŋ]

A glass of ..., please.
Bitte ein Glas ... ['bɪtə ˀaɪn glaːs]

A bottle of/Half a bottle of ..., please.
Bitte eine Flasche/eine halbe Flasche ...
['bɪtə ˀaɪnə 'flaʃə/ˀaɪnə 'halbə 'flaʃə]

With ice, please.
Mit Eis, bitte. [mɪt ˀaɪs 'bɪtə]

Enjoy your meal!
Guten Appetit! ['guːtn̩ ˀapə'tiːt]

Would you like anything else?
Haben Sie sonst noch einen Wunsch?
[haːbm̩ zi 'zɔnst nɔx aɪnn vʊnʃ]

Bring us ..., please.
Bitte bringen Sie uns ... ['bɪtə brɪŋŋ zi ˀʊns]

Could we have some more bread/water/wine, please?
Könnten wir noch etwas Brot/ Wasser/Wein bekommen?
['kœntn̩ viɐ nɔx ˌɛtvas 'broːt/'vasɐ/'vaɪn bə'kɔmm]

Cheers!
Zum Wohl! [tsʊm 'voːl]

Complaints

We need another ...
Wir brauchen noch ein ... [viɐ braʊxn̩ nɔx ˀaɪn]

Have you forgotten my ...?
Haben Sie mein ... vergessen? [haːbm̩ zi ˌmaɪn ... fɛ'gɛsn̩]

I didn't order that.
Das habe ich nicht bestellt. [das haːb ɪç nɪçt bə'ʃtɛlt]

The food is cold.
Das Essen ist kalt. [das ˀɛsn̩ ˀɪst kalt]

There's too much salt in the soup.
Die Suppe ist versalzen. [di 'zʊpə ˀɪst fɛ'zaltsn̩]

The meat's tough/too fatty.
Das Fleisch ist zäh/zu fett. [das flaɪʃ ɪst 'tsɛː/tsʊ 'fɛt]

The fish is not fresh.
Der Fisch ist nicht frisch.
[de fɪʃ ˀɪst nɪçt frɪʃ]

I'm afraid the wine is corked.
Es tut mir Leid, aber der Wein schmeckt nach Korken.
['ˀəs tuːt miɐ laɪt ˀabɐ de vaɪn ʃmɛkt nax 'kɔɐkŋ]

Take it back, please.
Nehmen Sie es bitte zurück. ['ne:mm zi əs 'bɪtə tsʊ'ʀʏk]

Fetch the manager, please.
Holen Sie bitte den Chef. ['ho:ln zi 'bɪtə den 'ʃɛf]

Don't confuse German *Chef* (= manager) with English "chef"
(= *Koch*).

The bill

Could I have the bill, please?
Die Rechnung, bitte. [di 'ʀɛçnʊŋ 'bɪtə] /
Bezahlen, bitte. [bə'tsa:ln 'bɪtə]

All together, please.
Bitte alles zusammen. ['bɪtə ˀaləs tsʊ'samm]

Separate bills, please.
Getrennte Rechnungen, bitte. [gə'tʀɛntə 'ʀɛçnʊŋŋ 'bɪtə]

There seems to be a mistake on the bill.
Die Rechnung scheint mir nicht zu stimmen.
[di 'ʀɛçnʊŋ ʃaɪnt miɐ nɪçt tsʊ 'ʃtɪmm]

I didn't have that. I had ...
Das habe ich nicht gehabt. Ich hatte ...
[das 'ha:bə ɪç nɪçt gə'hapt ˀɪç 'hatə ...]

Did you enjoy your meal?
Hat es geschmeckt? [hat ˀɛs gə'ʃmɛkt]

The food was excellent.
Das Essen war ausgezeichnet. [das ˀɛsn va: ˀaʊsgə'tsaɪçnət]

That's for you.
Das ist für Sie. [das ɪst fyɐ 'zi:]

Keep the change.
(Es) Stimmt so. [(ˀəs) 'ʃtɪmt zo:]

Drinks will be included on the bill with food. Service of 10%
is included and it is customary to round up the bill by about
10% or so.

Zum Weißen Adler – Meeting people

After arriving at the airport or driving through a city centre, you may be wondering what became of the German-speaking Old World. To find that and real-time natives, head to the nearest *Gasthaus*. They usually have a name beginning with *zum* or *zur: Zum Weißen Adler* – to the white eagle, *Zum Roten Ochsen* – to the red ox, or *Zur Post* – to the post office. The *Gasthaus* was traditionally an inn for travellers and anyone else looking for a place to eat or sleep. They also became good places to drink beer or wine, to meet people and socialize. This they have remained to the present day.

Even if they appear often quite reserved, Germans, Austrians and the Swiss pride themselves on being open and willing to exchange ideas. Furthermore, in any non-posh eating-and-drinking establishment any seat not taken is yours to sit down in for the asking: *„Ist hier noch frei?"* You can now strike up a conversation by asking about tomorrow's weather, satisfaction with the government, or what happened today in football. Sitting together with strangers is normal, unless you run into a couple who insist on being by themselves.

Don't be turned off if there aren't cuckoo clocks and alpine horns hanging from every wall. Some of these places can be very simple in decoration. There'll always be a small bar with beer on tap and dozens of bottles of schnapps and other forms of liquor above and below the bar. Somewhere not far away you'll also see that quintessence of Germanic drinking culture, the *Stammtisch* regulars' table, that means a no-go area for any stranger.

EATING AND DRINKING

Good evening.
Guten Abend! ['guːtn ˀaːbmt]

Can I sit here?
Ist hier noch frei? [ˀɪst hiɐ nɔx fʀaɪ]

Where are you from?
Wo kommen Sie her? [voː kɔmm ziː 'heɐ]

I come from England/the States.
Ich komme aus England/den USA.
[ˀɪç kɔmə aʊs ˀˀɛŋlant/den uːɛsˀˀaː]

What'll it be?
Was darf es sein? [vas da:f əs zaɪn]

I'd like a beer/a wine/a schnapps.
Ich hätte gern ein Bier/einen Wein/ einen Schnaps.
[ʔɪç ˈhɛtə gɛɛn ʔaɪn biɐ/ʔaɪnn vaɪn/ʔaɪnn ʃnaps]

What flavour?
Welche Geschmacksrichtung? [ˈvɛlçə gəˈʃmaks,ʀɪçtʊŋ]

A pint of mild (dark beer).
Ein großes Dunkles. [ʔaɪn ˈgʀo:səs dʊŋkləs]

A half-pint of lager.
Ein kleines Helles. [ʔaɪn ˈklaɪnəs ˈhɛləs]

Would you like another drink?
Möchten Sie noch etwas trinken? [ˈmœçtn zi nɔx ʔɛtvas ˈtʀɪŋkŋ]

Same again.
Das Gleiche noch einmal. [das ˈglaɪçə nɔx ʔaɪnma:l]

Here's to your health!
Zum Wohl! [tsʊm vo:l]

Cheers!
Prost! [pʀo:st]

What do you drink where you're from?
Was trinkt man bei Ihnen zu Hause?
[vas ˈtʀɪŋkt man baɪ ʔˈi:nn tsʊ haʊzə]

Did you see that game on TV between ... and ...?
Haben Sie das Spiel im Fernsehen zwischen ... und ... gesehen?
[ˈha:bm zi das ʃpi:l ʔɪm ˈfɛɐnze:n ˈtsvɪʃn ... ʔʊnt ... gəˈze:n]

What's your opinion of ...?
Was halten Sie von ...? [vas ˈhaltn zi fɔn]

I don't understand politics. I only pay taxes.
Ich verstehe nichts von Politik. Ich zahle nur Steuern.
[ʔɪç fɐˈʃte: nɪçts fɔn pɔlɪˈti:k ʔɪç ˈtsa:lə nuɐ ˈʃtɔjɐn]

I'd like the bill, please.
Die Rechnung, bitte. [di ˈʀɛçnʊŋ ˈbɪtə]

This round is on me.
Diese Runde übernehme ich. [ˈdi:zə ˈʀʊndə ʔˈybɐˈne:mə ʔˈɪç]

➤ also Groceries

appetizer	die Vorspeise [di ˈfoɐʃpaɪzə]
ashtray	der Aschenbecher [dɐ ʔˈaʃnbɛçɐ]
bone	der Knochen [dɐ knɔxn]
bowl	die Schüssel [di ʃʏsl]
breakfast	das Frühstück [das ˈfʀy:ʃtʏk]
children's portion	der Kinderteller [dɐ ˈkɪndɐtɛlɐ]

cook	der Koch [dɐ kɔx]
corkscrew	der Korkenzieher [dɐ ˈkɔɐkn̩tsiːɐ]
course	der Gang [dɐ ɡaŋ]
cover *(setting)*	das Gedeck [das ɡəˈdɛk]
cup	die Tasse [di ˈtasə]
cutlery	das Besteck [das bəˈʃtɛk]
dessert	der Nachtisch [dɐ ˈnaːxtɪʃ]
diabetic	diabetisch [diaˈbeːtɪʃ]
diabetic *(person)*	der Diabetiker/die Diabetikerin [dɐ diaˈbeːtɪkɐ/dɪ diaˈbeːtɪkəʀɪn]
diet	die Schonkost [di ˈʃoːnkɔst]
dinner	das Abendessen [das ˈ⁷aːbm̩t⁷ɛsn̩]
dish	das Gericht [das ɡəˈʀɪçt]
dish of the day	das Tagesgericht [das ˈtaːɡəsɡəʀɪçt]
draught	vom Fass [fɔm fas]
dressing	das Dressing [das ˈdʀɛsɪŋ]
drink	das Getränk [das ɡəˈtʀɛŋk]
fishbone	die Gräte [di ˈɡʀɛːtə]
fork	die Gabel [di ˈɡaːbl̩]
glass	das Glas [das ɡlaːs]
gourmet restaurant	das Feinschmeckerlokal [das ˈfaɪnʃmɛkɐloˌkaːl]
gravy	die (Braten)Soße [di (ˈbʀaːtn̩)zoːsə]
grill	der Rost [dɐ ʀɔst]
hard-boiled	hart gekocht [ˈhaːt ɡəˌkɔxt]
home-made	hausgemacht [ˈhaʊsɡəmaxt]
hors d'œuvre	die Vorspeise [di ˈfoɐʃpaɪzə]
hot *(temperature)*	heiß [haɪs]
hot *(spicy)*	scharf [ʃaːf]
hungry	hungrig [ˈhʊŋʀɪç]
ketchup	das Ketschup [das ˈkɛtʃap]
knife	das Messer [das ˈmɛsɐ]
lunch	das Mittagessen [das ˈmɪtak⁷ɛsn̩]
main course	die Hauptspeise [di ˈhaʊptʃpaɪzə]
mayonnaise	die Mayonnaise [di majoˈnɛːzə]
menu	die Speisekarte [di ˈʃpaɪzəkaːtə]
mustard	der Senf [dɐ zɛnf (zɛmf)]
napkin	die Serviette [di zɛˈvjɛtə]
non-alcoholic	alkoholfrei [⁷alkoˈhoːlfʀaɪ]
oil	das Öl [das ⁷øːl]
on tap	vom Fass [fɔm fas]
order	die Bestellung [di bəˈʃtɛlʊŋ]
pepper	der Pfeffer [dɐ ˈpfɛfɐ]
plate	der Teller [dɐ ˈtɛlɐ]
portion	die Portion [di pɔˈtsjoːn]
salad bar	das Salatbüfett [das zaˈlaːtbyˈfeː]
salt	das Salz [das zalts]

sauce	die Soße [di 'zoːsə]
saucer	die Untertasse [di ˀʊntɐtasə]
season	würzen [vvɐtsn̩]
seasoning	das Gewürz [das gə'vvɐts]
serviette	die Serviette [di zɛ'vjɛtə]
set meal	das Menü [das me'nyː]
slice	die Scheibe [di 'ʃaɪbə]
soup	die Suppe [di 'zʊpə]
soup plate	der Suppenteller [dɐ 'zʊpmtɛlɐ]
special (of the day)	das Tagesmenü [das 'taːgəsmeˌnyː]
speciality	die Spezialität [di ʃpetsjali'tɛːt]
spice	das Gewürz [das gə'vvɐts]
spoon	der Löffel [dɐ lœfl̩]
stain	der Fleck [dɐ flɛk]
starter	die Vorspeise [di 'foɐʃpaɪzə]
straw	der Strohhalm [dɐ 'ʃtʀoːhalm]
sugar	der Zucker [dɐ 'tsʊkɐ]
sweet	der Nachtisch [dɐ 'naːxtɪʃ]
sweetener	der Süßstoff [dɐ 'zyːʃtɔf]
tablecloth	das Tischtuch [das 'tɪʃtuːx]
teaspoon	der Teelöffel [dɐ 'teːlœfl̩]
tip	das Trinkgeld [das 'tʀɪŋkgɛlt]
toothpick	der Zahnstocher [dɐ 'tsaːnʃtɔxɐ]
tumbler	das Wasserglas [das 'vasɐglaːs]
vegetarian	vegetarisch [vega'taːʀɪʃ]
vegetarian (person)	der Vegetarier/die Vegetarierin [dɐ vega'taːʀɪɐ/dɪ vega'taːʀɪəʀɪn]
vinegar	der Essig [dɐ ˀɛsɪç]
waiter/waitress	der Kellner/die Kellnerin [dɐ 'kɛlnɐ/di 'kɛlnəʀɪn]
water	das Wasser [das 'vasɐ]
water glass	das Wasserglas [das 'vasɐglaːs]
wineglass	das Weinglas [das 'vaɪnglaːs]

Preparation/Cooking style

au gratin	überbacken [ˀybɐˈbakn̩]
baked	gebacken [ɡəˈbakn̩]
boiled	gekocht [ɡəˈkɔxt]
braised	geschmort [ɡəˈʃmoɐt]
broiled	gegrillt [ɡəˈɡʀɪlt]
cooked/done	gar [ɡaː]
fried	in der Pfanne gebraten [ˀɪn dɐ ˈpfanə ɡəˈbʀaːtn̩]
grilled	vom Grill [fɔm ˈɡʀɪl]
hot (spicy)	scharf [ʃaːf]
juicy	saftig [ˈzaftɪç]
lean	mager [ˈmaːɡɐ]
raw	roh [ʀoː]
roasted	gebraten [ɡəˈbʀaːtn̩]
smoked	geräuchert [ɡəˈʀɔɪçɐt]
soft-boiled	weich gekocht [ˈvaɪç ɡəˌkɔxt]
sour	sauer [ˈzaʊɐ]
spit-roasted	am Spieß gebraten [am ʃpiːs ɡəˈbʀaːtn̩]
steamed	gedämpft [ɡəˈdɛmpft], gedünstet [ɡəˈdʏnstət]
stuffed	gefüllt [ɡəˈfʏlt]
sweet	süß [zyːs]
tender	zart [tsaːt]
tough	zäh [tsɛː]
well-done	durchgebraten [ˈdʊʁçɡəbʀaːtn̩]

boiled
gekocht

simmered/ cooked
gegart

steamed
gedämpft

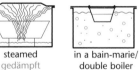

in a bain-marie/ double boiler
im Wasserbad

fried
gebraten

deep-fried
frittiert

grilled
gegrillt

garlic
der Knoblauch
[dɐ ˈknoːblaʊx]

onion
die Zwiebel
[di tsviːbl̩]

dill
der Dill [dɐ dɪl]

bay-leaves
die Lorbeerblätter *n pl*
[di ˈlɔɐbeɐˌblɛtɐ]

rosemary
der Rosmarin
[dɐ ˈʁoːsmaʁiːn]

marjoram
der Majoran
[dɐ ˈmajoʁaːn]

coriander
der Koriander
[dɐ koːriˈandə]

parsley
die Petersilie
[di peːtɐˈziːljə]

basil
das Basilikum
[das baˈziːlɪkʊm]

104

nutmeg die Muskatnuss [di mʊsˈkaːtnʊs]

chilli
der Chili
[dɐ ˈtsɪli]

pepperoni
die Peperoni
[di pɛpəˈroːni]

chives
der Schnittlauch
[dɐ ˈʃnɪtlaʊx]

sage
der Salbei
[dɐ ˈzalbaɪ]

chervil
der Kerbel
[dɐ kɛɐbl]

thyme
der Thymian
[dɐ ˈtyːmiaːn]

savory
das Bohnenkraut
[das ˈboːnnkʀaʊt]

lovage
der/das Liebstöckl
[dɐ/das ˈliːpʃtœkl]

105

I'd like ...
Ich hätte gern ...

I'd like ...
Ich hätte gern ...

Speisekarte

Frühstück — Breakfast

Frühstück	Breakfast
Schwarzer Kaffee [ʃvaːtsɐ ˈkafeː]	black coffee
Kaffee mit Milch [ˈkafe mɪt ˈmɪlç]	white coffee
Koffeinfreier Kaffee [kɔfeˈʔiːnfʀaɪɐ ˈkafeː]	decaffeinated coffee
Tee mit Milch/Zitrone [teː mɪt ˈmɪlç/tsɪˈtʀoːnə]	tea with milk/lemon
Schokolade [ʃokoˈlaːdə]	hot chocolate
Fruchtsaft [ˈfʀʊxtzaft]	fruit juice
Weiches Ei [vaɪçəs ʔaɪ]	soft-boiled egg
Rühreier [ˈʀyɐʔaɪɐ]	scrambled eggs
Brot/Brötchen [bʀoːt/bʀøːtçn̩]	bread/rolls
Toast [toːst]	toast
Butter [ˈbʊtɐ]	butter
Honig [ˈhoːnɪç]	honey
Marmelade [mamaˈlaːdə]	jam
Orangenmarmelade [oˈʀaŋʒnmaməˌlaːdə]	marmalade
Müsli [ˈmyːsli]	muesli
Jogurt [ˈjoːɡʊɐt]	yoghurt
Obst [ʔoːpst]	fruit

Most hotels have a breakfast buffet with a large selection of cheese, sausage, fruit, breakfast cereal, and juice. Bacon-and-eggs style breakfast can only be found in large international hotels. Smaller hotels may still offer "continental breakfast" – bread rolls, cheese, and jam. Tea is usually served with a slice of lemon; if you take milk, ask for it.

Vorspeisen — Hors d'œuvres

Vorspeisen	Hors d'œuvres
Austern f pl [ˈʔaʊstɐn]	oysters
Avocado [ʔavoˈkaːdo]	avocado
Garnelencocktail [gaˈneːlnˌkɔktɛɪl]	prawn cocktail
Hummer [ˈhʊmɐ]	lobster
Krabbencocktail [ˈkʀabm̩ˌkɔktɛɪl]	shrimp cocktail
Melone mit Schinken [meˈloːnə mɪt ˈʃɪŋkn̩]	melon with ham
Muscheln f pl [mʊʃln̩]	mussels
Räucherlachs [ˈʀɔɪçɐlaks]	smoked salmon

Schinken [ʃɪŋkŋ] . . . . ham
Weinbergschnecken ['vaɪnbɛɐkʃnɛkŋ] . . snails in garlic butter

Salate / Salads

Bohnensalat ['boːnnzalaːt] . . . . bean salad
Gemischter Salat [gə'mɪʃtɐ za'laːt] . . . . . mixed salad
Gurkensalat ['gʊɐkŋzalaːt] . . . . cucumber salad
Karottensalat [ka'ʀɔtnzalaːt] . . . . carrot salad
Kartoffelsalat [ka'tɔflzalaːt] . . . . potato salad
Krautsalat ['kʀaʊtzalaːt] . . . . coleslaw

Suppen / Soups

Bouillon [bʊl'jɔŋ] . . . . clear soup/consommé
Champignoncremèsuppe . . . . cream of mushroom soup
['ʃampɪnjɔŋˌkʀɛːmzʊpə]
Erbsensuppe ['ʔɛɐpsnˌzʊpə] . . . . pea soup
Fleischbrühe ['flaɪʃbʀyə] . . . . clear soup/consommé
Französische Zwiebelsuppe . . . . French onion soup
[fʀan'tsøːzɪʃə 'tsviːblzʊpə]
Gemüsesuppe [gə'myːzəzʊpə] . . . . vegetable soup
Gulaschsuppe ['gʊlaʃzʊpə] . . . . goulash soup
Hühnersuppe ['hyːnɐzʊpə] . . . . chicken soup
Ochsenschwanzsuppe . . . . oxtail soup
['ʔɔksnʃvantsˌzʊpə]
Spargelcremesuppe . . . . cream of asparagus soup
['ʃpaːglkʀɛːmˌzʊpə]
Tomatencremesuppe . . . . cream of tomato soup
[to'maːtnkʀɛːmˌzʊpə]

Eierspeisen / Egg dishes

(Käse-/Champignon-/Tomaten-) . . . . . (cheese/mushroom/tomato)
Omelett [('kɛːzə/'ʃampɪnjɔŋ/   omelette
to'maːtn)ˌʔɔmlɛt]
Rühreier ['ʀyɐ'ʔaɪɐ] . . . . scrambled eggs
Spiegeleier ['ʃpiːgl'ʔaɪɐ] . . . . fried eggs
Spiegeleier mit Schinken . . . . ham and eggs
['ʃpiːgl'ʔaɪɐ mɪt 'ʃɪŋkŋ]
Verlorene Eier [vɐ'loːʀənə 'ʔaɪɐ] . . . . poached eggs

Fisch / Fish

Fisch	Fish
Aal [ʔaːl]	eel
Austern [ʔaʊstɐn]	oysters
Bückling ['bʏklɪŋ]	kipper
Forelle [foˈʀɛlə]	trout
Garnelen [gaˈneːln]	prawns
Hummer ['hʊmɐ]	lobster
Kabeljau ['kaːbljaʊ]	cod
Karpfen [kaːpfn]	carp
Krabben [kʀabm]	shrimps
Krebs [kʀeːps]	crab
Lachs [laks]	salmon
Makrele [maˈkʀeːlə]	mackerel
Matjesfilet ['matʃəsfɪˌleː]	salted young herring
Muscheln [mʊʃln]	mussels
Räucherhering ['ʀɔɪçeheːʀɪŋ],	smoked herring, kipper
Scholle ['ʃɔlə]	plaice
Schwertfisch [ʃveɐtfɪʃ]	swordfish
Seezunge ['zeːtsʊŋə]	sole
T(h)unfisch ['tuːnfɪʃ]	tuna
Tintenfisch ['tɪntnfɪʃ]	squid

Geflügel / Poultry

Geflügel	Poultry
Ente [ʔɛntə]	duck
Fasan [faˈzaːn]	pheasant
Gans [gans]	goose
Hähnchen/Huhn ['hɛːnçn/huːn]	chicken
Pute ['puːtə]	turkey
Rebhuhn ['ʀeːphuːn]	partridge
Truthahn ['tʀuːthaːn]	turkey
Wachtel [vaxtl]	quail

Fleisch / Meat

Fleisch	Meat
Filet(steak) [fɪˈleːsteːk]	fillet/filet (steak)
Frikadellen [fʀɪkaˈdɛln]	meat balls
Hackfleisch (vom Rind) ['hakflaɪʃ (fɔm 'ʀɪnt)]	minced beef/ground beef
Hamburger ['hambʊɐgɐ]	hamburger
Hirsch [hɪɐʃ]	venison (red deer)
Kalbfleisch ['kalpflaɪʃ]	veal
Kaninchen [kaˈniːnçn]	rabbit
Kotelett ['kɔtlɛt]	chop/cutlet

Kutteln ['kʊtln] . . . . tripe
Lamm [lam] . . . . lamb
Leber ['le:bɐ] . . . . liver
Nieren ['ni:rən] . . . . kidneys
Reh [Re:] . . . . venison (roe deer)
Rindfleisch ['Rɪntflaɪʃ] . . . . beef
Rumpsteak ['Rʊmpste:k] . . . . rump steak
Schinken [ʃɪŋkn̩] . . . . ham
Schweinefleisch ['ʃvaɪnəflaɪʃ] . . . . pork
Spanferkel ['ʃpaːnfɛekl] . . . . sucking pig
Wildschwein ['vɪltʃvaɪn] . . . . wild boar
Würstchen ['vyɐstçn̩] . . . . sausages
Zunge ['tsʊŋə] . . . . tongue

Gemüse | Vegetables

Blumenkohl ['blu:mmko:l] . . . . cauliflower
Bratkartoffeln ['bRa:tka,tɔfln] . . . . fried potatoes
Brokkoli ['bRɔkoli] . . . . broccoli
Champignons ['ʃampɪnjɔŋs] . . . . . . mushrooms
Chicorée ['ʃɪkoRe] . . . . chicory
Erbsen [ʔɛɐpsn] . . . . peas
Fenchel [fɛnçl] . . . . fennel
Folienkartoffel ['fo:ljənka,tɔfl] . . . . baked potato
Frühlingszwiebeln ['fRy:lɪŋstsvi:bln] . . . . spring/green onions
grüne Bohnen [ˌgRy:nə 'bo:nn] . . . . French beans
Gurke ['gʊɐkə] . . . . cucumber
Karotten [ka'Rɔtn] . . . . carrots
Kartoffelbrei [ka'tɔflbRaɪ] . . . . mashed potato(es)
Kartoffeln [ka'tɔfln] . . . . potatoes
Knoblauch ['kno:blaʊx] . . . . garlic
Kresse ['kRɛsə] . . . . cress
Kürbis ['kyɛbɪs] . . . . pumpkin
Lauch [laʊx] . . . . leek
Maiskolben ['maiskɔlbm] . . . . corn-on-the-cob
Möhren ['mø:Rən] . . . . carrots
Ofenkartoffel [ʔo:fnka,tɔfl] . . . . baked potato
Paprikaschoten ['papRɪkaʃo:tn] . . . . peppers
Pommes frites [pɔm'fRɪts] . . . . chips/French fries
Rosenkohl ['Ro:znko:l] . . . . Brussel sprouts
Rösti ['Rœsti] . . . . hash brown potatoes
Rote Bete [ˌRo:tə 'be:tə] . . . . beetroot/beets
Rotkohl ['Ro:tko:l] . . . . red cabbage
Salzkartoffeln ['zaltska,tɔfln] . . . . . . boiled potatoes
Schwenkkartoffeln ['ʃvɛŋka,tɔfln] . . . . . . sauté(ed) potatoes
Spargel [ʃpa:gl] . . . . asparagus

114

Spinat [ʃpɪ'naːt]	spinach
Stangensellerie ['ʃtaŋŋˌzɛləʀi]	celery
Tomaten [to'maːtn̩]	tomatoes
Weißkohl ['vaɪskoːl]	cabbage
Zucchini [tsʊ'kiːni]	courgettes/zucchini
Zwiebeln [tsviːbln̩]	onions

Some vegetable names vary from region to region, for example *Karfiol* ("cauliflower" in Austria) and *Erdäpfel* ("potato" in Austria and Switzerland); "carrots" are *Möhren* and *Mohrrüben* in northern Germany, and *Karotten* elsewhere.

Käse / Cheese

Käse	Cheese
Blauschimmelkäse ['blaʊʃɪmlˌkɛːzə]	blue cheese
Frischkäse ['fʀɪʃkɛːzə]	cream cheese
Hüttenkäse ['hʏtn̩kɛːzə]	cottage cheese
Schafskäse ['ʃaːfskɛːzə]	sheep's milk cheese
Ziegenkäse ['tsiːgŋkɛːzə]	goat's milk cheese

The German-speaking countries are also becoming important producers of cheese. Typical hard cheeses are *Emmentaler* or, more tasty, *Appenzeller*, *Greyerzer* (*Gruyère*) and *Bergkäse*. Particularly pungent are *Harzer*, *Limburger* and *Handkäse*. Soft cheeses from France (*Camembert, Brie*) have become very popular and are also being produced domestically. A traditional dish of cheese is *Handkäse mit Musik*, served with caraway seeds, onions and vinegar.

Nachtisch / Obst / Dessert / Fruit

Nachtisch / Obst	Dessert / Fruit
Ananas [ˈʔananas]	pineapple
Birnen [bɪʀnn̩]	pears
Eis [ˈʔaɪs]	ice-cream
Eisbecher [ˈʔaɪsbɛçɐ]	sundae
Erdbeeren [ˈʔeɐtbeːʀən]	strawberries
Gebäck [gə'bɛk]	pastries
Kirschen [kɪʀʃn̩]	cherries
Kompott [kɔm'pɔt]	stewed fruit
Obstsalat [ˈʔoːpstzaˌlaːt]	fruit salad
Pfannkuchen ['pfankuːxn̩]	pancakes
Pfirsiche ['pfɪʀzɪçə]	peaches

Pflaumen [pflaʊmm]	plums
Rhabarber [ʀaˈbaːbɐ]	rhubarb
Schlagsahne [ˈʃlaːkzaːnə];	whipped cream
(Austria) Schlagobers [ˈʃlagobɐs]	
Stachelbeeren [ˈʃtaxlbeːʀən]	gooseberries
Vanillesoße [vaˈnɪlzoːsə]	custard

Germany, Switzerland and Austria are a cake-eater's paradise. The range of cakes and pastries is overwhelming. As well as different types of fruit cakes such as *Apfelkuchen*, *Käsekuchen* (cheesecake), there are many *Torten* (with layers of cream), e.g. *Schwarzwälder Kirschtorte* (Black Forest Cake). People like to go to a Café for their cake, or buy some to bring back home for coffee. In a restaurant, on the other hand, the choice of desserts may seem limited – ice cream or fruit salad, but also typical desserts, such as *Rote Grütze*, stewed red summer fruit served cold with cream or custard.

Getränke — Beverages

Alkoholische Getränke — Alcoholic drinks

Apfelwein [ˈʔapflvaɪn]	cider
Bier [biɐ]	beer

There are many different types of beer, and the names can vary, depending on the region. The most popular ones are *Export* or *Helles* (lager), *Pils* (a strong lager), *Alt* or *Bockbier* (dark beer) and *Weizenbier* (a light summer beer made from wheat). *Radler* or *Alsterwasser* is beer diluted with lemonade/lemon soda.

Wein [vaɪn]	wine
Champagner [ʃamˈpanjɐ]	champagne (from France)
Sekt [zɛkt]	champagne style wine (from outside France)
leicht [laɪçt]	light
lieblich [ˈliːplɪç]	sweet
rosé [ʀoˈzeː]	rosé
rot [ʀoːt]	red

trocken [ˈtʀɔkn̩]	dry
weiß [vais]	white
Weinschorle sauer [ˈvaɪnʃɔːlə ˈzauɐ]	wine diluted with mineral water
Weinschorle süß [ˈvaɪnʃɔːlə ˈzyːs]	wine diluted with lemonade/lemon soda
Weinbrand [ˈvaɪnbʀant]	brandy
Most [mɔst]	cider
Kognak [ˈkɔnjak]	cognac
Likör [lɪˈkøɐ]	liqueur
Gin [dʒɪn]	gin
Rum [ʀʊm]	rum
Whisky [ˈvɪski]	whisky
Wodka [ˈvɔtka]	vodka

After a meal you may be offered a *Schnaps*, a spirit often distilled from pears, cherries or plums. A sweeter variation is *Obstler*, a mixed fruit schnapps.

Germany is famous for its white wines. The red wines and rosé tend to be light. There are two basic wine categories: *Tafelwein* (table wine) and *Qualitätswein* (quality wine). *QbA* (*Qualitätswein besonderer Anbaugebiete*) means that the wine comes from one of eleven special regions. Further designations are: *Kabinett* (premium quality), *Spätlese* (late harvest, with a richer flavour), *Auslese* (from selected grapes). A rare speciality is *Eiswein* (ice wine) made from frost-bitten grapes.

Alkoholfreie Getränke	**Non-alcoholic drinks**
Alkoholfreies Bier [ˈʔalkoˈhoːlfʀaɪəs biɐ]	non-alcoholic/alcohol-free beer
Apfelsaft [ˈʔapflzaft]	apple juice

Apple juice is often drunk diluted with mineral water *(eine Apfelsaftschorle* or *ein gespritzter Apfelsaft)*. Another popular drink is *Spezi* (a mixture of cola and orange). American children will be disappointed that lemonade as in the US is unknown.

Cola [ˈkoːla]	coke
Eistee [ˈʔaɪsteː]	iced tea
Fruchtsaft [ˈfʀʊxtzaft]	fruit juice

Limonade [lɪmo'na:də]	lemonade/soda pop
Mineralwasser [mɪnə'ʀa:lvasə]	mineral water
mit Kohlensäure [mɪt 'ko:lnzɔɪʀə]	carbonated
ohne Kohlensäure ['ʔo:nə 'ko:lnzɔɪʀə] . .	still
Orangensaft	orange juice
[ʔo'ʀaŋʒnzaft/ʔo'ʀa:ʒnzaft]	
Tomatensaft [to'ma:tnzaft]	tomato juice
Tonic ['tɔnɪk]	tonic water
Eiskaffee ['ʔaɪskafe:]	iced coffee
Früchtetee ['fʀʏçtəte:]	fruit tea
(eine Tasse) Kaffee	(a cup of) coffee
[('ʔaɪnə 'tasə) ka'fe:]	
Koffeinfreier Kaffee	decaffeinated coffee
[kɔfe'ʔi:nfʀaɪɐ ka'fe:]	
Kräutertee ['kʀɔɪtete:]	herbal tea
Milch [mɪlç]	milk
Pfefferminztee ['pfɛfɐmɪntste:]	peppermint tea
Sahne ['za:nə]	cream
(eine Tasse/ein Glas) Tee	(a cup/glass of) tea
[('ʔaɪnə 'tasə/ʔaɪn gla:s) 'te:]	

Coffee is usually served with evaporated milk, normal milk, or cream. In Germany, when sitting outside, often you can only order *ein Kännchen,* a small pot for two cups. *Schümli* is Swiss-style frothy coffee. Italian coffees such as *Cappuccino* and *Espresso* are very popular. Austrian coffee houses offer a wide range of specialities such as *Melange* (milk coffee), *Schwarzer* (black coffee) or *kleiner Brauner* (small cup of coffee with milk or cream).

Österreichische Spezialitäten
Austrian specialities

G'spritzter ['kʃpʀɪtstɐ]	1/8 litre of wine diluted with the same amount of mineral water
Heuriger ['hɔɪʀɪgɐ]	young wine less than a year old
Backhendl ['bakhendl]	whole roast chicken
Brettljause ['bʀɛtljaʊzə]	a selection of cheeses and sliced cold meat

Cevapcici [tʃeˈvaptʃitʃi] . . . . spicy, grilled minced meat fingers
Dampfnudeln [ˈdampfnuːdln] . . . . yeast dumplings often eated with custard
Erdäpfel [ˈʔeɐdepfl] . . . . potatoes
Faschiertes [faˈʃietəs] . . . . minced/ground meat
Frittatensuppe [frɪˈdaːtnsupːe] . . . . . . clear soup with strips of pancake
Germknödel [ˈgɛɛmkneːdl] . . . . a yeast dumpling filled with plum jam
Geselchtes [ˈkselçtes)] . . . . smoked meat
Haxe [haksə] . . . . pork knuckles
Jause [ˈjaʊzə] . . . . afternoon snack
Kaiserschmarren [ˈkɛːzeʃmoɐn] . . . . . . Austrian pancakes with almonds and raisins
Kren [kʀeːn] . . . . horseradish
Marillen [maˈʀɪln] . . . . apricots
Nockerl [ˈnɔkel] . . . . dumpling
Schlagobers [ˈʃlagobɛs] . . . . whipped cream
Palatschinken [ˈpalatʃɪŋkn] . . . . pancakes with chocolate sauce
Paradeiser [paʀaˈdaɪzə] . . . . tomatoes
Sachertorte [ˈzaxɐtɐɐtə] . . . . rich chocolate cake with a thin layer of apricot jam
Schwammerl [ˈʃvamɐl] . . . . mushrooms
Semmel [semːl] . . . . bread roll
Surstelze [ˈsuːrstəltsə] . . . . pork knuckle
Tafelspitz [ˈtaːflʃpɪts] . . . . boiled beef served with horseradish
Topfen [ˈtɔpfn] . . . . *Quark:* thick, creamy dairy product
Topfenstrudel [ˈtɔpfnʃtʀuːdl] . . . . similar to apple strudel, but filled with *Topfen*

Schweizer Spezialitäten
Swiss specialities

Café crème [kaˈfeː ˈkʀɛːm] . . . . coffee with cream
Schale [ˈʃaːlə] . . . . coffee with milk
Berner Platte [ˈbærnər ˈplatːe] . . . . . . platter with different kinds of meat, boiled tongue, sausages and beans
Bündner Fleisch [ˈbyndnər flaɪʃ] . . . . . paper thin slices of air-dried beef
Bürli [ˈbyrli] . . . . bread rolls

Fladen [ˈflaːdn]	cake
Fondue [fɔnˈdyː]	small pieces of fillet of pork/beef on skewers dipped in hot oil, served with various sauces
Glacé [glaˈseː]	ice cream
Kabis [ˈxabis]	cabbage
Käsefondue [ˈkɛzəfɔndyː]	cheese fondue: hot melted cheese into which pieces of bread are dipped
Raclette [ˈraxlet]	slices of melted raclette cheese served with potatoes
Rahm [ʀaːm]	whipped cream
Rösti [ˈrøʃti]	hash brown potatoes
Rübli [ˈʀyːbli]	carrots
Züricher Rahmgeschnetzeltes [ˈtsyrxər ˈʀaːmgʃnɛtsltəs]	strips of veal in a creamy wine and mushroom sauce

Sightseeing and excursions

Tourists love it here
The German-speaking countries are in many ways a tourist's dream. The countries are filled with old, romantic castles and other wonders of bygone days; the countryside is very pretty and remarkably varied; there is an abundance of cultural attractions such as festivals and concerts. Connecting all of this is an excellent system of roads and public transportation. Only the weather can be somewhat disappointing at times. Tourist high-season is the summer, of course. If you come earlier, the crowds of tourists will be smaller, but the weather more unpredictable. The crowds also get smaller starting in September, and the weather is usually quite good on into October – but the days will be shorter.

For information about interesting sights, festivals and events follow the L-sign to the *Fremdenverkehrsamt* (tourist office). There is one in nearly every town. Before you leave, you can also check ahead by looking at a city's web page. Frankfurt, for example, is {www.frankfurt.de}.

Tourist Information

Where's the tourist office?
Wo ist das Fremdenverkehrsamt? [vo: ʔɪst das fʀɛmdnfɐˈkeːsʔamt]

I'd like a map of ..., please.
Ich hääte gern einen Stadtplan von ...
[ʔɪç ˈhɛtə gɛɐn ʔaɪnn ˈʃtatplaːn fɔn]

Have you got a calendar of events for this week?
Haben Sie einen Veranstaltungskalender für diese Woche?
[haːbm zi ʔaɪnn fɐʔanʃtaltʊŋskaˌlɛndɐ fyɐ ˈdiːzə ˈvɔxə]

Are there sightseeing tours of the town?
Gibt es Stadtrundfahrten? [gɪpt əs ˈʃtatʀʊntfaːtn]

Cultural attractions

Opening hours, guided tours, admission

Can you tell me what special attractions there are here?
Können Sie mir bitte sagen, welche Sehenswürdigkeiten es hier gibt? [kœnn zi miɐ ˈbɪtə zaːgn ˈvɛlçə ˈzeːnsvvɐdɪçkaɪtn əs hiɐ gɪpt]

You really must visit ...
Sie müssen unbedingt ... besichtigen.
[zi mʏsn ˈʔʊnbədɪŋt ... bəˈzɪçtɪgn]

When's the museum open?
Wann ist das Museum geöffnet? ['van ɪst das muˈzeʊm gəˈʔœfnət]

> Most museums and art galleries are closed on Mondays.

When does the tour start?
Wann beginnt die Führung? [van bəˈgɪnt di ˈfyːʀʊŋ]

Is there a tour in English, too?
Gibt es auch eine Führung auf Englisch?
[gɪpt əs aʊx ˀaɪnə ˈfyːʀʊŋ ˀaʊf ˀˀɛŋlɪʃ]

Two tickets, please.
Zwei Eintrittskarten, bitte! [tsvaɪ ˀˀaɪntʀɪtskaːtn ˈbɪtə]

Two adults and one child.
Zwei Erwachsene und ein Kind. [tsvaɪ ˀeˈvaksənə ˀʊnt ˀaɪn ˈkɪnt]

Are there reductions for ...
Gibt es Ermäßigungen für ... [gɪpt əs ˀeˈmɛːsɪgʊŋŋ fye]

children?
Kinder? [ˈkɪndɐ]

students?
Studenten? [ʃtʊˈdɛntn]

senior citizens?
Senioren? [zenˈjoːʀən]

groups?
Gruppen? [ˈgʀʊpm]

Is there an exhibition catalogue?
Gibt es einen Katalog zur Ausstellung?
[gɪpt əs aɪnn kataˈloːk tsʊɐ ˀˀaʊʃtɛlʊŋ]

What? Who? When?

Is this/that ...?
Ist das ...? [ˀɪst das]

When was the church built?
Wann wurde die Kirche erbaut? [ˈvan ˌvʊɐdə diː ˈkɪɐçə ˀeˈbaʊt]

When was this building restored?
Wann wurde dieses Gebäude restauriert?
[van ˌvʊɐdə ˈdiːzəs gəˈbɔɪdə ʀɛstaʊˈʀiɐt]

Who painted this picture?
Von wem ist dieses Bild? [fɔn veːm ˀɪst ˈdiːzəs bɪlt]

Have you got a poster of this picture?
Haben Sie das Bild als Poster? [ˈhaːbm zi das bɪlt ˀals ˈpoːstɐ]

Cultural attractions

alley	die Gasse [di ˈɡasə]
art	die Kunst [di kʊnst]
city centre	das Stadtzentrum [das ˈʃtattsɛntʁʊm]
district	der Stadtteil [dɐ ˈʃtataɪl]
emblem	das Wahrzeichen [das ˈvaːtsaɪçn]
emperor/empress	der Kaiser/die Kaiserin [dɐ ˈkaɪze/di ˈkaɪzəʁɪn]
findings	die Funde m pl [di fʊndə]
guide	der Fremdenführer/die Fremdenführerin [dɐ ˈfʁɛmdnfyːɐ/ˈfʁɛmdnfyːəʁɪn]
guided tour	die Führung [di ˈfyːʁʊŋ]
history	die Geschichte [di ɡəˈʃɪçtə]
home town	die Geburtsstadt [di ɡəˈbʊɐtʃtat], die Heimatstadt [di ˈhaɪmaːtʃtat]
house	das Haus [das haʊs]
king	der König [dɐ ˈkøːniç]
lane	die Gasse [di ˈɡasə]
market	der Markt [dɐ maːkt]
museum	das Museum [das muˈzeːʊm]
ethnic museum of mankind	das Volkskundemuseum [das ˈfɔlkskʊndəmuˌzeʊm]
park	der Park [dɐ paːk]
pedestrian precinct/zone	die Fußgängerzone [di ˈfuːsɡɛŋɐˌtsoːnə]
queen	die Königin [di ˈkøːnɪɡɪn]
to reconstruct	rekonstruieren [ʁekɔnstʁʊˈʔiːʁən]
religion	die Religion [di ʁelɪˈɡjoːn]
remains	die Überreste m pl [di ˈʔyːbɐʁɛstə]
to restore	restaurieren [ʁɛstaʊˈʁiːʁən]
road	die Straße [di ˈʃtraːsə]
sights	die Sehenswürdigkeiten f pl [di ˈzeːnsvyɐdɪçkaɪtn]
sightseeing tour of the town/city	die Stadtrundfahrt [di ˈʃtatʁʊntfaːt]
street	die Straße [di ˈʃtraːsə]
suburb	der Vorort [dɐ ˈfoɐˈʔɔɐt]
symbol	das Wahrzeichen [das ˈvaːtsaɪçn]
tour	die Besichtigung [di bəˈzɪçtɪɡʊŋ]
town centre/downtown	das Stadtzentrum [ˈʃtattsɛntʁʊm]

Architecture

abbey	die Abtei [di ʔapˈtaɪ]
altar	der Altar [dɐ ʔalˈtaː]
arch	der Bogen [dɐ ˈboːɡn]
archaeology	die Archäologie [di ʔaːçeoloˈɡiː]
architect	Architekt/Architektin [ʔaːçɪˈtɛkt/ʔaːçɪˈtɛkt ɪn]

architecture	die Architektur [di ʔaːçitɛkˈtuɐ]
bay	der Erker [dɐ ˈʔɛɐkɐ]
bay window	das Erkerfenster [das ˈʔɛɐkɐfɛnstɐ]
bridge	die Brücke [di ˈbʀʏkə]
building	das Gebäude [das gəˈbɔɪdə]
castle (fortress)	die Burg [di bʊɐk]
castle (palace)	das Schloss [das ʃlɔs]
cathedral	die Kathedrale [di kateˈdʀaːlə]
ceiling	die Decke [di ˈdɛkə]
cemetery	der Friedhof [dɐ ˈfʀiːtoːf]
chapel	die Kapelle [di kaˈpɛlə]
church	die Kirche [di ˈkɪɐçə]
cloister	der Kreuzgang [dɐ ˈkʀɔɪtsgaŋ]
column	die Säule [di ˈzɔɪlə]
convent	das(Nonnen)Kloster [das (ˈnɔnn)ˌkloːstɐ]
covered market	die Markthalle [di ˈmaːkthalə]
crypt	die Krypta [di kʀʏpta]
dome	die Kuppel [di kʊpl]
excavations	die Ausgrabungen f pl [di ˈʔaʊsgʀaːbʊŋŋ]
façade	die Fassade [di faˈsaːdə]
fortress	die Festung [di ˈfɛstʊŋ]
fountain	der (Spring)Brunnen [dɐ (ˈʃpʀɪŋ)bʀʊnn]
gable	der Giebel [dɐ giːbl]
gate	das Tor [das toɐ]
grave	das Grab [das gʀaːp]
graveyard	der Friedhof [dɐ ˈfʀiːtoːf]
inner courtyard	der Innenhof [dɐ ˈʔɪnnhoːf]
inscription	die Inschrift [di ˈʔɪnʃʀɪft]
mausoleum	das Mausoleum [das maʊzoˈleʊm]
memorial	die Gedenkstätte [di gəˈdɛŋkʃtɛtə]
monastery	das (Mönchs)Kloster [das (ˈmœnçs)ˌkloːstɐ]
monument (memorial edifice)	das Denkmal [das ˈdɛŋkmaːl]
monument (tomb)	das Grabmal [ˈgʀaːbmaːl]
opera	die Oper [di ˈʔoːpɐ]
palace	der Palast [dɐ paˈlast]
pilgrimage church	die Wallfahrtskirche [di ˈvalfaːtsˌkɪɐçə]
pillar	die Säule [di ˈzɔɪlə], der Pfeiler [dɐ ˈpfaɪlɐ]
portal	das Portal [das pɔ(ɐ)ˈtaːl]
pulpit	die Kanzel [di kantsl]
to rebuild	wieder aufbauen [viːdɐ ˈʔaʊfbaʊən]
roof	das Dach [das dax]
ruin	die Ruine [di ʀuˈʔiːnə]
square	der Platz [dɐ plats]
steeple	der Kirchturm [dɐ ˈkɪɐçtʊɐm]

125

temple	der Tempel [dɐ tɛmpl]
theatre	das Theater [das te'ˀaːtɐ]
tomb	das Grab [das ɡʀaːp]
tower	der Turm [dɐ tʊɐm]
town centre	die Innenstadt [di ˀɪnnʃtat]
the old town	die Altstadt [di ˀaltʃtat]
town hall	das Rathaus [das ʀaːthaʊs]
town walls	die Stadtmauern f pl [di ʃtatmaʊɐn]
treasure chamber	die Schatzkammer [di ʃatskamɐ]
triumphal arch	der Triumphbogen [dɐ tʀiˀʊmpfboːɡn]
university	die Universität [di ˀʊnivɛɐziˈtɛːt]
vault(s)	das Gewölbe [das ɡəˈvœlbə]
wall (*supportive structure*) . .	die Mauer [di ˈmaʊɐ]
wall (*inside partition of house*)	die Wand [di vant]
window	das Fenster [das ˈfɛnstɐ]
wing	der Flügel [dɐ flyːɡl]

Arts and artefacts

arts and crafts	das Kunstgewerbe [das ˈkʊnstɡəvɛɐbə]
bronze	die Bronze [di ˈbʀɔŋsə]
carpet	der Teppich [dɐ ˈtɛpɪç]
ceramics	die Keramik [di keˈʀaːmɪk]
china	das Porzellan [das pɔɐtsəˈlaːn]
copperplate	der Kupferstich [dɐ ˈkʊpfeʃtɪç]
copy	die Kopie [di koˈpiː]
cross	das Kreuz [das ˈkʀɔɪts]
crucifix	das Kruzifix [das ˈkʀʊtsifɪks]
drawing	die Zeichnung [di ˈtsaɪçnʊŋ]
etching	die Radierung [di ʀaˈdiːʀʊŋ]
exhibit	das Exponat [das ˀɛkspoˈnaːt]
exhibition	die Ausstellung [di ˀaʊʃtɛlʊŋ]
gallery	die Galerie [di ɡaləˈʀiː]
glass painting	die Glasmalerei [di ˈɡlaːsmaːləˌʀaɪ]
gold work	die Goldschmiedekunst [di ˈɡɔltʃmiːdəˌkʊnst]
graphic arts	die Grafik [di ˈɡʀaːfɪk]
lithograph; lithography	die Lithografie [di litoɡʀaˈfiː]
model	das Modell [das moˈdɛl]
mosaic	das Mosaik [das mozaˈˀiːk]
nude (*painting*)	der Akt [dɐ ˀakt]
original (*version*)	das Original [das ˀɔʀɪɡiˈnaːl]
painter	der Maler/die Malerin [dɐ ˈmaːlɐ/di ˈmaːləʀɪn]
painting (*picture or portrait*)	das Gemälde [das ɡəˈmɛːldə]
painting (*type of art*)	die Malerei [di maːləˈʀaɪ]
photography	die Fotografie [di fotoɡʀaˈfiː]
picture	das Bild [das bɪlt]

porcelain	das Porzellan [das pɔ(ɐ)tsə'laːn]
portrait	das Porträt [das pɔ(ɐ)'trɛː]
poster	das Plakat [das pla'kaːt]
pottery	die Töpferei [di tœpfə'ʀaɪ]
sculptor	der Bildhauer/die Bildhauerin [dɐ 'bɪlthaʊɐ/di 'bɪlthaʊəʀɪn]
sculpture	die Skulptur [di skʊlp'tuɐ]
silk-screen print	der Siebdruck [dɐ 'ziːpdʀʊk]
statue	die Statue [di 'ʃtaːtuə]
still life	das Stillleben [das 'ʃtɪleːbm̩]
tapestry	der Wandteppich [dɐ 'vanttɛpɪç]
terracotta	die Terrakotta [di tɛʀa'kɔta]
torso	der Torso [dɐ 'tɔɐzo]
vase	die Vase [di 'vaːzə]
water-colour (picture)	das Aquarell [das ʔakva'ʀɛl]
wood carving	die Schnitzerei [di ʃnɪtsə'ʀaɪ]
woodcut	der Holzschnitt [dɐ 'hɔltʃnɪt]

Styles and ages

ancient	antik [ʔan'tiːk]
art nouveau	der Jugendstil [dɐ 'juːgn̩tstiːl]
baroque	barock [ba'ʀɔk]
bronze age	die Bronzezeit [di 'bʀɔŋsətsaɪt]
Celtic	keltisch ['kɛltɪʃ]
century	das Jahrhundert [das ja'hʊndɐt]
Christianity	das Christentum [das 'kʀɪstntuːm]
classicism	der Klassizismus [dɐ klasɪ'tsɪsmʊs]
dynasty	die Dynastie [di dʏnas'tiː]
epoch	die Epoche [di ʔe'pɔxə]
expressionism	der Expressionismus [dɐ ʔɛkspʀesjo'nɪsmʊs]
Gothic	die Gotik [di 'goːtik]
Greek	griechisch ['gʀiːçɪʃ]
heathen	heidnisch ['haɪtnɪʃ]
impressionism	der Impressionismus [dɐ ʔɪmpʀesjo'nɪsmʊs]
mannerism	der Manierismus [dɐ ˌmaniː'ʀɪsmʊs]
Middle Ages	das Mittelalter [das 'mɪtlʔaltɐ]
modern	modern [mo'dɛɐn]
pagan	heidnisch ['haɪtnɪʃ]
prehistoric	vorgeschichtlich ['foɐgəʃɪçtlɪç]
prime	die Blütezeit [di 'blyːtətsaɪt]
Renaissance	die Renaissance [di ʀənɛ'sãːs]
rococo	das Rokoko [das 'ʀɔkoko]
Romanesque style/period	die Romanik [di ʀo'maːnɪk]
Romanticism	die Romantik [di ʀo'mantɪk]
Stone Age	die Steinzeit [di 'ʃtaɪntsaɪt]

127

When do we meet?
Wann treffen wir uns? [van 'tʀɛfn viɐ ʔʊns]

Where do we leave from?
Wo fahren wir los? [vo: 'fa:ʀən viɐ lo:s]

Will we pass ...?
Kommen wir an ... vorbei? [kɔmm viɐ ʔan ... fɔ'baɪ]

Are we going to see ..., too?
Besichtigen wir auch ...? [bə'zɪçtɪgn viɐ ʔaʊx ...]

amusement park	der Freizeitpark [dɐ 'fʀaɪtsaɪt,pa:k]
botanic gardens	der botanische Garten [dɐ bo'tanɪʃə 'ga:tn]
cave	die Höhle [di 'hø:lə]
cliff	die Klippe [di 'klɪpə]
country(side)	das Land [das 'lant]
day trip	der Tagesausflug [dɐ 'ta:gəs,ʔaʊsflu:k]
dripstone cave	die Tropfsteinhöhle [di 'tʀɔpfʃtaɪn,hø:lə]
excursion	der Ausflug [dɐ 'ʔaʊsflu:k]
fishing port	der Fischerhafen [dɐ 'fɪʃɐha:fn]
forest	der Wald [dɐ valt]
island	die Insel [di 'ʔɪnzl]
lake	der See [dɐ ze:]
market	der Markt [dɐ ma:kt]
mountains	das Gebirge [das gə'bɪʀgə]
mountain village	das Bergdorf [das 'bɛɐkdoɐf]
national park	der Nationalpark [dɐ natsjo'na:lpa:k]
nature reserve	das Naturschutzgebiet [das na'tuɐʃʊtsgəbi:t]
observatory	die Sternwarte [di 'ʃtɛɐnva:tə]
open-air museum	das Freilichtmuseum [das 'fʀaɪlɪçtmʊ,zeʊm]
place of pilgrimage	der Wallfahrtsort [dɐ 'valfa:ts,ʔɔɐt]
ravine	die Schlucht [di 'ʃlʊxt]
scenery	die Landschaft [di 'lantʃaft]
surroundings	die Umgebung [di ʔʊm'ge:bʊŋ]
tour	die Rundfahrt [di 'ʀʊntfa:t]
trip	der Ausflug [dɐ 'ʔaʊsflu:k]
valley	das Tal [das ta:l]
vantage point	der Aussichtspunkt [dɐ 'ʔaʊsɪçtspʊŋt]
view	die Aussicht [di 'ʔaʊsɪçt]
waterfall	der Wasserfall [dɐ 'vasefal]
wildlife park	der Wildpark [dɐ 'vɪltpa:k]
woods	der Wald [dɐ valt]
zoo	der Zoo [dɐ tso:]

Active holidays

Lots of opportunities
Germany is a very popular country. It offers fine scenery, from high mountains to beaches on the sea, and noteworthy cultural attractions. The weather in the summer is usually mild, although there can be rather high humidity in some areas. Regardless of the time of year, you'll have a lot to choose from, and you can take advantage of numerous sporting and cultural opportunities, from swimming and hiking to booking a language course to improve your German.

Bathing and swimming

Excuse me, is there a ... here?
Entschuldigen Sie bitte, gibt es hier ein ...
[ˀɛntˈʃʊldɪgn̩ zi ˈbɪtə gɪpt ɛs hiɐ ˀaɪn ...]
  swimming pool
  Schwimmbad? [ˈʃvɪmbaːt]
  outdoor pool
  Freibad? [ˈfʀaɪbaːt]
  indoor pool
  Hallenbad? [halnbaːt]

A/One ticket, please.
Eine Eintrittskarte, bitte! [ˀaɪnə ˀaɪntʀɪtska:tə ˈbɪtə]

Can you tell me where the ... are, please?
Können Sie mir bitte sagen, wo die ... sind?
[kœnn zi miɐ ˈbɪtə za:gn̩ vo: di ... zɪnt]
  showers
  Duschen [ˈduːʃn]
  changing rooms
  Umkleidekabinen [ˀʊmklaɪdəkaˌbiːnn]

Is the beach ...
Ist der Strand ... [ˀɪst dɐ ʃtʀant ...]
  sandy?
  sandig? [ˈzandɪç]
  pebbled/stony?
  steinig? [ˈʃtaɪnɪç]

Are there any sea urchins/jellyfish here?
Gibt es hier Seeigel/Quallen? [gɪpt əs hiɐ ˈzeːˀiːgl̩/ˈkvaln]

Is the current strong?
Ist die Strömung stark? [ˀɪst di ˈʃtʀøːmʊŋ ʃta:k]

Is it dangerous for children?
Ist es für Kinder gefährlich? [ˀɪst əs fyɐ ˈkɪndɐ gəˈfeɐlɪç]

When's low tide/high tide?
Wann ist Ebbe/Flut? [van ɪst 'ʔɛbə/'fluːt]

I'd like to rent ...
Ich möchte ... mieten. [ʔɪç 'mœçtə ... miːtn]

a deck chair.
einen Liegestuhl [ʔaɪnn 'liːgəʃtuːl]

a sunshade.
einen Sonnenschirm [ʔaɪnn 'zɔnnʃɪɐm]

a boat.
ein Boot [ʔaɪn 'boːt]

a pair of water skis.
ein Paar Wasserski [ʔaɪn paː 'vaseʃiː]

How much is it per hour/day?
Was kostet das pro Stunde/Tag? [vas 'kɔstət das pʁo 'ʃtʊndə/taːk]

air mattress	die Luftmatratze [di 'lʊftma,tʁatsə]
boat-hire	der Bootsverleih [dɐ 'boːtsfɐlaɪ]
children's pool	das Kinderbecken [das 'kɪndɐbɛkn]
lifeguard	der Bademeister/die Bademeisterin [dɐ 'baːdəmaɪstɐ/'baːdəmaɪstərɪn]
non-swimmer	der Nichtschwimmer [dɐ 'nɪçtʃvɪmɐ]
nudist beach	der FKK-Strand [dɐ ʔɛfkaː'kaːʃtʁant]
pedal boat/pedalo	das Tretboot [das 'tʁeːtboːt]
swimmer	der Schwimmer/die Schwimmerin [dɐ 'ʃvɪmɐ/di 'ʃvɪmərɪn]
to swim	schwimmen [ʃvɪmm]
volleyball	der Volleyball [dɐ 'vɔlɪbal]
to go water skiing	Wasserski fahren ['vaseʃiː 'faːʁən]
water wings	die Schwimmflügel *m pl* [di 'ʃvɪmflyːgl]
windbreak	der Windschirm [dɐ 'vɪntʃɪɐm]

Other sporting activities

Popular sports are soccer, tennis and cycling in summer and skiing in winter. Golf is becoming quite popular now, although golf courses are usually for members only.
The national pastime-sport is *Wandern,* something between hiking and walking. In almost any larger wooded area there'll be a parking area *(Wanderparkplatz),* complete with a map on a signboard showing possible routes and walking time.

What sort of sports facilities are there here?
Welche Sportmöglichkeiten gibt es hier?
['vɛlçə 'ʃpɔɐtmøːkliçkaɪtn gɪpt əs hie]

131

Is there ... here?
Gibt es hier ... [gɪpt əs hiɐ ...]
a golf course
einen Golfplatz? [ˀaɪnn 'gɔlfplats]
a tennis court
einen Tennisplatz? [ˀaɪnn 'tɛnɪsplats]

Where can I go ... here?
Wo kann man hier ... [voː kan man hiɐ ...]
fishing
angeln? [ˀaŋln]
hiking
wandern? ['vandɐn]

Where can I hire/rent ...?
Wo kann ich ... ausleihen? [voː 'kan ɪç ... ˀauslaɪn]

I'd like to take a beginner's course/an advanced course.
Ich möchte einen Kurs für Anfänger/ Fortgeschrittene machen.
[ˀɪç 'mœçtə ˀaɪnn kʊɐs fyɐ ˀanfɛŋɐ/ 'fɔɐtgəʃʀɪtənə maxn]

Water sport	
canoe	das Kanu [das 'kaːnu]
inflatable (boat)	das Schlauchboot [das 'ʃlauxboːt]
motorboat	das Motorboot [das 'moːtɔboːt]
pick-up service	der Rückholservice [dɐ 'ʀykhoːlˌsœɐvɪs]
regatta	die Regatta [di ʀe'gata]
to row	rudern ['ʀuːdɐn]
rowing boat	das Ruderboot [das 'ʀuːdɐboːt]
rubber dinghy	das Schlauchboot [das 'ʃlauxboːt]
to sail	segeln ['zeːgln]
sailing boat	das Segelboot [das 'zeːglboːt]
to surf	surfen ['sœɐfn]
surfboard	das Surfbrett [das 'sœɐfbʀɛt]
wind conditions	die Windverhältnisse n pl [di 'vɪntfɐˌhɛltnɪsə]
windsurfing	das Windsurfen [das 'vɪntsœɐfn]

Diving	
to dive	tauchen [tauxn]
diving equipment	die Taucherausrüstung [di 'tauxɐˀausʀystʊŋ]
diving goggles	die Taucherbrille [di 'tauxɐbʀɪlə]
snorkel	der Schnorchel [dɐ ʃnɔɐçl]
to go snorkelling	schnorcheln [ʃnɔɐçln]
wetsuit	der Neoprenanzug [dɐ neo'pʀeːnˌˀantsuːk]

Fishing

bait	der Köder [dɐ ˈkøːdɐ]
fishing licence	der Angelschein [dɐ ˈʔaŋlʃaɪn]
fishing rod	die Angel [di ˈʔaŋl]
fresh water	das Süßwasser [das ˈzyːsvasɐ]
to go fishing	angeln [ˈʔaŋln]
off season	die Schonzeit [di ˈʃoːntsaɪt]
salt water	das Salzwasser [das ˈzaltsvasɐ]

Ball games

ball	der Ball [dɐ bal]
basketball	der Basketball [dɐ ˈbaːskətbal]
football	der Fußball [dɐ ˈfuːsbal]
football pitch/football field	der Fußballplatz [dɐ ˈfuːsbalˌplats]
football match	das Fußballspiel [das ˈfuːsbalˌʃpiːl]
goal	das Tor [das toɐ]
goalkeeper	der Torwart [dɐ ˈtoɐvaːt]
half-time	die Halbzeit [di ˈhalptsaɪt]
handball	der Handball [ˈhantbal]
team	die Mannschaft [di ˈmanʃaft]
volleyball	der Volleyball [dɐ ˈvɔlɪbal]

Tennis and badminton

badminton (sport)	das Badminton [das ˈbɛtmɪntn]
doubles	das Doppel [das ˈdɔpl]
floodlight(s)	das Flutlicht [das fluːtlɪçt]
racquet	der Schläger [dɐ ˈʃlɛːgɐ]
shuttlecock	der Federball [dɐ ˈfeːdɐbal]
singles	das Einzel [das ˈʔaɪntsəl]
squash	das Squash [das skvɔʃ]
table tennis	das Tischtennis [das ˈtɪʃtɛnɪs]
tennis	das Tennis [das ˈtɛnɪs]
tennis racquet	der Tennisschläger [dɐ ˈtɛnɪʃlɛːgɐ]

Fitness and working out

aerobics	das Aerobic [das ʔɛˈʁɔbɪk]
body-building	das Bodybuilding [das ˈbɔdɪbɪldɪŋ]
fitness centre	das Fitnesscenter [das ˈfɪtnəsˌtsɛntɐ]
fitness training	das Konditionstraining [das kɔndɪˈtsjoːnstʁɛːnɪŋ]
gymnastics	die Gymnastik [di gʏmˈnastɪk]
jazz aerobics	die Jazzgymnastik [di ˈdʒɛsgʏmˌnastɪk]
jogging	das Jogging [das ˈdʒɔgɪŋ]
to jog	joggen [ˈdʒɔgn]
weight training	das Krafttraining [das ˈkʁaftʁɛːnɪŋ]

jacuzzi	der Whirlpool [dɐ ˈvœɐlpuːl]
massage	die Massage [maˈsaːʒə]
sauna	die Sauna [di ˈzaʊna]
solarium	das Solarium [das zoˈlaːʀiʊm]
swimming pool	das Schwimmbad [das ˈʃvɪmbaːt]
Turkish bath	das Dampfbad [das ˈdampfbaːt]

Cycling

bicycle/bike	das Fahrrad [das ˈfaːʀat]
crash helmet	der Fahrradhelm [dɐ ˈfaːʀatˌhɛlm]
to cycle	Rad fahren [ˈʀaːt ˈfaːʀən]
cycle path	der Fahrradweg [dɐ ˈfaːʀatveːk]
cycle tour	die Radtour [di ˈʀaːttuɐ]
cycling	der Radsport [dɐ ˈʀaːtʃpɔɐt]
flat tyre/tire	die Panne [di ˈpanə]
mountain bike	das Mountainbike [das ˈmaʊntnbaɪk]
pump	die Luftpumpe [di ˈlʊftpʊmpə]
racing bike	das Rennrad [das ˈʀɛnʀaːt]
repair kit	das Flickzeug [das ˈflɪktsɔɪk]
touring bike	das Tourenrad [das ˈtuːʀənʀaːt]
trekking bike	das Trekkingrad [das ˈtʀɛkɪŋʀaːt]

Hiking and mountaineering

I'd like to go for a hike in the mountains.
Ich möchte eine Bergtour machen.
[ˈʔɪç ˈmœçtə ˌʔaɪnə ˈbɛɐktuɐ maxn]

Can you show me an interesting route on the map?
Können Sie mir eine interessante Route auf der Karte zeigen?
[kœnn zi miɐ ˌʔaɪnə ˌʔɪntʀəˈsantə ˈʀuːtə ˈʔaʊf dɐ ˈkaːtə tsaɪɡn]

day trip	die Tagestour [di ˈtaːɡəstuɐ]
freeclimbing	das Freeclimbing [das ˈfʀiːklaɪmbɪŋ]
to hike	wandern [ˈvandɐn]
hiking map	die Wanderkarte [di ˈvandɐkaːtə]
hiking trail	der Wanderweg [dɐ ˈvandɐveːk]
mountaineering	das Bergsteigen [das ˈbɛɐkʃtaɪɡn]
path	der Pfad [dɐ pfaːt]
refuge hut/shelter	die Schutzhütte [di ˈʃʊtshʏtə]

Riding

horse	das Pferd [das pfeɐt]
ride, horse ride	der Ausritt [dɐ ˈaʊsʀɪt]
to ride	reiten [ˈʀaɪtn]

riding holiday	die Reiterferien *pl* [di ˈʀaɪtɐˌfeːʀiən]
riding school	die Reitschule [ˈʀaɪtʃuːlə]
saddle	der Sattel [dɐ zatl]

Golf

18-hole course	der 18-Loch-Platz [dɐ ˈaxtseːn lɔx plats]
club member	das Clubmitglied [das ˈklʊpˌmɪtgliːt]
clubhouse	das Clubhaus [das ˈklʊphaʊs]
day guest...........	der Tagesbesucher [dɐ ˈtaːgəsbəzuːxɐ]
golf	das Golf [das gɔlf]
golf club *(implement)*	der Golfschläger [dɐ ˈgɔlfʃlɛːgɐ]
golf course	der Golfplatz [dɐ ˈgɔlfplats]
to play a round of golf	eine Runde Golf spielen [ˈaɪnə ˈʀʊndə gɔlf ˈʃpiːln]
tee	das Tee [das tiː]
tee-off	der Abschlag [dɐ apʃlaːk]

Gliding

glider	das Segelflugzeug [das ˈzeːglfluːktsɔɪk]
gliding	das Segelfliegen [das ˈzeːglfliːgn]
hang-gliding	das Drachenfliegen [das ˈdʀaxnfliːgn]
parachute	der Fallschirm [dɐ ˈfalʃɪɐm]
parachuting	das Fallschirmspringen [das ˈfalʃɪɐmʃpʀɪŋŋ]
paraglider	der Gleitschirm [dɐ ˈglaɪtʃɪɐm]
take-off area	der Startplatz [dɐ ˈʃtaːtplats]

Winter holidays

A day ticket, please.
Eine Tageskarte, bitte. [ˈaɪnə ˈtaːgəskaːtə ˈbɪtə]

How many points does this ski lift cost?
Wie viele Punkte kostet dieser Skilift?
[ˈviː_filə ˈpʊŋktə ˈkɔstət diːzɐ ˈʃiːlɪft]

What time is the last trip up the mountain?
Um wie viel Uhr ist die letzte Bergfahrt?
[ˈʊm ˈviː_fil ˈuɐ ˈɪst di ˈlɛtstə ˈbɛɐkfaːt]

baby lift	Babylift [ˈbeːbilɪft]
bottom station, base terminal	die Talstation [di ˈtaːlʃtatsjoːn]
cable car	die Seilbahn [di ˈzaɪlbaːn]
cable railway	die (Stand)Seilbahn [di (ʃtant)zaɪlbaːn]
chair-lift	der Sessellift [dɐ ˈzɛslɪft]
cross-country ski course ...	die Loipe [di lɔɪpə]
cross-country skiing	der Langlauf [dɐ ˈlaŋlaʊf]
curling	das Curling [das ˈkəːlɪŋ]

day pass	der Tagespass [dɐ 'taːɡəspas]
downhill skiing	Ski alpin [ʃiː ʔal'piːn]
drag lift	der Schlepplift [dɐ 'ʃlɛplɪft]
funicular	die (Stand)Seilbahn [di (ʃtant)ˌzaɪlbaːn]
ice hockey	das Eishockey [das ʔaɪshɔkeː]
ice rink	die Eisbahn [di ʔaɪsbaːn]
to go ice skating	Schlittschuh laufen ['ʃlɪtʃuː laʊfn]
ice skates	die Schlittschuhe m pl [di ʃlɪtʃuːə]
middle station	die Mittelstation [di 'mɪtlʃtaˌtsjoːn]
ski	der Ski [dɐ ʃiː]
ski bindings	die Skibindungen f pl [di 'ʃiːbɪndʊŋŋ]
ski goggles	die Skibrille [di 'ʃiːbʀɪlə]
ski instructor	der Skilehrer/die Skilehrerin [dɐ 'ʃiːleːʀɐ/'ʃiːleːʀəʀɪn]
ski poles	die Skistöcke m pl [di 'ʃiːʃtœkə]
ski slope	die Skipiste [di 'ʃiːpɪstə]
to go skiing	Ski laufen ['ʃiː laʊfn]
skiing course	der Skikurs [dɐ 'ʃiːkʊɐs]
sledge	der Schlitten [dɐ ʃlɪtn]
snowboard	das Snowboard [das 'snoːbɔɐt]
summit station/top station	die Bergstation [di 'bɛɐkʃtaˌtsjoːn]
toboggan	der Schlitten [dɐ ʃlɪtn]
week('s) pass	der Wochenpass [dɐ 'vɔxnpas]

Other sports

athletics	die Leichtathletik [di 'laɪçtʔatˌleːtɪk]
bowling (tenpin)	das Bowling [das 'boːlɪŋ]
bowling (ninepin)	das Kegeln [das keːgln]
crazy golf	das Minigolf [das 'mɪnigɔlf]
inline skating	das Inlineskating [das ʔɪnlaɪnˌskeɪtɪŋ]
motor-racing	der Motorsport [dɐ 'moːtɔʃpɔɐt]
to go roller-skating	Rollschuh fahren ['ʀɔlʃuː 'faːʀən]
skateboard	das Skateboard [das 'skɛɪtbɔɐt]
to skateboard	Skateboard fahren ['skɛɪtbɔɐt 'faːʀən]

Sporting events

Can you tell me what sort of sporting events there are here?
Können Sie mir bitte sagen, welche Sportveranstaltungen es hier gibt? [kœnn zi miɐ 'bɪtə zaːgn 'vɛlçə 'ʃpɔɐtfɛˌʔanʃtaltʊŋŋ əs hiɐ gɪpt]

I'd like to see the football match.
Ich möchte mir das Fußballspiel ansehen.
[ʔɪç 'mœçtə miɐ das 'fuːsbalʃpiːl ʔanzeːn]

When/Where is it?
Wann/Wo findet es statt? [van/voː fɪndət əs ʃtat]

What's the score?
Wie steht's? [viː ʃteːts]

Two-one.
Zwei zu eins. [tsvaɪ tsʊ ʔaɪns]

Three all/three tied.
Drei-drei. [dʀaɪ dʀaɪ]

Foul!
Foul! [faʊl]

Good shot!
Schöner Schuss! [ˈʃøːne ʃʊs]

Goal!
Tor! [toɐ]

athlete	der Sportler/die Sportlerin [de ˈʃpɔɐtle/di ˈʃpɔɐtlərɪn]
championship	die Meisterschaft [di ˈmaɪsteʃaft]
contest	der Wettkampf [de ˈvɛtkamf]
corner kick	der Eckstoß [de ˈʔɛkʃtoːs]
cross	die Flanke [di flaŋkə]
cycle racing	das Radrennen [das ˈʀaːtʀɛnn]
defeat	die Niederlage [di ˈniːdelaːgə]
draw	unentschieden [ˈʔʊnɛntʃiːdn]
free kick	der Freistoß [de ˈfʀaɪʃtoːs]
game	das Spiel [ʃpiːl]
kickoff	der Anstoß [de ˈanʃtoːs]
to lose	verlieren [fɛˈliːʀən]
match	das Spiel [ʃpiːl]
offside	abseits [ˈʔapzaɪts]
pass	der Pass [de pas]
penalty kick	der Elfmeter [de ˈʔɛlfmeːte]
penalty box	der Strafraum [de ˈʃtʀaːfʀaʊm]
program(me)	das Programm [das pʀoˈgʀam]
race	das Rennen [das ʀɛnn]
referee	der Schiedsrichter [de ˈʃiːtsʀɪçte]
to score a goal	ein Tor schießen [ʔaɪn toɐ ʃiːsn]
sports ground	der Sportplatz [de ˈʃpɔɐtplats]
stadium	das Stadion [das ˈʃtaːdjon]
ticket	die Eintrittskarte [di ˈʔaɪntʀɪtsˌkaːtə]
ticket office	die Kasse [di ˈkasə]
umpire	der Schiedsrichter [de ˈʃiːtsʀɪçte]
victory/win	der Sieg [de ziːk]
to win	gewinnen [gəˈvɪnn]

Creative holidays

I'm interested in ...
Ich interessiere mich für ... [ˀɪç ˀɪntʀəˈsiːʀə mɪç fyɐ ...]

a pottery course.
einen Töpferkurs. [ˀaɪnn ˈtœpfekʊɐs]

a German course.
einen Deutschkurs. [ˀaɪnn ˈdɔɪtʃkʊɐs]

for beginners
für Anfänger [fyɐ ˀanfɛŋɐ]

for advanced learners
für Fortgeschrittene [fyɐ ˈfɔɐtgəʃʀɪtnə]

How many hours per day are we together?
Wie viele Stunden pro Tag arbeiten wir zusammen?
[ˈviː_fiːlə ˈʃtʊndn pʀo taːk ˀaːbaɪtn vie tsʊˈzamm]

Is the number of participants limited?
Ist die Teilnehmerzahl begrenzt? [ˀɪst di ˈtaɪlneːmɐtsaːl bəˈgʀɛntst]

When do I have to enrol(l) by?
Bis wann muss man sich anmelden?
[bis van mʊs man zɪç ˀanmɛldn]

Are the costs of materials included?
Sind die Materialkosten inklusive?
[zɪnt di matɛʀˀaːlkɔstn ˀɪŋklʊˈziːvə]

What should I bring along?
Was soll ich mitbringen? [vas zɔl ɪç ˈmɪtbʀɪŋŋ]

carpentry workshop	die Holzwerkstatt [di ˈhɔltsˌvɛɐkʃtat]
to cook	kochen [ˈkɔxn]
course	der Kurs [dɐ kʊɐs]
dance theatre	das Tanztheater [das ˈtantsteˌˀaːtɐ]
drama workshop	der Schauspielworkshop
	[dɐ ˈʃaʊʃpiːlˌwəːkʃɔp]
to draw	zeichnen [ˈtsaɪçnn]
drumming	das Trommeln [das ˈtʀɔmln]
meditation	die Meditation [di meditaˈtsjoːn]
oil painting	die Ölmalerei [di ˀøːlmaːləˌʀaɪ]
to paint	malen [maːln]
silk painting	die Seidenmalerei [di ˈzaɪdnmaːləˌʀaɪ]
to photograph	fotografieren [ˌfotogʀaˈfiːʀən]
workshop	der Workshop [dɐ ˈwəːkʃɔp]
yoga	das Yoga [das ˈjoːga]

Culture, fun and diversion
All year long you'll find countless opportunities for entertainment. The normal concert and theatre season is from autumn to spring, but during the summer there are numerous festivals, including outdoor performances. Most cities and larger towns have websites (e.g. www.heidelberg.de for Heidelberg) where you can find out what's going on and get valuable tips for booking or planning your stay.

Theatre – Concert – Cinema

Could you tell me what's on at the theatre tonight, please?
Könnten Sie mir bitte sagen, welches Stück heute Abend im Theater gespielt wird? [kœntn zi miɐ ˈbɪtə zaːgn̩ ˈvɛlçəs ʃtʏk ˈhɔɪtə ʔaːbmt ʔɪm teˈʔaːtɐ gəˈʃpiːlt vɪɐt]

What's on at the cinema / movies tomorrow night?
Was läuft morgen Abend im Kino?
[vas lɔɪft ˌmɔɐgn̩ ˈʔaːbmt ʔɪm ˈkiːno]

Are there concerts in the cathedral?
Werden im Dom Konzerte veranstaltet?
[veɐdn̩ ʔɪm ˈdoːm kɔnˈtsɛɐtə fɛˈʔanʃtaltət]

Can you recommend a good play?
Können Sie mir ein gutes Theaterstück empfehlen?
[ˈkœnn zi miɐ ʔaɪn ˈguːtəs teˈʔaːtɐʃtʏk ʔɛmpˈfeːln]

When does the performance start?
Wann beginnt die Vorstellung? [van bəˈgɪnt di ˈfoɐʃtɛlʊŋ]

Where can I get tickets?
Wo bekommt man Karten? [voː bəˈkɔmt man ˈkaːtn̩]

Two tickets for this evening, please.
Bitte zwei Karten für heute Abend.
[ˈbɪtə tsvaɪ ˈkaːtn̩ fyɐ ˈhɔɪtə ʔaːbmt]

Two seats at ..., please.
Bitte zwei Plätze zu ... [ˈbɪtə ˈtsvaɪ ˈplɛtsə tsʊ]

Can I have a programme, please?
Kann ich bitte ein Programm haben?
[kan ɪç ˈbɪtə ʔaɪn pʁoˈgram ˈhaːbm̩]

advance booking	der Vorverkauf [dɐ ˈfoɐfɐkaʊf]
box office	die Kasse [di ˈkasə]
cloakroom	die Garderobe [di gaˈdʁoːbə]
festival	das Festival [das ˈfɛstɪval]
interval/intermission	die Pause [di ˈpaʊzə]

140

performance	die Vorstellung [di ˈfoɐ̯ʃtɛlʊŋ]
program(me)	das Programmheft [das pʀoˈgʀamhɛft]
ticket	die Eintrittskarte [di ˈʔaɪ̯ntʀɪtskaːtə]

Theatre

1st/2nd row	erster/zweiter Rang [ˈeɐ̯stɐ/ˈtsvaɪ̯tɐ ʀaŋ]
act	der Akt [dɐ ˈʔakt]
actor/actress	Schauspieler/Schauspielerin
	[ˈʃaʊ̯ʃpiːlɐ/ ˈʃaʊ̯ʃpiːlɛʀɪn]
ballet	das Ballett [das baˈlɛt]
box	die Loge [di ˈloːʒə]
cabaret	das Kabarett [das kabaˈʀeː]
comedy	die Komödie [di koˈmøːdiə]
dancer	der Tänzer/die Tänzerin
	[dɐ tɛntsɐ/ di tɛntsəˈʀɪn]
drama	das Drama [das ˈdʀaːma]
encore	die Zugabe [di ˈtsuːgaːbə]
music hall	das Varietee [das vaʀiəˈteː]
musical	das Musical [das ˈmjuːzɪkl]
open-air theatre	das Freilufttheater [das ˈfʀaɪ̯lʊftəˌʔaːtɐ]
opera	die Oper [di ˈʔoːpɐ]
operetta	die Operette [di ʔopəˈʀɛtə]
performance	die Aufführung [di ˈʔaʊ̯fyːʀʊŋ]
play	das Schauspiel [das ˈʃaʊ̯ʃpiːl]
play	das Theaterstück [das teˈʔaːtɐʃtʏk]
premiere	die Premiere [di pʀəmˈjeːʀə]
production	die Inszenierung [di ʔɪntsəˈniːʀʊŋ]
programme (booklet)	das Programmheft [das pʀoˈgʀamhɛft]
revue	das Kabarett [das kabaˈʀeː]
stalls	das Parkett [das paˈkɛt]
tragedy	die Tragödie [di tʀaˈgøːdiə]
variety theatre	das Varietee [das vaʀiəˈteː]

Concerts

blues	der Blues [dɐ bluːs]
choir	der Chor [dɐ koɐ̯]
classical	die Klassik [di ˈklasɪk]
composer	der Komponist/die Komponistin
	[dɐ kɔmpoˈnɪst/di kɔmpoˈnɪstɪn]
concert	das Konzert [das kɔnˈtsɛɐ̯t]
chamber music concert	das Kammerkonzert
	[das ˈkamɐkɔnˌtsɛɐ̯t]
church concert	das Kirchenkonzert
	[das ˈkɪʁçnkɔnˌtsɛɐ̯t]
symphony concert	das Sinfoniekonzert
	[das zɪmfoˈniːkɔnˌtsɛɐ̯t]
piano recital	der Klavierabend [dɐ klaˈviːɐaːbmt]

conductor	der Dirigent/die Dirigentin [de diʀiˈgɛnt/di diʀiˈgɛntɪn]
jazz	der Jazz [de ˈdʒɛs]
orchestra	das Orchester [das ʔɔɐ̯ˈkɛstɐ]
pop	der Pop [de pɔp]
reggae	der Reggae [de ˈʀɛgeː]
rock	der Rock [de ʀɔk]
singer	der Sänger/die Sängerin [de ˈzɛŋɐ/di ˈzɛŋəʀɪn]
soloist	der Solist/die Solistin [de zoˈlɪst/di zoˈlɪstɪn]
traditional music	die Volksmusik [di ˈfɔlksmʊˌziːk]
folk music	der Folk [de foːk]

Cinema/Movie Theater

cast	die Besetzung [di bəˈzɛtsʊŋ]
cinema/movie theater	das Kino [das ˈkiːno]
drive-in cinema	das Freilichtkino [das ˈfʀaɪlɪçtkiːno]
arts cinema	das Programmkino [das pʀoˈgʀamkiːno]
directed by	die Regie [di ʀəˈʒiː]
dubbed	synchronisiert [zʏŋkroniˈziet]
film (Am movie)	der Film [de fɪlm]
action film	der Actionfilm [de ˈʔɛktʃnfɪlm]
black-and-white film	der Schwarzweißfilm [de ʃvaːtsˈvaɪsfɪlm]
cartoon	der Zeichentrickfilm [de ˈtsaɪçnˌtʀɪkfɪlm]
classic film	der Klassiker [de ˈklasɪkɐ]
comedy	die Komödie [di koˈmøːdiə]
documentary	der Dokumentarfilm [de dɔkʊmɛnˈtaːfɪlm]
drama	das Drama [das ˈdʀaːma]
science fiction film	der Sciencefictionfilm [de saɪnsˈfɪktʃnfɪlm]
short film	der Kurzfilm [de kʊɐ̯tsfɪlm]
thriller	der Thriller [de ˈθʀɪlɐ]
western	der Western [de ˈvɛstɐn]
film/movie actor	der Filmschauspieler [de ˈfɪlmʃaʊʃpiːlɐ]
film/movie actress	die Filmschauspielerin [di ˈfɪlmʃaʊʃpiːlərɪn]
leading role	die Hauptrolle [di ˈhaʊptʀɔlə]
movie	der Film [de fɪlm]
original version	die Originalfassung [di ʔoʀɪgɪˈnaːlfasʊŋ]
screen	die Leinwand [di ˈlaɪnvant]
screenplay, script	das Drehbuch [das ˈdʀeːbuːx]

special effects	die Spezialeffekte *m pl*
	[di ʃpeˈtsjaːleˌfɛktə]
subtitles	der Untertitel [dɐ ˈʔʊntɐtiːtl̩]
supporting role	die Nebenrolle [di ˈneːbmˌʀɔlə]

Nightlife

What is there to do here in the evenings?

Was kann man hier abends unternehmen?

[vas kan man hiɐ ˈʔaːbmts ˈʔʊntɐˈneːmm]

Is there a nice pub here?

Gibt es hier eine gemütliche Kneipe?

[gɪpt əs hiɐ ˌʔaɪnə gəˈmyːtlɪçə ˈknaɪpə]

How long are you open today?

Bis wann haben Sie heute auf? [bɪs van ˈhaːbm zi ˈhɔɪtə ˈʔaʊf]

Where can we go dancing?

Wo kann man hier tanzen gehen? [voː kan man hiɐ ˈtantsn geːn]

Shall we have another dance?

Wollen wir noch einmal tanzen? [vɔln viɐ nɔx ˈʔaɪnmaːl ˈtantsn]

In pubs and bars you don't normally pay for each individual
drink. The waiter or barkeeper keeps a record of your orders
(sometimes on your beer mat) and presents you with the total
when you leave. Closing times vary considerably; ask if in
doubt. In larger cities pubs and bars are often open until well
after midnight.

---

band	die Band [di bɛ(ː)nt]
bar	die Bar [di baː]
casino	das Spielkasino [das ˈʃpiːlkaˌziːno]
to dance	tanzen [tantsn]
dance band	die Tanzkapelle [di ˈtantskaˌpɛlə]
discotheque	die Diskothek [di dɪskoˈteːk]
folklore evening	der Folkloreabend [dɐ fɔlkˈloːʀəˌʔaːbmt]
gambling	das Glücksspiel [das ˈglʏkʃpiːl]
to go out	ausgehen [ˈʔaʊsgeːn]
night club	der Nachtklub [dɐ ˈnaxtklʊp]
pub	die Kneipe [di ˈknaɪpə]
show	die Show [di ʃoː]

Festivals and events

Could you tell me when the music festival takes place, please?
Könnten Sie mir bitte sagen, wann das Musikfestival stattfindet?
[kɛntn zi miɐ 'bɪtə za:gn van das mu'zi:kfɛstɪval 'ʃtatfɪndət]

from June to September
von Juni bis September [fɔn 'ju:ni bɪs zɛp'tɛmbɐ]
every year in August
jedes Jahr im August ['je:dəs ja: ʔɪm aʊ'gʊst]
every 2 years
alle zwei Jahre [ʔalə tsvaɪ 'ja:ʀə]

Typical festivals and events

ball . . . . der Ball [dɐ bal]
barbecue . . . . das Grillfest [das 'gʀɪlfɛst]
brass band . . . . die Blaskapelle [di 'bla:ska‚pɛlə]
carnival . . . . der Fasching [dɐ 'faʃɪŋ]
Christmas market . . . . der Weihnachtsmarkt
[dɐ 'vaɪnaxts‚ma:kt]
circus . . . . der Zirkus [dɐ 'tsɪʀkʊs]
dance (party) . . . . das Tanzfest [das 'tantsfɛst]
event . . . . die Veranstaltung [di fɐ'ʔanʃtaltʊŋ]
fair . . . . die Kirmes [di 'kɪʀməs]
fireworks display . . . . das Feuerwerk [das 'fɔɪɐvɛɐk]
flea market . . . . der Flohmarkt [dɐ 'flo:ma:kt]
flower show . . . . die Gartenschau [di 'ga:tnʃaʊ]
funfair . . . . der Jahrmarkt [dɐ 'ja:ma:kt]
garden party . . . . das Gartenfest [das 'ga:tnfɛst]
New Year's Eve party . . . . . die Silvester-Party [di zɪl'vɛstɐpa:ti]
parade . . . . der Umzug [dɐ 'ʔʊmtsu:k]
procession . . . . die Prozession [di pʀotsɛs'jo:n]
village fête . . . . das Dorffest [das 'dɔɐfɛst]

Shopping

Spending your money

Shopping is a natural activity, and you'll have no trouble doing it in the German-speaking countries. Restrictions in store hours have been liberalised recently, so you can take advantage of opportunities six days a week and well into the evening. If you're looking for clothes, a great time to shop is during the *Sommer-schlussverkauf* (summer clearance sale), from the end of July to the middle of August. This is when stores clear out their summer lines and drop prices often by as much as 30% or 40% to do so.

Questions

I'm looking for ...

Are you being served?
Werden Sie schon bedient? [veɐdn zi ʃon bəˈdiːnt]

Thank you, I'm just looking (a)round.
Danke, ich sehe mich nur um. [daŋkə ʔɪç zeː mɪç nuɐ ʔʊm]

I'd like ...
Ich hätte gern ... [ʔɪç hɛtə gɛɐn]

Have you got ...?
Haben Sie ...? [ˈhaːbm zi]

Can I get you anything else?
Darf es sonst noch (et)was sein? [daːf əs zɔnst nɔx (ʔɛt)vas zaɪn]

Bargaining and buying

How much is it?
Wie viel kostet es? [ˈviː_fil ˈkɔstət əs]

That's really expensive!
Das ist aber teuer! [das ɪst ʔabɐ ˈtɔɪɐ]

Good. I'll take it.
Gut, ich nehme es. [guːt ʔɪç ˈneːm əs]

Do you take credit cards?
Nehmen Sie Kreditkarten? [ˈneːmm zi kʁeˈdiːtˌkaːtn]

Shops

Excuse me, where can I find ...?
Entschuldigen Sie bitte, wo finde ich ...?
[ʔɛntʃʊldɪgŋ zi ˈbɪtə voː ˈfɪndə ʔɪç]

antique shop	das Antiquitätengeschäft [das ʔantɪkvɪ'tɛːtngəʃɛft]
art dealer	der Kunsthändler [dɐ 'kʊnst͜hɛntlɐ]
baker's	die Bäckerei [di bɛkə'ʀaɪ]
barber's	der (Herren)Friseur [dɐ('hɛʀən)fʀɪ'zøɐ]
book shop	die Buchhandlung [di 'buːxhantlʊŋ]
boutique	die Boutique [di bu'tiːk]
butcher's	die Metzgerei [di mɛtsgə'ʀaɪ]
cake shop	die Konditorei [di kɔndito'ʀaɪ]
candy store	das Süßwarengeschäft [das 'zyːsvaːʀəngəʃɛft]
chemist's (*pharmacy*)	die Apotheke [di ʔapo'teːkə]
cobbler	der Schuhmacher [dɐ 'ʃuːmaxɐ]
delicatessen	das Feinkostgeschäft [das 'faɪnkɔstgəʃɛft]
department store	das Kaufhaus [das 'kaʊfhaʊs]
dressmaker	der Schneider/die Schneiderin [dɐ 'ʃnaɪdɐ/ 'ʃnaɪdəʀɪn]
drugstore	die Drogerie [di dʀogə'ʀiː]
(*shop for toiletries*)	
dry cleaner's	die Reinigung [di 'ʀaɪnɪgʊŋ]
fishmonger's/fish dealer . . .	das Fischgeschäft [das 'fɪʃgəʃɛft]
flea market	der Flohmarkt [dɐ 'floːmaːkt]
florist's	das Blumengeschäft [das 'bluːmŋgəʃɛft]
food/grocery store	das Lebensmittelgeschäft [das 'leːbmsmɪtlgəʃɛft]
greengrocer's/fruit and . . . vegetable store	der Obst- und Gemüsehändler [dɐ ʔoːpst ʔʊnt gə'myːzəhɛntlɐ]
hairdresser's	der Friseur [dɐ fʀɪ'zøɐ]
health food shop	das Reformhaus [das ʀe'fɔɐmhaʊs]
jeweller's	der Juwelier [dɐ juve'liɐ]
launderette	der Waschsalon [dɐ 'vaʃzaˌlɔŋ]
laundry	die Wäscherei [di vɛʃə'ʀaɪ]
liquor store	das Spirituosengeschäft [das ʃpiʀitu'oːzŋgəʃɛft]
market	der Markt [dɐ maːkt]
newsagent's	der Zeitungshändler [dɐ 'tsaɪtʊŋshɛntlɐ]

off-licence	das Spirituosengeschäft [das ʃpiritu'o:zngǝʃɛft]
optician's	der Optiker [dɐ ˀɔptɪkɐ]
organic food shop	der Bioladen [der 'biola:dn]
perfumery	die Parfümerie [di pafʏmǝ'ʀi:]
photographic materials	die Fotoartikel m pl [di 'fo:toˀaˌtɪkl]
second-hand shop	der Trödelladen [dɐ 'tʀø:dlla:dn]
shoe shop	das Schuhgeschäft [das 'ʃu:gǝʃɛft]
shoemaker's	der Schuhmacher [dɐ 'ʃu:maxɐ]
souvenir shop	der Souvenirladen [dɐ zʊvǝ'niǝla:dn]
sports shop	das Sportgeschäft [das 'ʃpɔɐtgǝʃɛft]
stationer's	das Schreibwarengeschäft [das 'ʃʀaɪpva:ʀǝngǝʃɛft]
supermarket	der Supermarkt [dɐ 'zu:pɐma:kt]
sweet shop	das Süßwarengeschäft [das 'zy:sva:ʀǝngǝʃɛft]
tailor	der Schneider/die Schneiderin [dɐ 'ʃnaɪdɐ/ 'ʃnaɪdǝʀɪn]
tobacconist's/tobacco shop	der Tabakladen [dɐ 'tabakla:dn]
toy shop	das Spielwarengeschäft [das 'ʃpi:lva:ʀǝngǝʃɛft]
travel agency	das Reisebüro [das 'ʀaɪzǝbyˌʀo:]
watchmaker's	der Uhrmacher [dɐ ˀuɐmaxɐ]
wine merchant's	die Weinhandlung [di 'vaɪnhantlʊŋ]

Books, magazines and stationery

I'd like ...
Ich hätte gern ... [ˀɪç hɛtǝ gɛɐn ...]
a German newspaper.
eine deutsche Zeitung. [ˀaɪnǝ 'dɔɪtʃǝ 'tsaɪtʊŋ]
a magazine.
eine Zeitschrift. [ˀaɪnǝ 'tsaɪtʃʀɪft]
a travel guide.
einen Reiseführer. [ˀaɪnn 'ʀaɪzǝfyːʀɐ]
a hiking map for this area.
eine Wanderkarte dieser Gegend. [ˀaɪnǝ 'vandɐka:tǝ di:zɐ 'ge:gŋt]

Books, magazines and newspapers

comic	das Comicheft [das 'kɔmɪkhɛft]
cookbook	das Kochbuch [das 'kɔxbu:x]
daily paper	die Tageszeitung [di 'ta:gǝstsaɪtʊŋ]
detective novel	der Kriminalroman [dɐ kʀɪmi'na:lʀoˌma:n]
dictionary	das Wörterbuch [das 'vœɐtǝbu:x]
(glossy) magazine	die Illustrierte [di ɪlʊ'stʀiɐtǝ]

(news) magazine	die Zeitschrift [di 'tsaɪtʃʁɪft]
map *(of country area)*	die Landkarte [di 'lantka:tə]
newspaper	die Zeitung [di 'tsaɪtʊŋ]
novel	der Roman [de ʁoˈmaːn]
paperback	das Taschenbuch [das 'taʃnbuːx]
road map	die Straßenkarte [di 'ʃtʁaːsnkaːtə]
thriller	der Kriminalroman [de kʁɪmiˈnaːlʁomaːn]
town map	der Stadtplan [de 'ʃtatplaːn]
travel guide	der Reiseführer [de 'ʁaɪzəfyːʁe]
women's magazine	die Frauenzeitschrift [di 'fʁaʊntsaɪtʃʁɪft]

Stationery

ball-point pen	der Kugelschreiber [de 'kuːglʃʁaɪbe],
biro	der Kuli [de 'kuːli]
coloured pencil	der Farbstift [de 'faːpʃtɪft]
colouring book	das Malbuch [das 'maːlbuːx]
envelope	der Briefumschlag [de 'bʁiːfʊmʃlaːk]
eraser	der Radiergummi [de ʁaˈdie̯ˌgʊmi]
felt-tip pen	der Filzstift [de 'fɪltʃɪft]
floppy disks	die Disketten *f pl* [di dɪsˈkɛtn]
glue	der Klebstoff [de 'kleːpʃtɔf]
notepad	der Notizblock [de noˈtiːtsblɔk]
paper	das Papier [das paˈpie̯]
pencil	der Bleistift [de 'blaɪʃtɪft]
picture postcard	die Ansichtskarte [di ˈʔanzɪçtskaːtə]
sellotape®/scotch tape®	der Tesafilm® [de 'teːzafɪlm]
writing pad	der Block [de blɔk]
writing paper	das Briefpapier [das 'bʁiːfpaˌpie̯]

CDs and cassettes

➢ also "Electrical goods" and "Concert"

Do you have any CDs/cassettes by ...?
Haben Sie CDs/Kassetten von ...? ['haːbm zi tseˈdeːs/kaˈsɛtn fɔn ...]

I'd like a CD of typical Swiss music.
Ich hätte gern eine CD mit typisch Schweizer Musik.
[ʔɪç hɛtə gɛɐn ʔaɪnə tseˈdeː mɪt 'tyːpɪʃ ʃvaɪtse muˈziːk]

Can I have a quick listen to this, please?
Kann ich hier bitte kurz reinhören?
[kan ʔɪç hie 'bɪtə kʊɐts 'ʁaɪnhøːʁən]

cassette	die Kassette [di kaˈsɛtə]
CD	die CD [di tseˈdeː]
CD player	der CD-Spieler [de tseˈdeːʃpiːle]

Discman®	der tragbare CD-Spieler [de 'tra:kba:re tse'de: ʃpi:le]
DVD	die DVD [di defaʊ'de:]
headphones	der Kopfhörer [de 'kɔpfhø:re]
personal stereo	der Walkman® [de 'wɔ:kmɛn]
portable CD player	der tragbare CD-Spieler [de 'tra:kba:re tse'de:ʃpi:le]
speaker	der Lautsprecher [de 'laʊtʃprɛçe]
Walkman®	der Walkman® [de 'wɔ:kmɛn]

Electrical goods

➤ also "Photographic materials", "CDs and cassettes"

adapter	der Adapter [de ʔa'dapte]
alarm clock	der Wecker [de 'vɛke]
battery	die Batterie [di bata'ri:]
battery charger	das Ladegerät [das 'la:degɛrɛ:t]
extension lead/cord	die Verlängerungsschnur [di fe'lɛŋərʊŋʃnue]
flashlight, torch	die Taschenlampe [di 'taʃnlampe]
hair dryer	der Föhn [de fø:n]
light bulb	die Glühbirne [di 'gly:bɪrne]
pager	der Piepser [de 'pi:pse]
pocket calculator	der Taschenrechner [de 'taʃnrɛçne]

Fashion

➤ also Colours

Clothing

Can you please show me ...?
Können Sie mir bitte ... zeigen? ['kœnn zi mie 'bɪtə ... 'tsaɪgn]

Can I try it on?
Kann ich es anprobieren? [kan ɪç əs ʔanprobi:rən]

What size do you take?
Welche Größe haben Sie? ['vɛlçə 'grø:sə 'ha:bm zi:]

It's too ...
Das ist mir zu ... ['das ʔɪst mie tsʊ '...]
  tight/big.
  eng/weit. [ʔɛŋ/vaɪt]
  short/long.
  kurz/lang. [kʊets/laŋ]
  small/big.
  klein/groß. [klaɪn/gro:s]

It's a good fit. I'll take it.
Das passt gut. Ich nehme es. [das past 'guːt ʔɪç 'neːm əs]
It's not quite what I want(ed).
Das ist nicht ganz, was ich möchte.
[das ʔɪst nɪçt gants vas ɪç 'mœçtə]

anorak	der Anorak [dɐ ʔˈanoʀak]
bathing-cap	die Bademütze [di 'baːdəmʏtsə]
bathrobe	der Bademantel [dɐ 'baːdəmantl]
bikini	der Bikini [dɐ bi'kiːni]
blazer	der Blazer [dɐ 'bleːzɐ]
blouse	die Bluse [di 'bluːzə]
body stocking/body suit . . .	der Body [dɐ 'bɔdi]
bow-tie	die Fliege [di 'fliːgə]
bra	der Büstenhalter [dɐ 'bʏstnhaltɐ]
briefs	der (Herren)Slip [dɐ ('hɛʀən)slɪp]
cap	die Mütze [di 'mʏtsə]
cardigan	die Strickjacke [di 'ʃtʀɪkjakə]
coat	der Mantel [dɐ mantl]
cotton	die Baumwolle [di 'baʊmvɔlə]
dress	das Kleid [das klaɪt]
gloves	die Handschuhe m pl [di 'hantʃuːə]
hat	der Hut [dɐ huːt]
jacket	die Jacke [di 'jakə]
jeans	die Jeans [di 'dʒiːns]
jumper	der Pullover [dɐ pʊ'loːvɐ]
leggings	die Leggings [di 'lɛgɪŋs]
linen	das Leinen [das laɪnn]
panties	der (Damen)Slip [dɐ ('daːmən)slɪp]
pants (Am)	die Hose [di 'hoːzə]
pants (underwear)	die Unterhose [di 'ʊntɐhoːzə]
parka	der Anorak [dɐ ʔˈanoʀak]
pullover	der Pullover [dɐ pʊ'loːvɐ]
raincoat	der Regenmantel [dɐ 'ʀeːgŋmantl]
scarf (decorative)	das Halstuch [das 'halstuːx]
scarf (for keeping warm) . . .	der Schal [dɐ ʃaːl]
shirt	das Hemd [das hɛmt]
shorts	die kurze Hose [di 'kʊɐtsə 'hoːzə]
silk	die Seide [di 'zaɪdə]
silk stockings	die Seidenstrümpfe m pl
	[di 'zaɪdnʃtʀʏmpfə]
silk tights	die Seidenstrumpfhose
	[di 'zaɪdnʃtʀʊmpfhoːze]
skirt	der Rock [dɐ ʀɔk]
sleeve	der Ärmel [dɐ ʔɛɐml]
socks	die Socken f pl [di 'zɔkŋ]

stockings	die Strümpfe _m pl_ [di ˈʃtʀʏmpfə]
suit _(for men)_	der Anzug [dɐ ˈʔantsuːk]
suit _(for women)_	das Kostüm [das kɔsˈtyːm]
sun hat	der Sonnenhut [dɐ ˈzɔnnhuːt]
sweater	der Pullover [dɐ pʊˈloːvɐ]
swimming trunks	die Badehose [di ˈbaːdəhoːzə]
swimsuit	der Badeanzug [dɐ ˈbaːdəˌʔantsuːk]
tee-shirt	das T-Shirt [das ˈtiːʃœɐt]
tie	die Krawatte [di kʀaˈvatə]
tights	die Strumpfhose [di ˈʃtʀʊmpfhoːzə]
tracksuit	der Trainingsanzug [dɐ ˈtʀɛːnɪŋsˌʔantsuːk]
trousers	die Hose [di ˈhoːzə]
umbrella	der Schirm [dɐ ʃɪʀm]
underpants	die Unterhose [di ˈʊntɐhoːzə]
underwear	die Unterwäsche [di ˈʔʊntɐvɛʃə]
waistcoat, _(US)_ vest	die Weste [di ˈvɛstə]
vest _(undershirt)_	das Unterhemd [das ˈʊntɐhɛmt]
wool	die Wolle [di ˈvɔlə]

Dry cleaning

I'd like to have these things cleaned/washed.
Ich möchte diese Sachen reinigen/ waschen lassen.
[ˈʔɪç ˈmœçtə ˌdiːzə ˈzaxn ˈʀaɪnɪgn̩/vaʃn̩ lasn̩]

When will they be ready?
Wann sind sie fertig? [van zɪnt zi ˈfɛɐtɪç]

to dry-clean	chemisch reinigen [ˈçeːmɪʃ ˈʀaɪnɪgn̩]
to iron	bügeln [byːgln̩]
to press	plätten [plɛtn̩]

Groceries

What can I get you?
Was darf es sein? [vas daːf əs ˈzaɪn]

I'd like ..., please.
Geben Sie mir bitte ... [geːbm zi miɐ ˈbɪtə]

a pound of ...
ein Pfund ... [ˈʔaɪn pfʊnt]

ten slices of ...
10 Scheiben ... [ˈtseːn ʃaɪbm̩]

a piece of ...
ein Stück von ... [ˈʔaɪn ʃtʏk fɔn]

a packet of ...
eine Packung ... [ˈʔaɪnə ˈpakʊŋ]

a jar of ...
ein Glas ... [ˀaɪn glaːs]

a tin of ...
eine Dose ... [ˀaɪnə ˈdoːzə]

a bottle of ...
eine Flasche ... [ˀaɪnə ˈflaʃə]

a bag, please.
eine (Einkaufs)tüte. [ˀaɪnə (ˀaɪnkaʊfs)ˌtyːtə]

Could I try some of this?
Dürfte ich vielleicht etwas hiervon probieren?
[dʏɐft ɪç fiˌlaɪçt ˌɛtvas ˈhiɐfɔn pʁoˈbiːʁən]

Would a little bit more be OK?
Darf es auch etwas mehr sein? [daːf əs aʊx ˌˀɛtvas ˈmeɐ zaɪn]

No, thank you. That's all.
Danke, das ist alles. [ˈdaŋkə das ɪst ˀaləs]

Fruit	Obst
apples	die Äpfel *m pl* [di ˀɛpfl]
apricots	die Aprikosen *f pl* [di ˀapʁɪˈkoːzn]
bananas	die Bananen *f pl* [di baˈnaːnən]
blackberries	die Brombeeren *f pl* [di ˈbʁɔmbeːʁən]
blackcurrants	die schwarzen Johannisbeeren *f pl* [di ˈʃvaːtsn joˈhanɪsbeːʁən]
blueberries	die Heidelbeeren *f pl* [di ˈhaɪdlbeːʁən]
cherries	die Kirschen *f pl* [di kɪɐʃn]
coconut	die Kokosnuss [di ˈkoːkosnʊs]
cranberries	die Preiselbeeren *f pl* [di ˈpʁaɪzlbeːʁən]
dried	getrocknet [gəˈtʁɔknət]
fruit	das Obst [das ˀoːpst]
gooseberries	die Stachelbeeren *f pl* [di ˈʃtaxlbeːʁən]
grapefruit	die Grapefruit [di ˈgrepfruːt]
grapes	die Weintrauben *f pl* [di ˈvaɪntʁaʊbm]
lemons	die Zitronen *f pl* [di tsɪˈtʁoːnn]
mandarins	die Mandarinen *f pl* [di mandaˈʁiːnn]
melon	die Melone [di meˈloːnə]
oranges	die Apfelsinen *f pl* [di ˀapflˈziːnn]
peaches	die Pfirsiche *m pl* [di ˈpfɪɐzɪçə]
pears	die Birnen *f pl* [di bɪʁnn]
pineapple	die Ananas [ˀananas]
plums	die Pflaumen *f pl* [di pflaʊmm]
raspberries	die Himbeeren *f pl* [di ˈhɪmbeːʁən]
redcurrants	die roten Johannisbeeren *f pl* [di ʁoːtn joˈhanɪsbeːʁən]
strawberries	die Erdbeeren *f pl* [di ˀeɐtbeːʁən]
tangerines	die Tangerinen *f pl* [di tangəˈʁiːnn]

Vegetables

Vegetables	**Gemüse**
artichokes	die Artischocken f pl [di ʔaːtɪˈʃɔkn̩]
asparagus	der Spargel [ˈʃpaːgl̩]
aubergines	die Auberginen f pl [di ʔobɐˈʒiːnn̩]
avocado	die Avocado [di ʔavoˈkaːdo]
beans	die Bohnen f pl [di boːnn̩]
green beans	grüne Bohnen [ˌgʀyːnə ˈboːnn̩]
haricot beans	weiße Bohnen [ˌvaɪsə ˈboːnn̩]
kidney beans	rote Bohnen [ˌʀoːtə ˈboːnn̩]
beetroot/beet(s)	Rote Bete [ˌʀoːtə ˈbeːtə]
cabbage	der Kohl [dɐ koːl]
carrots	die Karotten f pl [di kaˈʀɔtn̩]
cauliflower	der Blumenkohl [ˈbluːmŋkoːl]
celeriac	der Sellerie [dɐ ˈzɛləʀiː]
celery	der Stangensellerie [dɐ ˈʃtaŋŋˌzɛləʀiː]
corn, maize	der Mais [dɐ maɪs]
cucumber	die Gurke [di ˈgʊɐkə]
fennel	der Fenchel [dɐ fɛnçl̩]
garlic	der Knoblauch [dɐ ˈknoːblaʊx]
horseradish	der Meerrettich [dɐ ˈmeːʀɛtɪç]
leek	der Lauch [dɐ laʊx]
lentils	die Linsen f pl [di lɪnzn̩]
lettuce	der Kopfsalat [dɐ ˈkɔpfsaˌlaːt]

Salat means: (1) "salad" as in "potato salad", "green salad", etc., and (2) "lettuce". To clarify, use *Kopfsalat* (lettuce) or *Kartoffelsalat, grüner Salat*, etc.

Don't be surprised if you encounter regional dialect words, different from those in this list, especially for sausages, bread rolls and cakes.

---

olives	die Oliven f pl [di ʔoˈliːvn̩]
onions	die Zwiebeln f pl [di tsviːbl̩n]
peas	die Erbsen f pl [di ʔɛɐpsn̩]
peppers	die Paprikaschoten f pl [di ˈpapʀɪkaˌʃoːtn̩]
potatoes	die Kartoffeln f pl [di kaˈtɔfl̩n]
pumpkin	der Kürbis [dɐ ˈkʏɐbɪs]
spinach	der Spinat [dɐ ʃpɪˈnaːt]
tomatoes	die Tomaten f pl [di toˈmaːtn̩]

Herbs and spices — Kräuter und Gewürze

Herbs and spices	**Kräuter und Gewürze**
basil	das Basilikum [das baˈziːlikʊm]
bay-leaves	die Lorbeerblätter n pl [di ˈlɔɐbeːɐˌblɛtɐ]
borage	der Borretsch [dɐ ˈbɔʀɛtʃ]

caraway seed(s)	der Kümmel [dɐ kʏml]
chervil	der Kerbel [dɐ kɛɐbl]
chilli	der Chili [dɐ 'tsɪli]
chives	der Schnittlauch [dɐ ʃnɪtlaʊx]
cinnamon	der Zimt [dɐ tsɪmt]
cloves	die Nelken f pl [di nɛlkn]
coriander	der Koriander [dɐ koʀi'andɐ]
dill	der Dill [dɐ dɪl]
garlic	der Knoblauch [dɐ 'knoːblaʊx]
ginger	der Ingwer [dɐ ʔiŋvɐ]
herbs	die Kräuter n pl [di 'kʀɔɪtɐ]
lovage	der/das Liebstöckel [dɐ/das 'liːpʃtœkl]
marjoram	der Majoran [dɐ 'ma(ː)joʀaːn]
mint	die Minze [di 'mɪntsə]
nutmeg	die Muskatnuss [di mʊs'kaːtnʊs]
oregano	der Oregano [dɐ ʔoʀe'gaːno]
paprika	der Paprika [dɐ 'papʀɪka]
parsley	die Petersilie [di peːte'ziːljə]
pepper	der Pfeffer [dɐ 'pfɛfɐ]
pepperoni	die Peperoni [di pɛpə'roːni]
rosemary	der Rosmarin [dɐ 'ʀoːsmaʀiːn]
saffron	der Safran [dɐ 'zafʀaːn]
sage	der Salbei [dɐ 'zalbaɪ]
savory	das Bohnenkraut [das 'boːnnkʀaʊt]
tarragon	der Estragon [dɐ ʔɛstʀagɔn]
thyme	der Thymian [dɐ 'tyːmiaːn]

Bread, cakes and sweets — Backwaren und Süßwaren

The German-speaking countries undoubtedly set the benchmark for bakery goods. What you'll find in every town and city is worthy of any hungry person's attention and would go far beyond the limits of this book. Follow your nose, go in and point, saying *Was ist das, bitte?*
Kuchen is something baked that is sweet, often combined with other words, like *Apfelkuchen* (apple pastry). *Torte* is roughly like a pie, that is, something sweet is spread over baked dough. *Gebäck* is a collective term used for small baked items, much like biscuits/cookies. *Brot* always means literally bread, and comes in countless delicious variations.

bread	das Brot [das bʀoːt]
brown rye bread	das Schwarzbrot [das 'ʃvaːtsbʀoːt]
white bread	das Weißbrot [das 'vaɪsbʀoːt]
wholemeal bread	das Vollkornbrot [das 'fɔlkɔɐnˌbʀoːt]

biscuits/cookies	die Kekse *m pl* [di ˈkeːksə]
cake	der Kuchen [dɐ ˈkuːxn]
candy	die Süßigkeiten *f pl* [di ˈzyːsɪçkaɪtn]
chocolate	die Schokolade [di ʃokoˈlaːdə]
chocolate bar	der Schokoriegel [dɐ ˈʃoːkoʀiːgl]
chocolates	die Pralinen *f pl* [di pʀaˈliːnn]
ice-cream	das Eis [das ˈʔaɪs]
jam/marmalade	die Marmelade [di maməˈlaːdə]

> *Marmelade* in German means any kind of jam. If you want orange marmelade, ask for *Orangenmarmelade*.

muesli	das Müsli [das ˈmyːsli]
rolls	die Brötchen *n pl* [di bʀøːtçn]
filled rolls	belegte Brötchen [bəˈleːktə bʀøːtçn]
sweets	die Süßigkeiten *f pl* [di ˈzyːsiçkaɪtn]
toast	der Toast [dɐ toːst]

Eggs and milk products Eier und Milchprodukte

butter	die Butter [di ˈbʊtɐ]
buttermilk	die Buttermilch [di ˈbʊtɐmɪlç]
cheese	der Käse [dɐ ˈkɛːzə]
cottage cheese	der Hüttenkäse [dɐ ˈhʏtnkɛːzə]
cream	die Sahne [ˈzaːnə]
sour cream	die saure Sahne [di zaʊʀə ˈzaːnə]
whipping cream	die Schlagsahne [ˈʃlaːkzaːnə]
cream cheese	der Frischkäse [dɐ ˈfʀɪʃkɛːzə]
eggs	die Eier *n pl* [di ˈʔaɪɐ]
milk	die Milch [mɪlç]
low-fat milk	fettarme Milch [ˈfɛtˀaːmə mɪlç]
yoghurt	der Joghurt [dɐ ˈjoːgʊɐt]

Meat Fleisch und Wurst

beef	das Rindfleisch [ˈʀɪntflaɪʃ]
chicken	das Hähnchen [das hɛːnçn]
chop	das Kotelett [ˈkɔtlɛt]
cold cuts/lunch meat	der Aufschnitt [dɐ ˈʔaʊfʃnɪt]
cutlet	das Kotelett [das ˈkɔtlɛt]
goulash	das Gulasch [das ˈgʊlaʃ]
ham	der Schinken [dɐ ʃɪŋkn]
cooked ham	gekochter Schinken [gəˈkɔxtɐ ʃɪŋkn]
smoked ham	roher Schinken [ʀoːɐ ʃɪŋkn]
lamb	das Lammfleisch [das ˈlamflaɪʃ]
liver sausage	die Leberwurst [di ˈleːbɐvʊɐst]
meat	das Fleisch [das flaɪʃ]
minced meat	das Hackfleisch [das ˈhakflaɪʃ]
pork	das Schweinefleisch [ˈʃvaɪnəflaɪʃ]

rabbit	das Kaninchen [ka'niːnçn]
salami	die Salami [di zaˈlaːmi]
sausage	die Wurst [di vʊɐst]
small sausages	die Würstchen *n pl* [di vvɛstçn]
	(e.g., frankfurters)
veal	das Kalbfleisch [ˈkalpflaɪʃ]

Fish and seafood / Fisch und Meeresfrüchte

bream	die Brasse [di ˈbʀasə]
cod	der Kabeljau [dɐ ˈkaːbljaʊ]
crab	der Krebs [dɐ kreːps]
eel	der Aal [dɐ ʔaːl]
herring	der Hering [dɐ ˈheːʀɪŋ]
lobster	der Hummer [dɐ ˈhʊmɐ]
mackerel	die Makrele [di maˈkʀeːlə]
mussels	die Muscheln *f pl* [di mʊʃln]
oysters	die Austern *f pl* [di ˈʔaʊstɐn]
perch	der Barsch [dɐ baːʃ]
plaice	die Scholle [di ˈʃɔlə]
prawns	die Garnelen *f pl* [di gaˈneːln]
salmon	der Lachs [dɐ laks]
shrimps	die Krabben *f pl* [di kʀabm]
sole	die Seezunge [di ˈzeːtsʊŋə]
squid	der Tintenfisch [dɐ ˈtɪntnfɪʃ]
swordfish	der Schwertfisch [dɐ ˈʃveɐtfɪʃ]
trout	die Forelle [di foˈʀɛlə]
tuna	der Thunfisch [dɐ ˈtuːnfɪʃ]

Miscellaneous / Dies und das

almonds	die Mandeln *f pl* [di ˈmandln]
butter	die Butter [di ˈbʊtɐ]
flour	das Mehl [das meːl]
honey	der Honig [dɐ ˈhoːnɪç]
margarine	die Margarine [di magaˈʀiːnə]
mayonnaise	die Mayonnaise [di maɪoˈneːzə]
mustard	der Senf [dɐ zɛnf/zɛmf]
noodles	die Nudeln *f pl* [di nuːdln]
nuts	die Nüsse *f pl* [di ˈnʏsə]
oil	das Öl [das ʔøːl]
olive oil	das Olivenöl [das ʔoˈliːvnˌʔøːl]
pasta	die Nudeln *f pl* [di nuːdln]
rice	der Reis[dɐ ʀaɪs]
salt	das Salz [das zalts]
sugar	der Zucker [dɐ ˈtsʊkɐ]
vegetable stock cube	der Gemüsebrühwürfel
	[dɐ gəˈmyːzəˌbryːvvɐfl]
vinegar	der Essig [dɐ ˈʔɛsɪç]

Drink   Getränke

> Wine and spirits are sold openly in all shops offering food or drink. The only restriction is that the buyer must be of age. Identification is rarely, if ever, demanded. If you are looking for especially good wine, there are specialist shops (*Weinhändler* – wine dealer) in almost every larger town or city.

apple juice . . . . der Apfelsaft [dɐ ˈʔapflzaft]
beer . . . . das Bier [das biɐ]
champagne . . . . der Champagner [dɐ ʃamˈpanjɐ]
coffee . . . . der Kaffee [dɐ ˈkafe:/kaˈfe:]
  decaffeinated coffee . . . . . der koffeinfreie Kaffee
                           [dɐ kɔfeˈʔiːnfraɪə ˈkafe:]
cocoa . . . . der Kakao [dɐ kaˈkaʊ]
lemonade . . . . die Limonade [lɪmoˈnaːdə]
mineral water . . . . das Mineralwasser [das mɪnəˈraːlvasɐ]
  sparkling . . . . mit Kohlensäure [mɪt ˈkoːl(ə)nzɔɪʀə]
  still . . . . ohne Kohlensäure [ˈʔoːnə ˈkoːl(ə)nzɔɪʀə]
orange juice . . . . der Orangensaft [dɐ ʔoˈʀaŋʒnzaft]
tea . . . . der Tee [dɐ te:]
  green tea . . . . der grüne Tee [dɐ ˈgryːnə ˈte:]
  fruit tea . . . . der Früchtetee [dɐ ˈfʀʏçtəte:]
  rosehip tea . . . . der Hagebuttentee [dɐ hagəˈbʊtnte:]
  camomile tea . . . . der Kamillentee [dɐ kaˈmɪl(ə)nte:]
  herbal tea . . . . der Kräutertee [dɐ ˈkʀɔɪtəte:]
  peppermint tea . . . . der Pfefferminztee [dɐ ˈpfɛfəmɪntste:]
  black tea . . . . der Schwarztee [dɐ ˈʃvaːtste:]
  tea bags . . . . der Teebeutel [dɐ ˈte:bɔɪtl]
wine . . . . der Wein [dɐ vaɪn]
  rosé wine . . . . Rosé(wein) [ʀoˈze:(vaɪn)]
  red wine . . . . Rotwein [ˈʀoːtvaɪn]
  white wine . . . . Weißwein [ˈvaɪsvaɪn]
  mulled wine . . . . Glühwein [ˈglyːvaɪn]

Hairdresser/Barber

Shampoo and blow dry, please.
Waschen und föhnen, bitte. [ˈvaʃn ˈʔʊnt føːnn ˈbɪtə]

Wash and cut, please.
Schneiden mit Waschen, bitte. [ˈʃnaɪdn mɪt ˈvaʃn ˈbɪtə]

Dry cut.
Schneiden ohne Waschen. [ˈʃnaɪdn ˈʔoːnə ˈvaʃn]

I'd like ...
Ich möchte ... [ˈʔɪç ˈmœçtə ...]

Just trim the ends.
Nur die Spitzen. [nuɐ di ˈʃpɪtsn̩]

Not too short, please.
Nicht zu kurz, bitte. [nɪçt tsʊ ˈkʊɐts ˈbɪtə]

A bit shorter.
Etwas kürzer. [ˈʔɛtvas ˈkʏɐtsɐ]

Thank you. That's fine.
Vielen Dank. So ist es gut. [ˌfiln ˈdaŋk ˈzoː ʔɪst əs ˈguːt]

bangs *(US)*	der Pony [dɐ ˈpɔni
beard	der Bart [dɐ baːt]
blond(e)	blond [blɔnt]
to blow dry	föhnen [føːnn̩]
to comb	kämmen [kɛmm̩]
curlers	die Lockenwickler *m pl* [di ˈlɔkŋvɪklɐ]
curls	die Locken *f pl* [di lɔkŋ]
dandruff	die Schuppen *f pl* [di ʃʊpm̩]
to do someone's hair	frisieren [fʁɪˈziɐn]
to dye	färben [fɛɐbm̩]
fringe	der Pony [dɐ ˈpɔni]
hair	das Haar [das haː]
greasy hair	fettiges Haar [ˈfɛtɪgəs haː]
dry hair	trockenes Haar [ˈtʁɔknəs haː]
hairstyle	die Frisur [di fʁɪˈzuɐ]
highlights	die Strähnchen *n pl* [di ˈʃtʁɛːnçn̩]
layered cut	der Stufenschnitt [dɐ ˈʃtuːfnʃnɪt]
moustache	der Schnurrbart [dɐ ˈʃnʊɐbaːt]
parting	der Scheitel [dɐ ʃaɪtl̩]
perm	die Dauerwelle [di ˈdaʊɐvɛlə]
to set	legen [ˈleːgn̩]
shampoo	das Shampoo [das ˈʃampu]
sideburns	die Koteletten *f pl* [di kɔtˈlɛtn̩]
to tint	tönen [tøːnn̩]

Household goods

bin liner	der Abfallbeutel [dɐ ˈʔapfalbɔɪtl̩]
bottle opener	der Flaschenöffner [dɐ ˈflaʃn̩ˀœfnɐ]
can opener	der Dosenöffner [dɐ ˈdoːznˀœfnɐ]
candles	die Kerzen *f pl* [di kɛɐtsn̩]
charcoal	die Grillkohle [di ˈgʁɪlkoːlə]
cling film	die Frischhaltefolie [di ˈfʁɪʃhaltəˌfoːljə]
clothes line	die Wäscheleine [di ˈvɛʃəlaɪnə]
clothes pegs	die Wäscheklammern *f pl* [di ˈvɛʃəklamɐn]

corkscrew	der Korkenzieher [dɐ ˈkɔɐkn̩tsiːɐ]
fire-lighter	der Grillanzünder [dɐ ˈɡʀɪlantsʏndɐ]
fork	die Gabel [di ˈɡaːbl̩]
garbage bag	der Abfallbeutel [dɐ ˈʔapfalbɔɪtl̩]
glass	das Glas [das glaːs]
grill	der Grill [dɐ gʀɪl]
ice box	die Kühltasche [di ˈkyːltaʃə]
ice pack	das Kühlelement [das ˈkyːlɛləˌmɛnt]
knife	das Messer [das ˈmɛsɐ]
methylated spirits	der Brennspiritus [dɐ ˈbʀɛnʃpiʀitʊs]
paper napkins/serviettes	die Papierservietten *f pl* [di paˈpiːɐzɛˌvjɛtn̩]
paraffin	das Petroleum [das peˈtʀoːleʊm]
plastic bag	der Plastikbeutel [dɐ ˈplastɪkbɔɪtl̩]
plastic cup/mug	der Plastikbecher [dɐ ˈplastɪkbɛçɐ]
plastic wrap	die Frischhaltefolie [di ˈfʀɪʃhaltəˌfoːljə]
pocket knife	das Taschenmesser [das ˈtaʃn̩mɛsɐ]
spoon	der Löffel [dɐ lœfl̩]
thermos (flask)	die Thermosflasche® [di ˈtɛɐmɔsflaʃə]
tin foil	die Alufolie [di ˈʔalufoːljə]
tin opener	der Dosenöffner [dɐ ˈdoːzn̩ʔœfnɐ]

Jewellery shop

bracelet	das Armband [das ˈʔaːmbant]
brooch	die Brosche [di ˈbʀɔʃə]
costume jewellery	der Modeschmuck [dɐ ˈmoːdəʃmʊk]
crystal	der Kristall [dɐ kʀɪsˈtal]
earrings	die Ohrringe *m pl* [di ˈʔoːʀɪŋə]
earstud	der Ohrstecker [dɐ ˈʔoɐʃtɛkɐ]
gold	das Gold [das ˈgɔlt]
jewellery	der Schmuck [dɐ ʃmʊk]
necklace	die Kette [di ˈkɛtə]
pearl	die Perle [di ˈpɛɐlə]
pendant	der Anhänger [dɐ ˈʔanhɛŋɐ]
platinum	das Platin [das ˈplaːtiːn]
ring	der Ring [dɐ ʀɪŋ]
silver	das Silber [das ˈzɪlbɐ]
stud earring	der Ohrstecker [dɐ ˈʔoɐʃtɛkɐ]
tiepin	die Krawattennadel [di kʀaˈvatnnaːdl̩]
travel alarm	der Reisewecker [dɐ ˈʀaɪəvɛkɐ]
waterproof watch	die wasserdichte Uhr [di ˈvasɐdɪçtə ˈʔuɐ]
wristwatch	die Armbanduhr [di ˈʔaːmbantˌʔuɐ]
ladies'	für Damen [fyɐ ˈdaːmən]
men's	für Herren [fyɐ ˈhɛʀən]

160

Optician

Could you repair these glasses for me, please.
Würden Sie mir bitte diese Brille reparieren?
['vvedn zi miɐ 'bɪtə 'diːzə 'bʀɪlə ʀɛpaˈʀiɐn]

I'm short-sighted/near-sighted.
Ich bin kurzsichtig. [ˀɪç bɪn 'kʊɐtsɪçtɪç]

I'm long-sighted/far-sighted.
Ich bin weitsichtig. [ˀɪç bɪn 'vaɪtsɪçtɪç]

What's your (visual) acuity?
Wie ist Ihre Sehstärke? ['vi ɪst iʀə 'zeːʃtɛɐkə]

... in the right eye, ... in the left eye.
rechts ..., links ... [ʀɛçts ... lɪŋks ...]

When can I pick up the glasses?
Wann kann ich die Brille abholen? [van kan ɪç di 'bʀɪlə ˀaphoːln]

I'd like ...
Ich hätte gern ... [ˀɪç 'hɛtə 'gɛɐn ...]

  some storage solution
  eine Aufbewahrungslösung [ˌˀaɪnə ˀaʊfbəvaːʀʊŋsˌløːzʊŋ]

  some cleansing solution
  eine Reinigungslösung [ˌˀaɪnə 'ʀaɪnɪgʊŋsˌløːzʊŋ]

  for hard/soft contact lenses.
  für harte/weiche Kontaktlinsen. [fyɐ 'haːtə/'vaɪçə kɔn'taktlɪnzn]

  some sunglasses.
  eine Sonnenbrille. [ˀaɪnə 'zɔnnbʀɪlə]

  some binoculars.
  ein Fernglas. [ˀaɪn 'fɛɐŋglaːs]

Photographic materials

> also Photos

I'd like ...
Ich hätte gern ... [ˀɪç 'hɛtə gɛɐn]

  a film for this camera.
  einen Film für diesen Fotoapparat.
  [ˀaɪnn 'fɪlm fyɐ 'diːzn 'foːtoˀapaˌʀaːt]

  a colour film (for slides).
  einen Farbfilm (für Dias). [ˀaɪnn 'faːpfɪlm (fyɐ 'diaːs)]

  a film with 36/24/12 exposures.
  einen Film mit sechsunddreißig/ vierundzwanzig/zwölf Auf-
  nahmen.
  [ˀaɪnn 'fɪlm mɪt 'zɛksʊnˌdʀasɪç/ 'fiɐʊnˌtsvantsɪç/tsvœlf ˀaʊfnaːmm]

... doesn't work/is broken.

... funktioniert nicht/ist kaputt. [fuŋktsjo'niet nɪçt/ɪst ka'put]

Can you repair/fix it?

Können Sie es reparieren? ['kœnn zi əs ʀɛpa'ʀien]

black-and-white film	der Schwarzweiß-Film [de ʃva:ts'vaɪsfɪlm]
camcorder	der Camcorder [de 'kamkhɔede]
digital camera	die Digitalkamera [di digi'ta:l̩,kaməʀa]
DVD	die DVD [di defaʊ'de:]
film speed	die Filmempfindlichkeit [di 'fɪlmɛmpfɪntlɪçkaɪt]
flash	das Blitzgerät [das 'blɪtsgəʀɛ:t]
lens	das Objektiv [das ʔɔbjɛk'ti:f]
light meter	der Belichtungsmesser [de bə'lɪçtʊŋs,mɛse]
Polaroid® camera	die Sofortbildkamera [di zo'fɔetbɪlt,kaməʀa]
self-timer	der Selbstauslöser [de 'zɛlpstaʊslø:ze]
shutter	der Auslöser [de 'ʔaʊslø:ze]
telephoto lens	das Teleobjektiv [das 'te:leʔɔbjɛk,ti:f]
tripod	das Stativ [das ʃta'ti:f]
video camera	die Videokamera [di 'vi:deo,kaməʀa]
video cassette	die Videokassette [di 'vi:deoka,sɛtə]
video film	der Videofilm [de 'vi:deofɪlm]
video recorder	der Videorekorder [de 'vi:deoʀe,kɔede]
viewfinder	der Sucher [de 'zu:xe]

Shoes and leather goods

I'd like a pair of shoes.

Ich hätte gern ein Paar Schuhe. [ʔɪç 'hɛtə gɛɛn ʔaɪn pa: 'ʃuə]

I take (shoe) size ...

Ich habe Schuhgröße ... [ʔɪç 'ha:bə 'ʃu:gʀø:sə]

They're too tight

Sie sind zu eng. [zi zɪnt tsʊ ʔɛŋ]

They're too big.

Sie sind zu groß. [zi zɪnt tsʊ gʀo:s]

backpack	der Rucksack [de 'ʀʊkzak]
bag	die Tasche [di 'taʃə]
bathing shoes	die Badeschuhe m pl [di 'ba:dəʃuə]
beach shoes	die Strandschuhe m pl [di 'ʃtʀantʃuə]
belt	der Gürtel [de gɣetl̩]
boots	die Stiefel m pl [di ʃti:fl̩]

bumbag/fanny pack ...... die Gürteltasche [di gʏɐtltaʃə]
gym shoes .... die Turnschuhe *m pl* [di 'tʊɐnʃuə]
handbag .... die Handtasche [di 'han(t)taʃə]
leather coat .... der Ledermantel [dɐ 'le:dɐmantl]
leather jacket .... die Lederjacke [di 'le:dɐjakə]
leather trousers .... die Lederhose [di 'le:dɐho:zə]
rubber boots .... die Gummistiefel *m pl* [di 'gʊmiʃti:fl]
rucksack .... der Rucksack [dɐ 'ʀʊkzak]
sandals .... die Sandalen *f pl* [di zan'da:ln]
shoe .... der Schuh [dɐ ʃu:]
shoe brush .... die Schuhbürste [di 'ʃu:bʏɐstə]
shoe cream .... die Schuhcreme [di 'ʃu:kʀɛ:m]
shoelaces .... die Schnürsenkel *m pl* [di 'ʃnyɐzɛŋkl]
shoulder bag .... die Umhängetasche [di 'ˀʊmhɛŋəˌtaʃə]
shoulder strap .... der Schulterriemen [də 'ʃʊltɐʀi:mm]
ski boots .... die Skistiefel *m pl* [di 'ʃi:ʃti:fl]
sneakers *(US)* .... die Turnschuhe *m pl* [di 'tʊɐnʃuə]
sole .... die Sohle [di 'zo:lə]
suitcase .... der Koffer [dɐ 'kɔfɐ]
travelling bag .... die Reisetasche [di 'ʀaɪzətaʃə]
trolley case .... der Trolleykoffer/die Trolleytasche [dɐ 'tʀɔlɪkɔfɐ/di 'tʀɔlɪtaʃə]
wellingtons .... die Gummistiefel *m pl* [di 'gʊmiʃti:fl]

Souvenirs

I'd like ...
Ich hätte gern ... [ˀɪç 'hɛtə gɛɐn]
a nice souvenir.
ein hübsches Andenken. [ˀaɪn 'hʏpʃəs 'ˀandɛŋkŋ]
something typical of this area.
etwas Typisches aus dieser Gegend.
[ˀɛtvas 'ty:pɪʃ ˀaʊs di:zɐ 'ge:gɛnt]

How much do you want to spend?
Wie viel wollen Sie ausgeben? ['vi:‿fi:l vɔln zi 'ˀaʊsge:bm]

I'd like something that's not too expensive.
Ich möchte etwas nicht zu Teures.
[ˀɪç 'mœçtə ˌˀɛtvas 'nɪç(t) tsʊ 'tɔɪrəs]

That's lovely.
Das ist aber hübsch. [das ɪst 'ˀabɐ hʏpʃ]

Thanks, but I didn't find anything (I liked).
Danke schön, ich habe nichts gefunden(, das mir gefällt).
['daŋkə ʃø:n ˀɪç 'ha:bə nɪçts gə'fʊndn (das miɐ gə'fɛlt)]

ceramics	die Keramik [di ke'ʀa:mɪk]
genuine	echt [ʔɛçt]
hand-made	handgemacht ['hantgəmaxt]
jewellery	der Schmuck [dɐ ʃmʊk]
local specialities	die regionalen Spezialitäten [di ʀegio'na:ln ʃpɛtsjali'tɛ:tn]
pottery	die Töpferwaren f pl [di 'tœpfɐva:ʀən]
souvenir	das Souvenir [das zʊvə'niɐ]
wood-carving	die Schnitzerei [di ʃnɪtsə'ʀaɪ]

Tobacco

A packet/pack of filter-tipped ..., please.
Eine Schachtel ... mit Filter, bitte! [ʔaɪnə ʃaxtl ... mɪt 'fɪltɐ 'bɪtə]

A carton of plain ..., please.
Eine Stange ... ohne Filter, bitte! [ʔaɪnə 'ʃtaŋə ...ʔo:nə 'fɪltɐ 'bɪtə]

Ten cigars/cigarillos, please.
Zehn Zigarren/Zigarillos, bitte. [tse:n tsɪ'gaʀən/tsɪga'ʀɪlo:s 'bɪtə]

A packet of cigarette tobacco, please.
Ein Päckchen Zigarettentabak, bitte.
[ʔaɪn pɛkçn 'tsɪgaʀɛtn̩tabak 'bɪtə]

A tin of pipe tobacco, please.
Eine Dose Pfeifentabak, bitte. [ʔaɪnə 'do:zə '(p)faɪfn̩tabak 'bɪtə]

ashtray	der Aschenbecher [dɐ ʔaʃnbɛçɐ]
cigar	die Zigarre [di tsɪ'gaʀə]
cigarette	die Zigarette [di tsɪga'ʀɛtə]
cigarillo	das Zigarillo [das tsɪga'ʀɪlo]
lighter	das Feuerzeug [das 'fɔɪɐtsɔɪk]
matches	die Streichhölzer n pl [di 'ʃtʀaɪçhœltsɐ]
pipe	die Pfeife [di 'pfaɪfə]

Toiletries

after-shave lotion	das Rasierwasser [das ʀa'ziɐvasɐ]
brush	die Bürste [di 'bʏɐstə]
comb	der Kamm [dɐ kam]
condom	das Kondom [kɔn'do:m]
cotton swabs	das Wattestäbchen [das 'vatəʃtɛ:pçn]
cotton wool	die Watte [di 'vatə]
cream	die Creme [di kʀɛ:m]
dental floss	die Zahnseide [di 'tsa:nzaɪdə]
deodorant	das Deo [das 'deo]
detergent (dishes)	das Spülmittel [das 'ʃpy:lmɪtl]
detergent (clothes)	das Waschmittel [das 'vaʃmɪtl]

165

dishcloth	das Spültuch [das ˈʃpyːltuːx]
flannel	der Waschlappen [dɐ ˈvaʃlapm̩]
hair gel	das Haargel [das ˈhaːɡeːl]
hairpins	die Haarklammern f pl [di ˈhaːklamɐn]
Kleenex®	das Tempo(taschentuch)® [das ˈtɛmpoˌtaʃntuːx]
lip balm	die Lippenpomade [di ˈlɪpmpomaːdə]
lipstick	der Lippenstift [dɐ ˈlɪpmʃtɪft]
mascara	die Wimperntusche [di ˈvɪmpɐntʊʃə]
mirror	der Spiegel [dɐ ˈʃpiːɡl̩]
moisturizing cream	die Feuchtigkeitscreme [di ˈfɔɪçtɪçkaɪtsˌkʀɛːm]
nail scissors	die Nagelschere [di ˈnaːɡlʃeːʀə]
nail varnish/polish	der Nagellack [dɐ ˈnaːɡllak]
nail varnish/polish remover	der Nagellackentferner [dɐ ˈnaːɡllakɛntˌfɛɐnɐ]
night cream	die Nachtcreme [di ˈnaxtkʀɛːm]
panty liners	die Slipeinlagen f pl [di ˈslɪpaɪnlaːɡn̩]
paper handkerchiefs	die Papiertaschentücher n pl [di paˈpiːɐˌtaʃnˈtyːçɐ]
perfume	das Parfüm [das paˈfyːm]
plaster	das Pflaster [das ˈpflastɐ]
powder	der Puder [dɐ ˈpuːdɐ]
protection factor	der Lichtschutzfaktor [dɐ ˈlɪçtʃʊtsˌfaktoɐ]
razor blade	die Rasierklinge [di ʀaˈziːɐklɪŋə]
sanitary towels/napkins	die Damenbinden f pl [di ˈdaːmmbɪndn̩]
scent	das Parfüm [das paˈfyːm]
shampoo	das Schampoo [das ˈʃampo/ˈʃampu]
shaver	der Rasierapparat [dɐ ʀaˈziːɐʔapaˌʀaːt]
shaving brush	der Rasierpinsel [dɐ ʀaˈziːɐpɪnzl̩]
shaving foam	der Rasierschaum [dɐ ʀaˈziːɐʃaʊm]
shower gel	das Duschgel [das ˈduːʃɡeːl]
soap	die Seife [di ˈzaɪfə]
sun cream	die Sonnencreme [di ˈzɔnnkʀɛːm]
suntan lotion	die Sonnenmilch [di ˈzɔnnmɪlç]
suntan oil	das Sonnenöl [das ˈzɔnnʔøːl]
tampons	die Tampons m pl [di ˈtampɔŋs]
mini/regular/super/super plus	mini/normal/super/super plus [ˈmiːni/nɔɐˈmaːl/ˈzuːpɐ/ˌzuːpɐ ˈplʊs]
tea-tree oil	das Teebaumöl [das ˈteːbaʊmʔøːl]
toilet paper	das Toilettenpapier [das toˈlɛtnpaˌpiːɐ]
toothbrush	die Zahnbürste [di ˈtsaːnbʏɐstə]
toothpaste	die Zahnpasta [di ˈtsaːnpasta]
toothpick	das Zahnstocher [dɐ ˈtsaːnʃtɔxɐ]
washcloth (US)	der Waschlappen [dɐ ˈvaʃlapm]
washing-up brush	die Spülbürste [di ˈʃpyːlbʏɐstə]

Health

In an emergency

If you have any need of medical assistance, you will find first-rate facilities and medical personnel in all the German-speaking countries. As anywhere else, expect standards in large cities to be higher than those in small towns. Particularly noteworthy are the university clinics in most cities. Here you will find highly-motivated doctors and assistants who almost always speak good English, should you be worried that your German won't be sufficient.

At the chemist's/pharmacy

Can you tell me where the nearest chemist's (with all-night service) is, please?
Können Sie mir sagen, wo die nächste Apotheke (mit Nachtdienst) ist?
[kœnn zi miɐ zaːgŋ voː di 'nɛːçstə ʔapo'teːkə (mɪt 'naxtdiːnst) ʔɪst]

Could you give me something for ..., please?
Könnten Sie mir bitte etwas gegen ... geben
[kœntn zi miɐ 'bɪtə ʔɛtvas geːgŋ ... geːbm]

You need a prescription for this.
Für dieses Mittel brauchen Sie ein Rezept.
[fyɐ 'diːzəs 'mɪtl bʁaʊxn zi ʔaɪn ʁe'tsɛpt]

➤also At the doctor's

aftersun lotion	die Sonnenbrandlotion [di 'zɔnnbʁantˌloʊʃən]
aspirin	das Aspirin [das ʔaspi'ʁiːn]
burns ointment	die Brandsalbe [di bʁantzalbə]
cardiac stimulant	das Kreislaufmittel [das 'kʁaɪslaʊfˌmɪtl]
condom	das Kondom [das kɔn'doːm]
cotton-wool/cotton	die Watte [di 'vatə]
cough mixture/syrup	der Hustensaft [de 'huːstnzaft]
disinfectant	das Desinfektionsmittel [das dezɪnfɛk'tsjoːnsmɪtl]
drops	die Tropfen *m pl* [di 'tʁɔpfn]
ear-drops	die Ohrentropfen *m pl* [di 'oːʁəntʁɔpfn]
elastic bandage	die Elastikbinde [di ʔe'lastɪkbɪndə]
eye-drops	die Augentropfen *m pl* [di 'ʔaʊgŋtʁɔpfn]
gauze bandage	die Mullbinde [di 'mʊlbɪndə]

168

glucose	der Traubenzucker [dɐ ˈtʀaʊbmtsʊkɐ]
headache tablets	die Kopfschmerztabletten f pl [di ˈkɔpfʃmɛɐtstaˌblɛtn]
insect repellent	das Mittel gegen Insektenstiche [das ˈmɪtl geːgn ˀɪnˈzɛktnʃtɪçə]
insulin	das Insulin [das ˀɪnzʊˈliːn]
laxative	das Abführmittel [das ˀˈapfyɐˌmɪtl]
medicine	das Medikament [das medɪkaˈmɛnt]
ointment	die Salbe [di ˈzalbə]
pain-killing tablets	die Schmerztabletten f pl [di ˈʃmɛɐtstaˌblɛtn]
pill	die Tablette [di taˈblɛtə]
plaster	das Pflaster [das ˈpflastɐ]
powder	der Puder [dɐ ˈpuːdɐ]
prescription	das Rezept [das ʀeˈtsɛpt]
remedy	das Mittel [das ˈmɪtl]
sedative	das Beruhigungsmittel [das bəˈʀʊɪgʊŋsmɪtl]
sleeping pills	die Schlaftabletten f pl [di ˈʃlaːftaˌblɛtn]
sunburn lotion	die Sonnenbrandlotion [di ˈzɔnnbʀantˌloʊʃən]
suppository	das Zäpfchen [das ˈtsɛpfçn]
tablet	die Tablette [di taˈblɛtə]
thermometer	das Fieberthermometer [das ˈfiːbɐɛmoˌmeːtɐ]
throat lozenges	die Halstabletten f pl [di ˈhalstaˌblɛtn]
tincture of iodine	die Jodtinktur [di ˈjoːtɪŋktuɐ]
tranquilliser	das Beruhigungsmittel [das bəˈʀʊɪgʊŋsmɪtl]
vitamin pills	die Vitamintabletten f pl [di vɪtaˈmiːntaˌblɛtn]

At the doctor's

> also Travelling with children

Could you recommend a/an ...?
Könnten Sie mir einen ... empfehlen?
[ˈkœntn zi miɐ ˀaɪnn ... ˀɛmpˈfeːln]

dentist
Zahnarzt [ˈtsaːnˀaːtst]

dermatologist
Hautarzt [ˈhaʊtˀaːtst]

doctor
Arzt/eine Ärztin [ˀaːtst/ˀaɪnə ˀˈɛɐtstɪn]

169

ear, nose and throat specialist
Hals-Nasen-Ohren-Arzt [hals‿na:zn↓ʔo:rən↓ʔa:tst]

eye specialist
Augenarzt [ʔaʊgn̩ʔa:tst]

general practitioner
praktischen Arzt ['pʀaktɪʃn ʔa:tst]

gynaecologist
Frauenarzt ['fʀaʊən̩ʔa:tst]

pediatrician
Kinderarzt ['kɪndɐʔa:tst]

urologist
Urologen [ʔuʀoˈlo:gn̩]

Beipackzettel	Medicine information / application leaflet
Zusammensetzung	Ingredients
Anwendungsgebiete	Areas of application
Gegenanzeigen	Contraindications
Wechselwirkungen	Interactions
Nebenwirkungen	Side-effects
Dosierungsanleitung:	Dosage:
1 x / mehrmals täglich einnehmen	Take once / several times per day
1 Tablette	1 tablet
20 Tropfen	20 drops
1 Messbecher	1 measuring cup
vor dem Essen	before meals
nach dem Essen	after meals
auf nüchternen Magen	on an empty stomach
unzerkaut mit etwas Flüssigkeit einnehmen	Swallow whole with water
in etwas Wasser auflösen	Dissolve in a small amount of water
im Mund zergehen lassen	Dissolve in your mouth
dünn auf die Haut auftragen und einreiben	Apply thin layer to skin and rub in
Erwachsene	adults
Säuglinge	infants
Schulkinder	schoolchildren
Kleinkinder	toddlers
Jugendliche	young adults
Für Kinder unzugänglich aufbewahren!	Keep away from children!

Where's his/her surgery/the doctor's office?
Wo ist seine/ihre Praxis? [voː ʔɪst ˌzaɪnə/ˌʔiːʀə ˈpʀaksɪs]

I'd like to make an appointment.
Ich möchte einen Termin ausmachen.
[ʔɪç ˈmœçtə ˀaɪnn tɛɐ̯ˈmiːn ˈausmaxn]

Medical complaints

What's the trouble?
Was für Beschwerden haben Sie? [ˈvas_fyɐ bəˈʃveɐdn ˈhaːbm ziː]

I've got a temperature.
Ich habe Fieber. [ʔɪç ˈhaːbə ˈfiːbɐ]

I often feel sick.
Mir ist oft schlecht. [miɐ̯ ʔɪst ˀɔft ˈʃlɛçt]

Sometimes I feel dizzy.
Mir ist manchmal schwindlig. [miɐ̯ ʔɪst ˈmançmaːl ˈʃvɪndlɪç]

I fainted.
Ich bin ohnmächtig geworden. [ʔɪç bɪn ˀˈoːnmɛçtɪç gəˈvɔɐdn]

I've got a bad cold.
Ich bin stark erkältet. [ˀʔɪç bɪn ʃtaːk ˀeˈkɛltət]

I've got ...
Ich habe ... [ʔɪç ˈhaːbə]
  a headache.
  Kopfschmerzen. [ˈkɔpfʃmɛɐtsn]
  a sore throat.
  Halsschmerzen. [ˈhalsʃmɛɐtsn]
  a cough.
  Husten. [huːstn]

I've been stung.
Ich bin gestochen worden. [ʔɪç bɪn gəˈʃtɔxn ˈvɔɐdn]

I've been bitten.
Ich bin gebissen worden. [ʔɪç bɪn gəˈbɪsn ˈvɔɐdn]

I've got an upset stomach.
Ich habe mir den Magen verdorben.
[ʔɪç ˌhaːbə miɐ̯ den ˈmaːgŋ veˈdɔɐbm]

I've got diarrhoea.
Ich habe Durchfall. [ʔɪç ˈhaːbə ˈdʊɐçfal]

I'm constipated.
Ich habe Verstopfung. [ʔɪç ˈhaːbə feˈʃtɔpfʊŋ]

The food doesn't agree with me.
Ich vertrage das Essen nicht. [ʔɪç feˈtʀaːgə das ˀˈɛsn nɪçt]

I can't stand the heat.
Ich vertrage die Hitze nicht. [ˀɪç fɛˈtʀaːgə di ˈhɪtsə nɪçt]

I've hurt myself.
Ich habe mich verletzt. [ˀɪç ˈhaːbə mɪç fɛˈlɛtst]

I fell down.
Ich bin gestürzt. [ˀɪç bɪn gəˈʃtʏɛtst]

Can you prescribe something for ...?
Können Sie mir bitte etwas gegen ... verschreiben?
[ˈkœnn zi miɐ ˈbɪtə ˀɛtvas ˈgeːgn̩ ... fɛˈʃʀaɪbm̩]

I usually take ...
Normalerweise nehme ich ... [nɔˈmaːlɐvaɪzə ˈneːm ɪç]

I've got high/low blood pressure.
Ich habe einen hohen/niedrigen Blutdruck.
[ˀɪç ˌhaːbə ˀaɪnn ˈhoːn/ˈniːdʀɪgn̩ ˈbluːtdʀʊk]

I'm a diabetic.
Ich bin Diabetiker/Diabetikerin. [ˀɪç bɪn diaˈbeːtɪkɐ/diaˈbeːtɪkəʀɪn]

I'm pregnant.
Ich bin schwanger. [ˀɪç bɪn ˈʃvaŋɐ]

I had ... recently
Ich hatte vor kurzem ... [ˀɪç ˌhatə foɐ ˈkʊɐtsm̩]

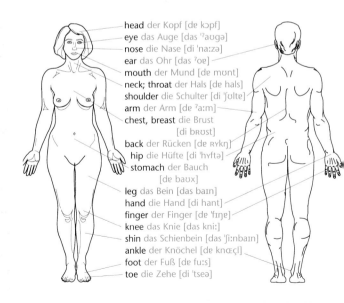

head der Kopf [dɐ kɔpf]
eye das Auge [das ˀaʊgə]
nose die Nase [di ˈnaːzə]
ear das Ohr [das ˀoɐ]
mouth der Mund [dɐ mʊnt]
neck; throat der Hals [dɐ hals]
shoulder die Schulter [di ˈʃʊltɐ]
arm der Arm [dɐ ˀaːm]
chest, breast die Brust [di bʀʊst]
back der Rücken [dɐ ʀʏkŋ]
hip die Hüfte [di ˈhʏftə]
stomach der Bauch [dɐ baʊx]
leg das Bein [das baɪn]
hand die Hand [di hant]
finger der Finger [dɐ ˈfɪŋɐ]
knee das Knie [das kniː]
shin das Schienbein [das ˈʃiːnbaɪn]
ankle der Knöchel [dɐ knœçl̩]
foot der Fuß [dɐ fuːs]
toe die Zehe [di ˈtseə]

What can I do for you?

Was kann ich für Sie tun? [vas kan ıç fye zi 'tu:n]

Where does it hurt?

Wo tut es weh? [vo: 'tu:t əs 've:]

I've got a pain here.

Ich habe hier Schmerzen. [ʔɪç 'ha:bə 'hiɐ 'ʃmɛɐtsn]

Uncover your arm, please.

Bitte, machen Sie Ihren Arm frei. ['bɪtə maxn zi ʔiɐn ʔa:m fʀaɪ]

Take off your clothes, please.

Bitte, machen Sie sich frei. ['bɪtə maxn zi zɪç 'fʀaɪ]

Take a deep breath.

Tief einatmen. [ti:f ʔaɪna:tmən]

Hold your breath.

Atem anhalten. [ʔa:təm ʔanhaltn]

I need to do a blood/urine test.

Ich brauche eine Blutprobe/ Urinprobe.

[ʔɪç ˌbʀaʊxə ˌʔaɪnə 'blu:tpʀo:bə/ʔu'ʀi:npʀo:bə]

You need a few days in bed.

Sie brauchen ein paar Tage Bettruhe.

[zi bʀaʊxn aɪn pa: 'ta:gə 'bɛtʀuə]

It's nothing serious.

Es ist nichts Ernstes. [ʔəs ɪst nɪçts (nɪks) ʔɛɐnstəs]

Have you got a vaccination card?

Haben Sie einen Impfpass? [ha(:b)m zi ʔaɪnn ʔɪmpfpas]

I've been vaccinated against ...

Ich bin gegen ... geimpft. [ʔɪç bɪn ge:gŋ ... gəʔɪmpft]

EU nationals are covered free of charge for medical and dental treatment in Germany and Austria on production of an E111 form. Visitors from non-EU countries should take out medical insurance before travelling.

In hospital

How long will I have to stay here?
Wie lange muss ich hier bleiben? [vi_'laŋə mʊs ɪç 'hiɐ blaɪbm]

I can't sleep.
Ich kann nicht einschlafen. [ˈʔɪç kan nɪçt ˈʔaɪnʃlaːfn]

Could you give me ..., please.
Geben Sie mir bitte ... [ˈgeːbm zi miɐ ˌbɪtə]
  a glass of water
  ein Glas Wasser [ˈʔaɪn glaːs ˈvasɐ]
  a pain–killing tablet
  eine Schmerztablette [ˌʔaɪnə ˈʃmɛɐtstaˌblɛtə]
  a sleeping-pill
  eine Schlaftablette [ˌʔaɪnə ˈʃlaːftaˌblɛtə]
  a hot-water bottle
  eine Wärmflasche [ˈʔaɪnə ˈvɛɐmflaʃə]

When can I get up?
Wann darf ich aufstehen? [van daːf ɪç ˈʔaʊfʃteːn]

Illnesses and afflictions

abscess	der Abszess [dɐ ʔapsˈɛs]
AIDS	das Aids [das ˈʔɛɪts]
be allergic to	allergisch sein gegen ... [ʔalɛˈgɪʃ zaɪn ˈgeːgn]
allergy	die Allergie [di ʔal(ɛ)ɐˈgiː]
angina	die Angina [di ʔaŋˈgiːna]
appendicitis	die Blinddarmentzündung [di ˈblɪntdaːmɛnˌtsʏndʊŋ]
asthma	das Asthma [das ˈʔastma]
attack	der Anfall [dɐ ˈʔanfal]
backache	die Rückenschmerzen m pl [di ˈʀʏknʃmɛɐtsn]
bleeding	die Blutung [di ˈbluːtʊŋ]
blood-poisoning	die Blutvergiftung [di ˈbluːtfɐgɪftʊŋ]
broken	gebrochen [gəˈbʀɔxn]
bronchitis	die Bronchitis [di bʀɔnˈçiːtɪs]
bruise (*caused by hitting*)	die Prellung [di ˈpʀɛlʊŋ]
bruise (*caused by pinching*)	die Quetschung [di ˈkvɛtʃʊŋ]
burn	die Verbrennung [di fɐˈbʀɛnʊŋ]
cancer	der Krebs [dɐ kʀeːps]
cardiac infarction	der Herzinfarkt [dɐ ˈhɛɐtsɪnfaːkt]
circulatory disorder	die Kreislaufstörung [di ˈkʀaɪslaʊfˌʃtøːʀʊŋ]
cold	die Erkältung [di ʔɛˈkɛltʊŋ]
colic	die Kolik [di ˈkoːlɪk]

174

concussion	die Gehirnerschütterung [di gə'hɪɐneˌʃytəʀʊŋ]
constipation	die Verstopfung [di feˈʃtɔpfʊŋ]
contagious	ansteckend [ˈʔanʃtɛkŋt]
cramp	der Krampf [dɐ kʀampf]
cut	die Schnittwunde [di ˈʃnɪtvʊndə]
diabetes	der Diabetes [dɐ diaˈbeːtəs]
diarrhoea	der Durchfall [dɐ ˈdʊɐçfal]
difficulty in breathing	die Atembeschwerden f pl [di ˈʔaːtmbəʃveːedn]
diphtheria	die Diphtherie [di dɪftəˈʀiː]
dizziness	das Schwindelgefühl [das ˈʃvɪndlgəfyːl]
to faint	in Ohnmacht fallen [ˈʔɪn ˈʔoːnmaxt faln]
fever	das Fieber [das ˈfiːbɐ]
fit	der Anfall [dɐ ˈʔanfal]
flu	die Grippe [di ˈgʀɪpə]
food poisoning	die Lebensmittelvergiftung [di ˈleːbmsmɪtlfɐˌgɪftʊŋ]
fracture	der Knochenbruch [dɐ ˈknɔxnbʀʊx]
growth	die Geschwulst [di gəˈʃvʊlst]
haemorrhoids	die Hämorriden f pl [di hɛmoˈʀiːdn]
hay fever	der Heuschnupfen [dɐ ˈhɔɪʃnʊpfn]
headache	die Kopfschmerzen m pl [di ˈkɔpfʃmɛɐtsn]
heart attack	der Herzinfarkt [dɐ ˈhɛɐtsɪnfaːkt]
heart defect	der Herzfehler [dɐ ˈhɛɐtsfeːlɐ]
heart trouble	die Herzbeschwerden f pl [ˈhɛɐtsbəʃveːedn]
heartburn	das Sodbrennen [das ˈzoːtbʀɛnn]
hernia	der Leistenbruch [dɐ ˈlaɪstnbʀʊx]
high blood pressure	der Bluthochdruck [dɐ ˈbluːthoːxdʀʊk]
hoarse	heiser [ˈhaɪzɐ]
to hurt	wehtun [ˈveːtuːn]
to hurt oneself	sich verletzen [zɪç fɐˈlɛtsn]
ill	krank [kʀaŋk]
illness	die Krankheit [di ˈkʀaŋkhaɪt]
impaired balance	die Gleichgewichtsstörungen f pl [di ˈglaɪçgəvɪçtsʃtøːʀʊŋŋ]
impaired vision	die Sehstörungen f pl [di ˈzeːʃtøːʀʊŋŋ]
indigestion	die Verdauungsstörung [di fɐˈdaʊʊŋʃtøːʀʊŋ]
infection	die Infektion [di ʔɪnfɛkˈtsjoːn]
inflammation	die Entzündung [di ʔɛnˈtsʏndʊŋ]
inflammation of the	die Mittelohrentzündung
middle ear	[di ˈmɪtlʔoɐɛnˌtsʏndʊŋ]
influenza	die Grippe [di ˈgʀɪpə]
to injure	verletzen [fɐˈlɛtsn]

injury	die Verletzung [di fɛ'lɛtsʊŋ]
insect bite	der Insektenstich [dɐ ʔɪn'zɛktnʃtɪç]
insomnia	die Schlaflosigkeit [di 'ʃla:flozɪçkaɪt]
jaundice	die Gelbsucht [di 'gɛlpzʊxt]
kidney stone	der Nierenstein [dɐ 'ni:ɐnʃtaɪn]
lumbago	der Hexenschuss [dɐ 'hɛksnʃʊs]
migraine	die Migräne [di mi'gʀɛ:nə]
miscarriage	die Fehlgeburt [di 'fe:lgəbʊɐt]
nausea	der Brechreiz [dɐ 'bʀɛçʀaɪts]
nephritis	die Nierenentzündung [di 'ni:ɐn'ʔɛnˌtsʏndʊŋ]
nose bleed	das Nasenbluten [das 'na:znblu:tn]
pain	die Schmerzen m pl [di 'ʃmɛɐtsn]
painful	schmerzhaft ['ʃmɛɐtshaft]
paralysis	die Lähmung [di 'lɛ:mʊŋ]
piles	die Hämorriden f pl [di hɛmoʀi:dn]
pneumonia	die Lungenentzündung [di 'lʊŋən'ʔɛnˌtsʏndʊŋ]
poisoning	die Vergiftung [di vɐ'gɪftʊŋ]
polio	die Kinderlähmung [di 'kɪndɐlɛ:mʊŋ]
pulled muscle	die Zerrung [di 'tsɛʀʊŋ]
rash	der Ausschlag [dɐ 'ʔaʊʃla:k]
rheumatism	das Rheuma [das 'ʀɔɪma]
rupture	der Leistenbruch [dɐ 'laɪstnbʀʊx]
sciatica	der Ischias [dɐ 'ʔɪʃias]
shivering fit	der Schüttelfrost [dɐ 'ʃʏtlfʀɔst]
sick	krank [kʀaŋk]
sinusitis	die Stirnhöhlenentzündung [di 'ʃtɪʀnhø:ln'ʔɛnˌtsʏndʊŋ]
sleeplessness	die Schlaflosigkeit [di 'ʃla:flozɪçkaɪt]
smallpox	die Pocken f pl [di pɔkŋ]
sore throat	die Halsschmerzen m pl [di 'halʃmɛɐtsn]
sprained	verstaucht [fɐ'ʃtaʊxt]
stitch	das Seitenstechen [das 'zaɪtnʃtɛçn]
stomach-ache	die Magenschmerzen m pl [di 'ma:gnʃmɛɐtsn]
stroke	der Schlaganfall [dɐ 'ʃla:kanfal]
sunburn	der Sonnenbrand [dɐ 'zɔnnbʀant]
sunstroke	der Sonnenstich [dɐ 'zɔnnʃtɪç]
swelling	die Schwellung [di 'ʃvɛlʊŋ]
swollen	geschwollen [gə'ʃvɔln]
tachycardia	das Herzrasen [das 'hɛɐtsʀa:zn]
temperature (fever)	das Fieber [das 'fi:bɐ]
tetanus	der Tetanus [dɐ 'tɛtanʊs]
tonsilitis	die Mandelentzündung [di 'mandl'ʔɛnˌtsʏndʊŋ]

torn ligament	der Bänderriss [dɐ ˈbɛndɐʀɪs]
tumour	die Geschwulst [di gəˈʃvʊlst]
typhoid	der Typhus [dɐ ˈtyːfʊs]
ulcer	das Geschwür [das gəˈʃvyɐ]
venereal disease	die Geschlechtskrankheit [di geˈʃlɛçtsˌkʀaŋkhaɪt]
whooping-cough	der Keuchhusten [dɐ ˈkɔɪçhuːstn]
wind	die Blähungen f pl [di ˈblɛːʊŋŋ]
wound	die Wunde [di ˈvʊndə]

Body – Doctor – Hospital

abdomen	der Unterleib [dɐ ˈʔʊntɐlaɪp]
anaesthetic	die Narkose [di naˈkoːzə]
appendix	der Blinddarm [dɐ ˈblɪntdaːm]
artificial limb	die Prothese [di pʀoˈteːzə]
bandage	der Verband [dɐ fɐˈbant]
bladder	die Blase [di ˈblaːzə]
to bleed	bluten [bluːtn]
blood	das Blut [das bluːt]
blood group	die Blutgruppe [di ˈbluːtgʀʊpə]
blood pressure (high/low) . .	der Blutdruck (hoher/niedriger) [dɐ ˈblutdʀʊk (ˈhoɐ/ˈniːdʀɪgɐ)]
bone	der Knochen [dɐ knɔxn]
bowel movement	der Stuhlgang [dɐ ˈʃtuːlgaŋ]
brain	das Gehirn [das gəˈhɪɐn]
to breathe	atmen [ˈʔaːtmən]
bronchial tubes	die Bronchien f pl [di ˈbʀɔnçɪən]
bypass	der Bypass [dɐ ˈbaɪpaːs]
certificate	das Attest [das ʔaˈtɛst]
chest	die Brust [di bʀʊst]
collarbone	das Schlüsselbein [das ˈʃlʏslbaɪn]
cough	der Husten [dɐ huːstn]
diagnosis	die Diagnose [di diaˈgnoːzə]
diet	die Diät [di diˈɛːt]
digestion	die Verdauung [di fɐˈdaʊʊŋ]
to disinfect	desinfizieren [dɛzɪnfɪˈtsiːʀən]
to dress (a wound)	verbinden [fɐˈbɪndn]
dressing	der Verband [dɐ fɐˈbant]
eardrum	das Trommelfell [das ˈtʀɔmlfɛl]
examination	die Untersuchung [di ʔʊntɐˈzuːxʊŋ]
face	das Gesicht [das gəˈzɪçt]
gall-bladder	die Gallenblase [di ˈgalnblaːzə]
gullet	die Speiseröhre [di ˈʃpaɪzəʀøːʀə]
health	die Gesundheit [di gəˈzʊnthaɪt]
health resort	der Kurort [dɐ ˈkuɐˌʔɔɐt]
hearing	das Gehör [das gəˈhøɐ]
heart	das Herz [das hɛɐts]

heart specialist	der Herzspezialist [dɐ ˈhɛɐtʃpɛtsjaˌlɪst]
hospital	das Krankenhaus [das ˈkʁaŋkn̩haʊs]
ill	krank [kʁaŋk]
infusion	die Infusion [di ʔɪnfʊˈzjoːn]
injection	die Spritze [di ˈʃpʁɪtsə]
intestines	der Darm [dɐ daːm]
joint	das Gelenk [das ɡəˈlɛŋk]
kidney	die Niere [di ˈniːʁə]
lip	die Lippe [di ˈlɪpə]
liver	die Leber [di ˈleːbɐ]
lungs	die Lunge [di ˈlʊŋə]
medical insurance card	die Verischertenkarte [dɪ fəˈzɪxɐtənkaːtə]
menstruation	die Menstruation [di mɛnstʁuaˈtsjon]
muscle	der Muskel [dɐ ˈmʊskl̩]
nerve	der Nerv [dɐ nɛɐf]
nervous	nervös [nɐˈvøːs]
nurse	die Krankenschwester [di ˈkʁaŋkn̩ʃvɛstɐ]
oesophagus	die Speiseröhre [di ˈʃpaɪzəʁøːʁə]
operation	die Operation [di ʔɔpəʁaˈtsjoːn]
pacemaker	der Herzschrittmacher [dɐ ˈhɛɐt(s)ʃʁɪtmaxɐ]
to perspire	schwitzen [ˈʃvɪtsn̩]
pregnancy	die Schwangerschaft [di ˈʃvaŋɐʃaft]
to prescribe	verschreiben [fɐˈʃʁaɪbm̩]
pulse	der Puls [dɐ pʊls]
pus	der Eiter [dɐ ʔaɪtɐ]
rib	die Rippe [di ˈʁɪpə]
scar	die Narbe [di ˈnaːbə]
sexual organs	die Geschlechtsorgane n pl [di ɡəˈʃlɛçtsʔɔˌɡaːnə]
sick	krank [kʁaŋk]
skin	die Haut [di haʊt]
sonogram	die Ultraschalluntersuchung [di ʔʊltʁaʃalʔʊnteˌzuːxʊŋ]
specialist	der Facharzt [dɐ ˈfaxaːtst]
spine	die Wirbelsäule [di ˈvɪʁblzɔɪlə]
splint	die Schiene [di ˈʃiːnə]
sting	der Stich [dɐ ʃtɪç]
stitch (stitches)	die Naht [naːt]
to stitch (up)	nähen [nɛːn]
stomach	der Magen [dɐ maːgn̩]
surgeon	der Chirurg/die Chirurgin [dɐ çɪˈʁʊɐk/di çɪˈʁʊɐɡɪn]
surgery *(hours)*	die Sprechstunde [di ˈʃpʁɛçʃtʊndə]
(operation)	die Operation [di ʔɔpəʁaˈtsjoːn]
to sweat	schwitzen [ˈʃvɪtsn̩]

throat	die Kehle [di keːlə]
tongue	die Zunge [ˈtsʊŋə]
tonsils	die Mandeln f pl [di ˈmandln]
ultrasound scan	die Ultraschalluntersuchung [di ˈʔʊltʀaʃalˈʔʊntɐˌzuːxʊŋ]
unconscious	bewusstlos [bəˈvʊstloːs]
urine	der Urin [dɐ ʔuˈʀiːn]
vaccination	die Impfung [di ˈʔɪmpfʊŋ]
vaccination card	der Impfpass [dɐ ˈʔɪmpfpas]
virus	das Virus [das ˈviːʀʊs]
visiting hours	die Besuchszeit [di bəˈzuːxstsaɪt]
to vomit	sich erbrechen [zɪç ʔeˈbʀɛçn]
waiting room	das Wartezimmer [das ˈvaːtətsɪmɐ]
ward	die Station [di ʃtaˈtsjoːn]
windpipe	die Kehle [di keːlə]
X-ray	die Röntgenaufnahme [di ˈʀœnçnʔaʊfnaːmə]
to X-ray	röntgen [ˈʀœnçn]

At the dentist's

I've got (terrible) toothache.
Ich habe (starke) Zahnschmerzen. [ʔɪç ˈhaːbə (ˈʃtaːkə) ˈtsaːnʃmɛɐtsn]

This upper/bottom tooth hurts.
Dieser Zahn oben/unten tut weh. [ˈdiːzɐ tsaːn ˈʔoːbm/ˈʔʊntn tuːt ˈveː]

This front/back tooth hurts.
Dieser Zahn vorn/hinten tut weh. [ˈdiːzɐ tsaːn foɐn/ˈhɪntn tuːt ˈveː]

I've lost a filling.
Ich habe eine Füllung verloren. [ʔɪç ˈhaːbə ˈʔaɪnə ˈfʏlʊŋ fɛˈloɐn]

I've broken a tooth.
Mir ist ein Zahn abgebrochen. [miɐ ʔɪst ʔaɪn tsaːn ˈʔapgəbʀɔxn]

I'll only do a temporary job.
Ich behandle ihn nur provisorisch. [ʔɪç bəˈhandlə ʔin nuɐ pʀoviˈzoːʀɪʃ]

I'd like an injection, please.
Geben Sie mir bitte eine Spritze. [ˈgeːbm zi miɐ ˈbɪtə ˌʔaɪnə ˈʃpʀɪtsə]

I don't want an injection.
Geben Sie mir keine Spritze. [ˈgeːbm zi miɐ ˈkaɪnə ˈʃpʀɪtsə]

brace	die Zahnspange [di ˈtsaːnʃpaŋə]
bridge	die Brücke [di ˈbʀʏkə]
cavity	das Loch [das lɔx]
crown	die Krone [di ˈkʀoːnə]

dentures	die Zahnprothese [di ˈtsaːnpʀoˌteːzə]
to extract	ziehen [tsiːn]
filling	die Füllung [di ˈfʏlʊŋ],
	die Plombe [di ˈplɔmbə]
gums	das Zahnfleisch [das ˈtsaːnflaɪʃ]
incisor	der Schneidezahn [dɐ ˈʃnaɪdətsaːn]
jaw	der Kiefer [dɐ ˈkiːfɐ]
molar	der Backenzahn [dɐ ˈbakn̩tsaːn]
tartar	der Zahnstein [dɐ ˈtsaːnʃtaɪn]
tooth	der Zahn [dɐ tsaːn]
tooth decay	die Karies [di ˈkaːʀiɛs]
toothache	die Zahnschmerzen *m pl*
	[di ˈtsaːnʃmɛɛtsn̩]
wisdom tooth	der Weisheitszahn [dɐ ˈvaɪshaɪtsaːn]

Essentials A to Z

Twenty-four hour language lab
Below you will find more practical phrases for situations "on the street". Keep in mind that a city's streets and walkways represent the world's greatest language lab. Get out there and try out your German. People are impressed if they see you're trying and will prove very helpful. *Viel Erfolg!* (Good luck!, literally, "much success")

Bank

Can you tell me where the nearest bank is, please?
Können Sie mir bitte sagen, wo hier eine Bank ist?
[kɛnn zi miɐ 'bɪtə zaːgn voː hiɐ ʔaɪnə 'baŋk ʔɪst]

I'd like to change £100 into euros.
Ich möchte einhundert Pfund in Euro wechseln.
[ʔɪç mœçtə ʔaɪnhʊndɛt pfʊnt ʔɪn ʔʔɔɪʁo 'vɛksln]

I'd like to change $150 into Swiss francs.
Ich möchte einhundertfünfzig Dollar in Schweizer Franken wechseln.
[ʔɪç mœçtə ʔaɪnhʊndɛtˌfʏnftsɪç 'dɔlaː ʔɪn 'ʃvaɪtsɐ fʁaŋkn vɛksln]

Can you tell me what the exchange rate is today, please?
Können Sie mir bitte sagen, wie heute der Wechselkurs ist?
[kɛnn zi miɐ 'bɪtə zaːgn viː hɔɪtə dɐ 'vɛkslkʊɐs ʔɪst]

I'd like to cash this traveller's-cheque.
Ich möchte diesen Reisescheck einlösen.
[ʔɪç 'mœçtə diːzn 'ʁaɪzəʃɛk ʔaɪnløːzn]

What's the maximum I can cash on one cheque?
Auf welchen Betrag kann ich ihn maximal ausstellen?
[ʔaʊf 'vɛlçn bəˈtʁaːk kan ɪç ʔiːn maksiˈmaːl ʔaʊʃtɛln]

Can I see your cheque card, please?
Ihre Scheckkarte, bitte. [ʔiːʁə 'ʃɛkaːtə 'bɪtə]

May I see ..., please?
Darf ich bitte ... sehen? [daːf ɪç 'bɪtə ... zeːn]
  your identity card
  Ihren Ausweis [ʔiːʁən ʔaʊsvaɪs]
  your passport
  Ihren Pass [ʔiːʁən 'pas]

Sign here, please.
Unterschreiben Sie bitte hier. [ʔʊntɐˈʃʁaɪbm zi 'bɪtə 'hiɐ]

account	das Konto [das 'kɔnto]
amount	der Betrag [de bə'tʀaːk]
automated teller machine . .	der Geldautomat [de 'gɛltaʊto‚maːt]
bank	die Bank [di baŋk]
banknote	der Geldschein [de 'gɛltʃaɪn]
cash	das Bargeld [das 'baːgɛlt]
cashpoint	der Geldautomat [de 'gɛltaʊto‚maːt]
cent	der Cent [de sɛnt]
change	das Kleingeld [das 'klaɪngɛlt]
to change	umtauschen ['ʔʊmtaʊʃn]
cheque (*Am* check)	der Scheck [de ʃɛk]
cheque card	die Scheckkarte [di 'ʃɛkaːtə]
chip card	die Chipkarte [di 'tʃɪpkaːtə]
coin	die Münze [di 'mʏntsə]
credit card	die Kreditkarte [di kʀediːtkaːtə]
currency	die Währung [di 'vɛːʀʊŋ]
euro	der Euro [de 'ʔɔɪʀo]
exchange	der Geldwechsel [de 'gɛltvɛksl]
exchange rate	der Wechselkurs [de 'vɛkslkʊɐs]
form	das Formular [das fɔmu'laː]
money	das Geld [das gɛlt]
to pay out	auszahlen ['ʔaʊstsaːln]
payment	die Zahlung [di 'tsaːlʊŋ]
Personal Identification	die Geheimzahl [di gə'haɪmtsaːl]
Number (PIN)	
receipt	die Quittung [di 'kvɪtʊŋ]
remittance	die Überweisung [di ʔybe'vaɪzʊŋ]
service charge	die Bearbeitungsgebühr [di bə'ʔaːbaɪtʊŋsgə‚byɐ]
signature	die Unterschrift [di 'ʔʊnteʃʀɪft]
Swiss francs	Schweizer Franken *m pl* [ʃvaɪtsə 'fʀaŋkŋ]
telegraphic transfer	die telegrafische Überweisung [di tele'gʀaːfɪʃə ʔy:be'vaɪzʊŋ]
transfer	die Überweisung [di ʔybe'vaɪzʊŋ]
traveller's cheque	der Reisescheck [de 'ʀaɪzəʃɛk]
to write a cheque	einen Scheck ausstellen [ʔaɪnn ʃɛk 'ʔaʊʃtɛln]

Lost-property office

> also Police

Could you tell me where the lost-property office/lost-and-found is, please?
Könnten Sie mir bitte sagen, wo das Fundbüro ist?
[ˈkœntn̩ zi miɐ ˈbɪtə zaːgn̩ voː das ˈfʊntbyˌʀoː ˀɪst]

I've lost ...
Ich habe ... verloren. [ˀɪç ˈhaːbə ... fɐˈloɐn]

I left my handbag on the train.
Ich habe meine Handtasche im Zug vergessen.
[ˀɪç ˈhaːbə ˈmaɪnə ˈhantaʃə ˀɪm tsuːk fɐˈɡɛsn̩]

Would you let me know if it turns up, please?
Würden Sie mich bitte benachrichtigen, wenn sie gefunden werden sollte?
[ˌvyɐdn̩ zi mɪç ˌbɪtə bəˈnaːxʀɪçtɪɡn̩ vɛn zi ɡəˈfʊndn̩ veɐdn̩ ˌzɔltə]

Here's the address of my hotel.
Hier ist meine Hotelanschrift. [ˈhiɐ ˀɪst ˈmaɪnə hoˈtɛlanʃʀɪft]

Here's my home address.
Hier ist meine Heimatadresse. [ˈhiɐ ˀɪst ˈmaɪnə ˈhaɪmataˌdʀɛsə]

Photos

> also Photographic materials

Could you take a photo of us?
Könnten Sie ein Foto von uns machen?
[ˈkœntn̩ zi ˀaɪn ˈfoːto fɔn ʊns maxn̩]

You only have to press this button.
Sie müssen nur auf diesen Knopf drücken.
[zi mʏsn̩ nuɐ ˀaʊf ˈdiːzn̩ ˈknɔpf dʀʏkn̩]

You set the distance like this.
Die Entfernung stellt man so ein. [di ˀɛntˈfɛɐnʊŋ ʃtɛlt man ˈzoː ˀaɪn]

May I take a photo of you?
Dürfte ich Sie wohl fotografieren? [dʏɐftə ˀɪç zi voːl fotoɡʀaˈfiːʀən]

Smile, please.
Bitte lächeln. [ˈbɪtə ˈlɛçl̩n]

We'll have a lovely reminder of our holiday.
So haben wir eine schöne Erinnerung an unseren Urlaub.
[zo ˈhaːbm̩ viɐ ˀaɪnə ˈʃøːnə ˀeˀˈʀɪneʀʊŋ ˀan ˌˀʊnzen ˀˈuɐlaʊp]

snapshot . . . . der Schnappschuss [dɐ ˈʃnapʃʊs]

Police

Could you tell me where the nearest police station is, please?
Könnten Sie mir bitte sagen, wo das nächste Polizeirevier ist?
[kœntn zi miɐ 'bɪtə za:gn̩ vo: das 'nɛːçstə pɔliˈtsaɪʀe̯viɐ ʔɪst]

I'd like to report ...
Ich möchte ... anzeigen. [ʔɪç 'mœçtə ... ʔantsaɪgn̩]
  a theft
  einen Diebstahl [ʔaɪnn̩ 'di:pʃta:l]
  a robbery
  einen Überfall [ʔaɪnn̩ ʔyːbɐfal]

My ... has been stolen.
Mir ist ... gestohlen worden. [miɐ ʔɪst ... gəˈʃto:ln̩ vɔɐdn̩]
  wallet
  meine Brieftasche ['maɪnə 'bʀi:ftaʃə]
  camera
  mein Fotoapparat [maɪn 'foto̯ʔapaˌʀa:t]
  car
  mein Auto [maɪn ʔaʊto]

My car has been broken into.
Mein Auto ist aufgebrochen worden.
[maɪn ʔaʊto ʔɪst ʔaʊfgəbʀɔxn̩ vɔɐdn̩]

... has been stolen from my car.
Aus meinem Auto ist ... gestohlen worden.
[ʔaʊs 'maɪ(nə)m ʔaʊto ʔɪst ... gəˈʃto:ln̩ vɔɐdn̩]

I've lost ...
Ich habe ... verloren. [ʔɪç 'ha:bə ... fɛ'loɐn̩]

My son/daughter is missing.
Mein Sohn/Meine Tochter ist verschwunden.
[maɪn 'zo:n/ˌmaɪnə 'tɔxtɐ ʔɪst fɛ'ʃvʊndn̩]

This man is pestering me.
Dieser Mann belästigt mich. ['di:zɐ man bə'lɛstɪçt mɪç]

Can you help me, please?
Können Sie mir bitte helfen? ['kœnn̩ zi miɐ 'bɪtə 'hɛlfn̩]

When exactly did this happen?
Wann genau ist das passiert? [van gə'naʊ ɪst das pa'siet]

Your name and address, please.
Ihren Namen und Ihre Anschrift, bitte.
[ʔiʀən 'na:mm̩ ʊnt ˌiʀə ʔanʃʀɪft 'bɪtə]

Please get in touch with your consulate.
Wenden Sie sich bitte an Ihr Konsulat.
['vɛndn̩ zi zɪç an iɐ kɔnzʊ'la:t]

to arrest	verhaften [fɐ'haftn]
to beat up	zusammenschlagen [tsʊ'zammʃla:gn]
to break into/open	aufbrechen ['ʔaʊfbrɛçn]
car radio	das Autoradio [das 'ʔaʊto,ra:djo]
car registration documents	der Kfz-Schein [dɐ ka'ʔef'tsɛtʃaɪn]
cheque/check	der Scheck [dɐ ʃɛk]
cheque card	die Scheckkarte [di 'ʃɛka:tə]
court	das Gericht [das gə'rɪçt]
credit card	die Kreditkarte [di 'kredi:tka:tə]
crime	das Verbrechen [das fɐ'brɛçn]
documents	die Papiere n pl [di pa'pi:rə]
drugs	das Rauschgift [das 'raʊʃgɪft]
guilt	die Schuld [ʃʊlt]
to harass	belästigen [bə'lɛstɪgn]
identity card	der Personalausweis [dɐ pɛrzo'na:laʊsvaɪs]
judge	der Richter/die Richterin [dɐ 'rɪçtɐ/di 'rɪçtərɪn]
key	der Schlüssel [dɐ 'ʃlysl]
lawyer	der Rechtsanwalt [dɐ 'rɛçtsanvalt], die Rechtsanwältin [dɪ 'rɛçtsanvɛltɪn]
to lose	verlieren [fɐ'li:rən]
mugging	der Überfall [dɐ 'ʔy:bɐfal]
papers	die Papiere n pl [di pa'pi:rə]
passport	der Reisepass [dɐ 'raɪzəpas]
pickpocket	der Taschendieb [dɐ 'taʃndi:p]
police	die Polizei [di pɔlɪ'tsaɪ]
police car	der Polizeiwagen [dɐ pɔlɪ'tsaɪva:gn]
police custody	die Untersuchungshaft [di ʔʊntɐ'zu:xʊŋshaft]
policeman/policewoman	der Polizist/die Polizistin [dɐ polɪ'tsɪst/di polɪ'tsɪstɪn]
prison	das Gefängnis [das gə'fɛŋnɪs]
purse	die Geldbörse [di 'gɛltbœrzə]
rape	die Vergewaltigung [di fɛgə'valtɪgʊŋ]
to report	anzeigen ['ʔantsaɪgn]
sexual harassment	die sexuelle Belästigung [di sɛksu'ɛlə bə'lɛstɪgʊŋ]
to smuggle	schmuggeln [ʃmʊgln]
theft	der Diebstahl [dɐ 'di:pʃta:l]
thief	der Dieb/die Diebin [dɐ di:p/di 'di:bɪn]

Can you tell me where ... is, please?
Können Sie mir bitte sagen, wo ... ist?
[kœnn zi miɐ 'bɪtə 'zaːgŋ voː ... ʔɪst]

the nearest post office
das nächste Postamt [das 'nɛːçstə 'pɔstʔamt]
the nearest letterbox/mailbox
der nächste Briefkasten [de 'nɛːçstə 'bʀiːfkastn]

How much does a letter/postcard cost ...
Was kostet ein Brief/eine Postkarte ...
[vas 'kɔstət ʔaɪn 'bʀiːf/ˌʔaɪnə 'pɔstkaːtə nax ...]

to the US?
in die USA? [ʔɪn di ʔuɛsˀʔaː]
to England?
nach England? [nax ʔɛŋlant]

I'd like to send this letter ...
Diesen Brief bitte per ... ['diːzn bʀif ˌbɪtə pɛɐ]
by airmail.
Luftpost. ['lʊftpɔst]
express.
Express. [ʔɛks'pʀɛs]

Three ... euro stamps, please.
Drei Briefmarken zu ... Euro, bitte!
[dʀaɪ 'bʀiːfmaːkŋ tsʊ ... ʔɔɪʀo 'bɪtə]

Do you have any special issue stamps?
Haben Sie Sondermarken? [haːbm zi 'zɔndɛmaːkŋ]

➢ also Bank

address	die Adresse [di ʔa'dʀɛsə]
addressee	der Empfänger [de ʔɛmp'fɛŋɐ]
by airmail	mit Luftpost [mɪt 'lʊftpɔst]
charge	die Gebühr [di gə'byɐ]
collection (of mail)	die Leerung [di 'leːʀʊŋ]
customs declaration	die Zollerklärung [di 'tsɔlɛklɛːʀʊŋ]
declaration of value	die Wertangabe [di 'veɐtangaːbə]
dispatch form	die Paketkarte [di pa'keːtkaːtə]
express letter	der Eilbrief [de ʔaɪlbʀiːf]
fax	das Telefax [das ('teːlə)faks]
fee	die Gebühr [di gə'byɐ]
to fill in	ausfüllen [ʔaʊsfʏln]
form	das Formular [das fɔmu'laː]
to forward	nachsenden ['naːxzɛndn]
letter	der Brief [de bʀiːf]
letterbox/mailbox	der Briefkasten [de 'bʀiːfkastn]

main post office	das Hauptpostamt
	[das 'haʊptˌpɔstˀamt]
parcel	das Paket [das paˈkeːt]
post code	die Postleitzahl [di 'pɔstlaɪtsaːl]
post office	das Postamt [das 'pɔstamt]
post office savings book	das Postsparbuch [das 'pɔstʃpaːbuːx]
postage	das Porto [das 'pɔʁto]
postcard	die Postkarte [di 'pɔstkaːtə]
poste restante	postlagernd ['pɔstlaːgɐnt]
registered letter	der Einschreibebrief
	[de ˀaɪnʃʁaɪbəbʁiːf]
to send on	nachsenden ['naːxzɛndn]
sender	der Absender/die Absenderin
	[de ˀapzɛndɐ/di ˀapzɛndərɪn]
small packet	das Päckchen [das pɛkçn]
special issue stamp	die Sondermarke [di 'zɔndemaːkə]
stamp	die Briefmarke [di 'bʁiːfmaːkə]
to stamp	frankieren [fʁaŋ'kiːɐn]
stamp machine	der Briefmarkenautomat
	[de 'bʁiːfmaːkŋˀaʊtoˌmaːt]
telex	das Telex [das 'teːlɛks]
weight	das Gewicht [das gə'vɪçt]
zip code	die Postleitzahl [di 'pɔstlaɪtsaːl]

Telephoning

Can you tell me where the nearest phone box/booth is, please?
Können Sie mir bitte sagen, wo die nächste Telefonzelle ist?
[kœnn zi miɐ 'bɪtə zaːgŋ 'vo di 'nɛːçstə teləˈfoːntsɛlə ˀɪst]

I'd like a phonecard, please.
Ich möchte bitte eine Telefonkarte.
[ˀɪç 'mœçtə bɪtə ˀaɪnə teləˈfoːnkaːtə]

What's the area code for ...?
Wie ist bitte die Vorwahl von ...? ['viː ˀɪst bɪtə di 'foɐvaːl fɔn]

I'd like to make a call to ...
Bitte ein Ferngespräch nach ... ['bɪtə ˀaɪn 'fɛɐngəʃpʁɛːç nax ...]

I'd like to make a reverse charge call/ collect call.
Ich möchte ein R-Gespräch anmelden.
[ˀɪç 'mœçtə ˀaɪn ˀɛɐgəʃpʁɛːç ˀanmɛldn]

Use booth number four.
Gehen Sie in Kabine Nummer vier. ['geːn zi ˀɪn kaˈbiːnə ˌnʊme 'fiɐ]

A telephone call

This is ... speaking.
Hier spricht ... ['hiɐ ʃpʀɪçt ...]

Good morning/afternoon, my name is ...
Guten Tag, mein Name ist ... [guːtn 'taːk maɪn 'naːmə ʔɪst]

Hello, who's speaking, please?
Hallo, mit wem spreche ich, bitte? ['halo: mɪt veːm ʃpʀɛç ɪç bɪtə]

Can I speak to Mr/Mrs ..., please?
Kann ich bitte Herrn/Frau ... sprechen?
['kan ɪç 'bɪtə hɛɐn/fʀaʊ ... ʃpʀɛçn]

I'm sorry, he's/she's not here.
Tut mir Leid, er/sie ist nicht da. [tuːt mɪɐ 'laɪt ɛɐ/zi ʔɪst nɪçt daː]

Can he call you back?
Kann er Sie zurückrufen? ['kan (e)ɐ zi tsʊ'ʀʏkʀuːfn]

Would you like to leave a message?
Möchten Sie eine Nachricht hinterlassen?
[mœçtn zi ʔaɪnə 'naːxɪçt hɪntɐ'lasn]

Would you tell him/her that I called?
Würden Sie ihm/ihr bitte sagen, ich hätte angerufen?
['vʏɐdn zi ʔiːm/ʔiɐ 'bɪtə 'zaːgn ʔɪç 'hɛtə ʔangəʀuːfn]

"The number you have dialled has not been recognized."
„Kein Anschluss unter dieser Nummer."
[kaɪn 'ʔanʃlʊs 'ʔʊntɐ diːzɐ 'nʊmɐ]

to answer the phone	abnehmen ['ʔapneːmm]
answering machine	der Anrufbeantworter [dɐ 'ʔanfuːfbə,ʔantvɔɐtɐ]
area code	die Vorwahlnummer [di 'foɐvaːl,nʊmɐ]
booking	die Voranmeldung [di 'foɐʔanmɛldʊŋ]
busy	besetzt [bə'zɛtst]
call	der Anruf [dɐ 'ʔanʀuːf]
to call	anrufen ['ʔanʀuːfn]
cellular phone	das Handy [das 'hɛndi]
charge	die Gebühr [di gə'byɐ]
connection	die Verbindung [di fɐ'bɪndʊŋ]
conversation	das Gespräch [das gə'ʃpʀɛːç]
to dial	wählen [vɛːln]
directory enquiries/assistance	die Auskunft [di 'ʔaʊskʊnft]
engaged	besetzt [bə'zɛtst]
international call	das Auslandsgespräch [das 'ʔaʊslantsgəʃpʀɛːç]
line	die Verbindung [di fɐ'bɪndʊŋ]
local call	das Ortsgespräch [das 'ʔɔɐtsgəʃpʀɛːç]

189

long-distance call	das Ferngespräch [das ˈfɛʁŋɡəʃpʁɛːç]
mobile (phone)	das Handy [das ˈhɛndi], das Mobiltelefon [das moˈbiːltelefoːn]
national code	die Vorwahlnummer [di ˈfoːʁvaːlˌnʊmɐ]
to phone	anrufen [ˈʔanʁuːfn̩]
phone call	der Anruf [dɐ ˈʔanʁuːf]
phone box/booth	die Telefonzelle [di teleˈfoːntsɛlə]
phone number	die Telefonnummer [di teleˈfoːnnʊmə]
phonecard	die Telefonkarte [di teleˈfoːnkaːtə]
receiver	der Hörer [dɐ ˈhøːʁɐ]
reverse charge call	das R-Gespräch [das ˈʔɛʁɡəʃpʁɛːç]
telephone	das Telefon [das ˈteːləfoːn]
telephone directory	das Telefonbuch [das teleˈfoːnbuːx]

Toilet and bathroom

Where is the toilet, please?
Wo ist bitte die Toilette? [voː ʔɪst ˈbɪtə di toˈlɛtə]

May I use your toilet?
Dürfte ich Ihre Toilette benutzen? [ˈdʏftə ʔɪç ˈʔiːʁə toˈlɛtə bəˈnʊtsn̩]

Would you give me the key for the toilet, please?
Würden Sie mir bitte den Schlüssel für die Toiletten geben?
[ˈvʏʁdn̩ zi miɐ ˈbɪtə den ˈʃlʏsl̩ fyɐ di toˈlɛtə geːbm̩]

clean	sauber [ˈzaʊbɐ]
cubicle	die Kabine [di kaˈbiːnə]
dirty	schmutzig [ˈʃmʊtsɪç]
flush the toilet	(die Toilette) spülen [(di toˈlɛtə) ʃpyːln]
Gents	Herren [ˈhɛʁən]
Ladies	Damen [daːmm̩]
Men's Room	die Herrentoilette [di ˈhɛʁəntoˌlɛtə]
sanitary towels	die Damenbinden f pl [di ˈdaːmmbɪndn̩]
soap	die Seife [di ˈzaɪfə]
tampons	die Tampons m pl [di ˈtampɔŋs]
toilet-paper	das Toilettenpapier [das toˈlɛtnpaˌpiɐ]
towel	das Handtuch [das ˈhan(t)tuːx]
washbasin	das Waschbecken [das ˈvaʃbɛkn̩]
Women's Room	die Damentoilette [di ˈdaːmmtoˌlɛtə]

A short guide to German grammar

Articles

The article indicates the gender of a noun. There are three genders in German: masculine, feminine and neuter, as well as four cases: nominative, accusative, genitive and dative.

	definite article				indefinite article			
	m	f	n	pl	m	f	n	pl
nom.	der	die	das	die	ein	eine	ein	*no article*
acc.	den	die	das	die	einen	eine	ein	*used with*
gen.	des	der	des	der	eines	einer	eines	*plural nouns*
dat.	dem	der	dem	den	einem	einer	einem	

Nouns

All German nouns are written with a capital letter.
There are three declensions: strong, weak and mixed. (These terms classify nouns according to their endings in the genitive case.)
Nouns which end in 's,' 'sch', 'ß/ss' and 'z ' always have an '-es' in the genitive case.
Some nouns are declined like adjectives.

1. Strong masculine and neuter nouns

	nom. plural: +e	nom. plural: umlaut+e	nom. plural: +er	nom. plural: umlaut+er
singular				
nom.	der Tag (the day)	der Traum (the dream)	das Kind (the child)	das Dach (the roof)
acc.	den Tag	den Traum	das Kind	das Dach
gen.	des Tag(e)s	des Traum(e)s	des Kind(e)s	des Dach(e)s
dat.	dem Tag(e)	dem Traum(e)	dem Kind(e)	dem Dach(e)
plural				
nom.	die Tage	die Träume	die Kinder	die Dächer
acc.	die Tage	die Träume	die Kinder	die Dächer
gen.	der Tage	der Träume	der Kinder	der Dächer
dat.	den Tagen	den Träumen	den Kindern	den Dächern

	nom. plural: +s	nom. plural: umlaut only	nom. plural: no change	nom. plural: no change
singular				
nom.	das Auto (the car)	der Vogel (the bird)	der Tischler (the carpenter)	der Lappen (the cloth)
acc.	das Auto	den Vogel	den Tischler	den Lappen
gen.	des Autos	des Vogels	des Tischlers	des Lappens
dat.	dem Auto	dem Vogel	dem Tischler	dem Lappen
plural				
nom.	die Autos	die Vögel	die Tischler	die Lappen
acc.	die Autos	die Vögel	die Tischler	die Lappen
gen.	der Autos	der Vögel	der Tischler	der Lappen
dat.	den Autos	den Vögeln	den Tischlern	den Lappen

2. Strong feminine nouns

	nom. plural: umlaut+e	nom. plural: umlaut only	nom. plural: +s
singular			
nom.	die Wand (the wall)	die Mutter (the mother)	die Bar (the bar)
acc.	die Wand	die Mutter	die Bar
gen.	der Wand	der Mutter	der Bar
dat.	der Wand	der Mutter	der Bar
plural			
nom.	die Wände	die Mütter	die Bars
acc.	die Wände	die Mütter	die Bars
gen.	der Wände	der Mütter	der Bars
dat.	den Wänden	den Müttern	den Bars

192

3. Weak masculine nouns

singular			
nom.	der Bauer (the farmer)	der Bär (the bear)	der Hase (the hare)
acc.	den Bauern	den Bären	den Hasen
gen.	des Bauern	des Bären	des Hasen
dat.	dem Bauern	dem Bären	dem Hasen
plural			
nom.	die Bauern	die Bären	die Hasen
acc.	die Bauern	die Bären	die Hasen
gen.	der Bauern	der Bären	der Hasen
dat.	den Bauern	den Bären	den Hasen

4. Weak feminine nouns

singular				
nom.	die Uhr (the clock)	die Feder (the feather)	die Gabe (the gift)	die Ärztin (the doctor)
acc.	die Uhr	die Feder	die Gabe	die Ärztin
gen.	der Uhr	der Feder	der Gabe	der Ärztin
dat.	der Uhr	der Feder	der Gabe	der Ärztin
plural				
nom.	die Uhren	die Federn	die Gaben	die Ärztinnen
acc.	die Uhren	die Federn	die Gaben	die Ärztinnen
gen.	der Uhren	der Federn	der Gaben	der Ärztinnen
dat.	den Uhren	den Federn	den Gaben	den Ärztinnen

5. Mixed masculine and neuter nouns

These are declined as strong nouns in the singular and weak nouns in the plural.

singular				
nom.	das Auge (the eye)	das Ohr (the ear)	der Name (the name)	das Herz (the heart)
acc.	das Auge	das Ohr	den Namen	das Herz
gen.	des Auges	des Ohr(e)s	der Namens	des Herzens
dat.	dem Auge	dem Ohr(e)	dem Namen	dem Herzen
plural				
nom.	die Augen	die Ohren	die Namen	die Herzen
acc.	die Augen	die Ohren	die Namen	die Herzen
gen.	der Augen	der Ohren	der Namen	der Herzen
dat.	den Augen	den Ohren	den Namen	den Herzen

6. Nouns declined as adjectives

masculine singular		
nom.	der Reisende	ein Reisender
	(the traveller)	
acc.	den Reisenden	einen Reisenden
gen.	des Reisenden	eines Reisenden
dat.	dem Reisenden	einem Reisenden

plural		
nom.	die Reisenden	Reisende
acc.	die Reisenden	Reisende
gen.	der Reisenden	Reisender
dat.	den Reisenden	Reisenden

feminine singular		
nom.	die Reisende	eine Reisende
acc.	die Reisende	eine Reisende
gen.	der Reisenden	einer Reisenden
dat.	der Reisenden	einer Reisenden

plural		
nom.	die Reisenden	Reisende
acc.	die Reisenden	Reisende
gen.	der Reisenden	Reisender
dat.	den Reisenden	Reisenden

neuter singular		
nom.	das Neugeborene	ein Neugeborenes
	(the new born [baby])	
acc.	das Neugeborene	ein Neugeborenes
gen.	des Neugeborenen	eines Neugeborenen
dat.	dem Neugeborenen	einem Neugeborenen

plural		
nom.	die Neugeborenen	Neugeborene
acc.	die Neugeborenen	Neugeborene
gen.	der Neugeborenen	Neugeborener
dat.	den Neugeborenen	Neugeborenen

There are three types of adjective declension: strong, weak and mixed.

The strong declension

is used when there is no article, pronoun or other word preceeding the adjective indicating the case (e.g. *manch(e)*, *mehrere* etc.). It is also used with cardinal numbers and expressions like *ein paar* and *ein bisschen*.

	m	f	n
singular			
nom.	guter Wein (good wine)	schöne Frau (beautiful woman)	liebes Kind (well-behaved child)
acc.	guten Wein	schöne Frau	liebes Kind
gen.	guten Wein(e)s	schöner Frau	lieben Kindes
dat.	gutem Wein(e)	schöner Frau	liebem Kind(e)
plural			
nom.	gute Weine	schöne Frauen	liebe Kinder
acc.	gute Weine	schöne Frauen	liebe Kinder
gen.	guter Weine	schöner Frauen	lieber Kinder
dat.	guten Weinen	schönen Frauen	lieben Kindern

The weak declension

is used with adjectives preceded by the definite article or with any other word already clearly showing the case of the noun (e.g. *diese(r,s)*, *folgende(r,s)* etc.).

	m	f	n
singular			
nom.	der gute Wein	die schöne Frau	das liebe Kind
acc.	den guten Wein	die schöne Frau	das liebe Kind
gen.	des guten Wein(e)s	der schönen Frau	des lieben Kindes
dat.	dem guten Wein	der schönen Frau	dem lieben Kind
plural			
nom.	die guten Weine	die schönen Frauen	die lieben Kinder
acc.	die guten Weine	die schönen Frauen	die lieben Kinder
gen.	der guten Weine	der schönen Frauen	der lieben Kinder
dat.	den guten Weinen	den schönen Frauen	den lieben Kindern

The mixed declension

is used with singular masculine and neuter nouns and the indefinite articles *ein* and *kein* and with the possessive pronouns *mein, dein, sein, unser, euer, ihr*.

	m	n
singular		
nom.	ein guter Wein (a good wine)	ein liebes Kind (a well-behaved child)
acc.	einen guten Wein	ein liebes Kind
gen.	eines guten Wein(e)s	eines lieben Kindes
dat.	einem guten Wein(e)	einem lieben Kind

Adverbs

- For the adverbial use of adjectives the unchanged basic form of the adjective is used.

Verbs

Present Tense

The basic ending of German verbs is '*-en*' (*machen, sagen, essen* etc.). To form the present tense remove the '*-en*' and add the corresponding personal endings to the stem of the verb. There is no continuous form in German , e.g. „*Ich gehe um acht Uhr ins Büro.*" can be translated as '*I go to the office at eight o'clock.*' (routine) or '*I'm going to the office at eight o'clock.*' (single event).

		machen (to do)	legen (to put)	sagen (to say)
I	ich	mache	lege	sage
you	du	machst	legst	sagst
he she it	er sie es	macht	legt	sagt
we	wir	machen	legen	sagen
you	ihr	macht	legt	sagt
they	sie	machen	legen	sagen

- The vowel '*-a-*' in some verbs changes to the umlaut '*-ä-*'.

tragen   ich trage, du trägst, er/sie/es trägt,
            wir tragen, ihr tragt, sie tragen

Auxilary verbs *haben*, *sein* and *werden*

Present tense

	sein (to be)	**haben** (to have)	**werden** (to become)
ich	bin	habe	werde
du	bist	hast	wirst
er sie es	ist	hat	wird
wir	sind	haben	werden
ihr	seid	habt	werdet
sie	sind	haben	werden

Past tense and past participle

	sein (to be)	**haben** (to have)	**werden** (to become)
ich	war	hatte	wurde
du	warst	hattest	wurdest
er sie es	war	hatte	wurde
wir	waren	hatten	wurden
ihr	wart	hattet	wurdet
sie	waren	hatten	wurden
past participle	bin gewesen	habe gehabt	bin geworden

Modal auxilaries

Here is a list of the most important ones. Note that most are irregular.

Present tense

	können (be able to)	**dürfen** (be allowed to)	**mögen** (like)	**müssen** (have to)	**sollen** (should)	**wollen** (want to)
ich	kann	darf	mag	muss	soll	will
du	kannst	darfst	magst	musst	sollst	willst
er sie es	kann	darf	mag	muss	soll	will
wir	können	dürfen	mögen	müssen	sollen	wollen
ihr	könnt	dürft	mögt	müsst	sollt	wollt
sie	können	dürfen	mögen	müssen	sollen	wollen

Past Tense

There are two tenses for the past in German, the imperfect and the present perfect. Both describe events which took place in the past. There is no past continuous form.

Gestern war ich krank.	Yesterday I was ill.
Letztes Jahr sind wir in Berlin gewesen.	Last year we were in Berlin.

To form the **imperfect**, the following verb endings are added to the stem of the verb:

	machen (to do)	**begegnen** (to meet)	**wetten** (to bet)
ich	machte	begegnete	wettete
du	machtest	begegnetest	wettetest
er sie es	machte	begegnete	wettete
wir	machten	begegneten	wetteten
ihr	machtet	begegnetet	wettetet
sie	machten	begegneten	wetteten

The **present perfect** is the most common way of referring to the past and is formed with the present tense of either *haben* (to have) or *sein* (to be) followed by the past participle of the verb. The past participle of regular verbs is formed by adding the prefix '*ge-*' and the ending '*-t*' to the stem.

machen	**ge-mach-t**	fragen	**ge-frag-t**
(to do)	(done)	(to ask)	(asked)

Most verbs take *haben* to form the present perfect:

Er hat es gemacht.	He's done it. / He did it.
Ich habe es gesagt.	I've said it. / I said it.

sein is used with verbs of motion and verbs that indicate a transition from one state to another. Many irregular verbs form the present perfect with the prefix '*ge-*', a vowel change and the ending '*-en*'.

Wir sind gefahren.	We drove.

Future

- The future tense is formed with auxiliary verb *werden* and the infinitive.

	fahren (to drive)	sein (to be)	haben (to have)	können (to be able to)
ich	werde fahren	werde sein	werde haben	werde können
du	wirst fahren	wirst sein	wirst haben	wirst können
er sie } es	wird fahren	wird sein	wird haben	wird können
wir	werden fahren	werden sein	werden haben	werden können
ihr	werdet fahren	werdet sein	werdet haben	werdet können
sie	werden fahren	werden sein	werden haben	werden können

- Often the present tense is also used to express the future.

Questions

Simple questions are formed by changing the order of subject and verb.

Es regnet.	It's raining.
Regnet es?	Is it raining?
Der Laden macht um 9 Uhr auf.	The shop opens at 9 o'clock.
Macht der Laden um 9 Uhr auf?	Does the shop open at 9 o'clock?

Negation

To negate a sentence add **nicht** after the main verb.

Sie wohnt in Berlin.	She lives in Berlin.
Er wohnt **nicht** in Berlin	He doesn't live in Berlin.

Nicht + **ein,eine,einen** etc. becomes **kein, keine, keinen** etc.

Ich habe eine Fahrkarte	I have a ticket.
Ich habe keine Fahrkarte	I don't have a ticket.

Pronouns agree with the gender and case/number of the noun they refer to.

1. Personal pronouns

nominative	accusative	genitive	dative
ich (I)	mich (me)	meiner	mir
du (you)	dich (you)	deiner	dir
er (he)	ihn (him)	seiner	ihm
sie (she)	sie (her)	ihrer	ihr
es (it)	es (it)	seiner	ihm
wir (we)	uns (us)	unser	uns
ihr (you)	euch (you)	euer	euch
sie (they)	sie (them)	ihrer	ihnen
Sie (you)	Sie (you)		

- **du** is the familiar form of address when speaking to family, friends and children.
- **Sie** is the polite form of address (for both the singular and plural).
- **ihr** is the familiar form of address used when speaking to more than one person.

2. Reflexive pronouns

These are used with reflexive verbs such as *sich freuen, sich waschen, sich bedanken.*

myself	mich	ich freue mich
yourself	dich *(familiar)*	du freust dich
	sich *(polite)*	Sie freuen sich
himself / herself / itself	sich	er/sie/es freut sich
ourselves	uns	wir freuen uns
yourselves	euch *(familiar)*	ihr freut euch
	sich *(polite)*	Sie freuen sich
themselves	sich	sie freuen sich

3. Possessive pronouns

	m	f	n	pl
singular				
nom.	mein	meine	mein	meine
acc.	meinen	meine	mein	meine
gen.	meines	meiner	meines	meiner
dat.	meinem	meiner	meinem	meinen

• *dein* (your), *sein* (his), *ihr* (her), *sein* (its) are declined like *mein* (my).

1st person plural (our)				
nom.	unser	uns(e)re	unser	uns(e)re
acc.	uns(e)ren unsern	uns(e)re	unser	unsre
gen.	uns(e)res	uns(e)rer	uns(e)res	uns(e)rer
dat.	uns(e)rem unserm	uns(e)rer	uns(e)rem unserm	uns(e)ren

2nd person plural (your)				
nom.	euer	eure	euer	eure
acc.	euren	eure	euer	eure
gen.	eures	eurer	eures	eurer
dat.	eurem	eurer	eurem	euren

3rd person plural (their)				
nom.	ihr	ihre	ihr	ihre
acc.	ihren	ihre	ihr	ihre
gen.	ihres	ihrer	ihres	ihrer
dat.	ihrem	ihrer	ihrem	ihren

A short guide to German pronunciation

Vowels

Vowel sounds in German can be **long** or **short**.

A vowel is usually **long** if it is followed by a <u>single</u> consonant:

Schlaf, schlafen, Kino, groß (exception: mit)

or if it is followed by a silent **h**:

mehr, mähen, hohlen

or if it is doubled:

Meer, Haar, Boot

The vowel combination **ie** is usually long:

wie viel, Ziel, ziehen

A vowel is usually **short** if it is followed by <u>two or more</u> consonants:

nass, Hund, Tisch, immer, Koch (exception: hoch)

or if it comes before **ck**:

Hecke, Rucksack, backen, Bäcker, Stücke

NB: if the root form of the word is long (e.g. sagen, groß) but the inflected form is followed by two consonants, the vowel remains long: gesagt, größte

Long and short 'a'

The **long a** sound – which can be written **a, aa** or **ah** – is like the English **a** in *car, calm, father*:

Glas, Haar, wahr, kam, Kahn

The **short a** sound is somewhere between the vowel sound in *fan* and *fun,* pronounced in a short, clipped way:

Land, danke, Stadt, Kamm, kann

Long and short 'e'

The **long e** sound – which can be written **e, ee** or **eh** – is like the English **a** in *bathe* or *hay* (but without sliding away into *ee* as the English does):

hebt, Meer, mehr, geht

The **short e** sound is like the **e** in *bed, net*:

Bett, Netz, wenn, leckt

Many German words end in a single unstressed **-e** or **-el**. This should be pronounced as in the final syllable of *Tina, sister* or *bubble, trouble*:

danke, Stelle, Gabel, Stachel

German words ending in a single unstressed -er should be pronounced very similarly but with the addition of a gently rolled **r** at the
end; contrast:

bitte – bitter; Fische – Fischer

Long and short 'i'

The **long i** sound is like the English **ee** in *feet* or the **ea** in *beach*:

Kilo, Bibel, wir

The **short i** sound is like the **i** in *bit*:

mit, mich

Long and short 'o'

The **long o** sound – which can be written **o**, **oo** or **oh** – is somewhere between the English **o** sound in *go* or *show* (but with the <u>lips</u>
more <u>rounded</u> and the <u>mouth</u> more <u>open</u>) and the **aw** sound in
lawn:

tot, Hose, Boot, Moos, froh, holen

The **short o** sound is like the **o** in *pot* only <u>shorter</u> and with a more
<u>rounded</u> mouth:

Sonne, Gott, hoffen, kochen

Long and short 'u'

The **long u** sound – which can be written **u** or **uh** – is like the
English **oo** in *hoot* or *rule* but with more <u>rounded</u> lips:

Fuß, gut, Ruf, Schule, Stuhl, Tuch, Uhr, zu

The **short u** sound is a shorter version of the vowel sound in *put* or
foot:

Fluss, Hund, Mutter, Suppe, unter, putzen

Long and short 'ä'

The **long ä** sound – which can be written **ä** or **äh** – is somewhere
between the vowel sounds in *day* (but without sliding away into *ee*
as the English does) and *dare*:

Mädchen, wählen, täglich, spät, Lärm

The **short ä** sound is like the **e** in *get, set*:

Männer, Hände, hätte, lästig

Long and short 'ö'

The **long ö** sound – which can be written **ö** or **öh** – sounds a bit
like the vowel sounds in *earth* and *learn* but said with <u>rounded</u> lips:

schön, böse, Flöte, Größe, Söhne, Höhle, hören, mögen

The **short ö** sound is a shorter, more clipped version of the above:

Löffel, Stöcke, Hölle, können, möchte

Long and short 'ü'

These are the hardest sounds in the German alphabet for the English speaker to master.

The **long ü** sound – which can be written **ü** or **üh** – is produced by saying an *ee* sound with <u>very rounded</u> lips.
Try saying *Tier* like this and with a bit of luck it should sound like *Tür*; try *spielen* too - this should come out as *'spülen'*.

früh, für, grün, müde, Schüler, Hügel, über

The **short ü** sound is a shorter, more clipped version of the above:

Stück, dünn, Küsse, hübsch, müssen

Groups of vowels

ai, ay, ei, ey sound like the **i** in '*mine*:

Mai, Main, Bayern, mein, Rhein, Speyer

au sounds like a shorter more clipped version of the **ow** in *now:*

Frau, braun, auch

äu, eu sound like the **oy** in *boy:*

Fräulein, Gebäude, neu, Freund

ie sounds like the **ee** in *deep* (but with a little more precision than in English):

die, viel, Lied, Bier, ziehen

When **ie** occurs at the end of a word, it can be pronounced in two separate ways: if the final syllable of the word is <u>stressed</u>, it is pronounced as the normal **ie** outlined above:

Biographie, Philosophie, Symphonie

But when it is <u>unstressed</u>, it is pronounced as two separate vowels:

Familie *(fa-mee-leeya)*

Consonants

b and **d** are usually pronounced as they are in English, except at the end of a word or syllable or before **s** or **t**, when the **b** sounds more like a **p** and the **d** sounds more like a **t**:

baden – Bad	Diebe – Dieb(stahl)	Handel – Hand
Hunde – Hund	leider – Leid	lieben – lieb(ster)
rauben – Raub	schreiben – Schreibtisch	wenden – Wand
gibt	siebter	Stadt

ch - has a multiplicity of regional variations but when it follows an **a, o, u** or **au** it is like the rather harsh guttural **ch** in the Scottish *Loch Ness*:

nach, lachen, Koch, Tochter, Buch, Kuchen, auch, rauchen

Otherwise it sounds a lot softer, rather like the **h** sound at the beginning of *hymn* or *humour*:

> brechen, ich, lächeln, möchte, Bücher, Küche, euch, geräuchert, Milch, welche, manche, Hähnchen, München, durch, Kirche

ch at the beginning of a word indicates a word that has been imported from a foreign language; if this is French then it sounds like **sh**:

> Chalet, Champagner, Chance, Chef

others sound like **k**:

> Chaos, Charakter, Cholera, Chor, Christ

or like the **ch** in *mich*:

> Chemie, chinesisch, Chirurg

and others are taken directly from languages like English and spoken as closely as possible to the original:

> Champion, Chart, Chat, checken

chs usually sounds like the **x** in *axe*:

> Lachs, sechs, wachsen, Wechsel
> (exceptions: machst [harsh 'ch'] nächste [soft 'ch'])

ck sounds like the English **k** and the vowel preceding it is always short and stressed:

> backen, Gepäck, Glück, lecker, Rock, zurück
> [Try these problem words: glücklich, schrecklich]

g is usually pronounced like the **g** in *gold* when it comes before a vowel:

> Geld, gelb

but at the end of a word or syllable or before **s** or **t**, it sounds more like a strangulated **k**:

> Berge – Berg   bürgen – Burg   fliegen – fliegt
> schlagen – Schlag(sahne)   tagen – Tag

ig at the end of a word, is pronounced just like the German **ich**, i.e. ending in a sound rather like the **h** in *hymn* or *humour*:

> fertig, Honig, hungrig, König, richtig, sonnig, zwanzig

gn, kn - both consonants are pronounced:

> Gnade, Kneipe, Knie, Knopf

h is clearly pronounced at the beginning of a word or second element in a compound noun:

> Haushalt, hier, holen, Buchhandlung

however, when it comes after a vowel, it is not usually sounded and the preceding vowel is lengthened:

> fahren, gehen, Lehrer, stehen

j sounds like the **y** in *yes*:

> ja, Jacke, jetzt, Johannes, Junge, Juni, Major

l sounds a little lighter and flatter than an English **l**, quite close to the sound in *million*:

alles, Liebe

ng always sounds like the nasal sound in *song, singer, ring,* even in the middle of a word (never like *finger*):

singen, schwanger, Engel, England, Zunge

q - as in English, **q** is always followed by a **u** but is pronounced **kv**:

Quittung, quer, Quiz

r has a multiplicity of regional variations but the basic sound when it occurs before a vowel is somewhere between a growl and a gargle made at the back of the throat:

drei, fahren, Frau, Jahre, Lehrerin, rot, Straße, trocken, warum

At the end of a word however, the **r** is hardly pronounced at all, rather as in the English words: *beer, brother, year*:

Bier, Bruder, Jahr

s sounds like the **s** in *sister*, except when it comes before a vowel, when it sounds like the **z** in *zoo*:

das, Glas, Maske, Maus, Pflaster, Reis
Masern, reisen, See, sie, Vase, Versicherung

sch sounds like the **sh** in *shoe*:

Geschichte, Schuh, Schule, schwimmen, Tisch, waschen

sp and **st** – when they occur at the <u>beginning</u> of a word or the beginning of the second element in a compound noun, or after unstressed *Ge* or *ge*, sound like **shp** and **sht**:

(Ball)Spiel, Sport, Sprache, (Haupt)Stadt, Stein, (Haupt)Straße, Gespräch, gesprochen, Gestank, gestohlen

Otherwise, they are pronounced as they would be in English:

Dienstag, Gast, ist, kosten, Liste, sagst

ss or **ß** is always pronounced like an English **ss**; when the preceding vowel is <u>short</u> it is written **ss**; when it comes after a <u>long</u> vowel or <u>diphthong</u> it is written **ß**:

besser, dass, muss, müssen, Pass, Schloss, Schlüssel, wissen
groß, Gruß, Grüße, schließen, Schoß, Spaß, Strauß, süß, weiß

th sounds like an English **t**:

Apotheke, Theater, Thema

tz is pronounced **ts**:

Blitz, Dutzend, jetzt, Metzger, Platz, plötzlich, putzen

v, f, ph sound like the English **f** in *before, father, from*:

bevor, Vater, vier, von, frei, für, Triumph, Typhus

206

In a few loan words from other languages however, **v** is pronounced as it is in English:

Klavier, Vase, Verb

w sounds like the English **v** in *very, video*:

Wasser, wenn, wieder, wir, Witwe, zuwinken

[Try these problem words:
Volkswagen, vorwärts, wievielte, wovon]

y – the pronunciation of the German **y** depends on the position of the letter in the word; if it occurs <u>within a word</u> it sounds like an **ü**:

Physik, Pyramide, Rhythmus, typisch

If **y** occurs at the beginning or end of a word, then it is pronounced in exactly the same way as it is in English:

Handy, Hobby, Yoga, Yucca,

z sounds like the **ts** in *cats, nuts* - even at the beginning of a word:

Herz, März, salzig, zehn, Zeit, Zimmer, zu, zwanzig

A

Aal m ['ʔaːl] eel

ab ['ʔap] from

abbestellen ['ʔapbəʃtɛln] *(tickets etc.)* cancel

Abblendlicht n ['ʔapblɛntlɪçt] dipped/dimmed headlights

abbrechen ['ʔapbʀɛçn] to stop

Abend m ['ʔaːbmt] evening, night

Abendessen n ['ʔaːbmt'ʔɛsn] dinner

abends ['ʔaːbms] in the evening

aber ['ʔaːbɐ] but

abfahren (von) ['ʔapfaː (ʀə)n fɔn] start (from), leave

Abfahrt f ['ʔapfaːt] departure

Abfall m ['ʔapfal] rubbish, garbage

Abfallbeutel m ['ʔapfalbɔɪtl] bin liner

Abfalleimer m ['ʔapfal'ʔaɪmɐ] bin

Abflug m ['ʔapfluːk] departure, take-off

Abführmittel n ['ʔapfyɐˌmɪtl] laxative

abgeben ['ʔapgeːbm] hand in, leave **abgelegen** ['ʔapgəleːgn] isolated

abholen ['ʔaphoːln] call for, pick up; **abholen lassen** ['ʔaphoːln lasn] send for

Abkürzung f ['ʔapkʰʏɐtsʊŋ] abbreviation; short-cut

ablehnen ['ʔapleːnn] decline, refuse

abnehmen ['ʔapneːmm] slim

abreisen (nach) ['ʔapʀaɪzn (nax)] leave (for)

absagen ['ʔapzaːgn] *(appointment)* cancel

Abschied nehmen ['ʔapʃiːt neːmm] say goodbye

abschleppen ['ʔapʃlɛpm] tow (away)

Abschleppseil n ['ʔapʃlɛpzaɪl] towrope

Abschleppwagen m ['ʔapʃlɛpvaːgn] breakdown vehicle

abschließen ['ʔapʃliːsn] to lock

abseits ['ʔapzaɪts] offside

Absender/in m/f ['ʔapzɛndɐ/ -dəʀɪn] sender

Abstand m ['ʔapʃtant] distance

abstellen ['ʔapʃtɛln] to park

Abszess m ['ʔaps'ʦɛs] abscess

Abtei f [ʔap'taɪ] abbey

Abteil n [ʔap'taɪl] compartment

Achtung ['ʔaxtʊŋ] attention; **Achtung!** ['ʔaxtʊŋ] look out!

Actionfilm m ['ʔɛktʃnfɪlm] action film

Adapter m [ʔa'daptɐ] adapter

Adresse f [ʔa'dʀɛsə] address

adressieren [ʔadʀɛ'siːʀən/-'siən] to address

Aerobic n [ʔɛ'ʀɔbɪk] aerobics

Agentur f [ʔagɛn'tʰuɐ] agency

ähnlich ['ʔɛːnlɪç] similar

Ahnung f ['ʔaːnʊŋ] idea

Akt m [ʔakt] *(play)* act; *(painting)* nude

Alarmanlage f [ʔa'laːmanlaːgə] alarm system

alkoholfrei [ʔalko'hoːlfʀaɪ] non-alcoholic

alle ['ʔalə] all

allein [ʔa'laɪn] alone

Allergie f [ʔal(ɛ)ɐ'giː] allergy

alles ['ʔaləs] everything

als ['ʔals] when; *(comparison)* than

also ['ʔalzoː] so, thus

alt ['ʔalt] old

Altar m [ʔal'taː] altar

Alter n ['ʔaltʰɐ] age

Alufolie f ['ʔalufoːljə] tin foil

Amerika [ʔaˈmeːʀɪkʰaː] America

Amerikaner/in *m/f* [ʔameʀiˈkaːnɐ/-ˈkaːnəʀɪn] American

Ampel *f* [ˈampl] traffic light

amputiert [ampuˈtiɐt] amputated

Amt *n* [ʔamt] office, department

amtlich [ˈʔamtlɪç] official

Ananas *f* [ˈʔananas] pineapple

anbieten [ˈʔanbiːtn] to offer

anders [ˈʔandɐs] different(ly)

anderswo [ˈʔandɛsvoː] elsewhere

Anfall *m* [ˈʔanfal] attack, fit

Anfang *m* [ˈʔanfaŋ] beginning

anfangen [ˈʔanfaŋŋ] begin

Angabe *f* [ˈʔangaːbə] statement

Angel *f* [ˈʔaŋl] fishing rod

Angelegenheit *f* [ˈʔangələgŋhaɪt] matter

angeln [ˈʔaŋln] go fishing

Angelschein *m* [ˈʔaŋlʃaɪn] fishing licence

angenehm [ˈʔangəneːm] agreeable, pleasant

Angina *f* [aŋˈgiːna] angina

Angst *f* [ʔaŋst] fear

anhalten [ˈʔanhaltn] to stop

Anhänger *m* [ˈʔanhɛŋɐ] pendant

Ankunft *f* [ˈʔankʊnft] arrival

Ankunftszeit *f* [ˈʔankʊnftˌtsaɪt] time of arrival

Anlage *f* [ˈʔanlaːgə] *(letter)* enclosure; park

Anlass *m* [ˈʔanlas] cause, reason

Anlasser *m* [ˈʔanlasɐ] starter (motor)

anlegen in [ˈʔanleːgŋ ʔɪn] dock at, land at

anmelden [ˈʔanmɛldn] announce; sich anmelden [zɪç ˈʔanmɛldn] register

Anmeldung *f* [ˈʔanmɛldʊŋ] registration

annehmen [ˈʔaneːmm] accept

Anorak *m* [ˈʔanoʀak] anorak

Anreisetag *m* [ˈʔanʀaɪzəˌtaːk] day of arrival

Anruf *m* [ˈʔanʀuːf] (phone) call

Anrufbeantworter *m* [ˈʔanfuːfbəˌʔantvɔɐte] answering machine

anrufen [ˈʔanʀuːfn] to call, to phone

anschauen [ˈʔanʃaʊn] look at

Anschluss *m* [ˈʔanʃlʊs] connection

Anschrift *f* [ˈʔanʃʀɪft] address

ansehen [ˈʔanzeːn] look at

Ansicht *f* [ˈʔanzɪçt] opinion, view

Ansichtskarte *f* [ˈʔanzɪçtskaːtə] picture postcard

anstatt [ʔanˈʃtat] instead of

ansteckend [ˈʔanʃtɛkŋt] contagious

anstrengend [ˈʔanʃtʀɛŋŋt] strenuous

antik [ʔanˈtiːk] ancient

Antiquitätengeschäft *n* [ʔanˈtɪkvɪˈtɛːtngəʃɛft] antique shop

Antwort *f* [ˈʔantvɔɐt] answer

antworten [ˈʔantvɔɐtn] to answer, to reply

anwenden [ˈʔanvɛndn] to use

Anwendung *f* [ˈʔanvɛndʊŋ] use

anwesend [ˈʔanveːznt] present

anzeigen [ˈʔantsaɪgŋ] to report

anziehen [ˈʔantsiːn] put on; sich anziehen [zɪç ˈʔantsiːn] dress, get dressed

Anzug *m* [ˈʔantsuːk] *(for men)* suit

anzünden [ˈʔantsʏndn] to light

Äpfel *m pl* [ˈɛpfl] apples

Apfelsinen *f pl* [ˈʔapflˈziːnn] oranges

Apotheke *f* [ʔapoˈteːkə] chemist's

Apparat *m* [ʔapʰaˈʀaːt] gadget; *(Foto~)* camera; *(Fernseh~)* television set

Appetit *m* [ʔapəˈtɪt] appetite

Aprikosen *f pl* [ʔapʀɪˈkoːzn] apricots

April [ʔaˈpʀɪl] April

Aquarell *n* [ʔakvaˈʀɛl] water-colour (picture)

Arbeit *f* [ˈʔaːbaɪt] work; job

arbeiten [ˈʔaːbaɪtn] to work

arbeitslos [ˈʔaːbaɪtsloːs] unemployed

Archäologie f [ˈʔaːçeoloˈgiː] archaeology

Architekt/Architektin [ˈʔaːçɪˈtɛkt/ˈʔaːçɪˈtɛkt ɪn] architect

Architektur f [ˈʔaːçitɛkˈtuɐ] architecture

ärgerlich [ˈʔɛɐɡelɪç] (adj) cross

arm [ˈʔaːm] poor

Armband n [ˈʔaːmbant] bracelet

Armbanduhr f [ˈʔaːmbantˌʔuɐ] wristwatch

Ärmel m [ˈʔɛeml] sleeve

Art f [ˈʔaːt] kind, sort

Artischocken f pl [ˈʔaːtɪˈʃɔkn] artichokes

Aschenbecher m [ˈʔaʃnbɛçɐ] ashtray

Aspirin n [ˈʔaspiˈʀiːn] aspirin

Asthma n [ˈʔastma] asthma

Atembeschwerden f pl [ˈʔaːtmbəʃveɐdn] difficulty in breathing

Atlantik m [ˈʔatˈlantʰɪk] Atlantic

atmen [ˈʔaːtmən] breathe

Attest n [ˈʔaˈtɛst] certificate

Auberginen f pl [ˈʔobeˈʒiːnn] aubergines

auch [ˈʔaʊx] also; too; auch nicht [ˈʔaʊx nɪç(t)] nor, neither

auf [ˈʔaʊf] on

aufbrechen [ˈʔaʊfbʀɛçn] break into/open

Aufenthalt m [ˈʔaʊfntʰalt] stay; (train) stop

Aufenthaltsraum m [ˈʔaʊfntaltsˌʀaʊm] lounge

auffordern [ˈʔaʊfɔɐdən] ask, invite

aufgeben [ˈʔaʊfgeːbm] (luggage) register

aufhalten, sich ~ [zɪç ˈʔaʊfhaltn] to stay

aufhören [ˈʔaʊfhøɐn] to stop

aufladen [ˈʔaʊflaːdn] put on, load

aufmachen [ˈʔaʊfmaxn] to open

aufpassen [ˈʔaʊfpasn] pay attention (to)

aufrufen [ˈʔaʊfʀuːfn] call (out)

aufschieben [ˈʔaʊfʃiːbm] postpone, put off

Aufschnitt m [ˈʔaʊfʃnɪt] cold cuts, lunch meat

aufschreiben [ˈʔaʊfʃʀaɪbm] write down

aufstehen [ˈʔaʊfʃteːn] get up

aufwachen [ˈʔaʊfvaxn] wake up

aufwärts [ˈʔaʊfvɛets] up(wards)

Aufzug m [ˈʔaʊftsuːk] elevator, lift

Auge n [ˈʔaʊgə] eye

Augentropfen m pl [ˈʔaʊgn̩tʀɔpfn] eye-drops

August [ˈʔaʊˈgʊst] August

aus [ˈʔaʊs] from; out of

Ausbildung f [ˈʔaʊsbɪlduŋ] education, training

Ausdruck m [ˈʔaʊsdʀʊk] expression

ausdrücklich [ˈʔaʊsdʀʏklɪç] explicit(ly)

Ausflug m [ˈʔaʊsfluːk] excursion, trip

ausfüllen [ˈʔaʊsfʏln] fill in

Ausgang m [ˈʔaʊsgaŋ] exit, way out

ausgeben [ˈʔaʊsgeːbm] spend

ausgehen [ˈʔaʊsgeːn] go out

ausgeschlossen [ˈʔaʊsgəʃlɔsn] impossible

ausgezeichnet [ˈʔaʊsgəˌtsaɪçnət] excellent

Ausgrabungen f pl [ˈʔaʊsgʀaːbʊŋŋ] excavations

Auskunft f [ˈʔaʊskʰʊnft] information; (Telefon~) telephone operator

Ausland, im/ins ~ [ɪm /ˈʔɪns ˈʔaʊslant] abroad

Ausländer/in m/f [ˈʔaʊslɛndɐ/ -lɛndəʀɪn] foreigner

ausländisch [ˈʔaʊslɛndɪʃ] foreign

Auslandsflug m [ˈʔaʊslantsfluːk] international flight

Auslandsgespräch *n* [ˈʔaʊslantsɡəʃprɛːç] international call

ausleihen [ˈʔaʊslaɪn] borrow

Auslöser *m* [ˈʔaʊsløːze] *(camera)* shutter release

ausmachen [ˈʔaʊsmaxn] *(light)* turn off, *(fire)* put out; agree

Auspuff *m* [ˈʔaʊspʊf] exhaust (pipe)

ausrichten [ˈʔaʊsrɪçtn] tell

ausruhen, sich ~ [zɪç ˈʔaʊsruːn] to rest

Aussage *f* [ˈʔaʊszaːɡə] statement

aussagen [ˈʔaʊszaːɡn] to state

Ausschlag *m* [ˈʔaʊʃlaːk] rash

aussehen [ˈʔaʊsɛːn] to look

außen [ˈʔaʊsn] outside

außer [ˈʔaʊsɐ] except

außerdem [ˈʔaʊsɐdeːm] besides

außergewöhnlich [ˈʔaʊsɐɡəvøːnlɪç] extraordinary

außerhalb [ˈʔaʊsɐhalp] outside

Aussicht *f* [ˈʔaʊszɪçt] view

Aussichtspunkt *m* [ˈʔaʊsɪçtspʊnt] vantage point

aussprechen [ˈʔaʊ(s)ʃprɛçn] pronounce

Ausstellung *f* [ˈʔaʊʃtɛlʊŋ] exhibition, show

aussuchen [ˈʔaʊsuːxn] pick out

Austausch *m* [ˈʔaʊstaʊʃ] exchange

austauschen [ˈʔaʊsthaʊʃn] to exchange

Austern *f pl* [ˈʔaʊstɐn] oysters

ausüben [ˈʔaʊsʔyːbm] *(profession)* practise

Ausverkauf *m* [ˈʔaʊsfɛkhaʊf] (clearance) sale

Auswahl *f* [ˈʔaʊsvaːl] choice

auszahlen [ˈʔaʊstsaːln] pay out

Auto *n* [ˈʔaʊthoː] car; Auto fahren [ˈʔaʊthoˌfaːn] drive a car

Autobahn *f* [ˈʔaʊtobaːn] freeway, motorway

Autobahnausfahrt *f* [ˈʔaʊtobaːnˌʔaʊsfaːt] (motorway) exit

Autobahngebühren *f* [ˈʔaʊtobaːnɡəˌbyːrən] motorway toll

Automat *m* [ˈʔaʊthoˈmaːt] vending machine

Automatikgetriebe *n* [ˈʔaʊtoˈmaːtɪkɡəˌtriːbə] automatic (transmission)

automatisch [ˈʔaʊthoˈmaːthɪʃ] automatic

Autoradio *n* [ˈʔaʊtoˌraːdjo] car radio

Avocado *f* [ˈʔavoˈkaːdo] avocado

B

Baby *n* [ˈbeːbiː] baby

Babyfon *n* [ˈbeːbifoːn] baby intercom

Babylift [ˈbeːbilɪft] baby lift

Babyschale *f* [ˈbeːbiʃaːlə] baby seat

Babysitter *m* [ˈbeːbisɪtɐ] babysitter

Bäckerei *f* [bɛkəˈraɪ] baker's

Badeanzug *m* [ˈbaːdəˌʔantsuːk] swimsuit

Badehose *f* [ˈbaːdəhoːzə] swimming trunks

Bademantel *m* [ˈbaːdəmantl] bathrobe

Bademeister/in *m/f* [ˈbaːdəmaɪstɐ/-tərɪn] lifeguard

baden [baːdn] to swim

Badeort *m* [ˈbaːdəʔɔet] seaside resort, beach resort

Badeschuhe *m pl* [ˈbaːdəʃuə] bathing shoes

Badewanne *f* [ˈbaːdəvanə] bath

Badezimmer *n* [ˈbaːdətsɪmɐ] bathroom

Badminton *n* [ˈbɛtmɪntn] badminton

Bahnhof *m* [ˈbaːnhoːf] station

bald [balt] soon

211

Balkon m [bal'kɔŋ] balcony
Ball m [bal] ball; *(event)* ball, dance
Ballett n [ba'lɛt] ballet
Bananen f pl [ba'na:nn] bananas
Band f [bɛ(:)nt] band
Bänderriss m ['bɛndeRɪs] torn ligament
Bank f [baŋk] bank; bench
Bar f [ba:] bar
bar zahlen ['ba: tsa:ln] pay (in) cash
Bargeld n ['ba:gɛlt] cash
barock [ba'Rɔk] baroque
Barsch m [ba:ʃ] *(fish)* perch
Bart m [ba:t] beard
Basilikum n [ba'zi:lıkʊm] basil
Basketball m ['ba:skətbal] basketball
Batterie f [batə'Ri:] battery
Bauch m [baʊx] stomach
Bauernhof m ['baʊenho:f] farm
Baum m [baʊm] tree
Baumwolle f ['baʊmvɔlə] cotton
beachten [bə'ʔaxtn] pay attention to
beantworten [bə'ʔantvɔetn] to reply, to answer
Bearbeitungsgebühr f [bə'ʔa:baɪtʊŋsgə,byɐ] service charge
bedauern [bə'daʊen] to regret
bedeutend [bə'dɔɪtnt] important
Bedeutung f [bə'dɔɪtʰʊŋ] meaning; importance
bedienen [bə'di:nn] serve
Bedienung f [bə'di:nʊŋ] service; waitress
beeilen, sich ~ [zıç bə'ʔaɪln] to hurry
beeindruckend [bə'ʔaɪndRʊkŋt] impressive
befahrbar [bə'fa:ba:] passable
befinden, sich ~ [zıç bə'fɪndn] be
befreundet sein [bə'fRɔɪndət zaɪn] be friends
befriedigt [bə'fRi:dıçt] satisfied

befürchten [bə'fvɛçtn] to fear, be afraid (of)
begegnen [bə'ge:kn (ə)n] meet
begeistert (von) [bə'gaɪstet fɔn] enthusiastic (about)
Beginn m [bə'gɪn] beginning
beginnen [bə'gɪnn] begin
begleiten [bə'glaɪtn] accompany
Begleitperson f [bə'glaɪtp(ɛ)ɐ,zo:n] accompanying person
begrüßen [bə'gRy:sn] greet, welcome
behalten [bə'haltn] keep
Behälter m [bə'hɛltʰɐ] container
behandeln [bə'handln] to treat
behaupten [bə'haʊptn] maintain; insist
Behinderte m/f [bə'hɪndetə] disabled person
behindertengerecht [bə'hɪndetngə,Rɛçt] suitable for the disabled
Behindertentoilette f [bə'hɪndetnto,lɛtə] toilet for the disabled
Behinderung f [bə'hɪndəRʊŋ] disability, handicap
Behörde f [bə'høedə] authorities
beide ['baɪdə] both
Beifall m ['baɪfal] applause
beige [be:ʃ] beige
Bein n [baɪn] leg
beinahe ['baɪna:] almost, nearly
Beispiel n ['baɪʃpi:l] example; **zum Beispiel** [tsʊm 'baɪʃpi:l] for example
beißen [baɪsn] to bite
bekannt [bə'kʰant] well-known; **bekannt machen** [bə'kʰant maxn] introduce
Bekannte m/f [bə'kantə] acquaintance, friend
Bekanntschaft f [bə'kʰantʃaft] acquaintance
bekommen [bə'kʰɔmm] get, receive

212

belästigen [bə'lɛstɪgn̩] bother, harrass (sexually)

belegte Brötchen [bə'le:ktə brø:tçn̩] filled rolls

beleidigen [bə'laɪdɪgn̩] to insult

Beleidigung f [bə'laɪdɪgʊŋ] insult

Belgien ['bɛlgɪən] Belgium

Belichtungsmesser m [bə'lɪçtʊŋsˌmɛsə] light meter

Beliebige, jeder ~ [ˌjeːdɐ bə'liːbɪgə] any

belohnen [bəloːnn̩] to reward

Belohnung f [bə'loːnʊŋ] reward

bemerken [bə'mɛɐkn̩] to notice; *(say)* to remark

bemühen, sich ~ [zɪç bə'myːn] try hard

benachrichtigen [bə'naːxrɪçtɪgn̩] inform

benötigen [bə'nøːtʰɪgn̩] need

benutzen [bə'nʊtsn̩] to use; *(means of transport)* to take

Benzinkanister m [bɛn'tsiːnkaˌnɪstə] petrol can

Benzinpumpe f [bɛn'tsiːnpʊmpə] petrol pump

beobachten [bə'ʔoːbaxtn̩] observe, watch

bequem [bə'kveːm] comfortable

berechnen [bə'rɛçn(ə)n] calculate

bereit [bə'raɪt] ready

bereits [bə'raɪts] already

Berg m [bɛɐk] mountain

Bergdorf n ['bɛɐkdoɐf] mountain village

Bergstation f ['bɛɐkʃtaˌtsjoːn] summit station, top station

Bergsteigen n ['bɛɐkʃtaɪgn̩] mountaineering/mountain climbing

Beruf m [bə'ruːf] job, profession

beruhigen, sich ~ [zɪç bə'rʊɪgn̩] calm down

Beruhigungsmittel n [bə'rʊɪgʊŋsmɪtl̩] sedative, tranquilliser

berühmt [bə'ryːmt] famous

berühren [bə'ryːrən /-'ryɐn] to touch

Berührung f [bə'ryːrʊŋ] contact

beschädigen [bə'ʃɛːdɪgn̩] to damage

Beschädigung f [bə'ʃɛːdɪgʊŋ] damage

Bescheid wissen [bə'ʃaɪt vɪsn̩] know

bescheinigen [bə'ʃaɪnɪgn̩] certify

Bescheinigung f [bə'ʃaɪnɪgʊŋ] statement

beschließen [bə'ʃliːsn̩] decide; make up one's mind

beschreiben [bə'ʃraɪbm̩] describe

besetzt [bə'zɛtst] *(seat)* occupied, taken; full; *(telephone)* engaged, busy

besichtigen [bə'zɪçtɪgn̩] to visit

Besichtigung f [bə'zɪçtɪgʊŋ] tour

besitzen [bə'zɪtsn̩] to own

Besitzer/in m/f [bə'zɪtsə/-'zɪtsərɪn] owner

besonders [bə'zɔndɐs] particularly, especially

besorgen [bə'zɔɐgn̩] get

besser ['bɛsə] better

bestätigen [bə'ʃtɛːtʰɪgn̩] confirm

beste(r, s) ['bɛstə (-tə, -təs)] best

bestechen [bə'ʃtɛçn̩] to bribe, to corrupt

bestechlich [bə'ʃtɛçlɪç] corrupt

Besteck n [bə'ʃtɛk] cutlery

bestehen auf [bə'ʃteːn ʔaʊf] insist on; **bestehen aus** ['bə'ʃteːn ʔaʊs] consist of

bestellen [bə'ʃtɛln̩] to order

Bestellung f [bə'ʃtɛlʊŋ] order

bestimmt [bə'ʃtɪmt] certain(ly)

Besuch m [bə'zuːx] visit

besuchen, jdn ~ [ˌjemandn bə'zuːxn̩] visit s. o., call on s. o.

Besuchszeit f [bə'zuːxstsaɪt] visiting hours

beten [be:tn̩] pray

betrachten [bə'traxtn̩] look at

Betrag m [bə'traːk] amount

betragen [bə'tʀa:gn̩] be, come/amount to

Betreuung f [bə'tʀɔɪʊŋ] care

Betrug m [bə'tʀu:k] swindle; fraud

betrügerisch [bə'tʀy:gəʀɪʃ] deceitful

betrunken [bə'tʀʊŋkn̩] drunk

Bett n [bɛt] bed; ins Bett gehen ['ʔɪns 'bɛt ge:n] go to bed

Bettdecke f ['bɛtdɛkə] blanket

Bettwäsche f ['bɛtvɛʃə] bed linen

beunruhigen, sich ~ [zɪç bə'ʔʊnʀʊɪgn̩] to worry

bevor [bə'foɐ] before

Bewohner/in m/f [bə'vo:nɐ/ -'vo:nəʀɪn] inhabitant

bewölkt [bə'vœlkt] (weather) cloudy

bewusst [bə'vʊst] aware

bewusstlos [bə'vʊstlo:s] unconscious

bezahlen [bə'tsa:ln̩] to pay

bezaubernd [bə'tsaʊbɐnt] charming

Biene f ['bi:nə] bee

Bier n [biɐ] beer

bieten [bi:tn̩] to offer

Bikini m [bi'ki:ni] bikini

Bild n [bɪlt] picture; illustration; painting

bilden [bɪldn̩] to form

Bildhauer/in m/f ['bɪlthaʊɐ/'bɪlthaʊəʀɪn] sculptor

billig ['bɪlɪç] cheap

Bioladen m ['biola:dn̩] organic food shop

Birnen f pl [bɪʀnn̩] pears

bis [bɪs] to; (time) til(l), until; bis jetzt [bɪs 'jɛtst] til(l) now

Bitte f ['bɪthə] request

bitten, jdn um etw. ~ [jemandn ʊm ˌʔɛtvas 'bɪtn̩] ask s.o. for s.th.

bitter ['bɪthə] bitter

Blähungen f pl ['blɛ:ʊŋŋ] (med) wind

Blase f ['bla:zə] bladder; blister

blau [blaʊ] blue

Blazer m ['ble:zɐ] blazer

bleiben [blaɪbm̩] remain, stay

Blick m [blɪk] look; view

blind [blɪnt] blind

Blinddarmentzündung f ['blɪntda:mɛnˌtsʏndʊŋ] appendicitis

Blinde m/f ['blɪndə] blind person

Blindenhund m ['blɪndnhʊnt] guide dog

Blindenschrift f ['blɪndnʃʀɪft] braille

Blinklicht n ['blɪŋklɪçt] indicator

Blitz m [blɪts] lightning

Blitzgerät n ['blɪtsgəʀɛ:t] (camera) flash

Block m [blɔk] writing pad

blöd(e) [blø:t / 'blø:də] silly, stupid

blond [blɔnt] blond(e)

Blues m [blu:s] blues

Blume f ['blu:mə] flower

Blumengeschäft n ['blu:mmgəʃɛft] florist's

Blumenkohl m ['blu:mmko:l] cauliflower

Blumenstrauß m ['blu:mmʃtʀaʊs] bunch of flowers

Bluse f ['blu:zə] blouse

Blut n [blu:t] blood

bluten [blu:tn̩] bleed

Blutgruppe f ['blu:tgʀʊpə] blood group

Bluthochdruck m ['blu:tho:xdʀʊk] high blood pressure

Blutung f ['blu:tʊŋ] bleeding

Blutvergiftung f ['blu:tfɐgɪftʊŋ] blood-poisoning

Bö f [bø:] gust of wind

Boden m [bo:dn̩] ground; floor

Bogen m ['bo:gn̩] arch

Bohnen f pl [bo:nn̩] beans

Bordkarte f ['bɔɐtka:tə] boarding card

böse ['bø:zə] evil; naughty; angry

botanischer Garten m [bo'tanɪʃə

'ga:tn] botanic garden
Botschaft f ['bo:tʃaft] embassy
Boutique f [bu'ti:k] boutique
Brand m [brant] fire
Bratensoße f ['bra:tnzo:sə] gravy
brauchen [brauxn] need, want;
(time) take
braun [braun] brown
Brechreiz m ['brɛçraɪts] nausea
breit [braɪt] broad, wide
Breite f ['braɪtə] width
Bremse f ['brɛmzə] brake; horsefly
Bremsflüssigkeit f
['brɛmsflysɪçkaɪt] brake fluid
Bremslichter f ['brɛmslɪçtə] brake
lights
brennen [brɛnn] to burn
Brennholz n ['brɛnhɔlts] firewood
Brennspiritus m ['brɛnʃpiritus]
methylated spirits
Brief m [bri:f] letter
Briefmarke f ['bri:f,ma:kə] *(pos-tage)* stamp
Briefmarkenautomat m
['bri:fma:knʔauto,ma:t] stamp
machine
Briefpapier n ['bri:fpapiɐ] writing
paper
Brieftasche f ['bri:ftʰaʃə] wallet,
billfold
Briefumschlag m ['bri:fumʃla:k]
envelope
bringen [('hee)brɪŋn] bring
Brombeeren f pl ['brɔmbe:rən]
blackberries
Bronchien f pl ['brɔnçɪən]
bronchial tubes
Bronchitis f [brɔn'çi:tɪs]
bronchitis
Bronze f ['brɔnsə] bronze
Brosche f ['brɔʃə] brooch
Brot n [bro:t] bread
Brötchen n pl [brø:tçn] rolls
Brücke f ['brʏkə] bridge
Bruder m ['bru:dɐ] brother
Brunnen m [('brunn] fountain,
well

Brust f [brust] chest
Buch n [bu:x] book
buchen [bu:xn] *(seat)* to book
Buchhandlung f ['bu:xhantlʊŋ]
book shop
Büchse f ['bʏksə] can, tin
buchstabieren [bux∫ta'bi:rən/
-'biɐn] to spell
Bucht f [buxt] bay
Buchung f ['bu:xʊŋ] booking
bügeln [by:gln] to iron
Bummel m [buml] stroll
Bungalow m ['bʊŋgalo:]
bungalow
Burg f [bʊɛk] *(fortress)* castle
Bürgschaft f ['bʏɛkʃaft] security
Büro n [by'ro:] office
Bürste f ['bʏɛstə] brush
Bus m [bʊs] bus
Busbahnhof m ['bʊs,ba:nho:f]
bus station
Busch m [bʊʃ] bush
Butter f ['bʊtɐ] butter
Buttermilch f ['bʊtɐmɪlç] butter-milk
Bypass m ['baɪpa:s] bypass

C

Café n [kʰa'fe:] café
Camcorder m ['kamkhɔedɐ] cam-corder
Camping n ['kɛmpɪŋ] camping
Campingführer m ['kɛmpɪŋfy:ʀɐ]
camping guide
Campingplatz m ['kɛmpɪŋplats]
camping site
CD f [tse'de:] CD
CD-Spieler m [tse'de:ʃpi:lɐ] CD
player
Champagner m [ʃam'panjɐ]
champagne
Chauffeur m [ʃɔ'føɐ] chauffeur,
driver
Chef/Chefin m/f [ʃɛf/ʃɛfɪn] boss,

head

chemisch reinigen ['çe:mɪʃ 'raɪnɪgn] dry-clean

Chipkarte f ['tʃɪpka:tə] chip card

Chirurg/Chirurgin m/f [çɪˈʀʊɐk/çɪˈʀʊɐgɪn] surgeon

Chor m [koɐ] choir

Christentum n ['kʀɪstntu:m] Christianity

Clubhaus n ['klʊphaʊs] clubhouse

Cousin/e m/f [kʰʊˈzɛŋ / kʰʊˈzi:nə] cousin

Creme f [kʀɛ:m] cream

Curling n ['kə:lɪŋ] curling

D

da [da:] *(place)* there; *(time)* then; *(reason)* as, because; **da sein** ['da:zaɪn] be present, be there

Dach n [dax] roof

dagegen sein [da'ge:gn zaɪn] be against s. th.

daheim [da'haɪm] at home

daher ['da:heɐ] therefore

damals ['da:ma (:)ls] then, at that time

Damen [da:mm] Ladies

Damenbinden f pl ['da:mmbɪndn] sanitary towels

Damenslip m ['da:mənslɪp] panties

danach [da'na:x] afterwards

danken ['daŋkn] thank

dann [dan] then

Darm m [da:m] intestines

dass [das] that

dasselbe [das'zɛlbə] the same

Datum n ['da:tʰʊm] date

dauern ['daʊen] to last

Dauerwelle f ['daʊevɛlə] perm

Deck n [dɛk] deck

Decke f ['dɛkə] ceiling

Defekt m [de'fɛkt] fault

dein [daɪn] your

denken (an) ['dɛŋkn ʔan] think (of)

Denkmal n ['dɛŋkma:l] monument

denn [dɛn] for; because

Deo n ['deo] deodorant

derselbe [de'zɛlbə] the same

deshalb ['dɛshalp] therefore

Desinfektionsmittel n [dezɪnfɛk'tsjo:nsmɪtl] disinfectant

desinfizieren [dezɪnfi'tsi:ʀən] disinfect

deutlich ['dɔɪtlɪç] distinct(ly), clear(ly)

deutsch [dɔɪtʃ] German

Deutsche m/f ['dɔɪtʃə] German

Deutschland ['dɔɪtʃlant] Germany

Dezember [de'tsɛmbɐ] December

Diabetes m [dia'be:təs] diabetes

Diabetiker/in m/f [dia'be:tɪkɐ/-kəʀɪn] *(person)* diabetic

diabetisch [dia'be:tɪʃ] diabetic

Diagnose f [dia'gno:zə] diagnosis

Diät f [di'ɛ:t] diet

dich [dɪç] you

dicht [dɪçt] *(crowd, fog etc.)* thick

dick [dɪk] thick, swollen; *(person)* stout, fat

Dieb/Diebin m/f [di:p/'di:bɪn] thief

Diebstahl m ['di:pʃta:l] theft

dienen [di:nn] to serve

Dienst m [di:nst] service

Dienstag ['di:nsta:k] Tuesday

diese ['di:zə] these, those

diese(r, s) ['di:zə/'di:zɐ/'di:zəs] that, this

Digitalkamera f [digi'ta:lˌkaməʀa] digital camera

Ding n [dɪŋ] thing

Diphtherie f [dɪftə'ʀi:] diphtheria

dir [diɐ] to/for you

direkt [di'ʀɛkt] direct

Dirigent/Dirigentin m/f [diʀi'gɛnt/diʀi'gɛntɪn] conductor

Diskothek f [dɪsko'te:k] discotheque

doch [dɔx] yet, however
Dokumentarfilm *m*
[dɔkumɛn'ta:fɪlm] documentary
Donnerstag ['dɔnɐsta:k] Thursday
Doppel *n* [dɔpl] doubles
doppelt [dɔplt] *(adj)* double; *(adv)* twice
Dorf *n* [dɔɐf] village
dort [dɔɐt] there
dorthin [dɔɐthɪn] *(location)* there
Dose *f* ['do:zə] tin, can
Dosenöffner *m* ['do:zn̩ʔœfnɐ] tin opener
Drachenfliegen *n* ['dʀaxnfli:gn̩] hang-gliding
Drama *n* ['dʀa:ma] drama
draußen ['dʀaʊsn̩] outside
Dressing *f* ['dʀɛsɪŋ] *(food)* dressing
drin [dʀɪn] inside
dringend [dʀɪŋŋt] urgent
drinnen [dʀɪnn̩] indoors
dritte(r, s) ['dʀɪtə (-tɐ, -təs)] third
du [du:] you
dumm [dʊm] stupid
dunkel [dʊŋkl] dark
dunkelblau [dʊŋkl'blaʊ] dark blue
dünn [dʏn] thin; slim, slender
durch [dʊɐç] through; *(quer ~)* across; by (means of)
durchaus nicht [dʊɐç'ʔaʊs nɪç(t)] not at all
Durchfall *m* ['dʊɐçfal] diarrhoea
durchgebraten ['dʊɐçgəbʀa:tn̩] well-done
Durchreise, auf der ~ ['ʔaʊf de 'dʊɐçʀaɪzə] passing through
durchschnittlich ['dʊɐçʃnɪtlɪç] average
dürfen [dʏɐfn̩] be allowed
dürftig ['dʏɐftɪç] *(sparse)* thin
Dusche *f* ['du:ʃə] shower
Duschgel *n* ['du:ʃge:l] shower gel
Duschsitz *m* ['du:ʃzɪts] shower seat
Dynastie *f* [dynas'ti:] dynasty

E

Ebbe *f* ['ʔɛbə] low tide
eben ['ʔe:bm̩] flat; smooth; *(time)* just now
Ebene *f* ['ʔe:bənə] plain
ebenerdig ['ʔe:bm̩ʔeedɪç] at ground level
echt [ʔɛçt] genuine
Ecke *f* ['ʔɛkʰə] corner
Ehefrau *f* ['ʔe:əfʀaʊ] wife
Ehemann *m* ['ʔe:əman] husband
Ehepaar *n* ['ʔe:əpa:] couple
eher ['ʔee] rather
Eier *n pl* ['ʔaɪɐ] eggs
eigen ['ʔaɪgn̩] own; peculiar, strange, odd, weird
Eigenschaft *f* ['ʔaɪgn̩ʃaft] quality, characteristic
eigentlich ['ʔaɪgn̩tlɪç] actual(ly)
Eigentümer/in *m/f*
['ʔaɪgn̩ty:me/-məʀɪn] owner
eilig ['ʔaɪlɪç] urgent; **es eilig haben** ['ʔəs 'ʔaɪlɪç ha:bm̩] be in a hurry
ein(e) ['ʔɪn /'ʔaɪnə] a, one
einchecken ['ʔaɪntʃɛkn̩] check in

einfach ['ʔaɪnfax] simple
Einfahrt *f* ['ʔaɪnfa:t] entrance
einfarbig ['ʔaɪnfaʀbɪç] plain
Eingang *m* ['ʔaɪngaŋ] entrance
einheimisch ['ʔaɪnhaɪmɪʃ] native, local
einig sein ['ʔaɪnɪç zaɪn] agree
einige ['ʔaɪnɪgə] some
einigen, sich ~ [zɪç 'ʔaɪnɪgn̩] agree
einkaufen ['ʔaɪnkʰaʊfn̩] buy, go shopping
einladen ['ʔaɪnla:dn̩] invite
einmal ['ʔaɪ (n)ma:l] once
einpacken ['ʔaɪnpʰakn̩] wrap, pack
eins ['ʔaɪns] one
einsam ['ʔaɪnza:m] lonely; secluded, isolated
Einschreibebrief *m*

['ʔaɪnʃRaɪbəbʀi:f] registered letter

einsteigen ['ʔaɪnʃtaɪgn] get in/on

eintreffen ['ʔaɪntʀɛfn] arrive (at)

Eintritt m ['ʔaɪntʀɪt] entrance, admission

Eintrittskarte f ['ʔaɪntʀɪts,kʰaːtʰə] (admission) ticket

Eintrittspreis m ['ʔaɪntʀɪtspʀaɪs] admission charge

Einwohner/in m/f ['ʔaɪnvoːnɐ/ -nəʀɪn] inhabitant

Einzel n ['ʔaɪntsəl] singles

einzelne, jeder ~ [,jeːdɐ 'ʔaɪntslnə] each

einzig ['ʔaɪntsɪç] only

Eis n ['ʔaɪs] ice

Eisbahn f ['ʔaɪsbaːn] ice rink

Eishockey n ['ʔaɪshɔkeː] ice hockey

Eiter m ['ʔaɪtɐ] pus

Elastikbinde f ['ʔeˈlastɪkbɪndə] elastic bandage

elektrisch ['ʔeˈlɛktʀɪʃ] electric

Eltern pl ['ʔɛltʰɐn] parents

empfangen ['ʔɛmpˈfaŋn] receive; greet, welcome

Empfänger m ['ʔɛmpˈfɛŋɐ] addressee

empfehlen ['ʔɛmpˈfeːln] recommend

Ende n ['ʔɛndə] end

endgültig ['ʔɛntgʏltʰɪç] definite; definitely

endlich ['ʔɛntlɪç] finally

Endstation f ['ʔɛntʃtatsjoːn] terminus

eng ['ʔɛŋ] narrow; *(clothes)* tight

England ['ʔɛŋlant] England

Engländer/in m/f ['ʔɛŋlɛndɐ/ -dəʀɪn] Englishman/-woman

englisch ['ʔɛŋlɪʃ] English

entdecken ['ʔɛntˈdɛkn] discover

Entfernung f ['ʔɛntˈfɛɐnʊŋ] distance

entgegengesetzt ['ʔɛntˈgeːŋgəˌzɛtst] opposite

entscheiden ['ʔɛntˈʃaɪdn] decide

entschuldigen ['ʔɛntˈʃʊldɪgn] to excuse; **sich ~** [zɪç 'ʔɛntˈʃʊldɪgn] apologize

Entschuldigung f ['ʔɛntˈʃʊldɪgʊŋ] apology; excuse; **Entschuldigung!** sorry!; **Ich bitte um Entschuldigung!** ['ɪç 'bɪtə 'ʊm ɛntˈʃʊldɪgʊŋ] I beg your pardon!; **Entschuldigung, ...** excuse me, ...

enttäuscht ['ʔɛntˈtʰɔɪʃt] disappointed

entweder ... oder ['ʔɛntveːdɐ ... 'ʔoːdɐ] either ... or

entwickeln ['ʔɛntˈvɪkln] develop

entzückend ['ʔɛnˈtsʏknt] charming, delightful

Entzündung f ['ʔɛnˈtsʏndʊŋ] inflammation

Epilepsie f [epilɛpˈsi] epilepsy

Epoche f ['ʔeˈpɔxə] epoch

er ['ʔeɐ] he

Erbsen f pl ['ʔɛɐpsn] peas

Erdbeeren f pl ['ʔeɐtbeːʀən] strawberries

Erde f ['ʔeɐdə] earth

Erdgeschoss n ['ʔeɐtgəʃɔs] ground floor, *(US)* first floor

Ereignis n ['ʔɛˈʔaɪknɪs] event

erfahren ['ʔeˈfaː(ʀə)n] learn, hear, experience; *(adj)* experienced

Erfolg m ['ʔeˈfɔlk] success

erfreut (über) ['ʔeˈfʀɔɪt ('ʔyːbɐ)] pleased (with), glad (of)

erhalten ['ʔeˈhaltn] receive, get

erholen, sich ~ [zɪç 'ʔeˈhoːln] recover

Erholung f ['ʔeˈhoːlʊŋ] rest

erinnern, sich ~ [zɪç ɐ'ʔɪnɐn] remember

Erkältung f ['ʔeˈkɛltʊŋ] cold

Ermäßigung f ['ʔeˈmɛːsɪgʊŋ] reduction

ernst ['ʔɛɐnst] serious

E-Rollstuhl m ['ʔeːˌʀɔlʃtuːl] electric wheelchair

erreichen ['ʔeˈʀaɪçn] to reach

Ersatz m ['ʔeˈzats] replacement; compensation

Ersatzreifen m ['ʔe'zatsʀaɪfn]
spare tyre

erschöpft ['ʔe'ʃœpft] exhausted

erschrecken ['ʔe'ʃʀɛkŋ] frighten,
startle; be alarmed

erschrocken ['ʔe'ʃʀɔkŋ] afraid,
alarmed

ersetzen ['ʔe'zɛtsn] replace

erst [eest] first of all; *(not later than)* only

erste(r, s) ['ʔeestə (-tə, -təs)] first

ertragen ['ʔe'tʀa:gŋ] to bear, to
stand

Erwachsene(r) m/f
['ʔe'vaks (ə)nə/'ʔe'vaks(ə)nə] adult

erwarten ['ʔe'va:tn] expect, wait
for

erwidern ['ʔe'vi:dən] to reply

erzählen ['ʔe'tsɛ:ln] tell

Erzeugnis n ['ʔe'tsɔɪknɪs] product

Erziehung f ['ʔe'tsiʊŋ] education

essbar ['ʔɛsba:] edible

essen ['ʔɛsn] eat

Essen n ['ʔɛsn] meal; food

Essig m ['ʔɛsɪç] vinegar

Esszimmer n ['ʔɛstsɪmɐ] (private)
dining room

Etagenbett n ['ʔe'ta:ʒnbɛt] bunk
bed

etwa ['ʔɛtva:] about

etwas ['ʔɛtvas] something; anything; a little

EU-Bürger/in ['ʔe'ʔu: bʀɐgɐ/
-gəʀɪn] EU citizen

euch ['ʔɔɪç] you

euer ['ʔɔɪɐ] your

Euro m ['ʔɔɪʀo] euro

Europa ['ʔɔɪ'ʀo:pʰa:] Europe

Europäer/in m/f ['ʔɔɪʀo'pɛːɐ/
-pɛːəʀɪn] European

europäisch ['ʔɔɪʀo'pʰɛ:ɪʃ] European

eventuell ['ʔevɛntʊ'(ʔ)ɛl] perhaps,
possible

Exponat n ['ʔɛkspo'na:t] exhibit

Expressionismus m
['ʔɛkspʀɛsjo'nɪsmus] expressionism

extra ['ʔɛkstʀa:] extra, special

F

Fabrik f [fa'bʀi (:)k] factory

Facharzt/-ärztin m/f
['faxa:tst/'fax'ʔɛɐtstɪn] specialist

Fähre f ['fɛ:ʀə] ferry

fahren [fa: (ʀə)n] go (by train, car
etc.); drive

Fahrer/in m/f ['fa:ʀɐ/'fa:ʀəʀɪn]
driver

Fahrgast m ['fa:gast] passenger

Fahrkartenautomat m
['fa:ka:tn'ʔʊto̩ma:t] ticket
machine

Fahrkartenschalter m
['fa:ka:tn̩ʃaltɐ] ticket office

Fahrplan m ['fa:pla:n] timetable

Fahrpreis m ['fa:pʀaɪs] fare

Fahrrad n ['fa:ʀat] bicycle, bike

Fahrradweg m ['fa:ʀatve:k] cycle
path

Fahrstuhl m ['fa:ʃtu:l] lift, elevator

Fahrt f [fa:t] journey, trip, voyage;
(car) drive

fair [feɐ] fair

fallen [faln] to fall

falls [fals] in case, if

Fallschirmspringen n
['falʃɪɐmʃpʀɪŋŋ] parachuting

falsch [falʃ] wrong; deceitful

Faltrollstuhl m ['falt̩ʀɔlʃtu:l]
folding wheelchair

Familie f [fa'mi:ljə] family

fangen [faŋŋ] to catch

färben [fɛɐbm] to dye

farbig ['faʀbɪç] coloured

Farbstift m ['fa:pʃtɪft] coloured
pencil

Fassade f [fa'sa:də] façade, front

fast [fast] almost, nearly

faul [faʊl] lazy; *(fruit)* rotten

Februar ['fe:bʀʊa:] February

Federball m ['fe:dəbal] shuttlecock; badminton

fehlen [fe:ln] be missing

Fehler m ['fe:lɐ] mistake; fault

Fehlgeburt f ['fe:lgəbʊɐt] miscarriage

fein [faɪn] fine; delicate; distinguished

Feinkostgeschäft n
['faɪnkɔstgəˌʃɛft] delicatessen

Feld n [fɛlt] field

Fell n [fɛl] fur, fleece

Fels m [fɛls] rock; cliff

Fenchel m [fɛnçl] fennel

Fenster n ['fɛnstɐ] window

Fensterplatz m ['fɛnstɐplats]
window seat

Ferien pl ['fe:ʁɪən ('feejən)] holidays, vacation

Ferienanlage f ['fe:ʁɪənʔanla:gə]
holiday camp

Ferienhaus n ['fe:ʁɪənhaʊs]
holiday home

Ferngespräch n ['fɛɐngəʃpʁɛ:ç]
long-distance call

Fernlicht n ['fɛɐnlɪçt] full beam,
high beam

Fernsehapparat m
['fɛɐnzeʔapaˌʁa:t]   (TV) set

Fernsehraum m ['fɛɐnze:ˌʁaʊm]
television lounge

fertig ['fɛɐtʰɪç] ready; finished

fest [fɛst] firm, solid, rigid

Fest n [fɛst] celebration(s), party

Festival n ['fɛstɪval] festival

feststellen ['fɛ(st)ʃtɛln] to state

Festung f ['fɛstʊŋ] fortress

fett [fɛt] fat; greasy

fettarme Milch ['fɛtʔa:mə mɪlç]
low-fat milk

feucht [fɔɪçt] moist, damp

Feuer n ['fɔɪɐ] fire

feuergefährlich ['fɔɪɐgəˌfeelɪç]
(in)flammable

Feuerlöscher m ['fɔɪɐlœʃɐ] fire
extinguisher

Feuermelder m ['fɔɪɐmɛldɐ] fire
alarm

Feuerwerk n ['fɔɪɐvɛɐk] fireworks
display

Feuerzeug n ['fɔɪɐtsɔɪk] lighter

Fieber n ['fi:bɐ] fever

Fieberthermometer n
['fi:bɐtɛɛmoˌme:tɐ] thermometer

Film m [fɪlm] film

Filmempfindlichkeit f
['fɪlmɛmpfɪntlɪçkaɪt] film speed

Filmschauspieler/-in m/f
['fɪlmʃaʊʃpi:lɐ/-ləʁɪn] film/movie
actor/actress

finden [fɪndn] to find

Finger m ['fɪŋɐ] finger

finster ['fɪnstɐ] dark

Firma f ['fɪʁma:] firm, company

Fischerhafen m ['fɪʃɛha:fn] fishing
port

Fischgeschäft n ['fɪʃgəʃɛft]
fishmonger's

fit [fɪt] fit

Fitnesscenter n ['fɪtnəsˌtsɛntɐ]
fitness centre

FKK-Strand m ['ʔɛfka'ka:ʃtʁant]
nudist beach

flach [flax] flat; level

Fläschchenwärmer m
['flɛʃçənvɛɛmɐ] bottle warmer

Flasche f ['flaʃə] bottle

Flaschenöffner m ['flaʃnʔœfnɐ]
bottle opener

Fleck m [flɛk] stain

Fleisch n [flaɪʃ] meat

Flickzeug n ['flɪktsɔɪk] repair kit

Fliege f ['fli:gə] fly

fliegen ['fli:gn] to fly

Flohmarkt m ['flo:ma:kt] flea
market

Flug m [flu:k] flight

Flügel m [fly:gl] wing

Fluggesellschaft f ['flu:kgəˌzɛlʃaft]
airline

Flughafen m ['flu:kha:fn] airport

Flughafenbus m ['flu:kha:fnˌbʊs]
airport bus

Flughafengebühr f
['flu:kha:fngəˌbyɐ] airport tax

Flugsteig m ['flu:kʃtaɪg] *(airport)*
gate

Fluss m [flʊs] river

flüssig ['flʏsɪç] liquid

Flut f [fluːt] high tide

Föhn m [føːn] hair dryer

föhnen [føːnn] to blow-dry

fordern ['fɔɐden] ask

Form f [fɔɐm] form, shape

Format n [fɔˈmaːt] *(paper)* size

Formular n [fɔmʊˈlaː] *(paper)* form

fort [fɔɐt] away

Foto n ['foto] photo

Fotografie f [fotogʀaˈfiː] photography

fotografieren [ˌfotogʀaˈfiːʀən] to photograph

Frage f ['fʀaːgə] question

fragen [fʀaːgn] ask

frankieren [fʀaŋˈkien] to stamp

französisch [fʀanˈtsøːzɪʃ] French

Frau f [fʀaʊ] woman; wife; Madam; Ms, Mrs

Fräulein n ['fʀɔ(ɪ)laɪn] young lady; Miss

frei [fʀaɪ] free; exempt; im Freien ['ɪm 'fʀaɪn] in the open air, outdoors

Freilichtkino n ['fʀaɪlɪçtkiːno] drive-in cinema

Freitag ['fʀaɪtaːk] Friday

Freizeitpark m ['fʀaɪtsaɪtˌpaːk] amusement park

fremd [fʀɛmt] strange; foreign; unknown

Fremde m/f ['fʀɛmdə] stranger; foreigner

Fremdenführer/in m/f ['fʀɛmdnfyːʀɐ/-fyːʀəʀɪn] guide

Freude f ['fʀɔɪdə] joy, pleasure

freuen, sich ~ (über) [zɪç 'fʀɔɪn (yːbɐ)] be pleased (with/about); sich ~ auf [zɪç 'fʀɔɪn ʔaʊf] look forward to

Freund/in m/f [fʀɔɪnt/'fʀɔɪndɪn] friend; boyfriend/girlfriend

freundlich ['fʀɔɪntlɪç] friendly, kind

Friedhof m ['fʀiːtoːf] cemetery, graveyard

frieren ['fʀiːʀən /fʀien] be cold, freeze

frisch [fʀɪʃ] fresh; *(clothing)* clean

Frischhaltefolie f ['fʀɪʃhaltəˌfoːljə] cling film

Friseur m [fʀiˈzøɐ] hairdresser's

Frisur f [fʀiˈzuɐ] hairstyle

froh [fʀoː] glad; happy; merry

Frost m [fʀɔst] frost

Frostschutzmittel n ['fʀɔstʃʊtsmɪtl] anti-freeze

Frühling m ['fʀyːlɪŋ] *(season)* spring

Frühstück n ['fʀyːʃtʏk] breakfast

frühstücken ['fʀyːʃtʏkn] have breakfast

Frühstücksbüfett n ['fʀyːʃtʏksbyˌfeː] buffet breakfast

Frühstücksraum m ['fʀyːʃtʏksʀaʊm] breakfast room

fühlen [fyːln] to feel

Führerschein m ['fyːʀɐʃaɪn] driving licence

Führung f ['fyːʀʊŋ] guided tour

funktionieren [fʊŋktsjoˈniːʀən/ -ˈnien] to work, to function

für [fyɐ] for

Furcht f [fʊɐçt] fear

fürchten ['fʏɐçtn] to fear; sich ~ (vor) [zɪç 'fʏɐçtn foɐ] be afraid (of)

fürchterlich ['fʏɐçtɐlɪç] terrible, dreadful, horrible

Fuß m [fuːs] foot

Fußball m ['fuːsbal] football

Fußballspiel n ['fuːsbalʃpiːl] football match

Fußgänger/in m/f ['fuːsgɛŋɐ/ -gɛŋəʀɪn] pedestrian

Fußgängerzone f ['fuːsgɛŋɐˌtsoːnə] pedestrian precinct/zone

G

Gabel f ['gaːbl] fork

Galerie f [galəˈʀiː] gallery

221

Gallenblase *f* ['galnbla:zə] gallbladder

Gang *m* [gaŋ] *(meal)* course; corridor; *(engine)* gear

ganz [gants] *(adj)* whole; entire, complete; *(adv)* quite

gar [ga:] cooked, done

gar nicht ['ga:_nɪç(t)] not at all

Garage *f* [ga'ʀa:ʒə] garage

Garantie *f* [gaʀan'tʰi:] guarantee

Garderobe *f* [ga'dʀo:bə] cloakroom

Garnelen *f pl* [ga'ne:ln] prawns

Garten *m* [ga:tn] garden

Gasflasche *f* [ga:sflaʃə] gas canister

Gaskartusche *f* ['ga:ska͜tuʃə] gas cartridge

Gaspedal *n* ['ga:speda:l] accelerator, gas pedal

Gasse *f* ['gasə] alley, lane

Gast *m* [gast] guest

Gastfreundschaft *f* ['gastfʀɔɪntʃaft] hospitality

Gastgeber/in ['gastge:bɐ / -bəʀɪn] host/hostess

gebacken [gə'bakn] baked

Gebäude *n* [gə'bɔɪdə] building

geben [ge:bm] give

Gebirge *n* [gə'bɪʀgə] mountains

geboren [gə'bo:ʀən / gə'boɐn] born

gebraten [gə'bʀa:tn] roasted

Gebrauch *m* [gə'bʀaʊx] use

gebrauchen [gə'bʀaʊx] to use

gebräuchlich [gə'bʀɔɪçlɪç] common

gebrochen [gə'bʀɔxn] broken

Gebühren *f pl* [gə'by:ʀən / -'byɐn] fees

Geburtsdatum *n* [gə'bʊɐtsda:tʊm] date of birth

Geburtsname *m* [gə'bʊɐtsna:mə] maiden name

Geburtsort *m* [gə'bʊɐtsˀɔɐt] place of birth

Geburtstag *m* [gə'bʊɐtstʰa:k] birthday

gedämpft [gə'dɛmpft] steamed

Gedenkstätte *f* [gə'dɛŋkʃtɛtə] memorial

Geduld *f* [gə'dʊlt] patience

gedünstet [gə'dʏnstət] steamed

Gefahr *f* [gə'fa:] danger

gefährlich [gə'fɛelɪç] dangerous

gefallen [gə'faln] to please

Gefallen *m* [gə'faln] favour

Gefängnis *n* [gə'fɛŋnɪs] prison

Gefäß *n* [gə'fɛ:s] container

Gefühl *n* [gə'fy:l] feeling

gefüllt [gə'fʏlt] stuffed

gegen [ge:gŋ] against; *(sport)* versus; towards; *(time)* about

Gegend *f* ['ge:gŋt] region, area, district

Gegenstand *m* ['ge:gŋʃtant] object

Gegenteil *n* ['ge:gŋtʰaɪl] opposite, contrary

gegenüber [gegŋˀy:bɐ] opposite

Geheimzahl *f* [gə'haɪmtsa:l] Personal Identification Number (PIN)

gehen [ge:n] to go; to walk

Gehirn *n* [gə'hɪʀn] brain

Gehirnerschütterung *f* [gə'hɪʀnɐʃʏtəʀʊŋ] concussion

Gehör *n* [gə'høɐ] hearing

gehören [gə'hø:ʀən / -'høɐn] belong to

gehörlos [gə'hø:elo:s] deaf

Gehörlose *m/f* [gə'hø:elo:zə] deaf person

geistig behindert ['gaɪstɪç bə'hɪndət] mentally handicapped

gekocht [gə'kɔxt] boiled, cooked

Gelände *n* [gə'lɛndə] ground; grounds

gelb [gɛlp] yellow

Geld *n* [gɛlt] money

Geldautomat *m* ['gɛltaʊto͜ma:t] automated teller machine, cashpoint

Geldbeutel *m* ['gɛltbɔɪtl] purse

Geldbörse *f* ['gɛltbœɐzə] purse

Geldschein *m* ['gɛltʃaɪn] banknote

Geldstrafe *f* ['gɛltʃtʀaːfə] *(monetary)* fine

gelegentlich [gəleːgntlɪç] occasional(ly)

Gelenk *n* [gəˈlɛŋk] joint

Gemälde *n* [gəˈmɛːldə] painting

gemeinsam [gəˈmaɪnza(ː)m] common; together

Gemüse *n* [gəˈmyːzə] vegetables

gemütlich [gəˈmyːtlɪç] comfortable, cosy

genau [gəˈnaʊ] exact(ly)

genauso … wie [gəˈnaʊzo … vi] just as … as

genießen [gəˈniːsn] enjoy

genug [gəˈnuːk] enough, sufficient

geöffnet [gəˈʔœfnət] open

Gepäck *n* [geˈpɛk] baggage, luggage

Gepäckaufbewahrung *f* [gəˈpɛkˌʔaʊfbəvaːʀʊŋ] baggage deposit, left-luggage office

Gepäckausgabe *f* [gəˈpɛkˌʔaʊsgaːbə] baggage/luggage reclaim

Gepäckschalter *m* [gəˈpɛkʃaltə] baggage/luggage counter

Gepäckwagen *m* [gəˈpɛkvaːgn] baggage/luggage car

gerade [g(ə)ˈʀaːdə] straight; *(time)* just

geradeaus [gʀaːdəˈʔaʊs] straight on/straight ahead

geräuchert [gəˈʀɔɪçɐt] smoked

Geräusch *n* [gəˈʀɔɪʃ] noise

gerecht [gəˈʀɛçt] just, fair

Gericht *n* [gəˈʀɪçt] *(food)* dish; (law) court

gering [gəˈʀɪŋ] little, small

gern [gɛɐn] gladly; nicht gern [nɪç(t) gɛɐn] reluctantly

Geruch *m* [gəˈʀu(ː)x] smell

Geschäft *n* [gəˈʃɛft] shop, store

Geschenk *n* [gəˈʃɛŋk] present, gift

Geschichte *f* [gəˈʃɪçtə] history; story

Geschirr *n* [gəˈʃɪɐ] crockery

Geschirrspülbecken *n* [gəˈʃɪɐspyːlbɛkŋ] sink

Geschirrspülmaschine *f* [gəˈʃɪɐspyːlmaʃɪnə] dishwasher

Geschirrtuch *n* [gəˈʃɪɐtuːx] tea towel

geschlossen [gəˈʃlɔsn] shut, closed

Geschmack *m* [gəˈʃmak] taste

geschmort [gəˈʃmoɐt] braised

Geschwindigkeit *f* [gəˈʃvɪndɪçkʰaɪt] speed

geschwollen [gəˈʃvɔln] swollen

Geschwulst *f* [gəˈʃvʊlst] tumour, growth

Geschwür *n* [gəˈʃvyɐ] ulcer

Gesellschaft *f* [gəˈzɛlʃaft] company

Gespräch *n* [gəˈʃpʀɛːç] conversation, talk

gestern ['gɛstɐn] yesterday

gesund [gəˈzʊnt] healthy

Getränk *n* [gəˈtʀɛŋk] drink

Getriebe *n* [gəˈtʀiːbə] gearbox, transmission

Gewicht *n* [gəˈvɪçt] weight

Gewinn *m* [gəˈvɪn] profit

gewinnen [gəˈvɪnn] to win

gewiss [gəˈvɪs] certain(ly), sure(ly)

gewöhnlich [gəˈvøːnlɪç] usual, ordinary

gewohnt [gəˈvoːnt] usual

gewöhnt sein [ˌʔɛtvas gəˈvøːnt zaɪn] be used to

Gewölbe *n* [gəˈvœlbə] vault(s)

Gewürz *n* [gəˈvʏɐts] spice, seasoning

Giebel *m* [giːbl] gable

Gift *n* [gɪft] poison

giftig ['gɪftɪç] poisonous

glänzend [glɛntsnt] splendid, glorious

Glas *n* [glaːs] glass

Glasmalerei *f* ['glaːsmaːləˌʀaɪ] glass painting

glauben [glaʊbm] believe

gleich [glaɪç] same; immediately,

at once

gleichfalls ['glaɪçfals] also; likewise

gleichzeitig ['glaɪçtsaɪtʰɪç] simultaneous(ly)

Gleis n [glaɪs] platform

Glück n [glʏk] luck; success

glücklich ['glʏklɪç] happy; lucky

Glückwunsch m ['glʏkvʊnʃ] congratulations

Glühbirne f ['gly:bɪrnə] light bulb

Gold n ['gɔlt] gold

Goldschmiedekunst f ['gɔltʃmi:də̩kʊnst] gold work

Golf n [gɔlf] golf

Golfclub m ['gɔlfklʊp] (establishment) golf club

Golfschläger m ['gɔlfʃlɛ:gɐ] (implement) golf club

Gotik f ['go:tik] Gothic

Gott m [gɔt] God

Grab n [gra:p] grave, tomb

Grabmal n ['gra:bma:l] (tomb) monument

Grafik f ['gra:fɪk] graphic arts

Gramm n [gram] gram(s)

Gras n [gra:s] grass

Gräte f ['grɛ:tə] fishbone

gratis ['gra:tɪs] free

gratulieren [gratʰʊ'li:rən / -'lien] congratulate

grau [graʊ] grey

Grenze f ['grɛntsə] border

Grieche/Griechin m/f ['gri:çə/'gri:çɪn] Greek

griechisch adj ['gri:çɪʃ] Greek

Grill m [grɪl] grill; vom Grill [fɔm 'grɪl] grilled

Grillkohle f ['grɪlko:lə] charcoal

Grippe f ['grɪpə] flu, influenza

groß [gro:s] big, large; tall; great

großartig ['gro:s(ʔ)a:tɪç] great

Größe f ['grø:sə] size; height

Großmutter f ['gro:smʊtɐ] grandmother

Großvater m ['gro:sfa:tʰɐ] grandfather

grün [gry:n] green

Grund m [grʊnt] reason, cause

grüne Bohnen [ˌgry:nə 'bo:nn] green beans

grüne Versicherungskarte f ['gry:nə fɐ'zɪçərʊnska:tə] green card

Gruppe f ['grʊpə] group

grüßen ['gry:sn] greet

gültig ['gʏltʰɪç] valid

Gummistiefel m pl ['gʊmiʃti:fl] rubber boots, wellingtons

Gurke f ['gʊɐkə] cucumber

Gürtel m [gʏɐtl] belt

gut [gu:t] (adj) good; (adv) well

Gutschein m ['gu:tʃaɪn] voucher

Gymnastik f [gʏm'nastɪk] gymnastics

H

Haar n [ha:] hair

Haargel n ['ha:ge:l] hair gel

Haarklammern f pl ['ha:klamɐn] hairpins

haben ['ha:bm] have

Hackfleisch n ['hakflaɪʃ] mince(d meat)

Hafen m ['ha:fn] port

Hähnchen n ['hɛ:nçn] chicken

Haken m ['ha:kŋ] hook

halb [halp] (adj/adv) half

Hälfte f ['hɛlftə] half

Halle f ['halə] hall

Hals m [hals] neck, throat

Halsschmerzen m pl ['halʃmɛɐtsn] sore throat

Halstabletten f pl ['halsta̩blɛtn] throat lozenges

Halstuch n ['halstu:x] (decorative) scarf

halt! [halt] halt!, stop!

haltbar ['haltba:] durable; ~ bis use by

Haltegriff m ['haltəgrɪf] handle

halten [haltn] hold; keep; last; stop

Haltestelle f ['haltəʃtɛlə] stop

Hand f [hant] hand

Handball m ['hantbal] handball

Handbike n ['hɛntbaɪk] hand-operated bike

Handbremse f ['hantbʀɛmzə] hand brake

Handgas n ['hantga:s] hand throttle

handgemacht ['hantgəmaxt] hand-made

Handlauf m ['hantlaʊf] handrail

Handschuhe m pl ['hantʃu:ə] gloves

Handtasche f ['han(t)taʃə] handbag

Handtuch n ['han(t)tu:x] towel

Handy n ['hɛndi] mobile (phone)

hart [ha:t] hard, solid

hässlich ['hɛslɪç] ugly

häufig ['hɔɪfɪç] frequent(ly)

Hauptbahnhof m ['haʊptba:nho:f (haʊpba:nof)] main station

Hauptpostamt n ['haʊpt.pɔst'amt] main post office

Hauptquartier n ['haʊptkva.tie] headquarters

Hauptrolle f ['haʊptʀɔlə] leading role

hauptsächlich ['haʊptzɛçlɪç] especially; mainly

Hauptsaison f ['haʊptzɛ.zɔŋ] high season

Hauptspeise f ['haʊptʃpaɪzə] main course

Hauptstadt f ['haʊptʃtat] capital

Hauptstraße f ['haʊptʃtra:sə] main street

Haus n [haʊs] house; im Haus ['ɪm haʊs] indoors

Hausbesitzer/in m/f ['haʊsbəzɪtsə/-bəzɪtsəʀɪn] landlord/landlady

Hausboot n ['haʊsbo:t] houseboat

hausgemacht ['haʊsgəmaxt] home-made

Hausnummer f ['haʊsnʊmə] house number

Haustiere n pl ['haʊsti:ʀə] pets

Haut f [haʊt] skin

heben [e:bm] to lift

heilig ['haɪlɪç] holy

Heiligabend [haɪlɪç 'ʔa:bmt] Christmas Eve

Heiliger Abend ['haɪlɪgɐ 'ʔa:bmt] Christmas Eve

Heilmittel n ['haɪlmɪtl] remedy

Heimat f ['haɪma:t] home, native country

Heimreise f ['haɪmʀaɪzə] return journey, trip home

heiraten ['haɪʀa:tn] marry

heiser ['haɪzɐ] hoarse

heiß [haɪs] hot

heißen [haɪsn] be called

heiter ['haɪtɐ] *(weather)* clear

heizen [haɪtsn] to heat

Heizung f ['haɪtsʊŋ] heating

hellblau [hɛl'blaʊ] light blue

Hemd n [hɛmt] shirt

herb [hɛɐp] *(wine)* dry

Herbst m ['hɛɐpst] autumn, *(US)* fall

Herd m [heɐt] cooker, stove

herein! [hɛ'ʀaɪn] come in!

Hering m ['he:ʀɪŋ] herring

Herr m [hɛɐ] gentleman; Mr

Herrenfriseur m ['hɛʀənfʀɪ'zøɐ] barber's

Herrenslip m ['hɛʀənslɪp] briefs

Herrentoilette f ['hɛʀənto.lɛtə] Gents, Men's Room

herrlich ['hɛɐlɪç] glorious, splendid, terrific

herum [hɛ'ʀʊm] around

Herz n [hɛɐts] heart

Herzbeschwerden f pl ['hɛɐtsbəʃveɐdn] heart trouble

Herzinfarkt m ['hɛɐtsɪnfa:kt] cardiac infarction, heart attack

herzlich ['hɛɐtslɪç] warm, sincere

Herzschrittmacher m ['hɛɐt(s)ʃʀɪtmaxɐ] pacemaker

Heuschnupfen m [ˈhɔɪʃnʊpfn] hay fever

heute [ˈhɔɪtə] today; **heute Morgen** [hɔɪtə ˈmɔɐgn̩] this morning; **heute Abend** [hɔɪtə ˈʔaːbmt] this evening; **heute Nacht** [hɔɪtʰ(ə) ˈnaxt] tonight

Hexenschuss m [ˈhɛksnʃʊs] lumbago

hier [hiɐ] here

Hilfe f [ˈhɪlfə] help, aid; **erste Hilfe** [ˌʔeɐstə ˈhɪlfə] first aid

Himmel m [hɪml] sky; heaven

hinausgehen [hɪˈnaʊsgeːn] go out, leave

hindern [ˈhɪndɐn] prevent, hinder

hinlegen [ˈhɪnleːgn̩] put down; sich ~ [zɪç ˈhɪnleːgn̩] lie down

hinter [ˈhɪntʰɐ] behind

hinterlassen [hɪntɐˈlasn̩] to leave

hinterlegen [hɪntʰɐˈleːgn̩] to deposit

hinzufügen [hɪnˈtsuːfyːgn̩] add

Hitze f [ˈhɪtsə] heat

hoch [hoːx] high

höchstens [høːçstns / høːkstns] at the most, at best

Hochzeit f [ˈhɔxtsaɪt] wedding

Hof m [hoːf] (court)yard

höflich [ˈhøːflɪç] polite

Höhe f [ˈhøːə] height

Höhepunkt m [ˈhøːəpʰʊŋkt] highlight; (career) peak, height; (film, play) climax

Höhle f [ˈhøːlə] cave

holen [hoːln] fetch, get

Holz n [hɔlts] wood

Holzschnitt m [ˈhɔltʃnɪt] woodcut

Honig m [ˈhoːnɪç] honey

hören [ˈhøːrən / høːn] hear

Hörer m [ˈhøːrɐ] receiver

Hose f [ˈhoːzə] trousers, (US) pants

hübsch [hʏpʃ] pretty, cute

Hüfte f [ˈhʏftə] hip

Hügel m [hyːgl] hill

Hund m [hʊnt] dog

hungrig [ˈhʊŋrɪç] hungry

Hupe f [ˈhuːpə] (car) horn

Husten m [huːstn̩] cough

Hustensaft m [ˈhuːstnzaft] cough mixture/syrup

Hut m [huːt] hat

Hütte f [ˈhʏtʰə] hut, cabin

I

ich [ʔɪç] I

Idee f [ʔiˈdeː] idea

Ihnen [ʔiːnn̩] (polite) to/for you

ihr [ʔiɐ] her, their

Illustrierte f [ɪlʊˈstriːɐtə] (glossy) magazine

Imbiss m [ʔɪmbɪs] snack

immer [ʔɪmɐ] always

Impfpass m [ʔɪm(p)fpas] vaccination card

Impfung f [ʔɪmpfʊŋ] vaccination

Impressionismus m [ʔɪmprɛsjoˈnɪsmʊs] impressionism

in [ʔɪn] in

inbegriffen [ʔɪnbəgrɪfn̩] included

Infektion f [ʔɪnfɛkˈtsjoːn] infection

informieren [ʔɪnfɔˈmiːrən/-ˈmiɐn] inform

Infusion f [ʔɪnfʊˈzjoːn] infusion

Inhalt m [ʔɪnhalt] contents

Inlandsflug m [ʔɪnlantsfluːk] domestic flight

innen [ʔɪnn̩] inside

Innenhof m [ʔɪnnhoːf] inner courtyard

Innenstadt f [ʔɪnnʃtat] town centre

Inschrift f [ʔɪnʃrɪft] inscription

Insekt n [ʔɪnˈzɛkt] insect

Insel f [ʔɪnzl] island

Insulin n [ʔɪnzʊˈliːn] insulin

Inszenierung f [ʔɪntsəˈniːrʊŋ] (stage) production

interessant [ʔɪntrəˈsant] interesting

interessieren, sich ~ (für) [zɪç

226

...'ɪntʁə'si:ʁən /-'siɐn fyɐ] be interested (in)
irisch ['ʔi:ʁɪʃ] Irish
Irland ['ʔɪʁlant] Ireland, Eire
irren, sich ~ [zɪç 'ʔɪʁən/'ʔɪɐn] be mistaken
Irrtum *m* ['ʔɪʁtʰu:m] mistake
Ischias *m* ['ʔɪʃias] sciatica

J

Jacke *f* ['jakə] jacket
Jahr *n* [ja:] year
Jahreszeit *f* ['ja:ʁəstsaɪt] season
Jahrhundert *n* [ja'hʊndet] century
jährlich ['jɛɐlɪç] annual(ly)
Jahrmarkt *m* ['ja:ma:kt] funfair
Jänner ['jɛnɐ] *(Austria)* January
Januar ['janʊa:] January
Jazz *m* ['dʒɛs] jazz
Jazzgymnastik *f* ['dʒɛsɡʏm,nastɪk] jazz aerobics
Jeans *f* ['dʒi:ns] jeans
jede(r, s) ['je:də(-dɐ, -dəs)] every, each
jedermann ['je:dɐman] everybody
jedoch [je'dɔx] however
jemand ['je:mant] somebody; anybody
jene(r,s) ['je:nə (-nɐ, -nəs)] that, *(pl)* those
jetzt [jɛtst] now
Jodtinktur *f* ['jo:tɪŋktuɐ] tincture of iodine
joggen ['dʒɔgn̩] to jog
Joghurt *m* ['jo:gʊɐt] yoghurt
Jugendstil *m* ['ju:gn̩tsti:l] art nouveau
Juli ['ju:li] July
jung [jʊŋ] young
Junge *m* ['jʊŋə] boy
Junggeselle *m* ['jʊŋgəzɛlə] bachelor
Juni ['ju:ni] June

Juwelier *m* [juve'liɐ] jeweller's

K

Kabarett *n* [kaba'ʁe:] cabaret
Kabine *f* [ka'bi:nə] cabin; cubicle
Kaffee *m* ['kafe:/ka'fe:] coffee
Kaffeemaschine *f* ['kafemaʃi:nə] coffee machine
Kai *m* [kaɪ] quay
Kalbfleisch *n* ['kalpflaɪʃ] veal
kalt [kʰalt] cold
Kamera *f* ['kaməʁa:] camera
Kamillentee *m* [ka'mɪl(ə)nte:] camomile tea
Kamm *m* [kam] comb
kämmen [kɛmm̩] to comb
Kanal *m* [kʰa'na:l] canal; channel
Kaninchen *n* [ka'ni:nçn] rabbit
Kanu *n* ['ka:nu] canoe
Kapelle *f* [ka'pɛlə] chapel
Kapitän *m* [kapi'tɛ:n] captain
kaputt [kʰa'pʰʊt] broken, out of order
Karfreitag [ka:'fʁaɪta:k] Good Friday
Karotten *f pl* [ka'ʁɔtn̩] carrots
Karte *f* ['ka:tə] ticket
Kartoffeln *f pl* [ka'tɔfln̩] potatoes
Käse *m* ['kɛ:zə] cheese
Kasse *f* ['kʰasə] cash-desk; box-office, ticket-office
Kassette *f* [ka'sɛtə] cassette
Kathedrale *f* [kate'dʁa:lə] cathedral
Katze *f* ['kʰatsə] cat
kaufen [kʰaʊfn̩] to buy
Kaufhaus *n* ['kaʊfhaʊs] department store
kaum [kʰaʊm] hardly, scarcely, barely
Kaution *f* [kʰaʊ'tsjo:n] security, down payment
Kehle *f* [ke:lə] throat
kein [kʰaɪn] no

227

keiner ['kʰaɪnɐ] nobody

Kellner/in m/f ['kɛlnɐ/'kɛlnəʀɪn] waiter/waitress

kennen [kʰɛnn] to know; **kennen lernen** ['kʰɛnnlɛɐnn] to meet

Keramik f [keˈʀaːmɪk] ceramics

Kerzen f pl [kɛɐtsn] candles

Ketschup n ['kɛtʃap] ketchup

Kette f ['kɛtə] chain; necklace

Keuchhusten m ['kɔɪçhuːstn] whooping-cough

Kfz-Schein m [kaˈʔɛfˈtsɛtʃaɪn] car registration documents

Kiefer m ['kiːfɐ] jaw; pine

Kilo n ['kiːlo] kilogram(s)

Kilometer m [ˌkiloˈmeːtɐ] kilometre

Kind n [kʰɪnt] child

Kinder n pl ['kɪndɐ] children **Kinderbecken** n ['kɪndɐbɛkn] children's pool

Kinderbetreuung f ['kɪndɐbətʀɔjʊŋ] babysitting service

Kinderbett n ['kɪndɐbɛt] cot

Kinderermäßigung f ['kɪndɐˈʔɛˈmɛːsɪgʊŋ] child reduction

Kinderkleidung f ['kɪndɐklaɪdʊŋ] children's clothing

Kinderkrankheit f ['kɪndɐˌkʀaŋkhaɪt] children's illness

Kinderlähmung f ['kɪndɐlɛːmʊŋ] polio

Kindernahrung f ['kɪndɐnaːʀʊŋ] baby food

Kindersitz m ['kɪndɐzɪts] child seat

Kinderspielplatz m ['kɪndɐʃpiːlplats] children's playground

Kinderteller m ['kɪndɐtɛlɐ] children's portion

Kino n ['kiːno] cinema, movie theater

Kirche f ['kɪʀçə] church

Kirchturm m ['kɪʀçtʊɐm] steeple

Kirmes f ['kɪʀməs] fair, fête

Kirschen f pl [kɪʀʃn] cherries

Kiste f ['kʰɪstə] box, chest

Klang m [klaŋ] sound

klar [klaː] clear

Klasse f ['klasə] class

Klassik f ['klasɪk] classical

Klassiker m ['klasɪkɐ] classic film

Klassizismus m [klasɪˈtsɪsmʊs] classicism

Kleid f [klaɪt] dress

Kleiderbügel m ['klaɪdɐbyːgl] coat hanger

Kleiderhaken m ['klaɪdɐhaːkn] peg

Kleidung f ['klaɪdʊŋ] clothing

klein [klaɪn] little, small

Klima n ['kliːmaː] climate

Klimaanlage f ['kliːmeˈʔanˌlaːgə] air-conditioning

Klingel f [klɪŋl] bell

Klippe f ['klɪpə] cliff

Kloster n ['kloːstɐ] monastery; convent

klug [kluːk] clever, intelligent

Kneipe f ['knaɪpə] pub

Knie n [kniː] knee

Knoblauch m ['knoːblaʊx] garlic

Knöchel m [knœçl] ankle

Knochen m [knɔxn] bone

Knochenbruch m ['knɔxnbʀʊx] fracture

Koch m [kɔx] cook

Kochbuch n ['kɔxbuːx] cookbook

kochen [kʰɔxn] to cook; (coffee, tea) make; (water) boil

Kocher m ['kɔxɐ] cooker

Köchin f ['kʰœxɪn] cook

Kochnische f ['kɔxniːʃə] kitchenette

Koffer m ['kʰɔfɐ] suitcase

Kofferraum m ['kɔfɐʀaʊm] boot, (US) trunk

Kohl m [koːl] cabbage

Kokosnuss f ['koːkosnʊs] coconut

Kolik f ['koːlɪk] colic

Kollege/Kollegin m/f

228

[kʰo'le:gə /kʰo'le:gɪn] colleague
kommen [kʰɔmm] come
Komödie f [ko'møːdiə] comedy
Kompass m ['kʰɔmpʰas] compass
Komponist/in m/f [kompo'nɪst/
-ɪn] composer
Konditorei f [kɔndito'ʀaɪ] cake
shop
Kondom n [kɔn'doːm] condom
König m ['køːniç] king
Königin f ['køːnɪgɪn] queen
können ['kʰœnn] be able to, can
Konsulat n [kʰɔnzʊ'laːt] consulate
Kontakt m [kʰɔn'tʰakt] contact
Konto n ['kʰɔnto] account
Kontrolleur/in m/f [kɔntʀo'lø:ɐ/
-'løʀɪn] inspector
kontrollieren [kʰɔntʀo'li:ʀən/
-'liːən] to control; to check
Konzert n [kɔn'tsɛɐt] concert
Kopf m [kɔpf] head
Kopfhörer m ['kɔpfhø:ʀe] head-
phones
Kopfkissen n ['kɔpfkɪsn] pillow
Kopfsalat m ['kɔpfsa,laːt] lettuce
Kopfschmerzen m pl
['kɔpfʃmɛɐtsn] headache
Kopfschmerztabletten f pl
['kɔpfʃmɛɐtsta,blɛtn] headache
tablets
Kopie f [ko'piː] copy
Korb m [kɔɐp] basket
Korkenzieher m ['kɔɐkŋtsi:ɐ]
corkscrew
Körper m ['kʰœɐpʰe] body
kosten [kʰɔstn] to cost
kostenlos ['kʰɔstnloːs] free (of
charge)
kostspielig ['kɔs(t)ʃpiːlɪç] ex-
pensive
Kostüm n [kɔs'tyːm] (women's)
suit
Kotelett n ['kɔtlɛt] chop, cutlet
Krabben f pl [kʀabm] shrimps
kräftig ['kʀɛftɪç] strong
Krafttraining n ['kʀaftʀɛːnɪŋ]
weight training

Krampf m [kʀampf] cramp
krank [kʀaŋk] ill, sick; **krank werden** ['kʀaŋk veɐdn] be taken ill, get
sick
Krankenhaus n ['kʀaŋknhaʊs]
hospital
Krankenkasse f ['kʀaŋknkasə]
health insurance scheme/company
Krankenschwester f
['kʀaŋknʃvɛstɐ] nurse
Krankenwagen m ['kʀaŋknvaːgn]
ambulance
Krankheit f ['kʀaŋkhaɪt] illness
Kräuter n pl ['kʀɔɪtɐ] herbs
Krawatte f [kʀa'vatə] tie
kreativ [kʀea'tiːf] creative
Krebs m [kʀeːps] cancer; crab
Kreditkarte f [kʀedi:tka:tə] credit
card
Kreislaufmittel n ['kʀaɪslaʊf,mɪtl]
cardiac stimulant
Kreislaufstörung f
['kʀaɪslaʊfˌʃtøːʀʊŋ] circulatory dis-
order
Kreuz n [kʀɔɪts] cross
Kreuzgang m ['kʀɔɪtsgaŋ] cloister
Kreuzung f ['kʀɔɪtsʊŋ] intersec-
tion, junction
kriegen [kʀiːgn] catch, get
Kriminalroman m
[kʀimi'naːlˌʀomaːn] thriller
Kristall n [kʀɪs'tal] crystal
Krone f ['kʀoːnə] crown
Krücke f ['kʀʏkə] crutch
Küche f ['kʰʏçə] kitchen
Kuchen m [kʊːxn] cake
Kugelschreiber m ['kuːglʃʀaɪbɐ]
ball-point pen
kühl [kʰyːl] cool
Kühlelement n ['kyːlʔeləˌmɛnt] ice
pack
Kühler m ['kyːlɐ] (car) radiator
Kühlschrank m ['kyːlʃʀaŋk] fridge,
refrigerator
Kühlwasser n ['kyːlvasɐ] cooling
water
Kuli m ['kuːli] biro

Kultur *f* [kʰʊl'tʰuɐ] culture
Kümmel *m* [kʏml] caraway seed(s)
Kunde/Kundin *m/f*
['kʰʊndə /'kʰʊndɪn] customer
Kunst *f* [kʊnst] art
Kunstgewerbe *n* ['kʊnstgəvɛɐbə]
arts and crafts
Kunsthändler/in *m/f*
['kʊnst,hɛntlɐ/-,hɛntlərɪn] art
dealer
Kuppel *f* [kʊpl] dome
Kupplung *f* ['kʊplʊŋ] *(car)* clutch
Kürbis *m* ['kʏɐbɪs] pumpkin
Kurs *m* [kʊɐs] course
Kurve *f* ['kʊɐvə] bend, curve
kurz [kʰʊɐts] short
kurze Hose *f* ['kʊɐtsə 'hoːzə]
shorts
Kurzfilm *m* [kʊɐtsfɪlm] short film
kurzfristig ['kʰʊɐtsfrɪstɪç] at short
notice
kürzlich ['kʏɐtslɪç] recently
Kurzschluss *m* ['kʊɐtsʃlʊs] short-
circuit
Kuss *m* [kʰʊs] kiss
küssen [kʰʏsn] to kiss
Küste *f* ['kʰʏstə] coast

L

lachen [laxn] to laugh
lächerlich ['lɛçɐlɪç] ridiculous
Ladegerät *n* ['laːdəgərɛːt] battery
charger
Laden *m* ['laːdn] shop, store
Lage *f* ['laːgə] situation; position,
location
Lähmung *f* ['lɛːmʊŋ] paralysis
Lammfleisch *n* ['lamflaɪʃ] *(meat)*
lamb
Lampe *f* ['lampə] lamp
Land *n* [lant] country; land
Landgut *n* ['lantguːt] estate
Landkarte *f* ['lantkʰaːtʰə] map
Landschaft *f* ['lantʃaft] scenery

Landsmann *m* ['lantsman] fellow
countryman
Landstraße *f* ['lantʃtraːsə] country
road
Landung *f* ['landʊŋ] landing
lang [laŋ] long
langsam ['laŋzaːm] slow(ly)
langweilig ['laŋvaɪlɪç] boring
Lärm *m* [lɛɐm] noise
lassen [lasn] to let; to leave
lästig ['lɛstɪç] annoying
laufen [laʊfn] to run; to go; to
walk
laut [laʊt] loud; noisy
Lautsprecher *m* ['laʊtʃprɛçɐ]
speaker
leben [leːbm] to live
Leben *n* [leːbm] life
Lebensmittel *n* ['leːbmsmɪtl] food
Lebensmittelgeschäft *n*
['leːbmsmɪtlgəʃɛft] food store,
grocery store
Lebensmittelvergiftung *f*
['leːbmsmɪtlfɐ,gɪftʊŋ] food poisoning
Leber *f* ['leːbɐ] liver
lebhaft ['leːphaft] lively
lecker ['lɛkɐ] tasty
Lederjacke *f* ['leːdɐjakə] leather
jacket
ledig ['leːdɪç] single
leer [leɐ] empty
Leerlauf *m* ['leɐlaʊf] *(gear)* neutral
Leerung *f* ['leːrʊŋ] collection (of
mail)
legen [leːgn] put
Leggings *f* ['lɛgɪŋs] leggings
lehren ['leːrən / leɐn] teach
leicht [laɪçt] easy; slight; *(weight)*
light
Leichtathletik *f* ['laɪçtʔatˌleːtɪk]
athletics
leider ['laɪdɐ] unfortunately
leihen [laɪn] lend; borrow
Leinen *n* [laɪnn] linen
leise ['laɪzə] quiet(ly)
Leistenbruch *m* ['laɪstnbrʊx]

hernia, rupture

Leiter/in *m/f* ['laɪtɐ/'laɪtərɪn] head, manager, boss

Leitung *f* ['laɪtʊŋ] *(telephone)* line

lernen ['lɛrnn] learn

lesen ['le:zn] read

letzte(r, s) ['lɛtstʰə (-tʰe, -tʰəs)] last

Leute *pl* ['lɔɪtʰə] people

Licht *n* [lɪçt] light

Lichtmaschine *f* ['lɪçtmaʃi:nə] dynamo, generator

Lichtschutzfaktor *m* ['lɪçtʃʊts‚faktoɐ] protection factor

lieb [li:p] nice; **jdn lieb haben** [jemandn 'li:p ha:bm] be fond of s.o.; **Liebe(r)** ['li:bə/'li:be] Dear

Liebe *f* ['li:bə] love

lieben [li:bm] to love

liebenswürdig ['li:bmsvɐdɪç] kind

lieber ['li:be] *(adv)* rather

Liebling *m* ['li:plɪŋ] darling; favourite

Lied *n* [li:t] song

liegen [li:gn] to lie

Liegewiese *f* ['li:gəvi:zə] sun- bathing area

Lift *m* [lɪft] elevator, lift

lila ['li:la] purple

Limonade *f* [lɪmo'na:də] lemonade

Linie *f* ['li:njə] line

linke(r, s) ['lɪŋkʰa (-kʰe, -kʰəs)] left(-hand)

links [lɪŋks] on the left, to the left

Linsen *f pl* [lɪnzn] lentils

Lippe *f* ['lɪpə] lip

Lippenstift *m* ['lɪpmʃtɪft] lipstick

Liter *m* ['li:te] litre

Loch *n* [lɔx] hole, puncture

Locken *f pl* [lɔkn] curls

Lockenwickler *m pl* ['lɔknvɪklə] curlers

Löffel *m* [lœfl] spoon

Loge *f* ['lo:ʒə] box

Lorbeerblätter *n pl*
['lɔɐbeɐ‚blɛtə] bay-leaves

Luft *f* [lʊft] air

lüften ['lʏftn] to air

Luftkissenboot *n* ['lʊftkɪsnbo:t] hovercraft

Luftpumpe *f* ['lʊftpʊmpə] pump

Lüge *f* ['ly:gə] lie

lügen [ly:gn] to (tell a) lie

Lunge *f* ['lʊŋə] lungs

Lungenentzündung *f*
['lʊŋən?ɛn‚tsʏndʊŋ] pneumonia

Lust *f* [lʊst] pleasure, joy; desire; lust

lustig ['lʊstɪç] merry, in a good mood; funny

luxuriös [lʊksʊri'ø:s] luxurious

M

machen ['maxn] do; make

Mädchen *n* ['mɛ:tçn] girl

Magen *m* [ma:gn] stomach

Magenschmerzen *m pl*
['ma:gnʃmeɐtsn] stomach-ache

mager ['ma:ge] lean, thin

Mahlzeit *f* ['ma:ltsaɪt] meal

Mai [maɪ] May

Makrele *f* [ma'kre:lə] mackerel

Mal *n* [ma:l] time

Malbuch *n* ['ma:lbu:x] colouring book

malen [ma:ln] to paint

Maler/in *m/f* ['ma:le/'ma:lərɪn] painter

Malerei *f* [ma:lə'raɪ] *(type of art)* painting

manchmal ['mançma:l] some- times

Mandarinen *f pl* [manda'ri:nn] mandarins

Mandelentzündung *f*
['mandl?ɛn‚tsʏndʊŋ] tonsilitis

Mandeln *f pl* ['mandln] almonds; tonsils

Mangel *m* [maŋl] defect, fault;

lack, shortage

Mann m [man] man; husband

Männer f [m] men

Mannschaft f ['manʃaft] team; crew

Mantel m [mantl] coat

Margarine f [maga'ʀi:nə] margarine

Marke f ['ma:kə] *(postage)* stamp

Markt m [ma:kt] market

Marmelade f [mamə'la:də] jam, marmalade

März [mɛɛts] March

Maschine f [ma'ʃi:nə] machine

Masern f pl ['ma:zɐn] measles

Massage f [ma'sa:ʒə] massage

Material n [matʰ (ə)ʀi'a:l] material

Matratze f [ma'tʀatsə] mattress

Mauer f ['mauɐ] *(external)* wall

Medikament n [medika'mɛnt] medicine

Meer n [meeɐ] sea

Mehl n [me:l] flour

mehr [meeɐ] more; **mehr als** ['meeɐ ʔals] more than

mein [main] my

meinen [mainn] to mean; think

meinetwegen ['mainət,ve:gn] I don't mind

Meinung f ['mainʊn] opinion, view

melden [mɛldn] announce; inform

Melone f [me'lo:nə] melon

Mensch m [mɛnʃ] person, man/woman; man

Menstruation f [mɛnstʀua'tsjon] menstruation

Menü n [me'ny:] set meal

merken [mɛɐkn] be aware of; **sich etw. ~** [zɪç ʔɛtvas 'mɛɐkn] remember s. th.

Messe f ['mɛsə] *(rel.)* mass; fair, exhibition

Messer n ['mɛsə] knife

Meter m ['me:tə] metre

Metzgerei f [mɛtsgə'ʀai] butcher's

mich [mɪç] me

Miete f ['mi:tə] rent

mieten ['mi:tn] to rent, to hire

Migräne f [mi'gʀɛ:nə] migraine

Mikrowelle f ['mi:kʀovɛlə] microwave

Milch f [mɪlç] milk

mild [mɪlt] mild

Millimeter m ['mɪli,me:tə] millimetre

mindestens ['mɪndəstns] at least

Minigolf n ['mɪnigɔlf] crazy golf

Minute f [mi'nu:tʰə] minute

mir [miɐ] (to) me

Missverständnis n ['mɪsfɛʃtɛntnɪs] misunderstanding

mit [mɪt] with

mitbringen ['mɪtbʀɪŋŋ] bring

Mittag m ['mɪtʰa:k] noon, midday

Mittagessen n ['mɪtak,ʔɛsn] lunch

Mitte f ['mɪtʰə] middle

mitteilen ['mɪtailn] inform

Mitteilung f ['mɪtʰailʊn] announcement; memo

Mittel n ['mɪtl] means; remedy

Mittelalter n ['mɪtl'ʔaltɐ] Middle Ages

Mittelohrentzündung f ['mɪtl'ʔoɐ'ʔɛn,tsyndʊn] inflammation of the middle ear

Mittwoch ['mɪtvɔx] Wednesday

Möbel n [mø'bl] furniture

Mobiltelefon n [mo'bi:ltelə,fo:n] mobile phone

Mode f ['mo:də] fashion

Modell n [mo'dɛl] model

modern [mo'dɛɐn] modern, up to date

Modeschmuck m ['mo:dəʃmʊk] costume jewellery

mögen ['mø:gn] to like; to want

möglich ['mø:klɪç] possible

Monat m ['mo:na:t] month

monatlich ['mo:natlɪç] monthly

Mond m [mo:nt] moon

Montag ['mo:nta:k] Monday

Morgen m ['mɔɐgn] morning

morgen früh/morgen Abend

[mɔʁgn̩ 'fʁy:/mɔɛgn̩ ˈʔaːbmt]
tomorrow morning/tomorrow
evening

morgens ['mɔɛgn̩s] in the
morning

Mosaik n [mozaˈʔiːk] mosaic

Motel n [moˈtɛl] motel

Motor m ['moːtoɐ] engine, motor

Motorboot n ['moːtɔboːt] motorboat

Motorhaube f ['moːtɔˌhaubə]
bonnet, *(US)* hood

Mountainbike n ['mauntnbaik]
mountain bike

Möwe f ['møːvə] seagull

Mücke f ['mʏkʰə] gnat, midge, mos-
quito

müde ['myːdə] tired

Müll m [mʏl] rubbish, garbage

Mullbinde f ['mʊlbɪndə] gauze
bandage

Mülltonne f ['mʏltʰɔnə] dustbin,
trashcan

Mumps m [mʊmps] mumps

Mund m [mʊnt] mouth

Mündung f ['mʏndʊŋ] *(river)*
mouth

Münze f ['mʏntsə] coin

Muscheln f pl [mʊʃln̩] mussels

Museum n [muˈzeːʊm] museum

Musical n ['mjuːzɪkl] musical

Musik f [muˈziːk] music; **Musik**
hören [muˈziːk ˈhøːʁən] listen to
music

musizieren [muzɪˈtsiːʁən] make
music

Muskatnuss f [mʊsˈkaːtnʊs] nutmeg

Muskel m ['mʊskl] muscle

Müsli n ['myːsli] muesli

müssen [mʏsn̩] have to, must

Mutter f ['mʊtʰɐ] mother

Mütze f ['mʏtsə] cap

nach [naːx] after; to

nach oben [nax ˈʔoːbm̩] up

nachher ['naːx(h)eɐ] afterwards

Nachmittag m ['naːxmɪtʰaːk]
afternoon

nachmittags ['naxmɪtaːks] in the
afternoon

nachprüfen ['naːxpʁyːfn̩] to
check

Nachricht f ['naːxʁɪçt] message;
news

Nachsaison f ['naːxzeˌzɔŋ] low
season, off-season

nachsehen ['naːxzeːn] to check

nachsenden ['naːxzɛndn̩] send on

nächste(r, s) ['nɛːçstə/'nɛːkstə
(-stə, -stəs)] next

Nacht f [naxt] night

Nachtisch m ['naːxtɪʃ] dessert,
sweet

Nachtklub m ['naxtklʊp] night
club

nachts [naxts] at night

Nachttisch m ['naxttɪʃ] bedside
table

nackt [nakt] naked, nude

Nagellack m ['naːgllak] nail
varnish/polish

Nagellackentferner m
['naːgllakɛntˌfɛɐnɐ] nail
varnish/polish remover

Nagelschere f ['naːglʃeːʁə] nail
scissors

nahe ['naː (ə)] near, close; **nahe
bei** [na: bai] close to

Nähe, in der ~ von ['ʔɪn dɐ 'nɛə
fɔn] near

nähen [nɛːn] sew, stitch (up)

nähere Angaben ['nɛəʁə
ˈʔanga:bm̩] particulars

Nahrung f ['naːʁʊŋ] food

Nahverkehrszug m
['naːfɐˌkeɐstsuːk] local train

Name m [naːmə] name

Narbe f ['naːbə] scar

Nase *f* ['na:zə] nose
Nasenbluten *n* ['na:znblu:tn] nosebleed
nass [nas] wet
Nationalitätskennzeichen *n* [natsjonalɪ'tɛ:tskɛntsaɪçn] international car index mark
Nationalpark *m* [natsjo'na:lpa:k] national park
Natur *f* [na'tʰuɐ] nature
natürlich [na'tʰyelɪç] natural(ly); of course
Naturschutzgebiet *n* [na'tuɐʃʊtsgəbi:t] nature reserve
Nebel *m* ['ne:bl] fog
neben ['ne:bm] next to, beside
Nebenkosten *f* ['ne:bmkɔstn] additional costs
nehmen [ne:mm] to take
nein [naɪn] no
Nelken *f pl* ['nɛlkn] cloves
nennen [nɛnn] to name, to call
Neoprenanzug *m* [neo'pʀe:n,ʔantsu:k] wetsuit
Nerv *m* [nɛɐf] nerve
nervös [nɛ'vø:s] nervous
nett [nɛt] nice
neu [nɔɪ] new
neugierig ['nɔɪgi:ʀɪç] curious
Neujahr [nɔɪ'ja:] New Year's Day
nicht [nɪçt] not; noch nicht [nɔx 'nɪç(t)] not yet
Nichtraucherabteil *n* ['nɪçtʀaʊxɐʔap,taɪl] no-smoking compartment
nichts [nɪçts / nɪks] nothing
nie [ni:] never
niemand ['ni:mant] nobody
Niere *f* ['ni:ʀə] kidney
Nierenstein *m* ['ni:ʀənʃtaɪn] kidney stone
nirgends ['nɪʀgŋ (t)s] nowhere
noch [nɔx] still
Norden *m* [nɔɐdn] north
Nordirland [nɔat'ʔɪɐlant] Northern Ireland
Nordsee *f* [di 'nɔɐtze:] North Sea

normal [nɔ'ma:l] normal; standard
normalerweise [nɔ'ma:lɐvaɪzə] normally, usually
Notausgang *m* ['no:tʔaʊsgaŋ] emergency exit
Notfall ['no:tfal] emergency
nötig ['nø:tɪç] necessary
Notizblock *m* [no'ti:tsblɔk] notepad
Notrufsäule *f* ['no:tʀufzɔɪlə] emergency telephone
notwendig ['no:tvɛndɪç] necessary
November [no'vɛmbɐ] November
nüchtern ['nʏçtɐn] sober
Nudeln *f pl* ['nu:dln] noodles, pasta
Nummer *f* ['nʊmɐ] number
nummerieren [nʊmə'ʀi:ʀən/-'ʀiɐn] to number
Nummernschild *n* ['nʊmɐnʃɪlt] number plate, *(US)* license plate,
nun [nu:n] now; well
nur [nuɐ] only
Nüsse *f pl* ['nʏsə] nuts

O

ob [ʔɔp] whether
oben [ʔo:bm] up
Objektiv *n* [ʔɔbjɛk'ti:f] lens
Obst *n* [ʔo:pst] fruit
Obst- und Gemüsehändler *m* [ʔo:pst ʔʊnt gə'my:zəhɛntlɐ] fruit and vegetable store, greengrocer's
obwohl [ʔɔp'vo:l] although
oder [ʔo:dɐ] or
offen [ʔɔfn] open
öffentlich [ʔʔœfntlɪç] public
offiziell [ʔɔfɪ'tsjɛl] official
öffnen [ʔʔœfn (ə)n] to open
Öffnungszeiten *f pl* [ʔʔœfnʊŋstsaɪtn] opening hours, hours of business
oft [ʔɔft] often
ohne [ʔʔo:nə] without

ohne Kohlensäure [ˈʔoːnə ˈkoːl(ə)nzɔɪʀə] still, uncarbonated

in Ohnmacht fallen [ˈʔɪn ˈʔoːnmaxt faln] to faint

Ohr *n* [ˈʔoɐ] ear

Ohrentropfen *m pl* [ˈʔoːʀəntʀɔpfn] ear-drops

Ohrringe *m pl* [ˈʔoːʀɪŋə] earrings

Oktober [ˈʔɔkˈtoːbɐ] October

Öl *n* [ˈʔøːl] oil

Ölgemälde *n* [ˈʔøːlgəˌmɛːldə] *(picture)* oil painting

Oliven *f pl* [ʔoˈliːvn] olives

Olivenöl *n* [ʔoˈliːvnˈʔøːl] olive oil

Ölmalerei *f* [ˈʔøːlmaːləˌʀaɪ] *(activity)* oil painting

Ölquelle *f* [ˈʔøːlˈkvɛlə] oil well

Ölwechsel *m* [ˈʔøːlvɛksl] oil change

Oper *f* [ˈʔoːpɐ] opera

Operation *f* [ˈʔɔpəʀaˈtsjoːn] operation; surgery

Operette *f* [ˈʔɔpəˈʀɛtə] operetta

Optiker *m* [ˈʔɔptɪkɐ] optician's

Orangensaft *m* [ˈʔoˈʀaŋʒnzaft] orange juice

Orchester *n* [ˈʔɔɐˈkɛstɐ] orchestra

Orden *m* [ˈʔɔedn] *(rel.)* order

ordinär [ˈʔɔdiˈnɛːɐ] vulgar

Ordnung *f* [ˈʔɔetnʊŋ] order

Original *n* [ˈʔʀɪgiˈnaːl] original

Originalfassung *f* [ˈʔoʀɪgɪˈnaːlfasʊŋ] original version

Ort *m* [ˈʔɔet] place; spot

Ortschaft *f* [ˈʔɔetʃaft] village, town

Ortsgespräch *n* [ˈʔɔetsgəʃpʀɛːç] local call

Osten *m* [ˈʔɔstn] east

Ostermontag [ˈʔoːstɐˈmoːntaːk] Easter Monday

Österreich [ˈʔøːstəʀaɪç] Austria

Österreicher/in *m/f* [ˈʔøːstəʀaɪçɐ/-ʀaɪçəʀɪn] Austrian

P

Paar [ˈpʰaː] pair; couple

paar, ein ~ [(ˈʔaɪ)n ˈpʰaː] a few

Päckchen *n* [pɛkçn] small packet

packen [pakŋ] to pack

Packung *f* [ˈpakʊŋ] box, pack

Paket *n* [paˈkeːt] parcel

Palast *m* [paˈlast] palace

Panne *f* [ˈpanə] breakdown, puncture

Pannendienst *m* [ˈpanndiːnst] breakdown service

Papier *n* [paˈpiɐ] paper; **Papiere** *n pl* [paˈpiːʀə] documents, papers

Papierservietten *f pl* [paˈpiɐzeˌvjɛtn] paper napkins/serviettes

Papiertaschentücher *n pl* [paˈpiɐˌtaʃntyːçɐ] paper handkerchiefs

Paprika *m* [ˈpapʀɪka] paprika

Paprikaschoten *f pl* [ˈpapʀɪkaʃoːtn] peppers

Parfüm *n* [paˈfyːm] perfume, scent

Parfümerie *f* [pafʏməˈʀiː] perfumery

Park *m* [ˈpʰaːk] park

parken [ˈpʰaːkŋ] to park

Parkett *n* [paˈkɛt] stalls

Pass *m* [pas] *(mountain)* pass

Passagier *m* [pasaˈʒiɐ] passenger

passen [ˈpʰasn] to fit; to suit

Pauschalpreis *m* [pauˈʃaːlpʀaɪs] flat rate

Pelz *m* [pɛlts] fur

Perle *f* [ˈpɛɐlə] pearl

Person *f* [pʰɐˈzoːn] person

Personalausweis *m* [p(ɛ)ezoˈnaːlˌʔausvaɪs] identity card

Personalien *pl* [pʰezoˈnaːljən] particulars, personal data

persönlich [pʰɐˈzøːnlɪç] personal

Petersilie *f* [peˈteˈziːljə] parsley

Petroleum *n* [peˈtʀoːleʊm] paraffin

Pfad *m* [(p)faːt] path

Pfand n [(p)fant] deposit; security
Pfeffer m ['pfɛfɐ] pepper
Pfeiler m ['pfaɪlɐ] pillar
Pferd n [pfeɐt] horse
Pfirsiche m pl ['pfɪɛzɪçə] peaches
Pflanze f [' (p)flantsə] plant
Pflaster n ['pflastɐ] plaster
pflegebedürftig
['pfle:gəbədvɛftɪç] in need of care
Pfund n [(p)fʊnt] pound(s)
Pilot m [pi'lo:t] pilot
Pilz m [pɪlts] mushroom; fungal
infection
Pkw m ['pe:kave:] car
Plakat n [pla'kʰa:t] poster
Planschbecken n ['planʃbɛkn]
paddling pool
Plastikbeutel m ['plastɪkbɔɪtl]
plastic bag
Platz m [plats] place; seat
Platzreservierung f
['platsʀeze,vi:ʀʊŋ] seat reservation
Plombe f ['plɔmbə] (tooth) filling
plötzlich ['plœtslɪç] suddenly
Polizei f [pɔli'tsaɪ] police
Polizeiwagen m [pɔli'tsaɪva:gŋ]
police car
Polizist/Polizistin m/f
[pɔli'tsɪst/pɔli'tsɪstɪn] police-
man/policewoman
Pony m ['pɔni] fringe
Portal n [pɔ(e)'ta:l] portal
Portier m [pɔe'tje:] porter
Portion f [pɔ'tsjo:n] portion
Porto n ['pɔeto] postage
Porträt n [pɔ(e)'tʀɛ:] portrait
Porzellan n [pɔ(e)tsə'la:n]
porcelain, china
Postamt n ['pɔstamt] post office
Postkarte f ['pɔstka:tə] postcard
postlagernd ['pɔstla:gɐnt] poste
restante
Postleitzahl f ['pɔstlaɪtsa:l] post
code
Postsparbuch n ['pɔstʃpa:bu:x]
post office savings book
praktisch ['pʀaktʰɪʃ] practical(ly)

Preis m [pʀaɪs] price; prize
Prellung f ['pʀɛlʊŋ] bruise
Premiere f [pʀəm'je:ʀə] premiere
Priester m [pʀi:stɐ] priest
prima ['pʀi:ma:] great
privat [pʀi'va:t] private
Probe f ['pʀo:bə] experiment, test,
trial
Problem n [pʀo'ble:m] problem
Produkt n [pʀo'dʊkt] product
Programmheft n [pʀo'gʀamhɛft]
(booklet) programme
Promillegrenze f
[pʀo'mɪlə,gʀɛntsə] legal alcohol
limit
Prospekt m [pʀos'pɛkt] prospectus, leaflet, brochure
Prothese f [pʀo'te:zə] artificial
limb
provisorisch [pʀovi'zo:ʀɪʃ]
provisional, temporary
Prozent n [pʀo'tsɛnt] percent
Prozession f [pʀotsɛs'jo:n] procession
Prüfung f ['pʀy:fʊŋ] examination,
test
Publikum n ['pʰʊblɪkʰʊm] public;
audience
Puder m ['pu:dɐ] powder
Pullover m [pʊ'lo:vɐ] jumper, pullover, sweater
Puls m [pʊls] pulse
pünktlich ['pʰʏŋktlɪç] punctual(ly);
on time
putzen ['pʰʊtsn] to clean

Q

Qualität f [kvali'tʰɛ:t] quality
Quelle f ['kvɛlə] source; spring
quer durch [kveɐ dʊɐç] straight
across/through
Quetschung f ['kvɛtʃʊŋ] bruise
Quittung f ['kvɪtʰʊŋ] receipt

Rabatt *m* [ʁaˈbat] discount
Rad *n* [ʁaːt] wheel
Rad fahren [ˈʁaːt ˈfaːʁən] to cycle
Radarkontrolle *f*
[ʁaˈdaːkɔnˌtʁɔlə] radar check
Radierung *f* [ʁaˈdiːʁʊŋ] etching
Radio *n* [ˈʁaːdjoː] radio
Radsport *m* [ˈʁaːtʃpɔɐt] cycling
Radtour *f* [ˈʁaːttuɐ] cycle tour
Rampe *f* [ˈʁampə] ramp
rasch [ʁaʃ] quick
Rasen *m* [ˈʁaːzn] lawn, grass
Rasierapparat *m* [ʁaˈziɐˀapaˌʁaːt]
shaver
Rasierklinge *f* [ʁaˈziːklɪŋə] razor
blade
Rasierpinsel *m* [ʁaˈziːpɪnzl]
shaving brush
Rasierschaum *m* [ʁaˈziːʃaʊm]
shaving foam
Rasierwasser *n* [ʁaˈziːvasɐ] after-
shave lotion
Rathaus *n* [ˈʁaːthaʊs] town hall
Rauch *m* [ʁaʊx] smoke
rauchen [ʁaʊxn] to smoke
Raucher/in *m/f*
[ˈʁaʊxɐ/ˈʁaʊxərɪn] smoker
Raucherabteil *n* [ˈʁaʊxɐˀapˌtaɪl]
smoking compartment
Raum *m* [ʁaʊm] space; room
rechnen [ˈʁɛçn(ə)n] calculate
Rechnung *f* [ˈʁɛçnʊŋ] bill, invoice
Recht *n* [ʁɛçt] right
rechte(r, s) [ˈʁɛçtə (-tɐ, -təs)]
right(-hand)
rechts [ʁɛçts] on the right, to the
right
Rechtsanwalt/-anwältin *m/f*
[ˈʁɛçtsanvalt/-anvɛltɪn] lawyer
rechtzeitig [ˈʁɛçtsaɪtʰɪç] in time
reden [ʁeːdn] to talk
Reformhaus *n* [ʁeˈfɔʁmhaʊs]
health food shop
regelmäßig [ˈʁeːglmɛːsɪç]
regular(ly)

Regen *m* [ˈʁeːgn] rain
Regenmantel *m* [ˈʁeːgŋmantl]
raincoat
Regenschauer *m* [ˈʁeːgŋʃaʊɐ]
shower
Regie *f* [ʁəˈʒiː] *(film)* direction;
directed by
Regierung *f* [ʁeˈgiːʁʊŋ] government
regnerisch [ˈʁeːknəʁɪʃ] rainy
reich [ʁaɪç] rich
reichen [ʁaɪçn] be sufficient; hand
over, pass
reif [ʁaɪf] ripe
Reifen *m* [ˈʁaɪfn] tyre
Reifenpanne [ˈʁaɪfnˌpanə] flat
tyre
reinigen [ˈʁaɪnɪgn] to clean
Reinigung *f* [ˈʁaɪnɪgʊŋ] drycleaner's
Reis *m* [ʁaɪs] rice
Reise *f* [ˈʁaɪzə] journey, trip
Reisebüro *n* [ˈʁaɪzəbyˌʁoː] travel
agency
Reiseführer *m* [ˈʁaɪzəˌfyːʁɐ] guide-
book
Reiseführer/in *m/f* [ˈʁaɪzəˌfyːʁɐ/
-ˌfyːʁərɪn] guide, courier
Reisegesellschaft *f*
[ˈʁaɪzəgəˌzɛlʃaft] party of tourists
reisen [ʁaɪzn] to travel
Reisende *m/f* [ˈʁaɪzndə] tourist
Reisepass *m* [ˈʁaɪzəpas] passport
Reisescheck *m* [ˈʁaɪzəʃɛk] travel-
ler's cheque
Reisetasche *f* [ˈʁaɪzətaʃə] travel-
ling bag
reißen [ʁaɪsn] to tear; to pull
reiten [ˈʁaɪtn] to ride
Reitschule *f* [ˈʁaɪtʃuːlə] riding
school
Religion *f* [ʁelɪˈgjoːn] religion
Renaissance *f* [ʁənɛˈsaːs] Renaissance
rennen [ʁɛnn] to run
Rennrad *n* [ˈʁɛnʁaːt] racing bike
Reparatur *f* [ʁɛpaʁaˈtuɐ] repair

reparieren [ʀɛpʰaˈʀiːʀən /-ˈʀiən] to repair

reservieren [ʀɛzəˈviːʀən /-ˈviən] to reserve

Reservierung f [ʀɛzəˈviːʀʊŋ] reservation

Rest m [ʀɛst] *(remainder)* rest

Rettungsboot n [ˈʀɛtʊŋsboːt] lifeboat

Rettungsring m [ˈʀɛtʊŋsʀɪŋ] life belt, *(US)* life preserver

Revue f [ʀeˈvyː] show

Rezept n [ʀeˈtsɛpt] prescription

Rezeption f [ʀɛtsɛpˈtsjoːn] reception

R-Gespräch n [ˈʔɛʀɡəʃpʀɛːç] reverse charge call

Rheuma n [ˈʀɔɪma] rheumatism

Richter/in m/f [ˈʀɪçtɐ/ˈʀɪçtəʀɪn] judge

richtig [ˈʀɪçtɪç] right; proper

Richtung f [ˈʀɪçtʊŋ] direction

riechen [ˈʀiːçn] to smell

Rindfleisch n [ˈʀɪntflaɪʃ] beef

Rock m [ʀɔk] skirt

roh [ʀoː] raw; **roher Schinken** [ʀoːɐ ʃɪŋkn] smoked ham

Rollschuhe m pl [ˈʀɔlʃuːə] roller skates

Rollstuhl m [ˈʀɔlʃtuːl] wheelchair

Rollstuhlfahrer/in m/f [ˈʀɔlʃtuːlˌfaːʀɐ/-ˌfaːʀəʀɪn] wheelchair user

Rollstuhlkabine f [ˈʀɔlʃtuːlkaˌbiːnə] wheelchair cabin

Roman m [ʀoˈmaːn] novel

röntgen [ˈʀœnçn] to X-ray

Röntgenaufnahme f [ˈʀœnçnˈʔaʊfnaːmə] X-ray

rosa [ˈʀoːza] pink

Rosmarin m [ˈʀoːsmaʀiːn] rosemary

rot [ʀoːt] red

Röteln f pl [ˈʀøːtln] German measles

Rotwein [ˈʀoːtvaɪn] red wine

Route f [ˈʀuːtʰə] route

Rücken m [ˈʀʏkŋ] back

Rückenschmerzen m pl [ˈʀʏkŋʃmɛɐtsn] backache

Rückfahrkarte f [ˈʀʏkfaːˌkaːtə] return ticket

Rückfahrt f [ˈʀʏkfaːt] return journey, trip back

Rückholservice m [ˈʀʏkhoːlœsɶɛvɪs] pick-up service

Rückkehr f [ˈʀʏkʰeɐ] return

Rücklicht n [ˈʀʏklɪçt] rear light, tail light

Rucksack m [ˈʀʊkzak] rucksack, backpack

Rückspiegel m [ˈʀʏkʃpiːɡl] rear-view mirror

rückwärts [ˈʀʏkvɛɐts] backwards

Rückwärtsgang m [ˈʀʏkvɛɐtsɡaŋ] reverse gear

Ruderboot n [ˈʀuːdɛboːt] rowing boat

rudern [ˈʀuːdən] to row

rufen [ˈʀuːfn] to call

Ruhe f [ʀuːə] rest; calm; silence

ruhen [ˈʀuːn] to rest

ruhig [ˈʀʊɪç] silent, quiet, calm

Ruine f [ʀuˈʔiːnə] ruin

rund [ʀʊnt] *(adj)* round

Runde f [ˈʀʊndə] round

Rundfahrt f [ˈʀʊntfaːt] round trip, tour

S

Saal m [zaːl] room; hall

Sache f [ˈzaxə] thing; matter, affair

Sack m [zak] sack; bag

Safaripark m [zaˈfaːʀipaːk] safari park

Safe m [sɛɪf/seːf] safe

Safran m [ˈzafraːn] saffron

saftig [ˈzaftɪç] juicy

sagen [ˈzaːɡn] say; tell

Sahne f [ˈzaːnə] cream

Saison f [zɛˈzɔŋ] season

Salami f [za'la:mi] salami

Salat m [za'la:t] salad

Salatbüfett n [za'la:tbγ'fe:] salad bar

Salbe f ['zalbə] ointment

Salbei m ['zalbaɪ] sage

Salz n [zalts] salt

sammeln [zamln] collect

Samstag ['zamsta:k] Saturday

Sandalen f pl [zan'da:ln] sandals

Sandburg f ['zantbʊɐk] sand-castle

Sandkasten m ['zantkastn] sand pit

Sänger/in m/f ['zɛŋɐ/'zɛŋəʀɪn] singer

Satz m [zats] sentence

sauber ['zaʊbɐ] clean

sauer ['zaʊɐ] sour

Sauger m ['zaʊɡɐ] teat

Saugflasche f ['zaʊkflaʃə] feeding bottle

Säule f ['zɔɪlə] column, pillar

Sauna f ['zaʊna] sauna

saure Sahne f [zaʊʀə 'za:nə] sour cream

Schachtel f [ʃaxtl] box

schade, wie ~! [vi 'ʃa:də] what a pity/shame!

Schaden m [ʃa:dn] damage

Schadenersatz m ['ʃa:dn?ɐˌzats] compensation

schaffen [ʃafn] make, create; manage; work

Schafsfell n ['ʃa:fsfɛl] fleece

Schal m [ʃa:l] scarf

Schalter m ['ʃaltɐ] switch

Schampoo n ['ʃampo/'ʃampu] shampoo

scharf [ʃa:f] *(spicy)* hot

Schatten m [ʃatn] shade, shadow

schätzen [ʃɛtsn] *(person)* to like; to estimate *(amount etc.)*

schauen ['ʃaʊn] to look

Schaufenster n ['ʃaʊfɛnstɐ] shop window

Schauspiel n ['ʃaʊʃpi:l] play

Schauspieler/in ['ʃaʊʃpi:lɐ/ -ʃpi:ləʀɪn] actor/actress

Scheck m [ʃɛk] cheque; *(US)* check

Scheibe f ['ʃaɪbə] slice

Scheibenwischer m ['ʃaɪbmvɪʃɐ] windscreen wiper

Scheinwerfer m ['ʃaɪnvɛɐfɐ] headlight

Scheitel m [ʃaɪtl] parting

schenken [ʃɛŋkn] give (as a present)

Scherz m [ʃɛɐts] joke

schicken [ʃɪkn] send

Schiebedach n ['ʃi:bədax] sunroof

Schienbein n ['ʃi:nbaɪn] shin

Schiene f ['ʃi:nə] splint

Schild n [ʃɪlt] sign

Schinken m [ʃɪŋkn] ham

Schirm m [ʃɪɐm] umbrella

Schlaf m [ʃla:f] sleep

Schlafcouch f ['ʃla:fkaʊtʃ] studio couch

schlafen [ʃla:fn] to sleep

Schlaflosigkeit f ['ʃla:flo:zɪçkaɪt] insomnia, sleeplessness

Schlaftabletten f pl ['ʃla:ftaˌblɛtn] sleeping pills

Schlafzimmer n ['ʃla:ftsɪmɐ] bedroom

Schlaganfall m ['ʃla:kanfal] stroke

Schläger m ['ʃlɛ:ɡɐ] racquet

Schlagsahne f ['ʃla:kza:nə] whipping cream

Schlange f ['ʃlaŋə] snake

schlank [ʃlaŋk] slim, slender

schlau [ʃlaʊ] clever

Schlauchboot n ['ʃlaʊxbo:t] rubber dinghy

schlecht [ʃlɛçt] bad; badly

schließen [ʃli:sn] to shut, to close

schlimm [ʃlɪm] bad

Schlitten m [ʃlɪtn] sledge, toboggan

Schlittschuh laufen ['ʃlɪtʃu:laʊfn] go ice skating

Schlittschuhe m pl ['ʃlɪtʃu:ə] ice skates

Schloss n [ʃlɔs] castle; *(door)* lock

239

Schlucht f ['ʃlʊxt] ravine

Schluss m [ʃlʊs] end

Schlüssel m ['ʃlʏsl] key

Schlüsselbein n ['ʃlʏslbaɪn] collar-bone

schmal [ʃmaːl] narrow; slim, thin

schmerzen [ʃmɛɐtsn] to hurt

schmerzhaft ['ʃmɛɐtshaft] painful

Schmerztabletten f pl ['ʃmɛɐtstaˌblɛtn] pain-killing tablets

Schmuck m [ʃmʊk] jewellery

Schmuggel m [ʃmʊgl] smuggle

schmuggeln [ʃmʊgln] to smuggle

schmutzig ['ʃmʊtsɪç] dirty

Schnappschuss m ['ʃnapʃʊs] snapshot

schnarchen [ʃnaːçn] to snore

Schnee m [ʃneː] snow

schneiden [ʃnaɪdn] to cut

Schneider/in m/f ['ʃnaɪdɐ/'ʃnaɪdərɪn] dressmaker, tailor

schnell [ʃnɛl] quick(ly), fast

Schnittwunde f ['ʃnɪtvʊndə] cut

Schnitzerei f [ʃnɪtsə'raɪ] wood-carving

Schnorchel m ['ʃnɔɐçl] snorkel

schnorcheln [ʃnɔɐçln] go snorkelling

Schnuller m ['ʃnʊlɐ] (baby's) dummy, (US) pacifier

Schnupfen m [ʃnʊpfn] cold

Schnurrbart m ['ʃnʊɐbaːt] moustache

Schokolade f [ʃoko'laːdə] chocolate

Schokoriegel m ['ʃoːkoriːgl] chocolate bar

schon [ʃoːn] already

schön [ʃøːn] beautiful(ly)

Schonkost f ['ʃoːnkɔst] diet

Schonzeit f ['ʃoːntsaɪt] off-season

schottisch ['ʃɔtʰɪʃ] Scottish

Schottland ['ʃɔtlant] Scotland

Schraube f ['ʃraʊbə] screw

schrecklich ['ʃrɛklɪç] terrible, terribly, awful(ly), dreadful(ly)

schreiben [ʃraɪbm] write

Schreibtelefon n ['ʃraɪpteləfoːn] keyboard telephone

Schreibwarengeschäft n ['ʃraɪpvaːrəngəʃɛft] stationer's

schreien ['ʃraɪn] to shout; to scream

schriftlich ['ʃrɪftlɪç] in writing

schüchtern ['ʃʏçtɐn] shy

Schuh m [ʃuː] shoe

Schuhbürste f ['ʃuːbʏɐstə] shoe brush

Schuhcreme f ['ʃuːkrɛːm] shoe cream

Schuhgeschäft n ['ʃuːgəʃɛft] shoe shop

Schuhmacher m ['ʃuːmaxɐ] cobbler, shoemaker's

Schuld f [ʃʊlt] guilt

Schule f ['ʃuːlə] school

Schulter f ['ʃʊltɐ] shoulder

Schuppen f pl [ʃʊpm] dandruff

Schüssel f ['ʃʏsl] bowl

Schutz m [ʃʊts] security

schwach [ʃvax] weak, feeble

Schwager m ['ʃvaːgɐ] brother-in-law

Schwägerin f ['ʃvɛːgərɪn] sister-in-law

Schwangerschaft f ['ʃvaŋɐʃaft] pregnancy

schwarz [ʃvaːts] black

Schwarzbrot n ['ʃvaːtsbroːt] brown rye bread

Schwarzweiß-Film m [ʃvaːts'vaɪsfɪlm] black-and-white film

schweigen [ʃvaɪgn] be silent, keep quiet

Schweinefleisch n ['ʃvaɪnəflaɪʃ] pork

Schweiz f [ʃvaɪts] Switzerland

Schweizer Franken m pl [ʃvaɪtsɐ 'fraŋkn] Swiss francs

Schweizer/in m/f ['ʃvaɪtsɐ/'ʃvaɪtsərɪn] Swiss (man/woman)

Schwellung *f* ['ʃvɛlʊŋ] swelling

schwer [ʃveɐ] heavy; *(illness)* serious; difficult

Schwerbehinderte *m/f* ['ʃveɐbəhɪndetə] severely handicapped person

schwerhörig ['ʃveɐhø:ʀɪç] hard of hearing

Schwertfisch *m* ['ʃveɐtfɪʃ] swordfish

Schwester *f* ['ʃvɛstɐ] sister

schwierig ['ʃvi:ʀɪç] difficult

Schwimmbad *n* ['ʃvɪmba:t] swimming pool

schwimmen [ʃvɪmm] to swim

Schwimmer/in *m/f* ['ʃvɪmɐ/'ʃvɪməʀɪn] swimmer

Schwimmflügel *m pl* ['ʃvɪmfly:gl] water wings

Schwimmkurs *m* ['ʃvɪmkuɐs] swimming lessons

Schwimmring *m* ['ʃvɪmʀɪŋ] rubber ring

Schwimmweste *f* ['ʃvɪmvɛstə] life jacket

Schwindelgefühl *n* ['ʃvɪndlgəfy:l] dizziness

schwitzen ['ʃvɪtsn] perspire, sweat

schwül [ʃvy:l] humid

See *f* [di ze:] sea

Seefahrt *f* ['ze:fa:t] voyage

seekrank ['ze:kʀaŋk] seasick

Seereise *f* ['ze:ʀaɪzə] voyage

Seezunge *f* ['ze:tsʊŋə] *(fish)* sole

Segelboot *n* ['ze:glbo:t] sailing boat

Segelfliegen *n* ['ze:glfli:gn] gliding

segeln ['ze:gln] to sail

Segeltörn *m* ['ze:gltœn] sailing cruise

sehbehindert ['se:bəhɪndet] partially sighted

sehen ['ze:n] see

Sehenswürdigkeiten *f pl* ['ze:nsvʏɐdɪçkaɪtn] sights

sehr [zeɐ] very; very much

Seide *f* ['zaɪdə] silk

Seidenmalerei *f* ['zaɪdnma:ləˌʀaɪ] silk painting

Seife *f* ['zaɪfə] soap

Seil *n* [zaɪl] rope

Seilbahn *f* ['zaɪlba:n] cable railway, funicular

sein [zaɪn] *(vb)* to be

sein [zaɪn] *(poss. pron.)* his; its

seit [zaɪt] since; for

Seite *f* ['zaɪtʰə] side; page

Sekunde *f* [ze'kʰʊndə] second

Selbstauslöser *m* ['zɛlpstaʊslø:zɐ] self-timer

Selbstbedienung *f* ['zɛlps (t)bədi:nʊŋ] self-service

selbstverständlich [zɛlp(st)fɐ'ʃtɛntlɪç] of course

Sellerie *m* ['zɛləʀi:] celeriac

selten [zɛltn] rare; seldom

senden ['zɛndn] send

Senf *m* [zɛnf (zɛmf)] mustard

September [zɛp'tɛmbɐ] September

servieren [zɛ'vi:ʀən /-'vien] serve

Serviette *f* [zɛ'vjɛtə] napkin, serviette

setzen [zɛtsn] put

sexuelle Belästigung *f* [sɛksu'ɛlə bə'lɛstɪgʊŋ] sexual harassment

Show *f* [ʃo:] show

sicher ['zɪçɐ] safe; sure, certain(ly)

Sicherheit *f* ['zɪçɐhaɪt] safety; security

Sicherheitsgebühr *f* ['zɪçɐhaɪtsgəˌbyɐ] security charge

Sicherheitsgurt *m* ['zɪçɐhaɪtsgʊɐt] seat belt

Sicherheitskontrolle *f* ['zɪçɐhaɪtskɔnˌtʀɔlə] security control

Sicherung *f* ['zɪçəʀʊŋ] fuse

Sicht *f* [zɪçt] visibility; view

sie [zi:] she, her; they, them

Sie [zi:] you

Silber *n* ['zɪlbɐ] silver

Silvester [sɪl'vɛstɐ] New Year's Eve

Sinfoniekonzert n [zɪmfoˈniːkɔnˌtsɛɛt] symphony concert

singen [zɪŋŋ] sing

Sitz m [zɪts] seat; (place of) residence; headquarters

sitzen [zɪtsn] sit

Sitzplatz m [ˈzɪtsplats] seat

Skateboard n [ˈskɛɪtbɔet] skateboard; **Skateboard fahren** [ˈskɛɪtbɔet ˈfaːrən] to skateboard

Ski m [ʃiː] ski

Skibindungen f pl [ˈʃiːbɪndʊŋŋ] ski bindings

Skibrille f [ˈʃiːbrɪlə] ski goggles

Skikurs m [ˈʃiːkʊes] skiing course

Skilehrer/in m/f [ˈʃiːleːʀɐ/-leːʀəʀɪn] ski instructor

Skistiefel m pl [ˈʃiːʃtiːfl] ski boots

Skistöcke m pl [ˈʃiːˈʃtœkə] ski poles

Skulptur f [skʊlpˈtuɐ] sculpture

Slipeinlagen f pl [ˈslɪpaɪnlaːgŋ] panty liners

so [zoː] so, thus

Socken f pl [ˈzɔkŋ] socks

Sodbrennen n [ˈzoːtbʀɛnn] heartburn

sofort [zoˈfɔet] at once

Sofortbildkamera f [zoˈfɔetbɪltˌkaməʀa] Polaroid® camera

Sohle f [ˈzoːlə] (shoe) sole

Sohn m [zoːn] son

Solarium n [zoˈlaːʀɪʊm] solarium

Solist/Solistin m/f [zoˈlɪst/zoˈlɪstɪn] soloist

sollen [zɔln] shall, should

Sommer m [ˈzɔmɐ] summer

Sondermarke f [ˈzɔndɐmaːkə] special issue stamp

sondern [ˈzɔndɐn] but

Sonnabend [ˈzɔnaːbmt] Saturday

Sonne f [ˈzɔnə] sun

Sonnenbrand m [ˈzɔnnbʀant] sunburn

Sonnencreme f [ˈzɔnnkʀɛːm] sun cream

Sonnenhut m [ˈzɔnnhuːt] sun hat

Sonnenmilch f [ˈzɔnnmɪlç] suntan lotion

Sonnenöl n [ˈzɔnnʔøːl] suntan oil

Sonnenstich m [ˈzɔnnʃtɪç] sunstroke

sonnig [ˈzɔnɪç] sunny

Sonntag [ˈzɔntaːk] Sunday

Sorge f [ˈzɔegə] worry

sorgen, sich ~ um [zɪç ˈzɔegŋ ʔʊm] be worried about

sorgfältig [ˈzɔekfɛltɪç] careful

Sorte f [ˈzɔetə] kind, sort

Soße f [ˈzoːsə] gravy, sauce

Souvenir n [zʊvəˈniɐ] souvenir

Souvenirladen m [zʊvəˈniɐlaːdn] souvenir shop

Spargel m [ʃpaːgl] asparagus

spärlich [ˈʃpɛːelɪç] (sparse) thin

Spaß m [ʃpaːs] joke; fun

spät [ʃpɛːt] late

spazieren gehen [ʃpaˈtsiːʀəngeːn /-ˈtsiɐngeːn] go for a walk

Spaziergang m [ʃpaˈtsiɐgaŋ] walk, stroll; **einen Spaziergang machen** [(ʔaɪn)n ʃpaˈtsiɐgaŋ maxn] go for a walk

Speisekarte f [ˈʃpaɪzəkaːtə] menu

Speiseröhre f [ˈʃpaɪzəʀøːʀə] gullet

Speisesaal m [ˈʃpaɪzəzaːl] dining room

Speisewagen m [ˈʃpaɪzəvaːgŋ] restaurant car

Spezialität f [ʃpetsjaliˈtɛːt] speciality

speziell [ʃpɛˈtsjɛl] special

Spiegel m [ʃpiːgl] mirror

Spiel n [ʃpiːl] game, match

spielen [ʃpiːln] to play

Spielkamerad/in m/f [ˈʃpiːlkaməˌʀaːt/-kaməˌʀaːdɪn] playmate

Spielkasino n [ˈʃpiːlkaˌziːno] casino

Spielsachen f pl [ˈʃpiːl zaːxn] toys

Spielwarengeschäft n [ˈʃpiːlvaːʀəngəˈʃɛft] toy shop

Spinat *m* [ʃpɪ'naːt] spinach

Spirituosengeschäft *n* [ʃpiʀitu'oːzngəʃɛft] off-licence

Sport *m* [ʃpɔɐt] sport

Sportgeschäft *n* ['ʃpɔɐtgəʃɛft] sports shop

Sportler/in *m/f* ['ʃpɔɐtle/'ʃpɔɐtləʀɪn] athlete

Sportplatz *m* ['ʃpɔɐtplats] sports ground, athletics field

Sprache *f* ['ʃpʀaːxə] language

sprechen [ʃpʀɛçn] speak

Sprechstunde *f* ['ʃpʀɛçʃtʊndə] *(hours)* surgery

Springbrunnen *m* ['ʃpʀɪŋbʀʊnn] fountain

Spritze *f* ['ʃpʀɪtsə] injection

Spülbürste *f* ['ʃpyːlbʏɐstə] washing-up brush

Spülmittel *n* ['ʃpyːlmɪtl] detergent, washing-up liquid

Spültuch *n* ['ʃpyːltuːx] dishcloth

Staat *m* [ʃtaːt] state, country

Staatsangehörigkeit *f* ['ʃtaːts,ʔangehøːʀɪçkaɪt] nationality

Stadion *n* ['ʃtaːdjon] stadium

Stadt *f* [ʃtat] town, city

Stadtmauern *f pl* ['ʃtatmaʊen] town/city walls

Stadtplan *m* ['ʃtatplaːn] town plan, city map

Stadtrundfahrt *f* ['ʃtatʀʊntfaːt] sightseeing tour of the town/city

Stadtteil *m* ['ʃtatʰaɪl] district

Stadtzentrum *n* ['ʃtattsɛntʀʊm] city centre

stammen aus [ʃtamm] come from

im Stande sein [ʔɪm'ʃtandə zaɪn] be able to

Standlicht *n* ['ʃtantlɪçt] sidelights

stark [ʃtaːk] strong; *(pain)* severe

Starthilfekabel *n* ['ʃtaːtʰɪlfəkaːbl] jump leads

Station *f* [ʃta'tsjoːn] station, stop; ward

Stativ *n* [ʃta'tiːf] tripod

statt [ʃtat] instead of

stattfinden ['ʃtatfɪndn] take place

Statue *f* ['ʃtaːtuə] statue

Stau *m* [ʃtaʊ] traffic jam

Staub *m* [ʃtaʊp] dust

stechen [ʃtɛçn] to sting, to bite

Steckdose *f* ['ʃtɛkdoːzə] power point, socket

Stecker *m* ['ʃtɛke] plug

stehen [ʃteːn] to stand

stehen bleiben ['ʃteːnblaɪbm] to stop, stand still

stehlen [ʃteːln] to steal

steil [ʃtaɪl] steep

Stein *m* [ʃtaɪn] stone

steinig ['ʃtaɪnɪç] stony

Stelle *f* ['ʃtɛlə] spot, place; job

stellen [ʃtɛln] put

Stellung *f* ['ʃtɛlʊŋ] job, position

Stempel *m* [ʃtɛmpl] stamp

Stern *m* [ʃtɛɐn] star

Sternwarte *f* ['ʃtɛɐnvaːtə] observatory

stets [ʃteːts] always

Steward/Stewardess *m/f* ['ʃtjuaːt/'ʃtjuadɛs] flight attendant, steward/stewardess

Stich *m* [ʃtɪç] sting, bite

Stiefel *m pl* [ʃtiːfl] boots

Stil *m* [stiːl (ʃtiːl)] style

still [ʃtɪl] quiet, silent; still, calm

Stillleben *n* ['ʃtɪleːbm] still life

Stimme *f* ['ʃtɪmə] voice; vote

stinken [ʃtɪŋkn] to smell, to stink

Stirnhöhlenentzündung *f* ['ʃtɪɐnhøːln?ɛn,tsʏndʊŋ] sinusitis

Stock *m* [ʃtɔk] stick

Stockwerk *n* ['ʃtɔkvɛɐk] floor, storey

Stoff *m* [ʃtɔf] material

stören [ʃtøɐn] disturb, bother

stornieren [ʃtɔ'niːen] cancel

Stoßstange *f* ['ʃtoːʃtaŋə] bumper

Strafe *f* ['ʃtʀaːfə] punishment; fine

Strafraum *m* ['ʃtʀaːfʀaʊm] penalty box

Strähnchen *n pl* ['ʃtʀɛːnçn] highlights

Strand *m* [ʃtʀant] beach

Strandschuhe *m pl* [ʃtʀantʃuə] beach shoes

Straße *f* [ʃtʀaːsə] street; road

Straßenbahn *f* [ʃtʀaːsnbaːn] streetcar, tram

Straßenkarte *f* [ʃtʀaːsnkaːtə] road map

Strecke *f* [ʃtʀɛkʰə] distance; *(railway)* line; road, route

Streichhölzer *n pl* [ʃtʀaɪçhœltsə] matches

streng [ʃtʀɛŋ] severe; strict

Strickjacke *f* [ʃtʀɪkjakə] cardigan

Strohhalm *m* [ʃtʀoːhalm] straw

Strom *m* [ʃtʀoːm] (large) river; *(electricity)* current

Strompauschale *f* [ʃtʀoːmpauʃaːlə] flat rate for electricity

Stromspannung *f* [ʃtʀoːmʃpanʊŋ] voltage

Strömung *f* [ʃtʀøːmʊŋ] *(water)* current

Strümpfe *m pl* [ʃtʀʏmpfə] stockings

Strumpfhose *f* [ʃtʀʊmpfhoːzə] tights

Stück *n* [ʃtʏk] piece; play

studieren [ʃtʊˈdiːʀən /-ˈdiən] to study

Stufe *f* [ʃtuːfə] step

Stufenschnitt *m* [ʃtuːfnʃnɪt] layered cut

Stuhl *m* [ʃtuːl] chair

Stuhlgang *m* [ʃtuːlɡaŋ] bowel movement

stumm [ʃtʊm] mute

Stunde *f* [ʃtʊndə] hour; lesson; eine halbe Stunde [(ˌʔaɪ)nə ˌhalbə ˈʃtʊndə] half an hour

stündlich [ʃtʏntlɪç] every hour, hourly

Sturm *m* [ʃtʊʀm] gale, storm

Sturz *m* [ʃtʊʀts] fall

stürzen [ʃtʏʀtsn] to fall

Sturzhelm *m* [ʃtʊʀtshɛlm] crash helmet

suchen [zuːxn] look for

Sucher *m* [zuːxɐ] viewfinder

Süden *m* [zyːdn] south

südlich von [zyːtlɪç fɔn] south of

Summe *f* [zʊmə] sum; amount

Supermarkt *m* [zuːpɐmaːkt] supermarket

Suppe *f* [zʊpə] soup

Suppenteller *m* [zʊpmtɛlɐ] soup plate

Surfbrett *n* [ˈsœːfbʀɛt] surfboard

surfen [ˈsœːfn] to surf

süß [zyːs] sweet

Süßigkeiten *f pl* [zyːsiçkaɪtn] sweets

Süßstoff *m* [zyːʃtɔf] sweetener

Süßwarengeschäft *n* [zyːsvaːʀənɡəʃɛft] sweet shop

Swimmingpool *m* [ˈsvɪmɪŋpuːl] *(private)* swimming pool

sympathisch [zʏmˈpʰaːtʰɪʃ] nice, pleasant

T

Tabak *m* [ˈtʰabak] tobacco

Tabakladen *m* [ˈtabaklaːdn] tobacconist's

Tablette *f* [taˈblɛtə] pill, tablet

Tacho(meter) *m* [ˌtaxo(ˈmeːtɐ)] speedometer

Tag *m* [tʰaːk] day; jeden ~ [jeːdn taːk] every day

Tagesausflug *m* [ˈtaːɡəsˌʔausfluːk] day trip

Tagesgericht *n* [ˈtaːɡəsɡəʀɪçt] dish of the day

Tageskarte *f* [ˈtaːɡəskaːtə] day ticket

Tagesmenü *n* [ˈtaːɡəsmeˌnyː] special (of the day)

Tagespass *m* [ˈtaːɡəspas] day pass

täglich [tɛːklɪç] daily

tagsüber ['ta:ks²y:bɐ] during the day

Tal n [ta:l] valley

Tampons m pl ['tampɔŋs] tampons

Tank m [taŋk] (petrol) tank

tanken ['thaŋkŋ] fill up

Tanz m [thants] dance

tanzen [tantsn] to dance

Tänzer/in m/f [tɛntsɐ/tɛntsə'ʁɪn] dancer

Tanzkapelle f ['tantska‚pɛlə] dance band

Tanztheater n ['tantste‚²a:tɐ] dance theatre

Tasche f ['thaʃə] pocket; bag

Taschenbuch n ['taʃnbu:x] paperback

Taschendieb/in m/f ['taʃndi:p/ -‚di:bɪn] pickpocket

Taschenmesser n ['taʃnmɛsɐ] pocket knife

Taschenrechner m ['taʃnʁɛçnɐ] pocket calculator

Tasse f ['tasə] cup

Taststock m ['tastʃtɔk] cane

Tätigkeit f ['tɛ:tɪçkaɪt] (job) work

taubstumm ['taupʃtʊm] deafmute

tauchen [taʊxn] to dive

Taucherausrüstung f ['taʊxɐ²aʊsʁystʊŋ] diving equipment

Taucherbrille f ['taʊxɐbʁɪlə] diving goggles

tauschen ['thaʊʃn] to exchange, to swap; (money) to change

täuschen, sich ~ [zɪç 'thɔɪʃn] be mistaken, be wrong

Taxifahrer/in m/f ['taksifa:ʁɐ/ -fa:ʁəʁɪn] taxi driver

Taxistand m ['taksi‚ʃtant] taxi rank/stand

Tee m [te:] tea

Teebeutel m ['te:bɔɪtl] tea bag

Teelöffel m ['te:lœfl] teaspoon

Teil m [thaɪl] part

teilnehmen (an) ['thaɪlne:mm (²an)] take part (in)

Telefon n ['te:ləfo:n] telephone

Telefonbuch n [telə'fo:nbu:x] telephone directory

telefonieren [thelefo'ni:ʁən/ -'nien] make a phone call, to phone

Telefonkarte f [telə'fo:nka:tə] phonecard

Telefonnummer f [telə'fo:nnʊmɐ] phone number

Telefonzelle f [telə'fo:ntsɛlə] phone box/booth

telegrafische Überweisung f [telə'gʁa:fɪʃə ²y:bɐ'vaɪzʊŋ] telegraphic transfer

Teleobjektiv n ['te:lə²ɔbjɛk‚ti:f] telephoto lens

Telex n ['te:lɛks] telex

Teller m ['tɛlɐ] plate

Tempel m [tɛmpl] temple

Temperatur f [‚tɛmpəʁa'tu:ɐ] temperature

Tennis n ['tɛnɪs] tennis

Tennisschläger m ['tɛnɪʃlɛ:gɐ] tennis racquet

Termin m [tʰɛ'mi:n] appointment; deadline

Terminal n ['tə:mɪnəl] terminal

Terrakotta f [tɛʁa'kɔta] terracotta

Terrasse f [te'ʁasə] terrace

Tetanus m ['tɛtanʊs] tetanus

teuer ['thɔɪɐ] dear, expensive

Theater n [te'²a:tɐ] theatre

Theaterkasse f [te'²a:te‚kasə] box-office

Thriller m ['θʁɪlɐ] thriller

Thunfisch m ['tu:nfɪʃ] tuna

Thymian m ['ty:mia:n] thyme

tief [tʰi:f] deep; low

Tier n [tʰiɐ] animal

Tintenfisch m ['tɪntnfɪʃ] squid

Tipp m [tʰɪp] (information) tip

Tisch m [tʰɪʃ] table

Tischtennis n ['tiʃtɛnɪs] table tennis

Tischtuch n ['tɪʃtu:x] tablecloth

Toast *m* [toːst] toast
Toaster *m* ['toːste] toaster
Tochter *f* ['tʰɔxtʰe] daughter
Toilette *f* [toˈlɛtə] lavatory, toilet
Toilettenpapier *n* [toˈlɛtnpaˌpiɐ]
toilet paper
toll [tɔl] wonderful
Tomaten *f pl* [toˈmaːtn] tomatoes
Ton *m* [toːn] sound, tone; *(colour)*
shade
tönen [tøːnn] to tint
Töpferei *f* [tœpfəˈʀaɪ] *(place)* pot-
tery
Töpfern ['tœpfen] *(activity)* pottery
Töpferwaren *f pl*
['tœpfeva:ʀən] *(product)* pottery
Tor *n* [toɐ] gate; *(sport)* goal
Torwart/in *m/f*
['toɐva:t/'toɐva:tin] goalkeeper
Tour *f* [tʰuɐ] tour, excursion, trip
Tourist/in *m/f* [tuˈʀɪst/tuˈʀɪstɪn]
tourist
tragen [tʀaːgn] carry; wear
Tragödie *f* [tʀaˈgøːdiə] tragedy
trampen [tʀɛmpm] hitchhike
Traum *m* [tʀaʊm] dream
träumen [tʀɔɪmm] to dream
traurig ['tʀaʊʀɪç] sad
treffen [tʀɛfn] meet
Trekkingrad *n* ['tʀɛkɪŋʀaːt]
trekking bike
Treppe *f* ['tʀɛpʰə] stairs, staircase;
steps
trinken [tʀɪŋkn] to drink
Trinkflasche *f* ['tʀɪŋkflaʃə] baby's
bottle
Trinkgeld *n* ['tʀɪŋkgɛlt] *(gratuity)*
tip
Trinkwasser *n* ['tʀɪŋkvasɐ] drinking water
trocken ['tʀɔkn] dry
Trödelladen *m* ['tʀøːdllaːdn]
second-hand shop
Trommelfell *n* ['tʀɔmlfɛl] eardrum
tropfen [tʀɔpfn] to drip; *(nose)* to
run
Tropfen *m pl* ['tʀɔpfn] drops

Tropfsteinhöhle *f*
['tʀɔpfʃtaɪnˌhøːlə] dripstone cave
trotzdem ['tʀɔtsdeːm] nevertheless
trüb [tʀyːp] *(liquid)* cloudy;
(weather) overcast, cloudy
Tuch *n* [tʰuːx] cloth
tun [tʰuːn] do
Tunnel *m* [tʰʊnl] tunnel
Tür *f* [tʰyɐ] door
Türbreite *f* ['tyɐbʀaɪtə] door
width
Türcode *m* ['tyɐkoːt] door code
türkisfarben [tʏɐˈkiːsfaːbm] turquoise
Turm *m* [tʊɐm] tower
Türöffner *m* ['tyɐˀœfnɐ] door
opener
Türschwelle *f* ['tyɐʃvɛlə] doorstep
Tüte *f* ['tʰyːtʰə] bag; *(ice cream)*
cone
Typhus *m* ['tyːfʊs] typhoid
typisch ['tʰyːpʰɪʃ] typical

U-Bahn *f* ['ˀuːbaːn] underground,
(US) subway
üben [ˀyːbm] practise
über [ˀyːbɐ] over
überall [ˀyːbɐˀal] everywhere
überbacken [ˀybɐˈbakn] au gratin
Überfall *m* [ˀyːbɐfal] mugging
Übergang *m* [ˀyːbɐgaŋ] crossing;
transition
überholen [ˀybɐˈhoːln] overtake,
pass
übermorgen [ˀyːbɐmɔɐgn] the
day after tomorrow
übernachten [ˀybɐˈnaxtn] stay
(overnight), spend the night
überqueren [ˀybɐˈkveːʀən/
-ˈkveɐn] to cross
Überreste *m pl* [ˀyːbɐʀɛstə]
remains

überschreiten [ˈyˈbɐʃraɪtn] to cross

übersetzen [ˈyˈbɐˈzɛtsn] translate

Überweisung f [ˈyˈbɐˈvaɪzʊŋ] remittance, transfer

üblich [ˈyˈplɪç] usual

Ufer n [ˈʔuˈfɐ] (river) bank; shore

Uhrmacher m [ˈʔuˈemaxɐ] watchmaker('s)

um [ˈʔʊm] around; (time) at, about

umbuchen [ˈʔʊmbuˈxn] change the booking

Umgebung [ˈʔʊmˈgeˈbʊŋ] surroundings

umgekehrt [ˈʔʊmgɐkʰeet] reverse

Umhängetasche f [ˈʔʊmhɛŋɐˌtaʃɐ] shoulder bag

umkehren [ˈʔʊmkʰeˈʀɐn/-kʰeen] turn back

umsonst [ˈʔʊmˈzɔnst] free (of charge); in vain

umsteigen [ˈʔʊmʃtaɪgn] to change (trains etc.)

umtauschen [ˈʔʊmtʰaʊʃn] to change, to exchange

Umweg m [ˈʔʊmveˈk] detour

Umwelt f [ˈʔʊmvɛlt] environment

umziehen, sich ~ [zɪç ˈʔʊmtsiˈn] to change (clothes)

unangenehm [ˈʔʊnangɐneˈm] unpleasant

unbedingt [ˈʔʊnbɐdɪŋt] really

und [ˈʔʊnt] and

unentschieden [ˈʔʊnɛntˌʃiˈdn] (sport) draw

unerfreulich [ˈʔʊnɐfʀɔɪlɪç] unpleasant

unerträglich [ˈʔʊnɐˌtʀɛˈklɪç] intolerable, unbearable

Unfall m [ˈʔʊnfal] accident

ungeeignet [ˈʔʊngɐˈʔaɪknɐt] unfit, unsuited

ungefähr [ˈʔʊngɐˌfee] about

ungern [ˈʔʊngɐɐn] reluctantly

ungewöhnlich [ˈʔʊngɐvøˈnlɪç] unusual

unglaublich [ˈʔʊnˈglaʊplɪç] in-credible

Unglück n [ˈʔʊnglʏkʰ] accident; misfortune

unglücklicherweise [ˌʔʊnglʏklɪçɐˈvaɪzɐ] unfortunately

Universität f [ˈʔʊniveˌɐziˈtʰɛːt] university

unmöglich [ˈʔʊnˌmøːglɪç] impossible

Unrecht haben [ˈʔʊnʀɛçt haːbm] be wrong

uns [ˈʔʊns] us

unser(e) [ˈʔʊnzɐ (-ʀɐ)] our

unten [ˈʔʊntn] below

unter [ˈʔʊntʰɐ] under; among

unterbrechen [ˈʔʊntʰɐˈbʀɛçn] interrupt

Unterführung f [ˈʔʊntʰɐˈfyːʀʊŋ] subway, underpass

unterhalb [ˈʔʊntʰɐhalp] below

unterhalten [ˈʔʊntɐˈhaltn] (feed) keep, maintain, support; entertain; sich ~ [zɪç ˈʔʊntʰɐˈhaltn] to talk; to amuse oneself

Unterhaltung f [ˈʔʊntʰɐˈhaltʰʊŋ] conversation; entertainment

Unterhemd n [ˈʔʊntɐhɛmt] vest

Unterhose f [ˈʔʊntɐhoːzɐ] pants

Unterkunft f [ˈʔʊntʰɐkʰʊnft] accommodation

Unternehmen n [ˈʔʊntɐneˈmm] firm

unterrichten [ˈʔʊntʰɐˈʀɪçtn] inform; teach

Unterrichtsstunde f [ˈʔʊntɐʀɪçtˌʃtʊndɐ] lesson

unterschreiben [ˈʔʊntʰɐˈʃʀaɪbm] to sign

Unterschrift f [ˈʔʊntʰɐʃʀɪft] signature

Untersuchung f [ˈʔʊntɐˈzuːxʊŋ] examination

Untersuchungshaft f [ˈʔʊntɐˈzuːxʊŋshaft] police custody

Untertasse f [ˈʔʊntɐtasɐ] saucer

Untertitel m [ˈʔʊntɐtɪtl] subtitles

Unterwäsche f [ˈʔʊntɐvɛʃɐ] underwear

unverschämt [ˈʔʊnfɛʃɛːmt]
impertinent, cheeky, rude

unwahrscheinlich [ˈʔʊnvaʃaɪnlɪç]
unlikely, improbable

unwichtig [ˈʔʊnvɪçtɪç] unimportant

Urin *m* [ʔuˈʀiːn] urine

Urlaub *m* [ˈʔuɐlaʊp] holidays, vacation

Ursache *f* [ˈʔuɐzaxə] cause, reason

Urteil *n* [ˈʔuɐtaɪl] judgement; opinion

V

Varietee *n* [vaʀiəˈteː] music hall, variety theatre

Vase *f* [ˈvaːzə] vase

Vater *m* [ˈfaːtʰɐ] father

Vaterland *n* [ˈfaːtɐlant] native country

Vegetarier/in
[vegeˈtaːʀɪɐ/vegeˈtaːʀɪərɪn] *(person)* vegetarian

vegetarisch [vegeˈtaːʀɪʃ]
vegetarian

Ventilator *m* [vɛntiˈlaːtoɐ] fan

Verabredung *f* [fɛˈʔapʀeːdʊŋ]
appointment; date

verabschieden, sich ~ [zɪç
fɛˈʔapʃiːdn] say goodbye

verändern [fɛˈʔɛndɐn] to change, alter

Veränderung *f* [fɛˈʔɛndəʀʊŋ]
change

Veranstaltung *f* [fɛˈʔanʃtaltʰʊŋ]
event

verantwortlich [fɛˈʔantvɔɐtlɪç]
responsible

Verband *m* [fɛˈbant] bandage, dressing

verbinden [fɛˈbɪndn] join, connect; *(med.)* to dress

Verbindung *f* [fɛˈbɪndʊŋ] connection

verboten [fɛˈboːtn] forbidden, prohibited

Verbrechen *n* [fɛˈbʀɛçn] crime

verbrennen [fɛˈbʀɛnn] to burn

Verbrennung *f* [fɛˈbʀɛnʊŋ] burn

verbringen [fɛˈbʀɪŋŋ] spend *(time)*

Verdauung *f* [fɛˈdaʊʊŋ] digestion

Verdauungsstörung *f*
[fɛˈdaʊʊŋʃtøːʀʊŋ] indigestion

verdorben [fɛˈdɔɐbm] spoiled; rotten; corrupt

Verein *m* [fɛˈʔaɪn] association, club

vereinbaren [fɛˈʔaɪnbaːʀən)n]
agree on

verfehlen [fɛˈfeːln] *(not attain)* to miss

Vergangenheit *f* [fɛˈgaŋŋhaɪt]
past

vergehen [fɛˈgeːn] *(time)* to pass

vergessen [fɛˈgɛsn] forget

Vergewaltigung *f* [fɛgeˈvaltɪgʊŋ]
rape

Vergiftung *f* [vɛˈgɪftʊŋ] poisoning

Vergnügen *n* [fɛˈgnyːgn] pleasure

verhaften [fɛˈhaftn] to arrest

Verhandlung *f* [fɛˈhandlʊŋ]
(court) trial

verheiratet [fɛˈhaɪʀaːtət] married

verhindern [fɛˈhɪndɐn] prevent

verirren, sich ~ [zɪç fɛˈʔɪʀən/
ˈʔɪʀən] lose one's way, get lost

Verkauf *m* [fɛˈkʰaʊf] sale

verkaufen [fɛˈkʰaʊfn] to sell

Verkehr *m* [fɛˈkʰeɐ] traffic

verkehren [fɛˈkeːʀən/ˈkeɐn] *(bus etc.)* to run

Verkehrsbüro *n* [fɛˈkeɐsbyˌʀoː]
tourist information office

verlängern [fɛˈlɛŋən] extend

Verlängerungsschnur *f*
[fɛˈlɛŋəʀʊŋʃnuɐ] extension lead

verlassen [fɛˈlasn] to leave

verletzen [fɛˈlɛtsn] injure

Verletzte *m/f* [fɛˈlɛtstə] injured person

Verletzung f [fɐˈlɛtsʊŋ] injury

verlieren [fɐˈliːʀən /-ˈliən] lose

Verlobte m/f [fɐˈloːptə] fiancé/fiancée

vermieten [fɐˈmiːtn] let (out), rent (out)

verpacken [fɐˈpakŋ] pack, wrap

Verpackung f [fɐˈpʰakʰʊŋ] packing, wrapping

verpassen [fɐˈpʰasn] to miss *(bus, opportunity)*

Verpflegung f [fɐˈ(p)fleːgʊŋ] food; board

verrechnen, sich ~ [zɪç fɐˈʀɛçn (ə)n] miscalculate, make a mistake

verreisen [fɐˈʀaɪzn] go on a journey

verrückt [fɐˈʀʏkt] mad, crazy

verschieben [fɐˈʃiːbm] put off, postpone

verschieden [fɐˈʃiːdn] different(ly)

verschließen [fɐˈʃliːsn] to lock

Verschluss m [fɐˈʃlʊs] *(door)* lock

verschreiben [fɐˈʃʀaɪbm] prescribe

Versicherung f [fɐˈzɪçəʀʊŋ] insurance

Verspätung f [fɐˈʃpɛːtʊŋ] delay

Verstand m [fɐˈʃtant] *(mind)* reason

verstaucht [fɐˈʃtaʊxt] sprained

verstehen [fɐˈʃteːn] understand

Verstopfung f [fɐˈʃtɔpfʊŋ] constipation

Versuch m [fɐˈzuːx] attempt, try; experiment, test

versuchen [fɐˈzuːxn] to try; to taste

vertauschen [fɐˈtaʊʃn] mistake for

Vertrag m [fɐˈtʀaːk] contract

Vertrauen n [fɐˈtʀaʊn] confidence

verunglücken [fɐˈʔʊnglʏkŋ] have an accident

verursachen [fɐˈʔuɐzaxn] to cause

Verwaltung f [fɐˈvaltʰʊŋ] administration

verwandt [fɐˈvant] related

verwechseln [fɐˈvɛksln] confuse, mix up

verwenden [fɐˈvɛndn] to employ, to use

Verwendung f [fɐˈvɛndʊŋ] use

verwitwet [fɐˈvɪtvət] widowed

verzögern [fɐˈtsøːgen] to delay

Videofilm m [ˈviːdeofɪlm] video film

Videokamera f [ˈviːdeoˌkaməʀa] video camera

Videokassette f [ˈviːdeokaˌsɛtə] video cassette

Videorekorder m [ˈviːdeoʀeˌkɔɐdɐ] video recorder

viel [fiːl] a lot of; much

vielleicht [fɪˈlaɪçt] perhaps, maybe

vielmehr [ˈfiːlmeɐ] rather

Viertelstunde f [fɪʀtlˈʃtʊndə] quarter of an hour

Virus n [ˈviːʀʊs] virus

Visum n [ˈviːzʊm] visa

Vogel m [foːgl] bird

Vogelschutzgebiet n [ˈfoːglʃʊtsgəbiːt] bird reserve

Volk n [fɔlk] people

voll [fɔl] full; crowded

vollenden [fɔlˈʔɛndn] to complete

Volleyball m [ˈvɔlɪbal] volleyball

völlig [ˈfœlɪç] complete(ly)

Vollkasko f [ˈfɔlkasko] fully comprehensive insurance

von [fɔn] from; of; by

vor [foɐ] in front of; before

Voranmeldung f [ˈfoɐʔanmɛldʊŋ] booking

im Voraus [ʔɪm ˈfoːʀaʊs] in advance

vorbei [fɔˈbaɪ] over, past

vorbeigehen [fɔˈbaɪgeːn] go by/past; pass

vorbereiten [ˈfoɐbəʀaɪtn] prepare

vorbestellen [ˈfoɐbəʃtɛln] to book

Vorfall m [ˈfoɐfal] incident

vorgestern [ˈfɔagɛsten] the day before yesterday

vorher [ˈfoɐheɐ] before

vorläufig ['foɐlɔɪfɪç] temporary

Vormittag m ['foɐmɪtʰaːk] morning

vormittags ['foɐmɪtaːks] in/during the morning

vorn [fɔɐn] in front

Vorname m ['foɐnaːmə] Christian name, first name

vornehm ['foɐneːm] distinguished, posh, noble

Vorort ['foɐˀɔɐt, 'foɐʃtat] suburb

Vorrat m ['foːraːt] stock, store, provisions

Vorsaison f ['foɐzeˌzɔn] low season, off-season

Vorschlag m ['foɐʃlaːk] suggestion

Vorschrift f ['foɐʃʀɪft] rule

Vorsicht f ['foɐzɪçt] caution

vorsichtig ['foɐzɪçtɪç] careful, cautious

Vorspeise f ['foɐʃpaɪzə] hors d'"uvre, starter

Vorstadt f ['foɐʃtat] suburb

vorstellen ['foɐʃtɛln] introduce

Vorstellung f ['foɐʃtɛlʊŋ] introduction; notion, idea; *(theatre)* performance

Vorteil m ['fɔɐtʰaɪl] advantage

vorüber [fo'ʀyːbɐ] past, over; gone

vorübergehen [fo'ʀyːbegeːn] *(time)* to pass

vorübergehend [fo'ʀyːbegeːnt] temporary

Vorverkauf m ['foɐfekaʊf] advance booking

Vorwahlnummer f ['foɐvaːlˌnʊmɐ] area code

vorwärts ['fɔɐvɛɐts] forward(s)

vorzeigen ['foɐtsaɪgn] to show

Vorzug m ['foɐtsuːk] advantage

wach [vax] awake

wagen [vaːgn] to dare

Wagenheber m ['vaːgnheːbɐ] jack

Wagennummer f ['vaːgnnʊmɐ] coach number

Wahl f [vaːl] choice

wählen ['vɛːln] to choose; to vote; *(telephone)* to dial

wahr [vaː] true

während ['vɛːʀənt (veːnt)] during; while

wahrscheinlich [va'ʃaɪnlɪç] probable; probably

Währung f ['vɛːʀʊŋ] currency

Wahrzeichen n ['vaːtsaɪçn] emblem, symbol; landmark

Wald m [valt] forest, woods

Wales [weɪls (veɪls)] Wales

Waliser/in m/f [va'liːze/va'liːzəʀɪn] Welshman/Welshwoman

walisisch [va'liːzɪʃ] Welsh

Wallfahrtsort m ['valfaːtsˀɔɐt] place of pilgrimage

Wand f [vant] wall

Wanderkarte f ['vandekaːtə] hiking map

wandern ['vanden] to hike, to ramble

Wanderung ['vandəʀʊŋ] hike

Ware f ['vaːʀə] product

warm [vaːm] warm; warmes Wasser ['kaltəs 'vasɐ] hot water

Wärme f ['vɛɐmə] heat

wärmen ['vɛɐmm] to heat, to warm

Warnblinkanlage f ['vaːnblɪŋkˀanlaːgə] hazard warning lights

Warndreieck n ['vaːndʀaɪɛk] warning triangle

warten (auf) [vaːtn (ˀaʊf)] wait (for)

Wartesaal m ['vaːtəzaːl] waiting room

Wartezimmer n ['vaːtətsɪmɐ] waiting room

was [vas] what

Waschbecken *n* ['vaʃbɛkn] wash-basin

Wäscheklammern *f pl* ['vɛʃəklamən] clothes pegs

Wäscheleine *f* ['vɛʃəlaɪnə] clothes line

waschen ['vaʃn] to wash

Wäscherei *f* [vɛʃə'ʀaɪ] laundry

Waschlappen *m* ['vaʃlapm] flannel

Waschmittel *n* ['vaʃmɪtl] *(clothes)* detergent

Waschraum *m* ['vaʃʀaʊm] washroom

Waschsalon *m* ['vaʃza,lɔŋ] launderette

Wasser *n* ['vasɐ] water

Wasserfall *m* ['vasɐfal] waterfall

Wasserglas *n* ['vasɐgla:s] tumbler

Wasserhahn *m* ['vasɐha:n] *(water)* tap

Wasserkanister *m* ['vasɐkan,ɪstɐ] water canister

Wasserski fahren ['vasɐʃi: 'fa:ʀən] go water-skiing

Wasserverbrauch *m* ['vasɐfɛbʀaʊx] water consumption

Watte *f* ['vatə] cotton wool

Wattestäbchen *n* ['vatəʃtɛ:pçn] cotton bud

Wechsel *m* [vɛksl] change; exchange

Wechselgeld *n* ['vɛkslgɛlt] *(money)* change

wechselhaft ['vɛkslhaft] changeable

Wechselkurs *m* ['vɛkslkʊɐs] exchange rate

wechseln [(gɛlt) vɛksln] to change *(money)*

wecken [vɛkn] wake

Wecker *m* ['vɛkɐ] alarm clock

weg [vɛk] away; gone

Weg *m* [ve:k] way; path; road

wegen [ve:gn] because of

weggehen ['vɛkge:n] go away, leave

Wegweiser *m* ['ve:kvaɪzɐ] *(directions)* sign

wehtun ['ve:tu:n] to hurt

weich [vaɪç] soft

weigern, sich ~ [zɪç 'vaɪgɐn] to refuse

Weihnachten ['vaɪnaxtn] Christmas

weil [vaɪl] because, since

Wein *m* [vaɪn] wine

Weinberg *m* ['vaɪnbɛɐk] vineyard

weinen [vaɪnn] to cry

Weinglas *n* ['vaɪngla:s] wineglass

Weinhandlung *f* ['vaɪnhantlʊŋ] wine merchant's

Weintrauben *f pl* ['vaɪntʀaʊbm] grapes

Weise *f* ['vaɪzə] way

Weisheitszahn *m* ['vaɪshaɪtsa:n] wisdom tooth

weiß [vaɪs] white

Weißbrot *n* ['vaɪsbʀo:t] white bread

Weißwein ['vaɪsvaɪn] white wine

weit [vaɪt] wide; *(distance)* long; far

Welt *f* [vɛlt] world

wenig ['ve:nɪç] little, few

wenigstens ['ve:(:)nɪkstns] at least

wenn [vɛn] if; when

werden [veɐdn] become

Werkstatt *f* ['vɛɐkʃtat] *(repairs)* garage

werktags ['vɛɐktʰa:ks] on weekdays

Werkzeug *n* ['vɛɐktsɔɪk] tools

Wertangabe *f* ['ve:ɐtanga:bə] declaration of value

wertlos ['ve:ɐtlo:s] worthless

Wertsachen *f pl* ['ve:ɐtzaxn] valuables

Wespe *f* ['vɛspə] wasp

Weste *f* ['vɛstə] waistcoat; *(US)* vest

Westen *m* ['vɛstn] west

Western *m* ['vɛstɐn] *(film)* western

Wettervorhersage *f*

['vɛtɐfoˌheːzaːgə] weather forecast
Wettkampf *m* ['vɛtkamf] competition, contest
wichtig ['vɪçtɪç] important
Wickeltisch *m* ['vɪkltɪʃ] baby's changing table
wie [viː] how; *(comparison)* like; wie schade! [vi ˈʃaːdə] what a pity/shame!
wieder ['viːdɐ] again
wiedergeben ['viːdɐgeːbm] give back, return
wiederholen [vidɐˈhoːln] to repeat
wiederkommen ['viːdɐkhɔmm] come back, return
Wiedersehen, auf ~ [ʔaʊf ˈviˈːdɐzeːn] goodbye
Wiese *f* ['viːzə] meadow
wild [vɪlt] wild(ly)
Willkommen *n* [vɪlˈkhɔmm] welcome
willkommen [vɪlˈkhɔmm] *(adj)* welcome; willkommen heißen [vɪlˈkhɔmm haɪsn] to welcome
Wimperntusche *f* ['vɪmpɐntuʃə] mascara
Wind *m* [vɪnt] wind
Windeln *f pl* ['vɪndln] nappies, *(US)* diapers
Windpocken *f pl* ['vɪntpɔkn] chickenpox
Windschutzscheibe *f* ['vɪntʃʊtʃaɪbə] windscreen, *(US)* windshield
Windstärke *f* ['vɪntʃtɛɐkə] windforce
Windsurfen *n* ['vɪntsœɐfn] windsurfing
Winkel *m* ['vɪŋkl] corner
Winter *m* ['vɪntɐ] winter
Winterreifen *m* ['vɪntɐʀaɪfn] winter tyres
wir [viɐ / vɐ] we
Wirbelsäule *f* ['vɪʀblzɔɪlə] spine
wirklich ['vɪʀklɪç] real; true; really, truly
wissen [vɪsn] know

Witz *m* [vɪts] joke
Woche *f* ['vɔxə] week
Wochenende *n* ['vɔxnʔɛndə] weekend
Wochenendpauschale *f* ['vɔxnʔɛntpaʊʃaːlə] weekend rate
wochentags ['vɔxnthaːks] on weekdays
wöchentlich ['vœçntlɪç] weekly; once a week
wohl [voːl] *(comfortable)* well
wohlwollend ['voːlvɔlnt] kind
wohnen [voːnn] to live, to stay
Wohnort *m* ['voːnʔɔɐt] place of residence
Wohnung *f* ['voːnʊŋ] flat, apartment
Wohnzimmer *n* ['voːntsɪmɐ] living room
Wolke *f* ['vɔlkə] cloud
Wolle *f* ['vɔlə] wool
wollen [vɔln] to want, to wish
Wort *n* [vɔɐt] word
Wunde *f* ['vʊndə] wound
wunderbar ['vʊndɐbaː] wonderful, marvellous
wundern, sich ~ (über) [zɪç ˈvʊnden (ˌʔybɐ)] be surprised (at/about)
Wunsch *m* [vʊnʃ] request
wünschen [vynʃn] to want; to wish for
Wurm *m* [vʊɐm] worm
Wurst *f* [vʊɐst] sausage
würzen [vvɛtsn] to season
wütend [vyːtnt] furious

Yoga *n* ['joːga] yoga

Z

zäh [tsɛ:] tough
Zahl f [tsa:l] number, figure
zahlen ['tsa:ln] to pay
zählen [tsɛ:ln] to count
Zahlung f ['tsa:lʊŋ] payment
Zahn m [tsa:n] tooth
Zahnbürste f ['tsa:nbʏɐstə] toothbrush
Zahnfleisch n ['tsa:nflaɪʃ] gums
Zahnpasta f ['tsa:npasta] toothpaste
Zahnschmerzen m pl ['tsa:nʃmɛɐtsn] toothache
Zahnstocher m ['tsa:nʃtɔxɐ] toothpick
Zäpfchen n ['tsɛpfçn] suppository
zart [tsa:t] *(soft)* tender
zärtlich ['tsɛɐtlɪç] tender, gentle
Zehe f ['tseə] toe
Zeichen n ['tsaɪçn] sign
Zeichensprache f ['tsaɪçnʃpra:xə] sign language
Zeichentrickfilm m ['tsaɪçnˌtrɪkfɪlm] cartoon
zeichnen ['tsaɪçn (ə)n] to draw
Zeichnung f ['tsaɪçnʊŋ] drawing
zeigen ['tsaɪgn] to show
Zeit f [tsaɪt] time
Zeitschrift f ['tsaɪtʃrɪft] *(news)* magazine
Zeitung f ['tsaɪtʰʊŋ] newspaper
Zeitungshändler m ['tsaɪtʊŋshɛntlɐ] newsagent's
Zelt n [tsɛlt] tent
zelten ['tsɛltn] to camp
Zentimeter m [ˌtsɛnti'me:tɐ] centimetre
zentral [tsɛn'tra:l] central
Zerrung f ['tsɛrʊŋ] pulled muscle
ziehen ['tsi:n] to pull
Ziel n [tsi:l] aim; target; goal; destination
ziemlich ['tsi:mlɪç] fairly, rather, pretty, quite
Zigarette f [tsɪga'rɛtə] cigarette

Zigarillo n [tsɪga'rɪlo] cigarillo
Zigarre f [tsɪ'garə] cigar
Zimmer n ['tsɪmɐ] room
Zimmermädchen n ['tsɪmɐmɛ:tçn] maid
Zimmertelefon n ['tsɪmɐteləˌfo:n] in-room telephone
Zirkus m ['tsɪrkʊs] circus
Zitronen f pl [tsi'tro:nn] lemons
Zoll m ['tsɔl] customs
Zollerklärung f ['tsɔlɛklɛ:rʊŋ] customs declaration
zollfrei ['tsɔlfraɪ] duty-free
Zollgebühren f pl ['tsɔlgəby:rən] customs duty
zollpflichtig ['tsɔl(p)flɪçtɪç] liable to duty
Zoo m [tso:] zoo
zornig ['tsɔɐnɪç] angry
zu [tsu (:)] to; shut, closed; too; **zu viel** [tsu'fi:l] too much
zubereiten ['tsu:bəraɪtn] prepare, cook; mix *(drinks)*
Zucker m ['tsʊkɐ] sugar
zuerst [tsu'ʔeɐst] (at) first
zufällig ['tsu:fɛlɪç] by chance
zufrieden [tsu'fri:dn] satisfied
Zug m [tsu:k] train
Zugang m ['tsu:gaŋ] access, entrance
zugänglich ['tsu:gɛŋlɪç] accessible
Zukunft f ['tsu:kʰʊnft] future
zukünftig ['tsu:kʰʏnftɪç] *(adj)* future
zulassen ['tsu:lasn] to register *(car)*
zulässig ['tsu:lɛsɪç] permitted, allowed
zuletzt [tsu'lɛtst] finally; last
zumachen ['tsu:maxn] to close, to shut
zunächst [tsu'nɛ:çst/-'nɛ:kst] first (of all)
Zündkerze f ['tsʏntkɛɐtsə] spark plug
Zündschlüssel m ['tsʏntʃlʏsl] ignition key
Zündung f ['tsʏndʊŋ] ignition

Zunge *f* ['tsʊŋə] tongue

zurück [tsʊ'ʀʏk] back

zurückbringen [tsʊ'ʀʏkbʀɪŋŋ] bring back

zurückfahren [tsʊ'ʀʏkfa: (ʀə)n] drive back, return

zurückgeben [tsʊ'ʀʏkge:bm] give back

zurückkehren [tsʊ'ʀʏkʰe:ʀən/ -kʰeen] come back, return

zurückweisen [tsʊ'ʀʏkvaɪzn] to refuse

zurzeit [tsʊɐ'tsaɪt] at the moment

zusagen ['tsu:za:gn̩] accept *(invitation)*

zusammen [tsʊ'zamm] together

zusammenschlagen [tsʊ'zammʃla:gn̩] beat up

Zusammenstoß *m* [tsʊ'zammʃto:s] collision, crash

zusätzlich ['tsu:zɛtslɪç] additional; in addition

zuschauen ['tsu:ʃaʊn] to watch

Zuschauer/in *m/f* ['tsu:ʃaʊɐ/'tsu:ʃaʊəʀɪn] viewer, spectator

Zustand *m* ['tsu:ʃtant] state, condition

zuständig ['tsu:ʃtɛndɪç] responsible

zweimal ['tsvaɪma:l] twice

zweite(r, s) ['tsvaɪtə (-tɐ/-təs)] second

zweitens ['tsvaɪtns] second(ly)

Zwiebeln *f pl* ['tsvi:bln] onions

zwischen ['tsvɪʃn] between; among

Zwischenfall *m* ['tsvɪʃnfal] incident

Zwischenlandung *f* ['tsvɪʃn‚landʊŋ] stopover

Zwischenstecker *m* ['tsvɪʃnʃtɛkɐ] adapter

English – German Dictionary

A

abbey die Abtei [di ˀapˈtaɪ]

abbreviation die Abkürzung [di ˀapkʀɛtsʊŋ]

able, be ~ to im Stande sein [ˀɪmˈʃtandə zaɪn], können [kœnn]

about ungefähr [ˀʊngəˈfeɐ], etwa [ˀɛtvaː]; (time) gegen [geːgŋ]

about noon gegen Mittag [ˈgeːgŋ ˈmɪtaːk]

abroad im/ins Ausland [ˀɪm/ˀɪns ˀaʊslant]

abscess der Abszess [dɐ ˀapsˈɛs]

accelerator das Gaspedal [das ˈgaːspedaːl]

accept annehmen [ˀaneːmm]; (invitation) zusagen [ˈtsuːzaːgŋ]

access der Zugang [dɐ ˈtsuːgaŋ]

accessible zugänglich [ˈtsuːgɛŋlɪç]

accident der Unfall [dɐ ˀʊnfal]; have an accident verunglücken [fɐˀʊnglʏkŋ]

accommodation die Unterkunft [di ˀʊntekʊnft]

accompany begleiten [bəˈglaɪtn]

accompanying person die Begleitperson [di bəˈglaɪtpɛɐˌzoːn]

account das Konto [das ˈkɔnto]

acquaintance die Bekanntschaft [di bəˈkantʃaft]; (person) der/die Bekannte [dɐ/di bəˈkantə]

across quer durch [kveɐ dʊɾç]

act der Akt [dɐ ˀakt]

action film der Actionfilm [dɐ ˀɛktʃnfɪlm]

actor/actress der Schauspieler/die Schauspielerin [dɐ ˈʃaʊʃpiːlɐ/di ˈʃaʊʃpiːlərɪn]

actual(ly) eigentlich [ˀaɪgŋtlɪç]

adapter der Adapter [dɐ ˀaˈdaptɐ], der Zwischenstecker [dɐ ˈtsvɪʃnʃtɛkɐ]

add hinzufügen [hɪnˈtsuːfyːgŋ]; in addition zusätzlich [ˈtsuːzɛtslɪç]; additional zusätzlich [ˈtsuːzɛtslɪç]

additional costs die Nebenkosten [di ˈneːbmkɔstn]

address die Anschrift [di ˀanʃʀɪft], die Adresse [di ˀaˈdʀɛsə]; (vb) adressieren [ˀadʀɛˈsiːrən/-ˈsien]

addressee der Empfänger [dɐ ˀɛmpˈfɛŋɐ]

administration die Verwaltung [di fɐˈvaltʊŋ]

admission charge der Eintrittspreis [dɐ ˀaɪntʀɪtspʀaɪs]

admission ticket die Eintrittskarte [di ˀaɪntʀɪtsˌkaɐtə]

adult der/die Erwachsene [dɐ/di ˀɛˈvaks(ə)nə]

advance booking der Vorverkauf [dɐ ˈfoɐfɛkaʊf]

advance, in ~ im Voraus [ˀɪm ˈfoːʀaʊs]

advantage der Vorzug [dɐ ˈfoɐtsuːk]; der Vorteil [dɐ ˈfɔɐtaɪl]

aerobics das Aerobic [das ˀɛˈʀɔbɪk]

afraid erschrocken [ˀɛˈʃʀɔkŋ]; be afraid (of) sich fürchten (vor) [zɪç ˈfʏɾçtn foɐ]; befürchten [bəˈfʏʀçtn]

after nach [naːx]

afternoon der Nachmittag [dɐ ˈnaːxmɪtaːk]; in the afternoon nachmittags [ˈnaːxmɪtaːks]

after-shave lotion das Rasierwasser [das ʀaˈziːevasə]

afterwards nachher [ˈnaːx(h)eɐ], danach [daˈnaːx]

again wieder [ˈviːdɐ]

against gegen [geːgŋ]; be against it dagegen sein [daˈgeːgŋ zaɪn]

age das Alter [das ˈʔaltɐ]

agency die Agentur [di ʔaɡɛnˈtuɐ]

agree sich einigen [zɪç ˈʔaɪnɪɡn̩]; einig sein [ˈʔaɪnɪç zaɪn]; *(on a date, time etc.)* ausmachen [ˈʔaʊsmaxn̩]; **agree on** vereinbaren [fɐˈʔaɪnba:(rə)n]

agreeable angenehm [ˈʔanɡəne:m]

aid die Hilfe [di ˈhɪlfə]; **first aid** erste Hilfe [ˌʔeːstə ˈhɪlfə]

aim das Ziel [das tsi:l]

air die Luft [di lʊft]; lüften [ˈlʏftn̩]

air-conditioning die Klimaanlage [di ˈkliːmaʔanˌla:ɡə]

airline die Fluggesellschaft [di ˈfluːkɡəˌzɛlʃaft]

airport der Flughafen [dɐ ˈfluːkhaːfn̩]

airport bus der Flughafenbus [dɐ ˈfluːkhaːfn̩ˌbʊs]

airport tax die Flughafengebühr [di ˈfluːkhaːfnɡəˌbyɐ]

alarm clock der Wecker [dɐ ˈvɛkɐ]

alarm system die Alarmanlage [di ʔaˈlaːmanlaːɡə]

alarmed erschrocken [ʔɐˈʃʀɔkn̩]

all alle [ˈʔalə]; ganz [ɡants]

allergy die Allergie [di ʔal(ɛ)ɐˈɡi:]

alley die Gasse [di ˈɡasə]

allowed zulässig [ˈtsuːlɛsɪç]; **be allowed** dürfen [dʏfn̩]

almonds die Mandeln *f pl* [di ˈmandl̩n]

almost fast [fast], beinahe [ˈbaɪnaːə]

alone allein [ʔaˈlaɪn]

already bereits [bəˈraɪts], schon [ʃoːn]

also auch [ʔaʊx], gleichfalls [ˈɡlaɪçfals]

altar der Altar [dɐ ʔalˈta:]

although obwohl [ʔɔpˈvoːl]

always immer [ˈʔɪmɐ], stets [ʃteːts]

ambulance der Krankenwagen [dɐ ˈkraŋkn̩vaːɡn̩]

America Amerika [ʔaˈmeːʀɪka:]

American der Amerikaner/die

Amerikanerin [dɐ ʔameʀɪˈkaːnɐ/di ʔameʀɪˈkaːnərɪn]

among zwischen [ˈtsvɪʃn̩]

amount der Betrag [dɐ bəˈtraːk]

amputated amputiert [ampuˈtiɐt]

amusement park der Freizeitpark [dɐ ˈfraɪtsaɪtˌpaːk]

ancient antik [ʔanˈtiːk]

and und [ʔʊnt]

angina die Angina [di ʔanˈɡiːna]

angry zornig [ˈtsɔɐnɪç]; böse [ˈbøːzə]

animal das Tier [das tiɐ]

ankle der Knöchel [dɐ knœçl̩]

announce melden [mɛldn̩], anmelden [ˈʔanmɛldn̩]

announcement die Mitteilung [di ˈmɪtaɪlʊŋ]

annoying lästig [ˈlɛstɪç]

annual(ly) jährlich [ˈjɛɐlɪç]

anorak der Anorak [dɐ ˈʔanoʀak]

answer die Antwort [di ˈʔantvɔɐt]; *(vb)* antworten [ˈʔantvɔɐtn̩], beantworten [bəˈʔantvɔɐtn̩]

answering machine der Anrufbeantworter [dɐ ˈʔanfuːfbəˌʔantvɔɐtɐ]

anti-freeze das Frostschutzmittel [das ˈfrɔstʃʊtsmɪtl̩]

antique shop das Antiquitätengeschäft [das ʔantɪkvɪˈtɛːtnɡəʃɛft]

any jeder Beliebige [ˌjeːdɐ bəˈliːbɪɡə]; *(in questions)* einige [ˈʔaɪnɪɡə]

anybody *(in questions)* jemand [ˈjeːmant]

anything *(in questions)* etwas [ˈʔɛtvas]

apartment die Wohnung [di ˈvoːnʊŋ]

apologize sich entschuldigen [zɪç ʔɛntˈʃʊldɪɡn̩]

appendicitis die Blinddarmentzündung [di ˈblɪntdaːmɛnˌtsʏndʊŋ]

appetite der Appetit [dɐ ʔapəˈtɪt]

applause der Beifall [dɐ ˈbaɪfal]

apples die Äpfel *m pl* [di ˈɛpfl̩]

appointment der Termin [dɐ tɐˈmiːn]; *(meeting)* die Verabredung

[di feˈʔapʀeːdʊŋ]
apricots die Aprikosen *f pl*
[di ˈʔapʀɪˈkoːzn]
April April [ˈʔaˈpʀɪl]
arch der Bogen [dɐ ˈboːgŋ]
archaeology die Archäologie
[di ˈʔaːçeoloˈgiː]
architect Architekt/Architektin
[ˈʔaːçɪˈtɛkt/ˈʔaːçɪˈtɛkt ɪn]
architecture die Architektur
[di ˈʔaːçitɛkˈtuːɐ]
area die Gegend [di ˈgeːgŋt]
area code die Vorwahlnummer
[di ˈfoeːvaːlˌnʊmɐ]
arm der Arm [dɐ ˈʔaːm]
around herum [hɐˈʀʊm]
arrest verhaften [fɐˈhaftn]
arrival die Ankunft [di ˈʔankʊnft]
arrive (at) eintreffen [ˈʔaɪntʀɛfn]
art die Kunst [di kʊnst]
art dealer der Kunsthändler
[dɐ ˈkʊnstˌhɛntlɐ]
art nouveau der Jugendstil
[dɐ ˈjuːgŋtstiːl]
artichokes die Artischocken *f pl*
[di ˈʔaːtɪˈʃɔkn]
artificial limb die Prothese
[di pʀoˈteːzə]
arts and crafts das Kunstgewerbe
[das ˈkʊnstgəvɛɐbə]
as *(reason)* da [daː]
ashtray der Aschenbecher
[dɐ ˈʔaʃnbɛçɐ]
ask fragen [fʀaːgŋ], fordern
[ˈfɔɐdɐn], auffordern [ˈʔaʊfɔɐdɐn];
ask s.o. for s.th. jdn um etw. bitten [ˈjemandn ʊm ˌʔɛtvas ˈbɪtn]
asparagus der Spargel [ˈʃpaːgl]
aspirin das Aspirin [das ˈaspiˈʀiːn]
association der Verein [dɐ feˈʔaɪn]
asthma das Asthma [das ˈʔastma]
at *(time)* um [ˈʔʊm]
athlete der Sportler/die Sportlerin
[dɐ ˈʃpɔɐtle/di ˈʃpɔɐtlɐrɪn]
athletics die Leichtathletik
[di ˈlaɪçtˈʔatˌleːtɪk]
Atlantic der Atlantik [dɐ ˈʔatˈlantɪk]

attack der Anfall [dɐ ˈʔanfal]
attention die Achtung [di
ˈʔaxtʊŋ]; **pay attention (to)** aufpassen [ˈʔaʊfpasn], beachten [bɐˈʔaxtn]
au gratin überbacken [ˈʔybɐˈbakn]
aubergines die Auberginen *f pl*
[di ˈʔobɐˈʒiːnn]
August August [ˈʔaʊˈgʊst]
Austria Österreich [das ˈʔøːstɐraɪç]
Austrian der Österreicher/die
Österreicherin [dɐ ˈʔøːstɐraɪçɐ/
di ˈʔøːstɐraɪçɐrɪn]
authorities die Behörde [di
bɐˈhøedə]
automated teller machine der
Geldautomat [dɐ ˈgɛltaʊtoˌmaːt]
automatic automatisch
[ˈʔautoˈmaːtɪʃ]
automatic (transmission) das
Automatikgetriebe [das
ˈʔautoˈmaːtɪkgəˌtriːbə]
autumn der Herbst [dɐ ˈhɛɐpst]
average durchschnittlich
[ˈdʊɐçʃnɪtlɪç]
avocado die Avocado [di
ˈʔavoˈkaːdo]
awake wach [vax]
aware bewusst [bɐˈvʊst]; **be
aware of** merken [mɛɐkŋ]
away weg [vɛk], fort [fɔɐt]
awful schrecklich [ˈʃʀɛklɪç]

B

baby das Baby [das ˈbeːbiː]
baby food die Kindernahrung
[di ˈkɪndɐnaːʀʊŋ]
baby intercom das Babyfon [das
ˈbeːbifoːn]
baby lift Babylift [ˈbeːbilɪft]
baby seat die Babyschale
[di ˈbeːbiʃaːlə]
baby's bottle die Trinkflasche
[di ˈtʀɪŋkflaʃə]
baby's changing table der

Wickeltisch [də 'vɪkltɪʃ]
babysitter der Babysitter
[də 'be:bisɪtɐ]
babysitting service die Kinderbetreuung [di 'kɪndebətRɔjʊŋ]
bachelor der Junggeselle
[də 'jʊŋgəzɛlə]
back der Rücken [də ʀʏkŋ]; (adv)
zurück [tsʊ'ʀʏk]
backache die Rückenschmerzen m
pl [di 'ʀʏkŋʃmɛɐtsn]
backwards rückwärts ['ʀʏkvɛɐts]
bad schlimm [ʃlɪm], schlecht [ʃlɛçt]
badly schlecht [ʃlɛçt]
badminton das Badminton [das
'bɛtmɪntn]
bag der Sack [də zak], die Tüte
[di 'ty:tə], die Handtasche [di
'han(t)taʃə]
baggage das Gepäck [das ge'pɛk]
baggage car der Gepäckwagen
[də gə'pɛkva:gŋ]
baggage deposit die Gepäckaufbewahrung [di
gə'pɛk˒aʊfbəva:ʀʊŋ]
baggage reclaim die Gepäckausgabe [di gə'pɛk˒aʊsga:bə]
baked gebacken [gə'bakŋ]
baker's die Bäckerei [di bɛkə'ʀaɪ]
balcony der Balkon [də bal'kɔn]
ball der Ball [də bal]; (festivity) der
Ball [də bal]
ballet das Ballett [das ba'lɛt]
ball-point pen der Kugelschreiber
[də 'ku:glʃʀaɪbɐ]
bananas die Bananen f pl
[di ba'na:nn]
band die Band [di bɛ(:)nt]
bandage der Verband [də fɛ'bant]
bank die Bank [di baŋk]; (river) das
Ufer [das '˒u:fɐ]
banknote der Geldschein
[də 'gɛltʃaɪn]
bar die Bar [di ba:]
barber's der (Herren)Friseur
[də('hɛʀən)fʀi'zøɐ]
baroque barock [ba'ʀɔk]

basil das Basilikum [das
ba'zi:likʊm]
basket der Korb [də kɔʀp]
basketball der Basketball
[də 'ba:skətbal]
bath die Badewanne
[di 'ba:dəvanə]
bathing shoes die Badeschuhe m
pl [di 'ba:dəʃuə]
bathrobe der Bademantel
[də 'ba:dəmantl]
bathroom das Badezimmer [das
'ba:dətsɪmɐ]
battery die Batterie [di batə'ʀi:]
battery charger das Ladegerät
[das 'la:dəgəʀɛ:t]
bay die Bucht [di bʊxt]
bay-leaves die Lorbeerblätter n pl
[di 'lɔɐbeɐblɛtɐ]
be sein [zaɪn], sich befinden [zɪç
bə'fɪndn]
beach der Strand [də ʃtʀant]
beach shoes die Strandschuhe m
pl [di 'ʃtʀantʃuə]
beans die Bohnen f pl [di bo:nn]
beard der Bart [də ba:t]
beat up zusammenschlagen
[tsʊ'zammʃla:gŋ]
beautiful schön [ʃø:n]
because weil [vaɪl]; da [da:];
because of wegen [ve:gŋ]
become werden [veɐdn]
bed das Bett [das bɛt]; go to bed
ins Bett gehen ['˒ɪns 'bɛt ge:n]
bed linen die Bettwäsche
[di 'bɛtvɛʃə]
bedroom das Schlafzimmer [das
'ʃla:ftsɪmɐ]
bedside table der Nachttisch
[də 'naxttɪʃ]
bee die Biene [di 'bi:nə]
beef das Rindfleisch ['ʀɪntflaɪʃ]
beer das Bier [das biɐ]
before vor [foɐ]; (conj) bevor
[bə'foɐ]; (previously) vorher
['foɐheɐ]
begin anfangen ['˒anfaŋŋ], begin-

nen [bə'gɪnn]

beginning der Anfang [de ˈʔanfaŋ], der Beginn [de bəˈgɪn]

behind hinter [ˈhɪntɐ]

beige beige [beːʃ]

Belgian der Belgier/die Belgierin [de ˈbɛlgɪɐ/di ˈbɛlgɪəʀɪn]

Belgium Belgien [ˈbɛlgɪən]

believe glauben [glaʊbm]

bell die Klingel [di klɪŋl]

belong to gehören [gəˈhøːʀən/-ˈhøːɐn]

below unterhalb [ˈʔʊntɐhalp], unten [ˈʔʊntn]

belt der Gürtel [de gʏɐtl]

bench die (Sitz)Bank [di (ˈzɪts)baŋk]

bend die Kurve [di ˈkʊɐvə]

beside neben [ˈneːbm]

besides außerdem [ˈʔaʊsedeːm]

best beste(r, s) [ˈbɛstə (-tɐ, -təs)]; **at best** höchstens [ˈhøːçstns/ˈhøːkstns]

better besser [ˈbɛsɐ]

between zwischen [ˈtsvɪʃn]

bicycle das Fahrrad [das ˈfaːʀat]

big groß [gʀoːs]

bike das Fahrrad [das ˈfaːʀat]

bikini der Bikini [de biˈkiːni]

bill die Rechnung [di ˈʀɛçnʊŋ]

bin der Abfalleimer [de ˈʔapfalˌʔaɪmɐ]

bin liner der Abfallbeutel [de ˈʔapfalbɔɪtl]

bird der Vogel [de foːgl]

bird reserve das Vogelschutzgebiet [das ˈfoːglʃʊtsgəbiːt]

biro der Kuli [de ˈkuːli]

birthday der Geburtstag [de gəˈbʊɐtstaːk]

bite (vb) beißen [baɪsn]

bitter bitter [ˈbɪtɐ]

black schwarz [ʃvaːts]

black-and-white film der Schwarzweiß-Film [de ʃvaːtsˈvaɪsfɪlm]

blackberries die Brombeeren f pl [di ˈbʀɔmbeːʀən]

bladder die Blase [di ˈblaːzə]

blanket die Bettdecke [di ˈbɛtdɛkə]

blazer der Blazer [de ˈbleːzɐ]

bleed bluten [bluːtn]

bleeding die Blutung [di ˈbluːtʊŋ]

blind blind [blɪnt]

blind person der/die Blinde [de/di ˈblɪndə]

blond(e) blond [blɔnt]

blood das Blut [das bluːt]

blood group die Blutgruppe [di ˈbluːtgʀʊpə]

blood-poisoning die Blutvergiftung [di ˈbluːtfɛɐgɪftʊŋ]

blouse die Bluse [di ˈbluːzə]

blow dry föhnen [føːnn]

blue blau [blaʊ]

blues der Blues [de bluːs]

boarding card die Bordkarte [di ˈbɔɐtkaːtə]

body der Körper [de ˈkœɐpɐ]

boil kochen [kɔxn]

boiled gekocht [gəˈkɔxt]

bone der Knochen [de knɔxn]

bonnet die Motorhaube [di ˈmoːtɔˌhaʊbə]

book das Buch [das buːx]; (vb) buchen [buːxn], vorbestellen [ˈfoɐbəʃtɛln]

book shop die Buchhandlung [di ˈbuːxhantlʊŋ]

booking die Buchung [di ˈbuːxʊŋ], die Voranmeldung [di ˈfoɐˌʔanmɛldʊŋ]

boot der Kofferraum [de ˈkɔfeʀaʊm]

boots die Stiefel m pl [di ˈʃtiːfl]

border die Grenze [di ˈgʀɛntsə]

boring langweilig [ˈlaŋvaɪlɪç]

born geboren [gəˈboːʀən (gəˈboɐn)]

borrow (aus)leihen [(ˈʔaʊs)laɪn]

boss der Leiter/die Leiterin [de ˈlaɪtɐ/di ˈlaɪtəʀɪn], der Chef/die Chefin [de ʃɛf/di ʃɛfɪn]

botanic gardens der botanische

Garten [de bo'tanɪʃə 'ga:tn]
both beide ['baɪdə]
bother belästigen [bə'lɛstɪgn], stören [ʃtøən]
bottle die Flasche [di 'flaʃə]
bottle opener der Flaschenöffner [de 'flaʃnˀœfnə]
bottle warmer der Fläschchenwärmer [de 'flɛʃçənvɛɛmə]
boutique die Boutique [di bu'ti:k]
bowel movement der Stuhlgang [de 'ʃtu:lgaŋ]
bowl die Schüssel [di ʃʏsl]
box die Kiste [di 'kɪstə], die Schachtel [di ʃaxtl], die Packung [di 'pakʊŋ]; *(theatre)* die Loge [di 'lo:ʒə]
box office die (Theater)Kasse [di (te'ˀa:te)kasə]
boy der Junge [de 'jʊŋə]
bracelet das Armband [das 'ˀa:mbant]
braille die Blindenschrift [di 'blɪndnʃʀɪft]
brain das Gehirn [das gə'hɪɐn]
braised geschmort [gə'ʃmoɐt]
brake die Bremse [di 'bʀɛmzə]
brake fluid die Bremsflüssigkeit [di 'bʀɛmsflʏsɪçkaɪt]
brake lights die Bremslichter [di 'bʀɛmslɪçte]
bread das Brot [das bʀo:t]
break into/open aufbrechen ['ˀaʊfbʀɛçn]
breakdown die Panne [di 'panə]
breakdown service der Pannendienst [de 'panndi:nst]
breakdown vehicle der Abschleppwagen [de 'ˀapʃlɛpva:gn]
breakfast das Frühstück [das 'fʀy:ʃtʏk]; **have breakfast** frühstücken ['fʀy:ʃtʏkn]
breakfast room der Frühstücksraum [de 'fʀy:ʃtʏksʀaʊm]
breathe atmen ['ˀa:tmən]
bridge die Brücke [di 'bʀʏkə]
briefs der (Herren)Slip [de (ˈhɛʀən)slɪp]

bring mitbringen ['mɪtbʀɪŋŋ]; *(her-)* bringen [(ˈheɐ)bʀɪŋŋ]; **bring back** zurückbringen [tsu'ʀʏkbʀɪŋŋ]
broad breit [bʀaɪt]
brochure der Prospekt [de pʀɔs'pɛkt]
broken kaputt [ka'pʊt]; *(bone)* gebrochen [gə'bʀɔxn]
bronchial tubes die Bronchien *f pl* [di 'bʀɔnçiən]
bronchitis die Bronchitis [di bʀɔn'çi:tɪs]
bronze die Bronze [di 'bʀɔnsə]
brooch die Brosche [di 'bʀɔʃə]
brother der Bruder [de 'bʀu:de]
brother-in-law der Schwager [de 'ʃva:ge]
brown braun [bʀaʊn]
brown (rye) bread das Schwarzbrot [das 'ʃva:tsbʀo:t]
bruise *(caused by hitting)* die Prellung [di 'pʀɛlʊŋ]; *(caused by pinching)* die Quetschung [di 'kvɛtʃʊŋ]
brush die Bürste [di 'bʏɐstə]
buffet breakfast das Frühstücksbüfett [das 'fʀy:ʃtʏksbʏˌfe:]
building das Gebäude [das gə'bɔɪdə]
bumper die Stoßstange [di 'ʃto:ʃtaŋə]
bunch of flowers der Blumenstrauß [de 'blu:mmʃtʀaʊs]
bungalow der Bungalow [de 'bʊŋgalo:]
bunk bed das Etagenbett [das ˀe'ta:ʒnbɛt]
burn die Verbrennung [di fe'bʀɛnʊŋ]; *(vb)* brennen [bʀɛnn]; verbrennen [fe'bʀɛnn]
bus der Bus [de bʊs]
bus station der Busbahnhof [de 'bʊs,ba:nho:f]
bush der Busch [de bʊʃ]
but aber ['ˀa:be]; sondern ['zɔnden]
butcher's die Metzgerei [di mɛtsgə'ʀaɪ]

butter die Butter [di 'bʊtɐ]

buttermilk die Buttermilch [di 'bʊtɐmɪlç]

buy kaufen [kaʊfn], einkaufen ['ʔaɪnkaʊfn]

by von [fɔn]; **by (means of)** durch [dʊɐç]

bypass der Bypass [dɐ 'baɪpaːs]

C

cabaret das Kabarett [das kaba'ʀɛː]

cabbage der Kohl [dɐ koːl]

cabin die Kabine [di ka'biːnə]

cable railway die (Stand)Seilbahn [di (ʃtant)ˌzaɪlbaːn]

café das Café [das ka'feː]

cake der Kuchen [dɐ kʊːxn]

cake shop die Konditorei [di kɔndito'ʀaɪ]

calculate rechnen ['ʀɛçn(ə)n], berechnen [bə'ʀɛçn(ə)n]

call der Anruf [dɐ 'ʔanʀuːf]; *(vb, phone)* anrufen ['ʔanʀuːfn]; *(shout)* rufen [ʀuːfn]; *(call out)* aufrufen ['ʔaʊfʀuːfn]; *(name)* nennen [nɛnn]; **be called** heißen [haɪsn]; **call for** *(pick up)* abholen ['ʔaphoːln]; **call on s.o.** jdn besuchen [jemandn bə'zuːxn]; **be called** heißen [haɪsn]

calm die Ruhe [di 'ʀuə]; *(adj)* ruhig [ʀʊɪç], still [ʃtɪl]; **calm down** sich beruhigen [zɪç bə'ʀʊɪgn]

camcorder der Camcorder [dɐ 'kamkhɔɐdɐ]

camera die Kamera [di 'kaməʀaː]

camomile tea der Kamillentee [dɐ ka'mɪl(ə)nteː]

camp *(vb)* zelten ['tsɛltn]

camping das Camping [das 'kɛmpɪŋ]

camping guide der Camping-führer [dɐ 'kɛmpɪŋfyːʀɐ]

camping site der Campingplatz [dɐ 'kɛmpɪŋplats]

can die Büchse [di 'bʏksə], die Dose [di 'doːzə]

canal der Kanal [dɐ ka'naːl]

cancel *(tickets etc.)* abbestellen ['ʔapbəʃtɛln]; *(appointment)* absagen ['ʔapzaːgn]; *(flight)* stornieren [ʃtɔ'niːɐn]

cancer der Krebs [dɐ kʀeːps]

candles die Kerzen *f pl* [di kɛɐtsn]

cane der Taststock [dɐ 'tastʃtɔk]

canoe das Kanu [das 'kaːnu]

cap die Mütze [di 'mʏtsə]

capital die Hauptstadt [di 'haʊptʃtat]

captain der Kapitän [dɐ kapi'tɛːn]

car das Auto [das 'ʔaʊtoː], der Wagen [dɐ 'vaːgn], der Pkw [dɐ 'peːkaveː]

car radio das Autoradio [das 'ʔaʊtoˌʀaːdjo]

car registration documents der Kfz-Schein [dɐ ka'ʔɛf'tsɛtʃaɪn]

caraway seed(s) der Kümmel [dɐ kʏml]

cardiac infarction der Herzin-farkt [dɐ 'hɛɐtsɪnfaːkt]

cardiac stimulant das Kreislauf-mittel [das 'kʀaɪslaʊfˌmɪtl]

cardigan die Strickjacke [di 'ʃtʀɪkjakə]

care die Betreuung [di bə'tʀɔɪʊŋ]; **in need of care** pflegebedürftig ['pfleːgəbədyɐftɪç]

careful vorsichtig ['foɐzɪçtɪç], sorg-fältig ['zɔɐkfɛltɪç]

carrots die Karotten *f pl* [di ka'ʀɔtn]

carry tragen [tʀaːgn]

cartoon der Zeichentrickfilm [dɐ 'tsaɪçnˌtʀɪkfɪlm]

in case falls [fals]

cash das Bargeld [das 'baːgɛlt]

cash: to pay (in) ~ bar zahlen ['baː tsaːln]

cashpoint der Geldautomat

[de 'gɛltaʊto,maːt]

casino das Spielkasino [das 'ʃpiːlka,ziːno]

cassette die Kassette [di ka'sɛtə]

castle *(fortress)* die Burg [di buɐk]; *(palace)* das Schloss [das ʃlɔs]

cat die Katze [di 'katsə]

catch fangen [faŋŋ]; *(train)* kriegen [kʁiːgŋ]

cathedral die Kathedrale [di kate'dʁaːlə]

cauliflower der Blumenkohl ['bluːmmkoːl]

cause die Ursache [di 'ʔuɐzaxə], der Anlass [de 'ʔanlas], der Grund [de gʁʊnt]; *(vb)* verursachen [fɐ'ʔuɐzaxn]

caution die Vorsicht [di 'foɐzɪçt]

cautious vorsichtig ['foɐzɪçtɪç]

cave die Höhle [di 'høːlə]

CD die CD [di tseːˈdeː]

CD player der CD-Spieler [de tseːˈdeːʃpiːlɐ]

ceiling die Decke [di 'dɛkə]

celebration(s) das Fest [das fɛst]

celeriac der Sellerie [de 'zɛlɐʁiː]

cemetery der Friedhof [de 'fʁiːtˌhoːf]

centimetre der Zentimeter [de ,tsɛnti'meːtɐ]

central zentral [tsɛn'tʁaːl]

century das Jahrhundert [das ja'hʊndɐt]

ceramics die Keramik [di ke'ʁaːmɪk]

certain *(adj)* gewiss [gə'vɪs], bestimmt [bə'ʃtɪmt], sicher ['zɪçɐ]; certainly *(adv)* gewiss [gə'vɪs], unbedingt ['ʔʊnbə'dɪŋt]

certificate das Attest [das ʔa'tɛst]

certify bescheinigen [bə'ʃaɪnɪgŋ]

chair der Stuhl [de ʃtuːl]

champagne der Champagner [de ʃam'panjɐ]

chance, by ~ zufällig ['tsuːfɛlɪç]

change der Wechsel [de vɛksl], die Veränderung [di fɐ'ʔɛndɐʁʊŋ]; *(money)* das Wechselgeld [das 'vɛkslgɛlt]; *(vb)* verändern [fɐ'ʔɛndɐn]; *(money)* wechseln [(gɛlt) vɛksln], umtauschen ['ʔʊmtaʊʃn]; *(trains)* umsteigen ['ʔʊmʃtaɪgŋ]; *(clothes)* sich umziehen [zɪç 'ʔʊmtsiːn]; change the booking umbuchen ['ʔʊmbuːxn]

changeable wechselhaft ['vɛkslhaft]

channel der Kanal [de ka'naːl]

chapel die Kapelle [di ka'pɛlə]

charcoal die Grillkohle [di 'gʁɪlkoːlə]

charming entzückend [ʔɛn'tsʏknt], bezaubernd [bə'tsaɪçnʊŋ]

cheap billig ['bɪlɪç]

check *(US)* der Scheck [de ʃɛk]; *(vb)* kontrollieren [kɔntʁo'liːʁən/ -'liən], nachprüfen ['naːxpʁyːfn], nachsehen ['naːxzeːn]; check in einchecken ['ʔaɪntʃɛkn]

cheeky unverschämt ['ʔʊnfɐʃɛːmt]

cheese der Käse [de 'kɛːzə]

chemist's die Apotheke [di ʔapoˈteːkə]

cherries die Kirschen *f pl* [di kɪɐʃn]

chest die Brust [di bʁʊst]; *(box)* die Kiste [di 'kɪstə]

chicken das Hähnchen [das hɛːnçn]

chickenpox die Windpocken *f pl* [di 'vɪntpɔkn]

child das Kind [das kɪnt]; children *(pl)* die Kinder *n pl* [di 'kɪndɐ]

child reduction die Kinderermäßigung [di 'kɪndɐʔɐ'mɛːsɪgʊŋ]

child seat der Kindersitz [de 'kɪndɐzɪts]

children's clothing die Kinderkleidung [di 'kɪndɐklaɪdʊŋ]

children's illness die Kinderkrankheit [di 'kɪndɐˌkʁaŋkhaɪt]

children's playground der Kinderspielplatz [de 'kɪndɐʃpiːlplats]

children's pool das Kinderbecken [das 'kɪndɐbɛkŋ]

children's portion der Kinderteller [dɐ 'kɪndetɛlɐ]

china das Porzellan [das pɔɐtsɐ'la:n]

chip card die Chipkarte [di 'tʃɪpka:tə]

chocolate die Schokolade [di ʃoko'la:də]

chocolate bar der Schokoriegel [dɐ 'ʃo:koʀi:gl]

choice die Auswahl [di 'ʔaʊsva:l], die Wahl [di va:l]

choir der Chor [dɐ koɐ]

choose wählen ['vɛ:ln]

chop das Kotelett ['kɔtlɛt]

Christian name der Vorname [dɐ 'foɐna:mə]

Christianity das Christentum [das 'kʀɪstntu:m]

Christmas Weihnachten ['vaɪnaxtn]

Christmas Eve Heiliger Abend ['haɪlɪgɐ 'ʔa:bmt], Heiligabend [ˌhaɪlɪç 'ʔa:bmt]

church die Kirche [di 'kɪʀçə]

cigar die Zigarre [di tsɪ'gaʀə]

cigarette die Zigarette [di tsɪga'ʀɛtə]

cigarillo das Zigarillo [das tsɪga'ʀɪlo]

cinema das Kino [das 'ki:no]

circulatory disorder die Kreislaufstörung [di 'kʀaɪslaʊfʃtø:ʀʊŋ]

circus der Zirkus [dɐ 'tsɪʀkʊs]

city centre das Stadtzentrum [das 'ʃtattsɛntʀʊm]

city map der Stadtplan [dɐ 'ʃtatpla:n]

class die Klasse [di 'klasə]

classic film der Klassiker [dɐ 'klasɪkɐ]

classical die Klassik [di 'klasɪk]

classicism der Klassizismus [dɐ klasɪ'tsɪsmʊs]

clean sauber ['zaʊbɐ]; (washing) frisch [fʀɪʃ]; (vb) putzen [pʊtsn], reinigen ['ʀaɪnɪgn]

clear klar [kla:]; (weather) heiter ['haɪtɐ]

clearance sale der Ausverkauf [dɐ 'ʔaʊsfɐkaʊf]

clever klug [klu:k], schlau [ʃlaʊ]

cliff die Klippe [di 'klɪpə]

climate das Klima [das 'kli:ma:]

cling film die Frischhaltefolie [di 'fʀɪʃhaltəˌfo:ljə]

cloakroom die Garderobe [di ga'dʀo:bə]

cloister der Kreuzgang [dɐ 'kʀɔɪtsgaŋ]

close (vb) schließen [ʃli:sn], zumachen ['tsu:maxn]

close (to) (adj) nahe (bei) ['na:(ə) baɪ]

closed geschlossen [gə'ʃlɔsn]

cloth das Tuch [das tu:x]

clothes line die Wäscheleine [di 'vɛʃəlaɪnə]

clothes pegs die Wäscheklammern f pl [di 'vɛʃəklamɐn]

clothing die Kleidung [di 'klaɪdʊŋ]

cloud die Wolke [di 'vɔlkə]

cloudy (liquid) trüb [tʀy:p]; (weather) bewölkt [bə'vœlkt]

cloves die Nelken f pl [di nɛlkn]

club der Verein [dɐ fɐ'ʔaɪn]

clubhouse das Clubhaus [das 'klʊphaʊs]

clutch die Kupplung [di 'kʊplʊŋ]

coach number die Wagennummer [di 'va:gnnʊmɐ]

coast die Küste [di 'kʏstə]

coat der Mantel [dɐ mantl]

coat hanger der Kleiderbügel [dɐ 'klaɪdɐby:gl]

cobbler der Schuhmacher [dɐ 'ʃu:maxɐ]

coconut die Kokosnuss [di 'ko:kosnʊs]

coffee der Kaffee [dɐ 'kafe:/ka'fe:]

coffee machine die Kaffeemaschine [di 'kafemaʃi:nə]

coin die Münze [di 'mʏntsə]

cold die Erkältung [di ʔe'kɛltʊŋ] , der Schnupfen [dɐ ʃnʊpfn]; (adj)

kalt [kalt]; be cold frieren
['fʀiːʀən/fʀiən]
cold cuts der Aufschnitt
[dɐ ʔ'aʊfʃnɪt]
cold water kaltes Wasser ['vaːməs
'vasɐ]
colic die Kolik [di 'koːlɪk]
collarbone das Schlüsselbein [das
'ʃlʏsl̩baɪn]
colleague der Kollege/die Kollegin
[dɐ ko'leːgə/di ko'leːgɪn]
collect sammeln [zaml̩n]
collection (of mail) die Leerung
[di 'leːʀʊŋ]
collision der Zusammenstoß
[dɐ tsu'zammʃtoːs]
coloured farbig ['faʀbɪç]
coloured pencil der Farbstift
[dɐ 'faːpʃtɪft]
colouring book das Malbuch [das
'maːlbuːx]
column die Säule [di 'zɔɪlə]
comb der Kamm [dɐ kam]; (vb)
kämmen [kɛmm]
come kommen [kɔmm]; come
back zurückkehren [tsu'ʀʏkeːʀən/
-keːn], wiederkommen
['viːdɛkɔmm]; come from stammen aus [ʃtamm ʔaʊs]; come in!
herein! [hɛ'ʀaɪn]
comedy die Komödie [di
ko'møːdiə]
comfortable bequem [bə'kveːm],
gemütlich [gə'myːtlɪç]
common (adj) gemeinsam
[gə'maɪnza(ː)m]; gebräuchlich
[gə'brɔɪçlɪç], gewöhnlich
[gə'vøːnlɪç]
company die Firma [di 'fɪʀmaː];
(people) die Gesellschaft
[di gə'zɛlʃaft]
compartment das Abteil [das
ʔap'taɪl]
compass der Kompass
[dɐ 'kɔmpas]
compensation der Ersatz
[dɐ ʔɛ'zats]; der Schadenersatz

[dɐ 'ʃaːdn̩ʔeˌzats]
complete ganz [gants]; (vb) vollenden [fɔl'ʔɛndn̩]
composer der Komponist/
die Komponistin [dɐ kɔmpo'nɪst/
di kɔmpo'nɪstɪn]
concert das Konzert [das kɔn'tsɛɛt]
concussion die Gehirnerschütterung [di gə'hɪʀnɛʃʏtəʀʊŋ]
condom das Kondom [das
kɔn'doːm]
conductor der Dirigent/die Diri-
gentin [dɐ diʀi'gɛnt/di diʀi'gɛntɪn]
confidence das Vertrauen [das
fɛ'tʀaʊn]
confirm bestätigen [bə'ʃtɛːtɪgŋ]
congratulate gratulieren
[gʀatu'liːʀən/-'liən]
congratulations der Glückwunsch [dɐ 'glʏkvʊnʃ]
connection der Anschluss [dɐ
ʔ'anʃlʊs], die Verbindung
[di fɛ'bɪndʊŋ]
consist of bestehen aus ['bə'ʃteːn
ʔaʊs]
constipation die Verstopfung
[di fɛ'ʃtɔpfʊŋ]
consulate das Konsulat [das
kɔnzʊ'laːt]
contact der Kontakt [dɐ kɔn'takt],
die Berührung [di bə'ʀyːʀʊŋ]
contagious ansteckend
[ʔ'anʃtɛkŋt]
container der Behälter [dɐ
bə'hɛltɐ], das Gefäß [das gə'fɛːs]
contents der Inhalt [dɐ ʔ'ɪnhalt]
contest der Wettkampf
[dɐ 'vɛtkampf]
contract der Vertrag [dɐ fɛ'tʀaːk]
contrary das Gegenteil [das
'geːgŋtaɪl]
control (vb) kontrollieren
[kɔntʀo'liːʀən/-'liən]
convent das (Nonnen)Kloster [das
('nɔnn),kloːstɐ]
conversation das Gespräch [das
gə'ʃpʀɛːç], die Unterhaltung

[di ˀʊntɐˈhaltʊŋ]

cook der Koch/die Köchin
[dɐ kɔx/di ˈkʰœxɪn]; *(vb)* kochen
[kɔxn]; zubereiten [ˈtsuːbəʀaɪtn]

cookbook das Kochbuch [das ˈkɔxbuːx]

cooked gar [gaː]

cooked ham gekochter Schinken [gəˈkɔxtɐ ʃɪŋkn]

cooker der Herd [dɐ heːɐt]; der Kocher [dɐ ˈkɔxɐ]

cool frisch [fʀɪʃ], kühl [kyːl]

cooling water das Kühlwasser [das ˈkyːlvasɐ]

copy die Kopie [di koˈpiː]

corkscrew der Korkenzieher [dɐ ˈkɔɐkntsiːɐ]

corner die Ecke [di ˀɛkə], der Winkel [dɐ ˈvɪŋkl]

corridor der Gang [dɐ gaŋ]

corrupt verdorben [fɐˈdɔɐbm], bestechlich [bəˈʃtɛçlɪç]

cost die Kosten *pl* [di kɔstn]; *(vb)* kosten [kɔstn]

costume jewellery der Modeschmuck [dɐ ˈmoːdəʃmʊk]

cosy gemütlich [gəˈmyːtlɪç]

cot das Kinderbett [das ˈkɪndɐbɛt]

cottage die Hütte [di ˈhʏtə]

cotton die Baumwolle [di ˈbaʊmvɔlə]

cotton swabs das Wattestäbchen [das ˈvatəʃtɛːpçn]

cotton wool die Watte [di ˈvatə]

cough der Husten [dɐ huːstn]

cough mixture/syrup der Hustensaft [dɐ ˈhuːstnzaft]

count *(vb)* zählen [tsɛːln]

country das Land [das lant]; native country das Vaterland [das ˈfaːtɐlant]; fellow countryman der Landsmann [dɐ ˈlantsman]

country road die Landstraße [di ˈlantʃtraːsə]

couple das Paar [das paː]; *(married)* das Ehepaar [das ˀeːəpaː]

course der Kurs [dɐ kʊɐs]; *(meal)*

der Gang [dɐ gaŋ]; of course selbstverständlich [zɛlp(st)fɐˈʃtɛntlɪç]; natürlich [naˈtyːlɪç]

cousin der Cousin/die Cousine [dɐ kʊˈzɛn/di kʊˈziːnə]

crab der Krebs [dɐ kreːps]

cramp der Krampf [dɐ krampf]

crash der Zusammenstoß [dɐ tsʊˈzammʃtoːs]

crash helmet der Sturzhelm [dɐ ˈʃtʊɐtshɛlm]

crazy verrückt [fɐˈʀʏkt]

crazy golf das Minigolf [das ˈmɪnigɔlf]

cream die Creme [di krɛːm]; *(cook)* die Sahne [di ˈzaːnə]

creative kreativ [kreaˈtiːf]

credit card die Kreditkarte [di kreˈdiːtkaːtə]

crew die Mannschaft [di ˈmanʃaft]

crime das Verbrechen [das fɐˈbrɛçn]

crockery das Geschirr [das gəˈʃɪɐ]

cross das Kreuz [das krɔɪts]; *(adj)* ärgerlich [ˀɛɐgɐlɪç]; *(vb)* überqueren [ˀyːbɐˈkveːʀən/-ˈkveːɐn], überschreiten [ˀyːbɐˈʃʀaɪtn]

crossing der Übergang [dɐ ˀyːbɐgaŋ]

crowded voll [fɔl]

crown die Krone [di ˈkroːnə]

crutch die Krücke [di ˈkrʏkə]

cry *(vb)* weinen [vaɪnn]

crystal der Kristall [dɐ krɪsˈtal]

cubicle die Kabine [di kaˈbiːnə]

cucumber die Gurke [di ˈgʊɐkə]

culture die Kultur [di kʊlˈtuɐ]

cup die Tasse [di ˈtasə]

curious neugierig [ˈnɔɪgiːʀɪç]

curlers die Lockenwickler *m pl* [di ˈlɔknvɪklɐ]

curling das Curling [das ˈkəːlɪŋ]

curls die Locken *f pl* [di lɔkn]

currency die Währung [di ˈvɛːʀʊŋ]

current *(electricity)* der Strom [dɐ ʃtroːm]; *(water)* die Strömung

[di 'ʃtʀøːmʊn]
curve die Kurve [di 'kʊɐvə]
customer der Kunde/die Kundin
[dɐ 'kʊndə/di 'kʊndɪn]
customs der Zoll [dɐ 'tsɔl]
customs declaration die Zollerklärung [di 'tsɔlɛklɛːʀʊn]
cut die Schnittwunde
[di 'ʃnɪtvʊndə]; (vb) schneiden
[ʃnaɪdn]
cutlery das Besteck [das bə'ʃtɛk]
cutlet das Kotelett [das 'kɔtlɛt]
cycle (vb) Rad fahren ['ʀaːt 'faːʀən]
cycle path der Fahrradweg [dɐ
'faːʀatveːk]
cycle tour die Radtour [di 'ʀaːttuɐ]
cycling der Radsport [dɐ 'ʀaːtʃpɔɐt]

D

daily täglich [tɛːklɪç]
damage die Beschädigung
[di bə'ʃɛːdɪgʊn], der Schaden
[dɐ ʃaːdn]; (vb) beschädigen
[bə'ʃɛːdɪgn], schaden [ʃaːdn]
damp feucht [fɔɪçt]
dance der Tanz [dɐ tants]; (vb) tanzen [tantsn]
dance band die Tanzkapelle
[di 'tantska͜pɛlə]
dance theatre das Tanztheater
[das 'tantste͜aːtɐ]
dancer der Tänzer/die Tänzerin
[dɐ tɛntsɐ/di tɛntsə'ʀɪn]
dandruff die Schuppen f pl
[di ʃʊpm]
danger die Gefahr [di gə'faː]
dangerous gefährlich [gə'fɛːlɪç]
dark dunkel [dʊŋkl], finster ['fɪnstɐ]
dark blue dunkelblau [dʊŋkl'blaʊ]
darling der Liebling [dɐ 'liːplɪn]
date das Datum [das 'daːtʊm];
(meeting) die Verabredung
[di fɛ'ʔapʀeːdʊn]; up to date
modern [mo'dɛɐn]

date of birth das Geburtsdatum
[das gə'bʊɐtsdaːtʊm]
daughter die Tochter [di 'tɔxtɐ]
day der Tag [dɐ taːk]
day of arrival der Anreisetag
[dɐ 'ʔanʀaɪzə͜taːk]
day pass der Tagespass
[dɐ 'taːgəspas]
day ticket die Tageskarte
[di 'taːgəskaːtə]
day trip der Tagesausflug
[dɐ 'taːgəs͜ʔaʊsfluːk]
deadline der Termin [dɐ tɛ'miːn]
deaf gehörlos [gə'høːloːs], taub
[taʊp]
deaf person der/die Gehörlose
[dɐ/di gə'høːloːzə]
deaf-mute (adj) taubstumm
['taʊpʃtʊm]
debt die Schuld [di ʃʊlt]
deceitful betrügerisch
[bə'tʀyːgəʀɪʃ]
December Dezember [de'tsɛmbɐ]
decide entscheiden ['ʔɛnt'ʃaɪdn],
beschließen [bə'ʃliːsn]
deck das Deck [das dɛk]
declaration of value die Wertangabe [di 'veɐtanga͜baə]
decline (vb) ablehnen ['ʔapleːnn]
deep tief [tiːf]
definite(ly) endgültig ['ʔɛntgʏltɪç]
delay die Verspätung [di
fɛ'ʃpɛːtʊn]; (vb) verzögern
[fɛ'tsøːgɛn]
delicatessen das Feinkostgeschäft
[das 'faɪnkɔstgə͜ʃɛft]
delightful entzückend ['ʔɛn'tsʏknt]
deodorant das Deo [das 'deo]
department store das Kaufhaus
[das 'kaʊfhaʊs]
departure die Abfahrt [di 'ʔapfaːt],
(flight) der Abflug [dɐ 'ʔapfluːk]
deposit die Kaution [di kaʊ'tsjoːn],
(on bottle) das Pfand [das (p)fant];
(vb) (Geld) hinterlegen [(gɛlt)
hɪntɐ'leːgn]
describe beschreiben [bə'ʃʀaɪbm]

dessert der Nachtisch [de 'na:xtɪʃ]

destination das (Reise)Ziel [das ('ʀaɪzə-)tsi:l]

detergent *(clothes)* das Waschmittel [das 'vaʃmɪtl]; *(dishes)* das Spülmittel [das 'ʃpy:lmɪtl]

detour der Umweg [de 'ʔumve:k]

develop entwickeln [ʔɛnt'vɪkln]

diabetes der Diabetes [de dia'be:təs]

diabetic *(person)* der Diabetiker/die Diabetikerin [de dia'be:tɪke/di dia'be:tɪkəʀɪn]; *(adj)* diabetisch [dia'be:tɪʃ]

diagnosis die Diagnose [di dia'gno:zə]

dial *(vb)* wählen ['vɛ:ln]

diarrhoea der Durchfall [de 'duɐçfal]

diet die Diät [di di'ɛ:t], *(food)* die Schonkost [di 'ʃo:nkɔst]

different(ly) verschieden [fe'ʃi:dn], anders ['ʔandɐs]

difficult schwierig ['ʃvi:ʀɪç], schwer [ʃveɐ]

difficulty in breathing die Atembeschwerden *f pl* [di 'ʔa:tmbəʃveɐdn]

digestion die Verdauung [di fe'daʊʊŋ]

digital camera die Digitalkamera [di digi'ta:l͜kaməʀa]

dining room *(hotel)* der Speisesaal [de 'ʃpaɪzəza:l]; *(private)* das Esszimmer [das 'ʔɛstsɪmɐ]

dinner das Abendessen [das 'ʔa:bmt'ʔɛsn]

diphtheria die Diphtherie [di dɪftə'ʀi:]

dipped headlights das Abblendlicht [das 'ʔapblɛntlɪçt]

direct direkt [di'ʀɛkt]

directed by die Regie [di ʀa'ʒi:]

direction *(way)* die Richtung [di 'ʀɪçtʊŋ]

dirty schmutzig ['ʃmʊtsɪç]

disability die Behinderung [di bə'hɪndəʀʊŋ]

disabled person der/die Behinderte [de/di bə'hɪndɐtə]

disappointed enttäuscht [ʔɛn'tɔɪʃt]

discotheque die Diskothek [di dɪsko'te:k]

discount der Rabatt [de ʀa'bat]

discover entdecken [ʔɛnt'dɛkn]

dish *(meal)* das Gericht [das gə'ʀɪçt]

dish of the day das Tagesgericht [das 'ta:gəsgəʀɪçt]

dishcloth das Spültuch [das 'ʃpy:ltu:x]

dishwasher die Geschirrspülmaschine [di gə'ʃɪʀʃpy:lmaʃɪnə]

disinfect desinfizieren [dezɪnfɪ'tsi:ʀən]

disinfectant das Desinfektionsmittel [das dezɪnfɛk'tsjo:nsmɪtl]

distance der Abstand [de 'ʔapʃtant], die Entfernung [di 'ʔɛnt'fɛɐnʊŋ], die Strecke [di 'ʃtʀɛkə]

distinct deutlich ['dɔɪtlɪç]

distinguished fein [faɪn], vornehm ['foɐne:m]

district die Gegend [di 'ge:gŋt], der Stadtteil [de 'ʃtataɪl]

disturb stören [ʃtøɐn]

dive tauchen [taʊxn]

diving equipment die Taucherausrüstung [di 'taʊxɐʔaʊsʀystʊŋ]

diving goggles die Taucherbrille [di 'taʊxɐbʀɪlə]

dizziness das Schwindelgefühl [das 'ʃvɪndlgəfy:l]

do tun [tu:n], machen ['maxn]

dock at anlegen in [ʔ'anle:gŋ ʔɪn]

documentary der Dokumentarfilm [de dɔkumɛn'ta:ɐfɪlm]

documents die Papiere *n pl* [di pa'pi:ʀə]

dog der Hund [de hʊnt]

dome die Kuppel [di kʊpl]

domestic flight der Inlandsflug

[deˈ ⁷ɪnlantsfluːk]
done *(cooked)* gar [gaː]
door die Tür [di tyɐ]
door code der Türcode
[deˈ ˈtyɐkoːt]
door opener der Türöffner
[deˈ ˈtyɐ⁷œfnɐ]
door width die Türbreite
[di ˈtyɐbraɪtə]
doorstep die Türschwelle
[di ˈtyɐʃvɛlə]
double doppelt [dɔplt]
doubles das Doppel [das dɔpl]
drama das Drama [das ˈdraːma]
draw zeichnen [ˈtsaɪçnn]; *(sport)*
unentschieden spielen [ˈ⁷ʊnɛntʃiːdn
ʃpiːln]
drawing die Zeichnung
[di ˈtsaɪçnʊŋ]
dreadful schrecklich [ˈʃrɛklɪç],
fürchterlich [ˈfvɛçtelɪç]
dream der Traum [deˈ traʊm]; *(vb)*
träumen [trɔɪmm]
dress das Kleid [das klaɪt]; *(vb)* sich
anziehen [zɪç ⁷antsiːn]; *(med.)* verbinden [feˈbɪndn]
dressing *(med)* der Verband
[deˈ feˈbant]; *(cook)* das Dressing
[das ˈdrɛsɪŋ]
dressmaker der Schneider/die
Schneiderin [deˈ ˈʃnaɪdeˈ/di
ˈʃnaɪdəʀɪn]
drink das Getränk [das gəˈtrɛŋk];
(vb) trinken [trɪŋkn]
drinking water das Trinkwasser
[das ˈtrɪŋkvasə]
dripstone cave die Tropfsteinhöhle [di ˈtrɔpfʃtaɪnˌhøːlə]
drive die Fahrt [di faːt]; *(vb)* fahren
[faː(ʀə)n]; **drive a car** Auto fahren
[ˈ⁷aʊto_faːn]; **drive back** zurückfahren [tsʊˈʀʏkfaː(ʀə)n]
drive-in cinema das Freilichtkino
[das ˈfraɪlɪçtkiːno]
driver der Chauffeur [deˈ ʃɔˈføɐ],
der Fahrer/die Fahrerin
[deˈ ˈfaːʀɐ/di ˈfaːʀəʀɪn]

driving licence der Führerschein
[deˈ ˈfyːʀɐʃaɪn]
drops die Tropfen *m pl* [di ˈtrɔpfn]
drunk betrunken [bəˈtrʊŋkn]
dry trocken [ˈtrɔkn]; *(wine)* herb
[hɛɐp], trocken [ˈtrɔkn]
dry-clean chemisch reinigen
[ˈçeːmɪʃ ˈraɪnɪgŋ]
drycleaner's die Reinigung
[di ˈraɪnɪgʊŋ]
dummy der Schnuller [deˈ ˈʃnʊlɐ]
durable haltbar [ˈhaltbaː]
during während [ˈvɛːʀənt]
during the day tagsüber
[ˈtaːksʔyːbɐ]
during the morning vormittags
[ˈfɔɐmɪtaːks]
dust der Staub [deˈ ʃtaʊp]
dustbin die Mülltonne
[di ˈmʏltɔnə]
duty die Zollgebühren *f pl*
[di ˈtsɔlgəbyːʀən]
duty-free zollfrei [ˈtsɔlfʀaɪ]
duty-free shop zollfreier Laden
[ˈtsɔlfʀaɪe laːdn]
dye *(vb)* färben [fɛɐbm]
dynamo die Lichtmaschine
[di ˈlɪçtmaʃiːnə]
dynasty die Dynastie [di dʏnasˈtiː]

E

each jede(r, s) [ˈjeːdə(-deˈ, -dəs)]
ear das Ohr [das ⁷oɐ]
ear-drops die Ohrentropfen *m pl*
[di ⁷oːʀəntrɔpfn]
eardrum das Trommelfell [das
ˈtrɔmlfɛl]
earrings die Ohrringe *m pl*
[di ⁷oːʀɪŋə]
earth die Erde [di ⁷eɐdə]
east der Osten [deˈ ⁷ɔstn]
Easter Monday Ostermontag
[ˌ⁷oːsteˈmoːˈntaːk]
easy leicht [laɪçt]

eat essen [ˈɛsn]
edible essbar [ˈʔɛsbaː]
education die Erziehung [di ʔeˈtsiːʊŋ], die Ausbildung [di ʔaʊsbɪldʊŋ]
eel der Aal [de ʔaːl]
eggs die Eier *n pl* [di ʔaɪe]
Eire Irland [ˈʔɪelant]
either ... or entweder ... oder [ˈʔɛntveːde ... ʔoːde]
elastic bandage die Elastikbinde [di ʔeˈlastɪkbɪndə]
electric elektrisch [ʔeˈlɛktrɪʃ]
electric wheelchair der E-Rollstuhl [de ˈʔeːˌrɔlʃtuːl]
elevator *(US)* der Fahrstuhl [de ˈfaːʃtuːl], der Aufzug [de ˈʔaʊftsuːk], der Lift [de lɪft]
elsewhere anderswo [ˈʔandesvoː]
embassy die Botschaft [di ˈboːtʃaft]
emblem das Wahrzeichen [das ˈvaːtsaɪçn]
emergency der Notfall [de ˈnoːtfal]
emergency brake die Handbremse [di ˈhantbrɛmzə]
emergency exit der Notausgang [de ˈnoːtʔaʊsɡaŋ]
emergency telephone die Notrufsäule [di ˈnoːtrufzɔɪlə]
empty leer [leːe]
enclosure *(letter)* die Anlage [di ˈʔanlaːɡə]
end das Ende [das ˈʔɛndə], der Schluss [de ʃlʊs]
engaged *(telephone)* besetzt [bəˈzɛtst]
engine der Motor [de ˈmoːtoe]
England England [ˈʔɛŋlant]
English englisch [ˈʔɛŋlɪʃ]; **Englishman/-woman** der Engländer/die Engländerin [de ˈʔɛŋlɛndə/di ˈʔɛŋlɛndərɪn]
enjoy genießen [ɡəˈniːsn]
enough genug [ɡəˈnuːk]
entertainment die Unterhaltung [di ʔʊntɐˈhaltʊŋ]

enthusiastic (about) begeistert (von) [bəˈɡaɪstɐt fɔn]
entire ganz [ɡants]
entrance die Einfahrt [di ˈʔaɪnfaːt], der Eingang [de ˈʔaɪnɡaŋ]; der Zugang [de ˈtsuːɡaŋ], *(fee)* der Eintritt [de ˈʔaɪntrɪt]
envelope der Briefumschlag [de ˈbriːfʊmʃlaːk]
environment die Umwelt [di ˈʔʊmvɛlt]
epilepsy die Epilepsie [di epilɛpˈsiː]
epoch die Epoche [di ˈʔeˈpɔxə]
especially hauptsächlich [ˈhaʊptzɛçlɪç], besonders [bəˈzɔndɐs]
estate das Landgut [das ˈlantɡuːt]
etching die Radierung [di raˈdiːrʊŋ]
EU citizen EU-Bürger/EU-Bürgerin [ˈʔeˈʔu: byrɡe/ˈʔeˈʔu: byrɡərɪn]
euro der Euro [de ˈʔɔɪro]
Europe Europa [ˈʔɔɪˈroːpaː]
European der Europäer/die Europäerin [de ˈʔɔɪroˈpɛːe/di ˈʔɔɪroˈpɛːərɪn]; europäisch [ˈʔɔɪroˈpɛːɪʃ]
evening der Abend [de ˈʔaːbmt]; **in the evening** abends [ˈʔaːbms]
event das Ereignis [das ˈʔeˈʔaɪknɪs], die Veranstaltung [di fɐˈʔanʃtaltʊŋ]
every jede(r, s) [ˈjeːdə(-de, -dəs)]
every day jeden Tag [jeːdn taːk]
every hour stündlich [ˈʃtʏntlɪç]
everybody jedermann [ˈjeːdeman]
everything alles [ˈʔaləs]
everywhere überall [ˈʔybeˈʔal]
evil böse [ˈbøːzə]
exact(ly) genau [ɡəˈnaʊ]
examination die Untersuchung [di ʔʊntɐˈzuːxʊŋ]
example das Beispiel [das ˈbaɪʃpiːl]; **for example** zum Beispiel [tsʊm ˈbaɪʃpiːl]
excavations die Ausgrabungen *f pl* [di ˈʔaʊsɡraːbʊŋn]
excellent ausgezeichnet [ˈʔaʊsɡəˈtsaɪçnət]

except außer [ʔaʊsɐ]

exchange der Austausch [de ʔaʊstaʊʃ], der Wechsel [de vɛksl]; (vb) tauschen [taʊʃn], austauschen [ʔaʊstaʊʃn]

exchange rate der Wechselkurs [de ˈvɛkslkʊɐs]

excursion der Ausflug [de ʔaʊsfluːk], die Tour [di tuɐ]

excuse die Entschuldigung [di ʔɛntˈʃʊldɪɡʊŋ]; (vb) entschuldigen [ʔɛntˈʃʊldɪɡn]

exhaust der Auspuff [de ʔaʊspʊf]

exhausted erschöpft [ʔeˈʃœpft]

exhibit das Exponat [das ʔɛkspoˈnaːt]

exhibition die Ausstellung [di ʔaʊʃtɛlʊŋ]

exit der Ausgang [de ʔaʊsɡaŋ]; (motorway) die (Autobahn)Ausfahrt [di (ʔaʊtobaːn-) ˌʔaʊsfaːt]

expect erwarten [ʔeˈvaːtn]

expensive kostspielig [ˈkɔs(t)ʃpiːlɪç], teuer [ˈtɔɪɐ]

experienced erfahren [ʔeˈfaː(ʀə)n]

explicit(ly) ausdrücklich [ˈʔaʊsdʀʏklɪç]

expression der Ausdruck [de ʔaʊsdʀʊk]

expressionism der Expressionismus [de ʔɛkspʀɛsjoˈnɪsmʊs]

extend verlängern [feˈlɛŋen]

extension lead/cord die Verlängerungsschnur [di feˈlɛŋeʀʊŋˌʃnuɐ]

extra extra [ˈʔɛkstʀaː]

extraordinary außergewöhnlich [ˌʔaʊsɐɡəˈvøːnlɪç]

eye das Auge [das ʔaʊɡə]

eye-drops die Augentropfen m pl [di ʔaʊɡn̩tʀɔpfn]

F

façade die Fassade [di faˈsaːdə]

factory die Fabrik [di faˈbʀi(ː)k]

---

faint (vb) in Ohnmacht fallen [ʔɪn ʔoːnmaxt faln]

fair (fête) die Kirmes [di ˈkɪɐməs]; (exhibition) die Messe [di ˈmɛsə]; (adj) gerecht [ɡəˈʀɛçt], fair [fɛɐ]; (weather) schön [ʃøːn]

fairly ziemlich [ˈtsiːmlɪç]

fall der Sturz [de ʃtʊɐts]; (US) der Herbst [de ˈhɛɐpst]; (vb) stürzen [ʃtʏɐtsn], fallen [faln]

family die Familie [di faˈmiːljə]

famous berühmt [bəˈʀyːmt]

fan der Ventilator [de vɛntiˈlaːtoɐ]

far weit [vaɪt]

fare der Fahrpreis [de ˈfaːpʀaɪs]

farm der Bauernhof [de ˈbaʊɐnhoːf]

fashion die Mode [di ˈmoːdə]

fast schnell [ʃnɛl]

fat fett [fɛt]; (person) dick [dɪk]

father der Vater [de ˈfaːtɐ]

fault der Fehler [de ˈfeːlɐ], der Mangel [de maŋl], der Defekt [de deˈfɛkt]

fear die Angst [di ʔaŋst], die Furcht [di fʊɐçt]; (vb) fürchten [fʏɐçtn], befürchten [bəˈfʏɐçtn]

February Februar [ˈfeːbʀʊaː]

feeble schwach [ʃvax]

feeding bottle die Saugflasche [di ˈzaʊkflaʃə]

feel fühlen [fyːln]

feeling das Gefühl [das ɡəˈfyːl]

fees die Gebühren f pl [di ɡəˈbyːʀən/ -ˈbyɐn]

fennel der Fenchel [de fɛnçl]

ferry die Fähre [di ˈfɛːʀə]

festival das Festival [das ˈfɛstɪval]

fever das Fieber [das ˈfiːbɐ]

few wenig [ˈveːnɪç]; a few ein paar [(ʔaɪ)n ˈpaː]

fiancé/fiancée der/die Verlobte [de/di feˈloːptə]

field das Feld [das fɛlt]

figure die Nummer [di ˈnʊmɐ], die Zahl [di tsaːl]

fill in ausfüllen [ˈʔaʊsfʏln]

fill up tanken [taŋkn]

filled rolls belegte Brötchen [bə'le:ktə brø:tçn]

filling *(med.)* die Plombe [di 'plɔmbə]

film der Film [de fɪlm]

film actor/actress der Filmschauspieler/die Filmschauspielerin [de 'fɪlmʃauʃpi:le/di 'fɪlmʃauʃpi:ləRɪn]

film speed die Filmempfindlichkeit [di 'fɪlmɛmpfɪntlɪçkaɪt]

finally zuletzt [tsʊ'lɛtst], endlich ['ʔɛntlɪç]

find finden [fɪndn]

fine *(punishment)* die Strafe [di 'ʃtRa:fə], die Geldstrafe [di 'gɛltʃtRa:fə]; *(thin)* fein [faɪn]

finger der Finger [de 'fɪŋe]

fire das Feuer [das 'fɔɪe], der Brand [de bRant]

fire alarm der Feuermelder [de 'fɔɪemɛlde]

fire extinguisher der Feuerlöscher [de 'fɔɪelʃe]

firewood das Brennholz [das 'bRɛnhɔlts]

fireworks display das Feuerwerk [das 'fɔɪevɛek]

firm die Firma [di 'fɪRma:], das Unternehmen [das ʔʊnte'ne:mm]; *(adj)* fest [fɛst]

first erste(r, -s) ['ʔeestə (-te, -təs)]; first (of all) zunächst [tsʊ'nɛ:çst/ -'nɛ:kst]; (at) first zuerst [tsʊ'ʔeest]

first name der Vorname [de 'foena:mə]

fishbone die Gräte [di 'gRɛ:tə]

go fishing angeln ['ʔaŋln]

fishing licence der Angelschein [de 'ʔaŋlʃaɪn]

fishing port der Fischerhafen [de 'fɪʃeha:fn]

fishing rod die Angel [di 'ʔaŋl]

fishmonger's das Fischgeschäft [das 'fɪʃgəʃɛft]

fit der Anfall [de 'ʔanfal]; *(adj)* fit

[fɪt]; *(vb)* passen [pasn]

fitness centre das Fitnesscenter [das 'fɪtnəsˌtsɛnte]

flannel der Waschlappen [de 'vaʃlapm]

flash das Blitzgerät [das 'blɪtsgəRɛ:t]

flat *(apartment)* die Wohnung [di 'vo:nʊŋ]; *(flat tyre)* (Reifen)Panne [('Raɪfn)ˌpanə]; *(adj)* eben ['ʔe:bm]

flat rate der Pauschalpreis [de pau'ʃa:lpRaɪs]

flat rate for electricity die Strompauschale [di 'ʃtRo:mpauʃa:lə]

flea market der Flohmarkt [de 'flo:ma:kt]

fleece das (Schafs)Fell [das ('ʃa:fs-)fɛl]

flight der Flug [de flu:k]

flight attendant der Steward/die Stewardess [de 'stjua:t/di: 'stjuadɛs]

floor der Boden [de bo:dn]; *(storey)* das Stockwerk [das 'ʃtɔkvɛek]

florist's das Blumengeschäft [das 'blu:mmgəʃɛft]

flour das Mehl [das me:l]

flower die Blume [di 'blu:mə]

flu die Grippe [di 'gRɪpə]

fly die Fliege [di 'fli:gə]; *(vb)* fliegen [fli:gn]

fog der Nebel [de 'ne:bl]

folding wheelchair der Faltrollstuhl [de 'faltˌRɔlʃtu:l]

fond, be ~ of s.o. jdn lieb haben [jemandn 'li:p ha:bm]

food das Essen [das 'ʔɛsn], das Lebensmittel [das 'le:bmsmɪtl]

food poisoning die Lebensmittelvergiftung [di 'le:bmsmɪtlfeˌgɪftʊŋ]

food store das Lebensmittelgeschäft [das 'le:bmsmɪtlgəʃɛft]

foot der Fuß [de fu:s]

football der Fußball [de 'fu:sbal]

football match das Fußballspiel [das 'fu:sbalʃpi:l]

for für [fye]; *(time)* seit [zaɪt];

(reason) denn [dɛn]

foreign fremd [frɛmt], ausländisch ['ʔaʊslɛndɪʃ]

foreigner der Ausländer/ die Ausländerin [de 'ʔaʊslɛndɐ/ di 'ʔaʊslɛndərɪn]; der/die Fremde [de/di 'frɛmdə]

forest der Wald [de valt]

forget vergessen [fe'gɛsn]

fork die Gabel [di 'ga:bl]

form die Form [di fɔɐm]; *(paper)* das Formular [das fɔmʊ'la:]; *(vb)* bilden [bɪldn]

fortress die Festung [di 'fɛstʊŋ]

forward(s) vorwärts ['fɔɐvɛɐts]; look forward to sich freuen auf [zɪç 'frɔɪn ʔaʊf]

fountain der (Spring)Brunnen [de ('ʃprɪŋ)brʊnn]

fracture der Knochenbruch [de 'knɔxnbrʊx]

fraud der Betrug [de bə'tru:k]

free gratis ['gra:tɪs], frei [fraɪ], kostenlos ['kɔstnlo:s], umsonst ['ʔʊm'zɔnst]

freeway die Autobahn [di 'ʔaʊtoba:n]

freeze *(vb)* frieren ['fri:rən/fri:ɐn]

French französisch [fran'tsø:zɪʃ]

frequently häufig ['hɔɪfɪç]

fresh frisch [frɪʃ]

Friday Freitag ['fraɪta:k]

fridge der Kühlschrank [de 'ky:lʃraŋk]

friend der Freund/die Freundin [de frɔɪnt/'di frɔɪndɪn], der/die Bekannte [de/di bə'kantə]; be friends befreundet sein [bə'frɔɪndət zaɪn]

friendly freundlich ['frɔɪntlɪç]

frighten erschrecken ['ʔe'ʃrɛkŋ]

fringe *(hair)* der Pony [de 'pɔni]

from ab [ʔap]; von [fɔn], aus [ʔaʊs]

front, in ~ vorn [fɔɐn]; in front of vor [foɐ]

frost der Frost [de frɔst]

fruit das Obst [das 'ʔo:pst]

fruit and vegetable store der Obst- und Gemüsehändler [de 'ʔo:pst 'ʔʊnt gə'my:zəhɛntlə]

full voll [fɔl]

full beam das Fernlicht [das 'fɛɐnlɪçt]

fully comprehensive insurance die Vollkasko [di 'fɔlkasko]

fun der Spaß [de ʃpa:s]

funfair der Jahrmarkt [de 'ja:ma:kt]

fungal infection der Pilz [de pɪlts]

funicular die (Stand)Seilbahn [di ('ʃtant)zaɪlba:n]

funny lustig ['lʊstɪç]

fur das Fell [das fɛl], der Pelz [de pɛlts]

furious wütend [vy:tnt]

furniture die Möbel *n pl* [di mø:bl]

fuse *(electricity)* die Sicherung [di 'zɪçərʊŋ]

future die Zukunft [di 'tsu:kʊnft]; *(adj)* zukünftig ['tsu:kʏnftɪç]

G

gable der Giebel [de gi:bl]

gadget der Apparat [de ʔapa'ra:t]

gale der Sturm [de ʃtʊɐm]

gall-bladder die Gallenblase [di 'galnbla:zə]

gallery die Galerie [di galə'ri:]

game das Spiel [das ʃpi:l]

garage die Garage [di ga'ra:ʒə]; *(for repairs)* die Werkstatt [di 'vɛɐkʃtat]

garbage der Müll [de mʏl]

garden der Garten [de ga:tn]

garlic der Knoblauch [de 'kno:blaʊx]

gas canister die Gasflasche [di ga:sflaʃə]

gas cartridge die Gaskartusche

[di 'ga:ska,tʊʃə]

gas pedal das Gaspedal [das 'ga:speda:l]

gas pump *(US)* die Benzinpumpe [di bɛn'tsi:npʊmpə]

gas tank *(US)* der Tank [dɐ taŋk]

gate das Tor [das toɐ]; *(airport)* der Flugsteig [dɐ 'flu:kʃtaɪg]

gauze bandage die Mullbinde [di 'mʊlbɪndə]

gear der Gang [dɐ gaŋ]

gearbox das Getriebe [das gə'tRi:bə]

generator die Lichtmaschine [di 'lɪçtmaʃi:nə]

gentleman der Herr [dɐ hɛɐ]

Gents Herren ['hɛRən]

genuine echt ['ʔɛçt]

German der/die Deutsche [dɐ/di 'dɔɪtʃə]; *(adj)* deutsch [dɔɪtʃ]

German measles die Röteln *f pl* [di Rø:tln]

Germany Deutschland ['dɔɪtʃlant]

get *(receive)* bekommen [bə'kɔmm], kriegen [kRi:gn]; *(obtain)* besorgen [bə'zɔɐgn]; *(fetch)* holen [ho:ln]; **get in/on** einsteigen ['ʔaɪnʃtaɪgn]; **get up** aufstehen ['ʔaʊfʃte:n]

gift das Geschenk [das gə'ʃɛŋk]

girl das Mädchen [das 'mɛ:tçn]

give geben [ge:bm]; **give back** wiedergeben ['vi:dɐge:bm], zurückgeben [tsʊ'Rʏkge:bm]

glad froh [fRo:]; **glad (of)** erfreut (über) ['ʔe'fRɔɪt ('ʔy:bɐ)]

gladly gern [gɛɐn]

glass das Glas [das gla:s]

glass painting die Glasmalerei [di 'gla:sma:lə,Raɪ]

gliding das Segelfliegen [das 'ze:glfli:gn]

glorious herrlich ['hɛɐlɪç]

gloves die Handschuhe *m pl* [di 'hantʃu:ə]

gnat die Mücke [di 'mʏkə]

go gehen [ge:n], fahren [fa:(Rə)n],

reisen [Raɪzn]; **go away** weggehen ['vɛk(g)e:n]; **go out** hinausgehen [hɪ'naʊsge:n]; *(in the evening)* ausgehen ['ʔaʊsge:n]

goal das Tor [das toɐ]

goalkeeper der Torwart [dɐ 'toɐva:t]

God der Gott [dɐ gɔt]

gold das Gold [das 'gɔlt]

gold work die Goldschmiedekunst [di 'gɔltʃmi:də,kʊnst]

golf das Golf [das gɔlf]

golf club *(implement)* der Golfschläger [dɐ 'gɔlfʃlɛ:gɐ]; *(establishment)* der Golfclub ['gɔlfklʊp]

good gut [gu:t]

Good Friday Karfreitag [ka:'fRaɪta:k]

goodbye auf Wiedersehen ['ʔaʊf 'vi(:)dɐze:n]; **say goodbye** Abschied nehmen ['ʔapʃi:t ne:mm], sich verabschieden [zɪç fɐ'ʔapʃi:dn]

Gothic die Gotik [di 'go:tik]

government die Regierung [di Re'gi:Rʊŋ]

gram(s) das Gramm [das gRam]

grandfather der Großvater [dɐ 'gRo:sfa:tɐ]

grandmother die Großmutter [di 'gRo:smʊtɐ]

grapes die Weintrauben *f pl* [di 'vaɪntRaʊbm]

graphic arts die Grafik [di 'gRa:fɪk]

grass das Gras [das gRa:s]; *(lawn)* der Rasen [dɐ Ra:zn]

grave das Grab [das gRa:p]

graveyard der Friedhof [dɐ 'fRi:to:f]

gravy die (Braten)Soße [di ('bRa:tn)zo:sə]

great großartig ['gRo:s(ʔ)a:tɪç], prima ['pRi:ma:]; *(important)* groß [gRo:s]

Greek der Grieche/die Griechin ['gRi:çə/'gRi:çɪn]; *(adj)* griechisch ['gRi:çɪʃ] green grün [gʀy:n]

green beans grüne Bohnen [ˌgʀy:nə ˈbo:nn̩]

green card die grüne Versicherungskarte [di ˈgry:nə fɐˈzɪçəʀʊŋska:tə]

greengrocer's der Obst- und Gemüsehändler [dɐ ʔo:pst ʔʊnt gəˈmy:zəhɛntlɐ]

greet begrüßen [bəˈgʀy:sn̩], grüßen [ˈgʀy:sn̩]

grey grau [gʀaʊ]

grill der Grill [dɐ gʀɪl]

grilled vom Grill [fɔm ˈgʀɪl]

grocery store das Lebensmittelgeschäft [das ˈle:bmsmɪtlgəˌʃɛft]

ground der Boden [dɐ bo:dn̩], das Gelände [das gəˈlɛndə]

ground-floor das Erdgeschoss [das ˈʔeɐdgəʃɔs]

group die Gruppe [di ˈgʀʊpə]

growth die Geschwulst [di gəˈʃvʊlst]

guarantee die Garantie [di gaʀanˈti:]

guest der Gast [dɐ gast]

guide der Fremdenführer/die Fremdenführerin [dɐ ˈfʀɛmdnfy:ʀɐ/di ˈfʀɛmdnfy:ʀəʀɪn], (book) der Reiseführer [dɐ ˈʀaɪzəˌfy:ʀɐ]

guide dog der Blindenhund [dɐ ˈblɪndnhʊnt]

guided tour die Führung [di ˈfy:ʀʊŋ]

guilt die Schuld [di ʃʊlt]

gullet die Speiseröhre [di ˈʃpaɪzəʀø:ʀə]

gums das Zahnfleisch [das ˈtsa:nflaɪʃ]

gust of wind die Bö [di bø:]

gymnastics die Gymnastik [di gʏmˈnastɪk]

hair das Haar [das ha:]

hair dryer der Föhn [dɐ fø:n]

hair gel das Haargel [das ˈha:ge:l]

hairdresser's der Friseur [dɐ fʀiˈzø:ɐ]

hairpins die Haarklammern *f pl* [di ˈha:klamən]

hairstyle die Frisur [di fʀiˈzu:ɐ]

half die Hälfte [di ˈhɛlftə]; *(adj)* halb [halp]

hall die Halle [di ˈhalə]; der Saal [dɐ za:l]

ham der Schinken [dɐ ʃɪŋkn̩]

hand die Hand [di hant]; *(vb)* reichen [ʀaɪçn̩]; hand in abgeben [ˈʔapge:bm]

hand brake die Handbremse [di ˈhantbʀɛmzə]

hand throttle *(car)* das Handgas [das ˈhantga:s]

handbag die Handtasche [di ˈhan(t)taʃə]

handball der Handball [ˈhantbal]

handicap die Behinderung [di bəˈhɪndəʀʊŋ]

handle der Haltegriff [dɐ ˈhaltəgʀɪf]

hand-made handgemacht [ˈhantgəmaxt]

hand-operated bike das Handbike [das ˈhɛntbaɪk]

handrail der Handlauf [dɐ ˈhantlaʊf]

hang-gliding das Drachenfliegen [das ˈdʀaxnfli:gn̩]

happy froh [fʀo:], glücklich [ˈglʏklɪç]

hard hart [ha:t]

hard of hearing schwerhörig [ˈʃveɐhø:ʀɪç]

hardly kaum [kaʊm]

hat der Hut [dɐ hu:t]

have haben [ˈha:bm]; have to müssen [mʏsn̩]

hay fever der Heuschnupfen

[dɐ 'hɔɪʃnʊpfn]

hazard warning lights die Warnblinkanlage [di 'vaːnblɪŋkˀanlaːgə]

he er [ˀee]

head der Kopf [dɐ kɔpf]; *(boss)* der Leiter/die Leiterin [dɐ 'laɪtɐ/di 'laɪtəʀɪn], der Chef/die Chefin [dɐ ʃɛf/di ʃɛfɪn]

headache die Kopfschmerzen *m pl* [di 'kɔpfʃmɛɛtsn]

headache tablets die Kopfschmerztabletten *f pl* [di 'kɔpfʃmɛɛtsta,blɛtn]

headlight der Scheinwerfer [dɐ 'ʃaɪnvɛɛfɐ]

headphones der Kopfhörer [dɐ 'kɔpfhøːʀe]

headquarters der Sitz [dɐ zɪts], das Hauptquartier [das 'haʊptkva,tiɐ]

health food shop das Reformhaus [das ʀeˈfɔɐmhaʊs]

healthy gesund [gəˈzʊnt]

hear hören ['høːʀən/høən]

hearing das Gehör [das gəˈhøɐ]

heart das Herz [das hɛɛts]

heart attack der Herzinfarkt [dɐ 'hɛɛtsɪnfaːkt]

heart trouble die Herzbeschwerden *f pl* ['hɛɛtsbəʃveɐdn]

heartburn das Sodbrennen [das 'zoːtbʀɛnn]

heat die Wärme [di 'vɛɛmə], die Hitze [di 'hɪtsə]; *(vb)* wärmen [vɛɛmm], heizen [haɪtsn]

heating die Heizung [di 'haɪtsʊŋ]

heaven *(rel)* der Himmel [dɐ hɪml]

heavy schwer [ʃveɐ]

height die Größe [di 'gʀøːsə], die Höhe [di 'høə]; *(of career)* der Höhepunkt [dɐ 'høəpʊŋkt]

help die Hilfe [di 'hɪlfə]

her *(pronoun)* sie [ziː], ihr [ˀiɐ]; *(possessive pronoun)* ihr [ˀiɐ]

herbs die Kräuter *n pl* [di 'kʀɔɪtɐ]

here hier [hiɐ]

hernia der Leistenbruch

[dɐ 'laɪstnbʀʊx]

herring der Hering [dɐ 'heːʀɪŋ]

high hoch [hoːx]

high beam das Fernlicht [das 'fɛɐnlɪçt]

high blood pressure der Bluthochdruck [dɐ 'bluːthoːxdʀʊk]

high season die Hauptsaison [di 'haʊptzɛ,zɔŋ]

high tide die Flut [di fluːt]

highlight der Höhepunkt [dɐ 'høəpʊŋkt]

highlights die Strähnchen *n pl* [di 'ʃtʀɛːnçn]

hike die Wanderung [di 'vandəʀʊŋ]; *(vb)* wandern ['vandɐn]

hiking map die Wanderkarte [di 'vandeka:tə]

hill der Hügel [dɐ hyːgl]

hinder hindern ['hɪndɐn]

hip die Hüfte [di 'hʏftə]

hire mieten ['miːtn]

his sein [zaɪn]

history die Geschichte [di gəˈʃɪçtə]

hitchhike trampen [tʀɛmpm]

hoarse heiser ['haɪzɐ]

hole das Loch [das lɔx]

holiday camp die Ferienanlage [di 'feːʀiənˀanla:gə]

holiday home das Ferienhaus [das 'feːʀiənhaʊs]

holy heilig ['haɪlɪç]

home das Heim [das haɪm], das Haus [das haʊs]; *(country)* die Heimat [di 'haɪma:t]; at home daheim [daˈhaɪm]

home-made hausgemacht ['haʊsgəmaxt]

honey der Honig [dɐ 'hoːnɪç]

hook der Haken [dɐ ha:kŋ]

horn die Hupe [di 'huːpə]

hors d'"uvre die Vorspeise [di 'foɐʃpaɪzə]

horse das Pferd [das pfeɐt]

hospital das Krankenhaus [das 'kʀaŋkŋhaʊs]

hospitality die Gastfreundschaft

[di 'gastfʀɔɪntʃaft]
host/hostess der Gastgeber/
die Gastgeberin [dɐ 'gastge:bɐ/
di 'gastge:bərɪn]
hot *(temperature)* heiß [haɪs];
(spicy) scharf [ʃa:f]
hot water warmes Wasser ['kaltəs
'vasɐ]
hour die Stunde [di 'ʃtʊndə]; a
quarter of an hour eine Viertelstunde [(ˌʔaɪ)nə fʀɛtl'ʃtʊndə]; half
an hour eine halbe Stunde [(ˌʔaɪ)nə
ˌhalbə 'ʃtʊndə]; ; hours of business die Öffnungszeiten *f pl*
[di 'ʔœfnʊŋstsaɪtn]
hourly stündlich ['ʃtʏntlɪç]
house das Haus [das haʊs]
house number die Hausnummer
[di 'haʊsnʊmɐ]
houseboat das Hausboot [das
'haʊsbo:t]
hovercraft das Luftkissenboot [das
'lʊftkɪsnbo:t]
how wie [vi:]; how many wie
viele [vi: 'fi:lə]; how much wie viel
[vi: 'fi:l]
however jedoch [je'dɔx], doch
[dɔx]
humid schwül [ʃvy:l]
hungry hungrig ['hʊŋʀɪç]
hurry sich beeilen [zɪç bə'ʔaɪln]; be
in a hurry es eilig haben ['əs 'ʔaɪlɪç
ha:bm]
hurt schmerzen [ʃmɛɐtsn], wehtun
['ve:tu:n]
husband der Ehemann
[dɐ 'ʔe:əman]
hut die Hütte [di 'hʏtə]

I

I ich ['ɪç]
ice das Eis [das 'ʔaɪs]
ice hockey das Eishockey [das
'ʔaɪshɔke:]

ice pack das Kühlelement [das
'ky:lɛləmɛnt]
ice rink die Eisbahn [di 'ʔaɪsba:n]
ice skates die Schlittschuhe *m pl*
[di 'ʃlɪtʃu:ə]
go ice skating Schlittschuh laufen
['ʃlɪtʃu: laʊfn]
idea die Idee [di 'ʔi'de:]; no idea!
keine Ahnung! ['kaɪnə 'ʔa:nʊŋ]
identity card der Personalausweis
[dɐ p(ɛ)ezo'na:l,'ʔaʊsvaɪs]
if wenn [vɛn], falls [fals]
ignition die Zündung [di 'tsʏndʊŋ]
ignition key der Zündschlüssel
[dɐ 'tsʏntʃlʏsl]
ill krank [kʀaŋk]; be taken ill
krank werden ['kʀaŋk veɐdn]
illness die Krankheit [di
'kʀaŋkhaɪt]
illustration das Bild [das bɪlt]
impertinent unverschämt
['ʔʊnfɐʃɛ:mt]
important bedeutend [bə'dɔɪtnt],
wichtig ['vɪçtɪç]
impossible ausgeschlossen
['ʔaʊsgəʃlɔsn], unmöglich
['ʔʊnˌmø:glɪç]
impressionism der Impressionismus [dɐ 'ʔɪmpʀɛsjo'nɪsmʊs]
impressive beeindruckend
[bə'ʔaɪndʀʊknt]
improbable unwahrscheinlich
['ʔʊnvaʃaɪnlɪç]
in in ['ʔɪn]
incident der Vorfall [dɐ 'foɐfal],
der Zwischenfall [dɐ 'tsvɪʃnfal]
included inbegriffen ['ʔɪnbəgʀɪfn]
incredible unglaublich
['ʔʊn'glaʊplɪç]
indicator *(car)* das Blinklicht [das
'blɪŋklɪçt]
indigestion die Verdauungsstörung [di fɐ'daʊʊnʃtø:ʀʊŋ]
indoors drinnen [dʀɪnn], im Haus
['ʔɪm haʊs]
infection die Infektion
[di 'ʔɪnfɛk'tsjo:n]

inflammable feuergefährlich
['fɔɪɛgəfeelɪç]

inflammation die Entzündung
[di ʔɛn'tsʏndʊŋ]

inflammation of the middle ear die Mittelohrentzündung
[di 'mɪtlʔoeʔɛn,tsʏndʊŋ]

influenza die Grippe [di 'gʀɪpə]

inform benachrichtigen
[bə'na:xʀɪçtɪgŋ], informieren
['ʔɪnfɔ'mi:ʀən/-'mien], mitteilen
['mɪtaɪln]

information die Auskunft
[di ʔ'aʊskʊnft]

infusion die Infusion
[di 'ɪnfʊ'zjo:n]

inhabitant der Bewohner/
die Bewohnerin [de bə'vo:ne/
di bə'vo:nəʀɪn], der Einwohner/
die Einwohnerin [de ʔ'aɪnvo:ne/
di ʔ'aɪnvo:nəʀɪn]

injection die Spritze [di 'ʃpʀɪtsə]

injure verletzen [fe'lɛtsn]

injured person der/die Verletzte
[de/di fe'lɛtstə]

injury die Verletzung [di fe'lɛtsʊŋ]

inner courtyard der Innenhof
[de ʔ'ɪnnho:f]

in-room telephone das Zimmertelefon [das 'tsɪmetelə,fo:n]

inscription die Inschrift
[di ʔ'ɪnʃʀɪft]

insect das Insekt [das ʔɪn'zɛkt]

inside innen [ʔ'ɪnn], drin [dʀɪn]

insist behaupten [bə'haʊptn];
insist on bestehen auf [bə'ʃte:n
ʔaʊf]

insomnia die Schlaflosigkeit
[di 'ʃla:flo:zɪçkaɪt]

inspector der Kontrolleur/
die Kontrolleurin [de kɔntʀo'løe/
di kɔntʀo'løʀɪn]

instead of statt [ʃtat], anstatt
[ʔ'an'ʃtat]

insulin das Insulin [das ʔ'ɪnzʊ'li:n]

insult die Beleidigung
[di bə'laɪdɪgŋ]; (vb) beleidigen
[bə'laɪdɪgŋ]

insurance die Versicherung
[di fe'zɪçəʀʊŋ]

intelligent klug [klu:k]

interested, be ~ (in) sich interessieren (für) [zɪç ʔɪntʀə'si:ʀən/-'sien
(fyɐ)]

interesting interessant
['ɪntʀə'sant]

international call das Auslandsgespräch [das ʔ'aʊslantsgə,ʃpʀɛ:ç]

international car index mark
das Nationalitätskennzeichen [das
natsjonalɪ'tɛ:tskɛntsaɪçn]

international flight der Auslandsflug [de ʔ'aʊslantsflu:k]

interrupt unterbrechen
[ʔʊnte'bʀɛçn]

intersection die Kreuzung
[di 'kʀɔɪtsʊŋ]

intestines der Darm [de da:m]

intolerable unerträglich
[ʔʊne,tʀɛ:klɪç]

introduce vorstellen ['foeʃtɛln],
bekannt machen [bə'kant maxn]

introduction die Vorstellung
[di 'foeʃtɛlʊŋ]

invite einladen [ʔ'aɪnla:dn]

Ireland Irland [ʔ'ɪʀelant]; Northern Ireland Nordirland [nɔat'ʔɪʀelant]

Irish irisch [ʔ'i:ʀɪʃ]

iron (metal) das Eisen [das ʔ'aɪzn];
(implement) das Bügeleisen [das
'by:gl'ʔaɪzn]; (vb) bügeln [by:gln]

island die Insel [di ʔ'ɪnzl]

isolated abgelegen [ʔ'apgəle:gŋ],
einsam [ʔ'aɪnza:m]

its sein [zaɪn]

J

jack der Wagenheber [de
'va:gŋhe:be]

jacket die Jacke [di 'jakə]

jam die Marmelade [di mamə'la:də]

277

January Januar ['janʊaː], *(Austria)* Jänner ['jɛnɐ]
jaw der Kiefer [dɐ 'kiːfɐ]
jazz der Jazz [dɐ 'dʒɛs]
jazz aerobics die Jazzgymnastik [di 'dʒɛsɡʏmˌnastɪk]
jeans die Jeans [di 'dʒiːns]
jeweller's der Juwelier [dɐ juve'liɐ]
jewellery der Schmuck [dɐ ʃmʊk]
job die Arbeit [di 'ʔaːbaɪt]; *(position)* die Stellung [di 'ʃtɛlʊŋ]
jog *(vb)* joggen ['dʒɔɡŋ]
joint das Gelenk [das ɡə'lɛŋk]
joke der Spaß [dɐ ʃpaːs], der Scherz [dɐ ʃɛɐts], der Witz [dɐ vɪts]
journey die Fahrt [di faːt], die Reise [di 'ʀaɪzə]; **go on a journey** verreisen [fɐ'ʀaɪzn]; **return journey** die Rückfahrt [di 'ʀʏkfaːt]; **journey home** die Heimreise [di 'haɪmʀaɪzə]
judge der Richter/die Richterin [dɐ 'ʀɪçtɐ/di 'ʀɪçtəʀɪn]
juicy saftig ['zaftɪç]
July Juli ['juːli]
jump leads das Starthilfekabel [das 'ʃtaːthɪlfəkaːbl]
jumper der Pullover [dɐ pʊ'loːvɐ]
junction die Kreuzung [di 'kʀɔɪtsʊŋ]
June Juni ['juːni]
just *(time)* gerade [ɡ(ə)'ʀaːdə]; **just as ... as** genauso ... wie [ɡə'naʊzo ... vi]

K

keep behalten [bə'haltn]; halten ['haltn]
ketchup das Ketschup [das 'kɛtʃap]
key der Schlüssel [dɐ 'ʃlʏsl]
keyboard telephone das Schreibtelefon [das 'ʃʀaɪptelefoːn]
kidney die Niere [di 'niːʀə]
kidney stone der Nierenstein [dɐ 'niːʀənʃtaɪn]
kilogram(s) das Kilo [das 'kiːlo]
kilometre der Kilometer [dɐ ˌkilo'meːtɐ]
kind die Art [di ʔaːt], die Sorte [di 'zɔɐtə]; *(adj)* freundlich ['fʀɔɪntlɪç]
king der König [dɐ 'køːnɪç]
kiss der Kuss [dɐ kʊs]; *(vb)* küssen ['kʏsn]
kitchen die Küche [di 'kʏçə]
kitchenette die Kochnische [di 'kɔxniːʃə]
knee das Knie [das kniː]
knife das Messer [das 'mɛsɐ]
know kennen ['kɛnn], wissen ['vɪsn];

L

Ladies Damen ['daːmn]
lady die Dame [di 'daːmə]
lake der See [dɐ zeː]
lamb das Lamm [das lam]; *(meat)* das Lammfleisch [das 'lamflaɪʃ]
lamp die Lampe [di 'lampə]
land das Land [das lant]; *(vb)* landen ['landn]; **land at** *(ship)* anlegen in ['ʔanleːɡn ʔɪn]
landing die Landung [di 'landʊŋ]
landlord/landlady der Hausbesitzer/die Hausbesitzerin [dɐ 'haʊsbəzɪtsɐ/di 'haʊsbəzɪtsəʀɪn]
lane die Gasse [di 'ɡasə]
language die Sprache [di 'ʃpʀaːxə]
large groß [ɡʀoːs]
last *(adj)* letzte(r, -s) ['lɛtstə (-tɐ, -təs)]; *(adv)* zuletzt [tsʊ'lɛtst]; *(vb)* halten ['haltn], dauern ['daʊɐn]
late spät [ʃpɛːt]
laugh *(vb)* lachen ['laxn]
launderette der Waschsalon [dɐ 'vaʃzaˌlɔn]
laundry die Wäscherei [di vɛʃə'ʀaɪ]
lavatory die Toilette [di to'lɛtə]
lawn der Rasen [dɐ ʀaːzn]

lawyer der Rechtsanwalt/die Rechtsanwältin [dɐ 'ʀɛçtsanvalt/di 'ʀɛçtsanvɛltɪn]

laxative das Abführmittel [das 'ʔapfyɐˌmɪtl]

layered cut der Stufenschnitt [dɐ 'ʃtuːfnʃnɪt]

lazy faul [faʊl]

leading role die Hauptrolle [di 'haʊptʀɔlə]

leaflet der Prospekt [dɐ pʀɔs'pɛkt]

lean mager ['maːgɐ]

learn lernen [lɛɐnn]

least, at ~ mindestens ['mɪndəstns], wenigstens ['veː(ː)nɪkstns]

leather jacket die Lederjacke [di 'leːdɐjakə]

leave abfahren (von) [ʔapfaː(ʀə)n fɔn], verlassen [fɐ'lasn], weggehen ['vɛkgeːn]; *(room)* hinausgehen [hɪ'naʊsgeːn]; *(behind)* hinterlassen [hɪntɐ'lasn]; **leave (for)** abreisen (nach) [ʔapʀaɪzn (nax)]

left(-hand) linke(r, -s) ['lɪŋkə (-kɐ, -kəs)]; **on the left, to the left** links [lɪŋks]

left-luggage office die Gepäckaufbewahrung [di gə'pɛkʔaʊfbəvaːʀʊŋ]

leg das Bein [das baɪn]

legal alcohol limit die Promillegrenze [di pʀo'mɪləˌgʀɛntsə]

leggings die Leggings *pl* [di 'lɛgɪŋs]

lemonade die Limonade [lɪmo'naːdə]

lemons die Zitronen *f pl* [di tsɪ'tʀoːnn]

lend leihen [laɪn]

lens das Objektiv [das ʔɔbjɛk'tiːf]

lentils die Linsen *f pl* [di lɪnzn]

lesson die Unterrichtsstunde [di ʔʊntɐʀɪçtʃtʊndə]

let *(permit)* lassen [lasn]; *(apartment etc.)* vermieten [fɐ'miːtn]

letter der Brief [dɐ bʀiːf]

lettuce der Kopfsalat [dɐ 'kɔpfsaˌlaːt]

level *(adj)* flach [flax]

liable to duty zollpflichtig ['tsɔl(p)flɪçtɪç]

license plate das Nummernschild [das 'nʊmɐnʃɪlt]

lie die Lüge [di 'lyːgə]; *(vb)* lügen [lyːgn]; *(in horizontal position)* liegen [liːgn]; **lie down** sich hinlegen [zɪç 'hɪnleːgn]

life das Leben [das leːbm]

life belt/life preserver der Rettungsring [dɐ 'ʀɛtʊŋsʀɪŋ]

life jacket die Schwimmweste [di 'ʃvɪmvɛstə]

lifeboat das Rettungsboot [das 'ʀɛtʊŋsboːt]

lifeguard der Bademeister/die Bademeisterin [dɐ 'baːdəmaɪstɐ/di 'baːdəmaɪstəʀɪn]

lift der Aufzug [dɐ 'ʔaʊftsuːk], der Fahrstuhl [dɐ 'faːʃtuːl]; *(ski-)* der Lift [dɐ lɪft]; *(vb)* heben [eːbm]

light das Licht [das lɪçt]; *(adj weight)* leicht [laɪçt]; *(vb)* anzünden ['ʔantsʏndn]

light blue hellblau [hɛl'blaʊ]

light bulb die Glühbirne [di 'glyːbɪrnə]

light meter der Belichtungsmesser [dɐ bə'lɪçtʊŋsˌmɛsɐ]

lighter das Feuerzeug [das 'fɔɪɐtsɔɪk]

lightning der Blitz [dɐ blɪts]

like *(comparison)* wie [viː]; *(vb)* mögen ['møːgn]

line die Linie [di 'liːnjə]; *(railway)* die Strecke [di 'ʃtʀɛkə]; *(telephone)* die Leitung [di 'laɪtʊŋ]

linen das Leinen [das laɪnn]

lip die Lippe [di 'lɪpə]

lipstick der Lippenstift [dɐ 'lɪpmʃtɪft]

liquid flüssig ['flʏsɪç]

listen to music Musik hören [mʊ'ziːk 'høːʀən]

litre der Liter [dɐ 'liːtɐ]

little klein [klaɪn]; *(not much)* wenig ['veːnɪç]

live *(vb)* leben [le:bm], wohnen [vo:nn]

lively lebhaft ['le:phaft]

liver die Leber [di 'le:bɐ]

living room das Wohnzimmer [das 'vo:ntsɪmɐ]

local einheimisch ['ʔaɪnhaɪmɪʃ]

local call das Ortsgespräch [das 'ʔɔɐtsgəʃprɛ:ç]

local train der Nahverkehrszug [dɐ 'na:fɐˌkeːestsu:k]

lock das Schloss [das ʃlɔs]; *(vb)* verschließen [fɐ'ʃliːsn], abschließen ['ʔapʃliːsn]

lonely einsam ['ʔaɪnzaːm]

long lang [laŋ]; *(far)* weit [vaɪt]

long-distance call das Ferngespräch [das 'fɛɐngəʃprɛ:ç]

look der Blick [dɐ blɪk]; *(vb)* sehen [se:n], schauen ['ʃaʊn]; **look at** anschauen ['ʔanʃaʊn], ansehen ['ʔanzeːn]; **look for** suchen ['zuːxn]; **look like** aussehen ['ʔaʊseːn]; **look out!** Achtung! ['ʔaxtʊŋ]

lose verlieren [fɐ'liːrən/-'liːɐn]; **lose one's way** sich verirren [zɪç fɐ'ʔɪrən]

lost, get ~ sich verirren [zɪç fɐ'ʔɪɐn]

loud laut [laʊt]

lounge das Wohnzimmer [das 'voːntsɪmɐ]; *(hotel)* der Aufenthaltsraum [dɐ 'ʔaʊfnthalts,ʀaʊm]

love die Liebe [di 'liːbə]; *(vb)* lieben [liːbm]

low tief [tiːf]

low season die Vorsaison [di 'foːɐze,zɔŋ]; die Nachsaison [di 'naːxze,zɔŋ]

low tide die Ebbe [di ʔɛbə]

low-fat milk fettarme Milch ['fɛtʔaːmə mɪlç]

luck das Glück [das glʏk]

lucky glücklich ['glʏklɪç]

luggage das Gepäck [das gɐ'pɛk]

luggage counter der Gepäck-

luggage reclaim die Gepäckausgabe [di gɐ'pɛkʔaʊsgaːbə]

luggage van der Gepäckwagen [dɐ gɐ'pɛkvaːgŋ]

lumbago der Hexenschuss [dɐ 'hɛksnʃʊs]

lunch das Mittagessen [das 'mɪtakˌʔɛsn]

lunch meat der Aufschnitt [dɐ 'ʔaʊfʃnɪt]

lungs die Lunge [di 'lʊŋə]

luxurious luxuriös [lʊksuʀiˈøːs]

M

machine die Maschine [di ma'ʃiːnə]

mackerel die Makrele [di ma'kʀeːlə]

mad verrückt [fɐ'ʀʏkt]

Madam Frau [fʀaʊ]

magazine *(glossy)* die Illustrierte [di ɪlʊ'stʀiːetə]; *(news)* die Zeitschrift [di 'tsaɪtʃʀɪft]

maid das Zimmermädchen [das 'tsɪmɐmɛːtçn]

maiden name der Geburtsname [dɐ gə'bʊɐtsnaːmə]

main course die Hauptspeise [di 'haʊptʃpaɪzə]

main post office das Hauptpostamt [das 'haʊptˌpɔstʔamt]

main station der Hauptbahnhof [dɐ 'haʊptbaːnhoːf ('haʊpbaːnoːf)]

main street die Hauptstraße [di 'haʊptʃtʀaːsə]

maintain behaupten [bə'haʊptn]

make *(produce)* machen ['maxn], schaffen [ʃafn]; *(coffee, tea)* kochen [kɔxn]; **make good** *(damage)* ersetzen ['ʔeˈzɛtsn]

man der Mann [dɐ man]; *(mankind)* der Mensch [dɐ mɛnʃ]

mandarins die Mandarinen *f pl*

[di manda'ʀiːnn]

map die Landkarte [di 'lantkaːtə]

March März [mɛɐts]

margarine die Margarine
[di magaˈʀiːnə]

market der Markt [dɐ maːkt]

marmalade die Marmelade
[di mamɐˈlaːdə]

married verheiratet [fɐˈhaɪʀaːtət]

marry heiraten [ˈhaɪʀaːtn]

marvellous wunderbar
[ˈvʊndɐbaː]

mascara die Wimperntusche
[di ˈvɪmpɐntʊʃə]

mass (rel) die Messe [di ˈmɛsə]

massage die Massage [maˈsaːʒə]

match das Spiel [ʃpiːl]

matches die Streichhölzer n pl
[di ˈʃtʀaɪçhœltsɐ]

material das Material [das
mat(ə)ʀiˈaːl], der Stoff [dɐ ʃtɔf]

matter die Angelegenheit
[di ˈʔangəleːgn̩haɪt], die Sache
[di ˈzaxə]

mattress die Matratze
[di maˈtʀatsə]

May Mai [maɪ]

maybe vielleicht [fɪˈlaɪçt]

mayonnaise die Mayonnaise
[di maɪoˈneːzə]

me mich [mɪç], mir [miɐ]

meadow die Wiese [di ˈviːzə]

meal das Essen [das ˈʔɛsn], die
Mahlzeit [di ˈmaːltsaɪt]

meaning die Bedeutung
[di bəˈdɔɪtʊŋ]

means das Mittel [das ˈmɪtl]

measles die Masern f pl [ˈmaːzɐn]

meat das Fleisch [das flaɪʃ]

medicine das Medikament [das
medɪkaˈmɛnt]

meet treffen [tʀɛfn], begegnen
[bəˈgeːkn(ə)n]; kennen lernen
[ˈkɛnlɐnn]

melon die Melone [di meˈloːnə]

memorial die Gedenkstätte
[di gəˈdɛŋkʃtɛtə]

men die Männer [di m]

men's für Herren [fyɐ ˈhɛʀən]

Men's Room die Herrentoilette
[di ˈhɛʀəntoˌlɛtə]

menstruation die Menstruation
[di mɛnstʀuaˈtsjon]

mentally handicapped geistig
behindert [ˈgaɪstɪç bəˈhɪndɐt]

menu die Speisekarte [di
ˈʃpaɪzəkaːtə]

merry lustig [ˈlʊstɪç], froh [fʀoː]

message die Nachricht
[di ˈnaːxʀɪçt]

methylated spirits der Brennspiritus [dɐ ˈbʀɛnʃpiʀɪtʊs]

metre der Meter [dɐ ˈmeːtɐ]

microwave die Mikrowelle
[di ˈmiːkʀovɛlə]

middle die Mitte [di ˈmɪtə]

Middle Ages das Mittelalter [das
ˈmɪtlʔaltɐ]

midge die Mücke [di ˈmʏkə]

migraine die Migräne
[di miˈgʀɛːnə]

mild mild [mɪlt]

milk die Milch [mɪlç]

millimetre der Millimeter
[dɐ ˈmɪliˌmeːtɐ]

minced meat das Hackfleisch [das
ˈhakflaɪʃ]

mind, I don't ~ meinetwegen
[ˈmaɪnətˌveːgn̩]

minute die Minute [di miˈnuːtə]

mirror der Spiegel [dɐ ʃpiːgl]

miscalculate sich verrechnen [zɪç
fɐˈʀɛçn(ə)n]

miscarriage die Fehlgeburt
[di ˈfeːlgəbʊɐt]

misfortune das Unglück [das
ˈʔʊnglʏk]

Miss das Fräulein [das ˈfʀɔ(ɪ)laɪn]

miss (vb) verfehlen [fɐˈfeːln]; verpassen [fɐˈpasn]; be missing fehlen
[feːln]

mistake Fehler [ˈfeːlɐ], der Irrtum
[dɐ ˈʔɪʀtuːm]; mistake for vertauschen [fɐˈtaʊʃn], verwechseln

[fe'vɛksln]; make a mistake einen Fehler machen [(ˀaɪn)n 'feːlɐ maxn], sich verrechnen [zɪç fe'ʀɛçn(ə)n]; be mistaken sich täuschen [zɪç 'tɔɪʃn], sich irren [zɪç 'ˀɪʀən/'ˀɪen]

misunderstanding das Missverständnis [das 'mɪsfɛʃtɛntnɪs]

mobile (phone) das Handy [das 'hɛndi], das Mobiltelefon [das mo'biːltelɐfoːn]

model das Modell [das mo'dɛl]

modern modern [mo'dɛen]

moist nass [nas], feucht [fɔɪçt]

monastery das (Mönchs)Kloster [das ('mœnçs)ˌkloːstɐ]

Monday Montag ['moːntaːk]

money das Geld [das gɛlt]

month der Monat [dɐ 'moːnaːt]

monthly monatlich ['moːnatlɪç]

monument *(memorial edifice)* das Denkmal [das 'dɛŋkmaːl]; *(tomb)* das Grabmal ['gʀaːbmaːl]

moon der Mond [dɐ moːnt]

more mehr [meɐ]; **more than** mehr als ['meɐ ˀals]

morning der Morgen [dɐ mɔʁgŋ], der Vormittag [dɐ 'foɐmɪtaːk]; **in the morning** morgens ['mɔʁgŋs]

mosaic das Mosaik [das mozaˀiːk]

most, at the ~ höchstens [høːçstns/høːkstns]

motel das Motel [das mo'tɛl]

mother die Mutter [di mʊtɐ]

motive der Grund [dɐ gʀʊnt]

motor der Motor [dɐ 'moːtoɐ]

motorboat das Motorboot [das 'moːtɔboːt]

motorway die Autobahn [di ˀaʊtobaːn]

motorway toll die Autobahngebühren [di ˀaʊtobaːŋgəˌbyːʀən]

mountain der Berg [dɐ bɛɐk]

mountain bike das Mountainbike [das 'maʊntnbaɪk]

mountain village das Bergdorf [das 'bɛɐkdoɐf]

mountaineering/mountain climbing das Bergsteigen [das 'bɛɐkʃtaɪgŋ]

mountains das Gebirge [das gə'bɪʁgə]

moustache der Schnurrbart [dɐ 'ʃnʊɐbaːt]

mouth der Mund [dɐ mʊnt]; *(river)* die Mündung [di 'mʏndʊŋ]

movie actor/actress der Filmschauspieler/ die Filmschauspielerin [dɐ 'fɪlmʃaʊʃpiːlɐ/di 'fɪlmʃaʊʃpiːlərɪn]

movie theater das Kino [das 'kiːno]

Mr Herr [hɛɐ]

Mrs Frau [fʀaʊ]

much viel [fiːl]

muesli das Müsli [das 'myːsli]

mugging der Überfall [dɐ 'ˀyːbɐfal]

mumps der Mumps [dɐ mʊmps]

muscle der Muskel [dɐ 'mʊskl]

museum das Museum [das mu'zeːʊm]

music die Musik [di mu'ziːk]

music hall das Varietee [das vaʀiə'teː]

musical das Musical [das 'mjuːzɪkl]

mussels die Muscheln *f pl* [di mʊʃln]

mustard der Senf [dɐ zɛnf (zɛmf)]

mute stumm [ʃtʊm]

my mein [maɪn];

myself mich [mɪç], mir [miɐ]; I did it myself ich habe es selbst gemacht ['ˀɪç haːbə (ˀə)s 'zɛlpst gəˌmaxt]

N

nail scissors die Nagelschere [di 'naːglʃeːʀə]

nail varnish/polish der Nagellack [dɐ 'naːgllak]

nail varnish/polish remover
der Nagellackentferner
[deˈnaːgllakɛntˌfɛenɐ]
naked nackt [nakt]
name der Name [deˈnaːmə]; *(vb)*
nennen [nɛnn]
napkin die Serviette [di zeˈvjɛtə]
nappies die Windeln *f pl*
[di vɪndln]
narrow schmal [ʃmaːl], eng [ʔɛŋ]
national park der Nationalpark
[deˈnatsjoˈnaːlpaːk]
nationality die Staatsangehörigkeit
[diˈʃtaːtsˌʔangehøːʁɪçkaɪt]
native einheimisch [ʔaɪnhaɪmɪʃ]
natural natürlich [naˈtyelɪç]
nature die Natur [di naˈtue]
nature reserve das Naturschutzgebiet [das naˈtueʃʊtsgəbiːt]
naughty böse [ˈbøːzə]
nausea der Brechreiz
[deˈbʁɛçʁaɪts]
near nahe [ˈnaː(ə)], in der Nähe
von [ʔɪn deˈnɛə fɔn], bei [baɪ]
nearly beinahe [ˈbaɪnaː], fast [fast]
necessary nötig [ˈnøːtɪç], notwendig [ˈnoːtvɛndɪç]
neck der Hals [de hals]
necklace die Kette [di ˈkɛtə]
need brauchen [bʁaʊxn], benötigen [bəˈnøːtɪgŋ]
neither auch nicht [ʔaʊx nɪç(t)]
nerve der Nerv [de nɛef]
nervous nervös [neˈvøːs]
neutral der Leerlauf [deˈleelaʊf]
never nie [niː]
nevertheless trotzdem
[ˈtʁɔtsdeːm]
new neu [nɔɪ], frisch [fʁɪʃ]
New Year's Day Neujahr [nɔɪˈjaː]
New Year's Eve Silvester [sɪlˈvɛstə]
newsagent's der Zeitungshändler
[deˈtsaɪtʊŋshɛntlə]
newspaper die Zeitung
[di ˈtsaɪtʊŋ]
next nächste(r, s) [ˈnɛːçstə/ˈnɛːkstə
(-stɐ, -stəs)]; **next to** neben

[ˈneːbm]
nice nett [nɛt], lieb [liːp], sympathisch [sʏmˈpaːtɪʃ]
night die Nacht [di naxt]; der
Abend [deˈʔaːbmt]; **at night**
nachts [naxts]
night club der Nachtklub
[deˈnaxtklʊp]
no nein [naɪn]; *(not any)* kein
[kaɪn]
nobody keine(r, s) [ˈkaɪnə (-nɐ,
-nəs)], niemand [ˈniːmant]
noise das Geräusch [das gəˈʁɔɪʃ],
der Lärm [deˈlɛɐm]
noisy laut [laʊt]
non-alcoholic alkoholfrei
[ˈʔalkoˈhoːlfʁaɪ]
noon der Mittag [deˈmɪtaːk]
nor auch nicht [ʔaʊx nɪçt]
normal normal [nɔˈmaːl]
normally normalerweise
[nɔˈmaːlevaɪzə]
north der Norden [de nɔedn]
North Sea die Nordsee
[di ˈnɔetzeː]
nose die Nase [di ˈnaːzə]
nose bleed das Nasenbluten [das
ˈnaːznbluːtn]
no-smoking compartment
das Nichtraucherabteil [das
ˈnɪçtʁaʊxəˈʔapˌtaɪl]
not nicht [nɪçt]; **not at all** gar
nicht [ˈgaː nɪç(t)], durchaus nicht
[dʊeçˈʔaʊs nɪç(t)]; **not yet** noch
nicht [nɔx ˈnɪç(t)]
notepad der Notizblock
[de noˈtiːtsblɔk]
nothing nichts [nɪçts/nɪks]
notice das Schild [das ʃɪlt]; *(vb)*
bemerken [bəˈmɛekŋ]
notion die Vorstellung
[di ˈfoeʃtɛlʊŋ]
novel der Roman [de ʁoˈmaːn]
November November [noˈvɛmbə]
now nun [nuːn], jetzt [jɛtst]; **till
now** bis jetzt [bɪs ˈjɛtst]
nowhere nirgends [ˈnɪʁegŋ(t)s]

nude *(adj)* nackt [nakt]; *(painting)* der Akt [de ˀakt]

nudist beach der FKK-Strand [de ˀɛfkaːkaːʃtʀant]

number die Nummer [di 'nʊmɐ]; *(vb)* nummerieren [nʊməˈʀiːʀən/ -'ʀiən]

number plate das Nummernschild [das 'nʊmɐnʃɪlt]

nurse die Krankenschwester [di 'kʀaŋknʃvɛstɐ]

nutmeg die Muskatnuss [di mʊsˈkaːtnʊs]

nuts die Nüsse *f pl* [di 'nʏsə]

O

object der Gegenstand [de 'geːgnʃtant]

observatory die Sternwarte [di 'ʃtɛʀnvaːtə]

occasionally gelegentlich [gəˈleːgntlɪç]

occupied *(seat)* besetzt [bəˈzɛtst]

October Oktober [ˀɔkˈtoːbɐ]

of von [fɔn]; *(material)* aus [ˀaʊs]

off season die Schonzeit [di 'ʃoːntsaɪt]

offer *(vb)* anbieten [ˀanbiːtn], bieten [biːtn]

office das Büro [das byˈʀoː]; *(position)* das Amt [das ˀamt]

official *(adj)* amtlich [ˀamtlɪç], offiziell [ˀɔfɪˈtsjɛl]

off-licence das Spirituosengeschäft [das ʃpiʀituˈoːzngəʃɛft]

off-season die Vorsaison [di 'foɐzɛˌzɔŋ]; die Nachsaison [di 'naːxzɛˌzɔŋ]

offside abseits [ˀapzaɪts]

often oft [ˀɔft]

oil das Öl [das ˀøːl]

oil change der Ölwechsel [de 'ˀøːlvɛksl]

oil painting die Ölmalerei [di 'ˀøːlmaːləˌʀaɪ]

ointment die Salbe [di 'zalbə]

old alt [ˀalt]

olive oil das Olivenöl [das ˀoˈliːvnˀøːl]

olives die Oliven *f pl* [di ˀoˈliːvn]

on *(switch)* an [ˀan]; *(position)* auf [ˀaʊf]

once einmal [ˀaɪ(n)maːl]; **at once** sofort [zoˈfɔɐt], gleich [glaɪç]

one *(adj)* ein(e) [ˀaɪn/ˀaɪnə], *(numeral)* eins [ˀaɪns]

onions die Zwiebeln *f pl* [di tsviːbln]

only nur [nuɐ], *(not before)* erst [ˀeɐst]; *(adj)* einzig [ˀaɪntsɪç]

open offen [ˀɔfn], geöffnet [gəˈˀœfnət]; *(vb)* öffnen [ˀœfn(ə)n], aufmachen [ˀaʊfmaxn]; **in the open air** im Freien [ˀɪm 'fʀaɪn]

opening hours die Öffnungszeiten *f pl* [di ˀœfnʊŋstsaɪtn]

opera die Oper [di ˀoːpɐ]

operation die Operation [di ˀɔpəʀaˈtsjoːn]

operetta die Operette [di ˀopəˈʀɛtə]

opinion die Meinung [di 'maɪnʊŋ]

opposite das Gegenteil [das 'geːgntaɪl]; *(adj)* entgegengesetzt [ˀɛntˈgeːgŋgəzɛtst]; *(prep)* gegenüber [gegnˈˀyːbɐ]

optician's der Optiker [de 'ˀɔptikɐ]

or oder [ˀoːdɐ]

orange juice der Orangensaft [de ˀoˈʀaŋʒnzaft]

oranges die Apfelsinen *f pl* [di ˀapflˈziːnn]

orchestra das Orchester [das ˀɔɐˈkɛstɐ]

order *(tidiness)* die Ordnung [di ˀɔɐtnʊŋ]; *(rel)* der Orden [de ˀɔɐdn]; *(restaurant)* die Bestellung [di bəˈʃtɛlʊŋ]; *(vb)* bestellen [bəˈʃtɛln]; **out of order** kaputt [kaˈpʊt]

ordinary gewöhnlich [gə'vø:nlɪç]

organic food shop der Bioladen [de 'biola:dn]

original das Original [das ʔɔrɪgi'na:l], **original version** die Originalfassung [di oʀɪgi'na:lfasʊŋ]

ought to sollen [zɔln]

our unser(e) [ʔʊnzɐ (-ʀə)]

outside außen [ʔaʊsn], außerhalb [ʔaʊsɐhalp], draußen [dʀaʊsn]

over *(prep)* über [ʔy:bɐ]; *(adv at an end)* vorüber [fo'ʀy:bɐ], vorbei [fɔ'baɪ]

overtake überholen [ʔy:bɐ'ho:ln]

own eigen [ʔaɪgn]; *(vb)* besitzen [bə'zɪtsn]

owner der Besitzer/die Besitzerin [de bə'zɪtsɐ/di bə'zɪtsəʀɪn], der Eigentümer/die Eigentümerin [de ʔaɪgnty:mɐ/di ʔaɪgnty:məʀɪn]

oysters die Austern *f pl* [di ʔaʊstɐn]

P

pacemaker der Herzschrittmacher [de 'hɛet(s)ʃʀɪtmaxɐ]

pack die Packung [di 'pakʊŋ]; *(vb)* packen [pakn], einpacken [ʔaɪnpakn], verpacken [fe'pakn]

packing die Verpackung [di fe'pakʊŋ]

paddling pool das Planschbecken [das 'planʃbɛkn]

page die Seite [di 'zaɪtə]

pain die Schmerzen *m pl* [di 'ʃmɛetsn]

painful schmerzhaft ['ʃmɛetshaft]

pain-killing tablets die Schmerztabletten *f pl* [di 'ʃmɛetsta,blɛtn]

paint die Farbe [di 'fa:bə]; *(vb)* malen [ma:ln]

painter der Maler/die Malerin [de 'ma:lɐ/di 'ma:ləʀɪn]

painting *(picture)* das Gemälde [das gə'mɛ:ldə]; *(type of art)* die Malerei [di ma:lə'ʀaɪ]

pair das Paar [das pa:]

palace der Palast [de pa'last]

panties der (Damen)Slip [de ('da:mən)slɪp]

pants *(underwear)* die Unterhose [di 'ʊnteho:zə]; *(US)* die Hose [di 'ho:zə]

panty liners die Slipeinlagen *f pl* [di 'slɪpaɪnla:gn]

paper das Papier [das pa'piɐ]

paper handkerchiefs die Papiertaschentücher *n pl* [di pa'piɐ,taʃnty:çɐ]

paper napkins/serviettes die Papierservietten *f pl* [di pa'piɐze,vjɛtn]

paperback das Taschenbuch [das 'taʃnbu:x]

papers die Papiere *n pl* [di pa'pi:ʀə]

paprika der Paprika [de 'papʀɪka]

parachuting das Fallschirmspringen [das 'falʃɪemʃpʀɪŋŋ]

paraffin das Petroleum [das pe'tʀo:leʊm]

paralysis die Lähmung [di 'lɛ:mʊŋ]

parcel das Paket [das pa'ke:t]

pardon, I beg your ~! Ich bitte um Entschuldigung [ʔɪç 'bɪtə ʔʊm ɛnt'ʃʊldɪgʊŋ]

parents die Eltern *n pl* [di ʔɛltɐn]

park die Anlage [di ʔanla:gə]; der Park [de pa:k]; *(vb)* abstellen [ʔapʃtɛln], parken ['pa:kn]

parsley die Petersilie [di pe:te'zi:ljə]

part der Teil [de taɪl]

partially sighted sehbehindert ['se:bəhɪndɐt]

particularly besonders [bə'zɔndɐs]

particulars die Personalien *f pl* [di pɛzo'na:ljən], nähere Angaben ['nɛɐʀə ʔanga:bm]

parting der Scheitel [de ʃaɪtl]

party das Fest [das fɛst]

285

pass *(mountain)* der Pass [dɐ pas]; *(vb)* reichen [ʀaɪçn]; *(time)* vergehen [fɐˈgeːn], vorübergehen [foˈʀyːbɐgeːn], vorbeigehen [fɔˈbaɪgeːn]; *(overtake)* überholen [ˈyːbɐhoːln]

passable befahrbar [bɐˈfaːbaː]

passenger der Fahrgast [dɐ ˈfaːgast], der Passagier [dɐ pasaˈʒiɐ]

passing through auf der Durchreise [ˈʔaʊf dɐ ˈdʊɐçʀaɪzə]

passport der Reisepass [dɐ ˈʀaɪzəpas]

past die Vergangenheit [di fɐˈgaŋnhaɪt]; *(adj adv)* vorüber [foˈʀyːbɐ], vorbei [fɔˈbaɪ]

pasta die Nudeln *f pl* [di nuːdln]

path der Weg [dɐ veːk], der Pfad [dɐ (p)faːt]

patience die Geduld [di gəˈdʊlt]

pay zahlen [ˈtsaːln], bezahlen [bəˈtsaːln]; **pay out** auszahlen [ˈʔaʊstsaːln]

payment die Zahlung [di ˈtsaːlʊŋ]

peaches die Pfirsiche *m pl* [di ˈpfɪʀzɪçə]

pearl die Perle [di ˈpɛɐlə]

pears die Birnen *f pl* [di bɪʀnn]

peas die Erbsen *f pl* [di ˈʔɛpsn]

pedestrian der Fußgänger/die Fußgängerin [dɐ ˈfuːsgɛŋɐ/di ˈfuːsgɛŋəʀɪn]

pedestrian precinct/zone die Fußgängerzone [di ˈfuːsgɛŋɐˌtsoːnə]

peg der Kleiderhaken [dɐ ˈklaɪdɐhaːkn]

penalty box der Strafraum [dɐ ˈʃtraːfʀaʊm]

pendant der Anhänger [dɐ ˈʔanhɛŋɐ]

people das Volk [das fɔlk], Leute *pl* [ˈlɔɪtə]

pepper der Pfeffer [dɐ ˈpfɛfɐ]

peppers die Paprikaschoten *f pl* [di ˈpapʀɪkaʃoːtn]

percent das Prozent [das pʀoˈtsɛnt]

perch der Barsch [dɐ baːʃ]

performance *(theatre)* die Vorstellung [di ˈfoɐʃtɛlʊŋ]

perfume das Parfüm [das paˈfyːm]

perfumery die Parfümerie [di pafʏməˈʀiː]

perhaps vielleicht [fɪˈlaɪçt]; eventuell [ˈʔevɛntʊˈ(ʔ)ɛl]

perm die Dauerwelle [di ˈdaʊɐvɛlə]

permitted zulässig [ˈtsuːlɛsɪç]

person die Person [di pɐˈzoːn]; der Mensch [dɐ mɛnʃ]

personal persönlich [pɐˈzøːnlɪç]

Personal Identification Number (PIN) die Geheimzahl [di gəˈhaɪmtsaːl]

perspire schwitzen [ˈʃvɪtsn]

petrol can der Benzinkanister [dɐ bɛnˈtsiːnkaˌnɪstɐ]

petrol pump die Benzinpumpe [di bɛnˈtsiːnpʊmpə]

petrol tank der Tank [dɐ taŋk]

pets die Haustiere *n pl* [di ˈhaʊstiːʀə]

phone das Telefon [das ˈteːlefoːn]; *(vb)* telefonieren [teləfoˈniːʀən/-ˈniɐn], anrufen [ˈʔanʀuːfn]

phone box/booth die Telefonzelle [di teləˈfoːntsɛlə]

phone call der Anruf [dɐ ˈʔanʀuːf]; make a phone call telefonieren [teləfoˈniːʀən/-ˈniɐn]

phone number die Telefonnummer [di teləˈfoːnnʊmɐ]

phonecard die Telefonkarte [di teləˈfoːnkaːtə]

photograph das Foto [das ˈfoto]; *(vb)* fotografieren [ˌfotoɡʀaˈfiːʀən]

photography die Fotografie [di fotoɡʀaˈfiː]

pick out aussuchen [ˈʔaʊsuːxn]

pickpocket der Taschendieb/die Taschendiebin [dɐ ˈtaʃndiːp/di ˈtaʃnˌdiːbɪn]

pick-up service der Rückholservice [dɐ ˈʀʏkhoːlˌœsœvɪs]

picture das Bild [das bɪlt]

picture postcard die Ansichts-karte [di ˈʔanzɪçtskaːtə]

piece das Stück [das ʃtʏk]

pier der Pier [dɐ piɐ]

pill die Tablette [di taˈblɛtə]

pillar die Säule [di ˈzɔɪlə], der Pfeiler [dɐ ˈpfaɪlɐ]

pillow das Kopfkissen [das ˈkɔpfkɪsn̩]

pilot der Pilot/die Pilotin [dɐ piˈloːt/di piˈloːtɪn]

pineapple die Ananas [ˈʔananas]

pink rosa [ˈʀoːza]

pity, what a ~! wie schade! [vi ˈʃaːdə]

place die Stelle [di ˈʃtɛlə], der Platz [dɐ plats], der Ort [dɐ ˈʔɔʀt]

place of birth der Geburtsort [dɐ gəˈbuːɐtsˈʔɔʀt]

place of pilgrimage der Wall-fahrtsort [dɐ ˈvalfaːtsˌʔɔʀt]

place of residence der Wohnort [dɐ ˈvoːnˈʔɔʀt]

plain die Ebene [di ˈʔeːbənə]; *(adj)* einfarbig [ˈʔaɪnfaʀbɪç]

plant die Pflanze [di ˈ(p)flantsə]

plaster das Pflaster [das ˈpflastɐ]

plastic bag der Plastikbeutel [dɐ ˈplastɪkbɔɪtl̩]

plate der Teller [dɐ ˈtɛlɐ]

platform das Gleis [das glaɪs]

play das Schauspiel [das ˈʃaʊʃpiːl]; *(vb)* spielen [ʃpiːln̩]

playmate der Spielkamerad/die Spielkameradin [dɐ ˈʃpiːlkaməˌʀaːt/di ˈʃpiːlkaməˌʀaːdɪn]

pleasant sympathisch [symˈpaːtɪʃ], angenehm [ˈʔangənəːm]

please bitte [ˈbɪtə]; *(vb)* gefallen [gəˈfaln̩]; **be pleased (with/about)** sich freuen (über) [zɪç ˈfʀɔɪn (ˌʔybɐ)]

pleasure die Freude [di ˈfʀɔɪdə], das Vergnügen [das fɐˈgnyːgn̩]

plug der Stecker [dɐ ˈʃtɛkɐ]

pneumonia die Lungenentzün-dung [di ˈlʊŋənˈʔɛnˌtsʏndʊŋ]

pocket die Tasche [di ˈtaʃə]

pocket calculator der Taschen-rechner [dɐ ˈtaʃnʀɛçnɐ]

pocket knife das Taschenmesser [das ˈtaʃnmɛsɐ]

poison das Gift [das gɪft]

poisoning die Vergiftung [di vɐˈgɪftʊŋ]

poisonous giftig [ˈgɪftɪç]

Polaroid® camera die Sofortbild-kamera [di zoˈfɔɐtbɪltˌkaməʀa]

police die Polizei [di pɔliˈtsaɪ]

police car der Polizeiwagen [dɐ pɔliˈtsaɪvaːgn̩]

police custody die Untersu-chungshaft [di ˈʔʊntɐˈzuːxʊŋshaft]

policeman/policewoman der Polizist/die Polizistin [dɐ pɔliˈtsɪst/di pɔliˈtsɪstɪn]

polio die Kinderlähmung [di ˈkɪndɐlɛːmʊŋ]

polite höflich [ˈhøːflɪç]

poor arm [ˈʔaːm]

porcelain das Porzellan [das pɔ(ɐ)tsəˈlaːn]

pork das Schweinefleisch [ˈʃvaɪnəflaɪʃ]

port der Hafen [dɐ ˈhaːfn̩]; *(wine)* der Portwein [der ˈpɔ(ɐ)tvaɪn]

portal das Portal [das pɔ(ɐ)ˈtaːl]

porter der Portier [dɐ pɔɐˈtjeː]

portion die Portion [di pɔˈtsjoːn]

portrait das Porträt [das pɔ(ɐ)ˈtʀɛː]

posh vornehm [ˈfoɐneːm]

position *(location)* die Lage [di ˈlaːgə]; *(profession)* die Stellung [di ˈʃtɛlʊŋ]

possible möglich [ˈmøːklɪç]; even-tuell [ˈʔevɛntʊ(ˈ)ɛl]

post code die Postleitzahl [di ˈpɔstlaɪtsaːl]

post office das Postamt [das ˈpɔstamt]

post office savings book das Postsparbuch [das ˈpɔstʃpaːbuːx]

postage das Porto [das ˈpɔɐto]

postcard die Postkarte

[di 'pɔstkaːtə]

poste restante postlagernd
['pɔstlaːgɛnt]

poster das Plakat [das plaˈkaːt]

postpone verschieben [fɛˈʃiːbm̩],
aufschieben [ˈʔaʊfʃiːbm̩]

potatoes die Kartoffeln *f pl*
[di kaˈtɔfln̩]

pottery *(workshop)* die Töpferei
[di tœpfəˈʀaɪ]; *(products)* die Töpferwaren *f pl* [di ˈtœpfevaˈʀən];
(activity) Töpfern [ˈtœpfen]

pound(s) das Pfund [das (p)fʊnt]

powder der Puder [dɐ ˈpuːdɐ]

power point die Steckdose
[di ˈʃtɛkdoːzə]

practical praktisch [ˈpʀaktɪʃ]

practise *(vb)* üben [ˈʔyːbm̩]; *(profession)* ausüben [ˈʔaʊsˈʔyːbm̩]

prawns die Garnelen *f pl*
[di gaˈneːln̩]

pray beten [beːtn̩]

pregnancy die Schwangerschaft
[di ˈʃvaŋɐʃaft]

premiere die Premiere
[di pʀəmˈjeːʀə]

prepare vorbereiten [ˈfoɐbəʀaɪtn̩],
zubereiten [ˈtsuːbəʀaɪtn̩]

prescribe verschreiben [fɛˈʃʀaɪbm̩]

prescription das Rezept [das
ʀeˈtsɛpt]

present das Geschenk [das gəˈʃɛŋk];
(adj) anwesend [ˈʔanveːznt]; **be
present** da sein [ˈdaːzaɪn]

pretty *(adj)* hübsch [hʏpʃ]; *(adv)*
ziemlich [ˈtsiːmlɪç]

prevent verhindern [fɛˈhɪndɐn],
hindern [ˈhɪndɐn]

price der Preis [dɐ pʀaɪs]

priest der Priester [dɐ pʀiːstɐ]

prison das Gefängnis [das
gəˈfɛŋnɪs]

private privat [pʀɪˈvaːt]

prize der Preis [dɐ pʀaɪs]

probable wahrscheinlich
[vaˈʃaɪnlɪç]

probably wahrscheinlich

[vaˈʃaɪnlɪç]

problem das Problem [das
pʀoˈbleːm]

procession die Prozession
[di pʀɔtsɛsˈjoːn]

product das Erzeugnis [das
ˈʔeˈtsɔɪknɪs], das Produkt [das
pʀoˈdʊkt], die Ware [di ˈvaːʀə]

production *(theatre)* die Inszenierung [di ˈʔɪntsəˈniːʀʊŋ]

profession der Beruf [dɐ bəˈʀuːf]

profit der Gewinn [dɐ gəˈvɪn]

programme *(booklet)* das Programmheft [das pʀoˈgʀamhɛft]

prohibited verboten [fɛˈboːtn̩]

pronounce aussprechen
[ˈʔaʊ(s)ʃpʀɛçn̩]

proper richtig [ˈʀɪçtɪç]

prospectus der Prospekt
[dɐ pʀosˈpɛkt]

protection factor der Lichtschutzfaktor [dɐ ˈlɪçtʃʊtsˌfaktoɐ]

provisional provisorisch
[pʀovɪˈzoːʀɪʃ]

provisions der Vorrat [dɐ ˈfoːʀaːt]

pub die Kneipe [di ˈknaɪpə]

public das Publikum [das
ˈpʊblɪkʊm]; *(adj)* öffentlich
[ˈʔœfntlɪç]

pull ziehen [tsiːn̩]

pulled muscle die Zerrung
[di ˈtsɛʀʊŋ]

pullover der Pullover [dɐ pʊˈloːvɐ]

pulse der Puls [dɐ pʊls]

pump die Luftpumpe
[di ˈlʊftpʊmpə]

pumpkin der Kürbis [dɐ ˈkʏɐbɪs]

punctual pünktlich [ˈpʏŋktlɪç]

puncture das Loch [das lɔx]; *(flat
tyre)* die Panne [di ˈpanə]

punishment die Strafe [di ˈʃtʀaːfə]

purple lila [ˈliːla]

purse der Geldbeutel [dɐ
ˈgɛltbɔɪtl], die Geldbörse [di
ˈgɛltbœɐzə]; *(handbag)* die Handtasche [di ˈhan(t)taʃə]

pus der Eiter [dɐ ˈʔaɪtɐ]

put legen [le:gn], stellen [ʃtɛln], setzen [zɛtsn]; **put down** hinlegen ['hɪnle:gn]; **put off** verschieben [fɛ'ʃi:bm], aufschieben ['ʔaʊfʃi:bm]; **put on** *(dress)* anziehen ['ʔantsi:n]

quality die Qualität [di kvalɪ'tɛ:t], die Eigenschaft [di 'ʔaɪgnʃaft]

quay der Kai [de kaɪ]

queen die Königin [di 'kø:nɪgɪn]

question die Frage [di 'fʀa:gə]

quick schnell [ʃnɛl]; rasch [ʀaʃ]

quiet leise ['laɪzə], ruhig [ʀʊɪç]

quite *(entirely)* ganz [gants]; *(somewhat)* ziemlich

rabbit das Kaninchen [ka'ni:nçn]

race das Rennen [das ʀɛnn]

racing bike das Rennrad [das 'ʀɛnʀa:t]

racquet der Schläger [de 'ʃlɛ:ge]

radar check die Radarkontrolle [di ʀa'da:kɔn,tʀɔlə]

radiator der Kühler [de 'ky:le]

radio das Radio [das 'ʀa:djo]

rain der Regen [de 'ʀe:gn]

raincoat der Regenmantel [de 'ʀe:gnmantl]

rainy regnerisch ['ʀe:knəʀɪʃ]

ramble wandern ['vanden]

ramp die Rampe [di 'ʀampə]

rape die Vergewaltigung [di fegə'valtɪgʊn]; *(vb)* vergewaltigen [fegə'valtɪgn]

rare selten [zɛltn]

rash der Ausschlag [de 'ʔaʊʃla:k]

rather lieber ['li:be], vielmehr ['fi:lmee], eher ['ʔee]; *(somewhat)* ziemlich ['tsi:mlɪç]

ravine die Schlucht [di 'ʃlʊxt]

raw roh [ʀo:]

razor blade die Rasierklinge [di ʀa'zieklɪnə]

reach erreichen [ʔe'ʀaɪçn]

read lesen [le:zn]

ready fertig ['fɛetɪç], bereit [bə'ʀaɪt]

real wirklich ['vɪʀeklɪç]

really unbedingt ['ʔʊnbədɪnt]; wirklich ['vɪʀeklɪç]

rear light das Rücklicht [das 'ʀʏklɪçt]

rear-view mirror der Rückspiegel [de 'ʀʏkʃpi:gl]

reason der Anlass [de 'ʔanlas], der Grund [de gʀʊnt]

receipt die Quittung [di 'kvɪtʊn]

receive erhalten [ʔe'haltn], empfangen [ʔɛmp'fann]

receiver der Hörer [de 'hø:ʀe]

recently kürzlich ['kʀɛtslɪç]

reception die Rezeption [di ʀetsɛp'tsjo:n]

recommend empfehlen [ʔɛmp'fe:ln]

recover sich erholen [zɪç ʔe'ho:ln]

red rot [ʀo:t]

red wine Rotwein ['ʀo:tvaɪn]

reduction die Ermäßigung [di e'mɛ:sɪgʊn]

refrigerator der Kühlschrank [de 'ky:lʃʀank]

refuse zurückweisen [tsʊ'ʀʏkvaɪzn], sich weigern [zɪç 'vaɪgen], ablehnen ['ʔaple:nn]

region die Gegend [di 'ge:gnt]

register sich anmelden [zɪç 'ʔanmɛldn]; *(luggage)* aufgeben ['ʔaʊfge:bm]; *(car)* zulassen ['tsu:lasn]

registered letter der Einschreibebrief [de 'ʔaɪnʃʀaɪbəbʀi:f]

registration die Anmeldung [di 'ʔanmɛldʊn]

regret das Bedauern [das bə'daʊen]; *(vb)* bedauern [bə'daʊen]

regular regelmäßig ['ʀe:glmɛ:sɪç]

related verwandt [fe'vant]

religion die Religion [di ʀelɪ'gjo:n]

reluctantly ungern ['ʔʊngɛen], nicht gern [nɪç(t) gɛen]

remain bleiben [blaɪbm]

remains die Überreste *m pl* [di ˈʔyːbɐʀɛstə]

remark *(vb)* bemerken [bəˈmɛɐ̯kŋ]

remedy das Heilmittel [das ˈhaɪlmɪtl̩]

remember sich erinnern [zɪç ɐˈʔɪnɐn]; remember s. th. sich etw. merken [zɪç ˈʔɛtvas ˈmɛɐ̯kŋ]

remittance die Überweisung [di ˈʔybɐˈvaɪzʊŋ]

Renaissance die Renaissance [di ʀənɛˈsaːs]

rent die Miete [di ˈmiːtə]; *(vb)* mieten [ˈmiːtn̩], vermieten [fɐˈmiːtn̩]

repair die Reparatur [di ʀɛpaʀaˈtuɐ̯]; *(vb)* reparieren [ʀɛpaˈʀiːʀən/-ˈʀiɐn]

repair kit das Flickzeug [das ˈflɪktsɔɪk]

repeat *(vb)* wiederholen [vidɐˈhoːln̩]

replace ersetzen [ʔɛˈzɛtsn̩]

replacement der Ersatz [dɐ ʔɛˈzats]

reply die Antwort [di ˈʔantvɔet]; *(vb)* antworten [ˈʔantvɔɐtn̩], beantworten [bəˈʔantvɔɐtn̩], erwidern [ʔɛˈviːdɐn]

report der Bericht; *(vb, a crime)* anzeigen [ˈʔantsaɪgn̩]

request die Bitte [di ˈbɪtə]

reservation die Reservierung [di ʀɛzɛˈviːʀʊŋ]

reserve reservieren [ʀɛzɛˈviːʀən/-ˈviɐn]

responsible zuständig [ˈtsuːʃtɛndɪç], verantwortlich [fɐˈʔantvɔɐtlɪç]

rest die Ruhe [di ˈʀuə], die Erholung [di ʔɛˈhoːlʊŋ]; *(remainder)* der Rest [dɐ ʀɛst]; *(vb)* ruhen [ʀuːn̩], sich ausruhen [zɪç ˈʔaʊsʀuːn̩]

restaurant car der Speisewagen [dɐ ˈʃpaɪzəvaːgn̩]

return die Rückkehr [di ˈʀʏkeɐ̯]; *(vb)* wiederkommen [ˈviːdɐkɔmm], zurückkehren [tsuˈʀʏkeːʀən/

-keɐn]; *(give back)* wiedergeben [ˈviːdɐgeːbm̩]

return ticket die Rückfahrkarte [di ˈʀʏkfaːˌkaːtə]

reverse umgekehrt [ˈʔʊmgəkeɐt]

reverse charge call das R-Gespräch [das ˈʔɛɐgəʃpʀɛːç]

reverse gear der Rückwärtsgang [dɐ ˈʀʏkvɛɐtsgaŋ]

reward die Belohnung [di bəˈloːnʊŋ]; *(vb)* belohnen [bəloːnn̩]

rheumatism das Rheuma [das ˈʀɔɪma]

rice der Reis [dɐ ʀaɪs]

rich reich [ʀaɪç]

ride *(vb)* reiten [ˈʀaɪtn̩]

ridiculous lächerlich [ˈlɛçɐlɪç]

riding school die Reitschule [ˈʀaɪtʃuːlə]

right das Recht [das ʀɛçt]; *(adj)* richtig [ˈʀɪçtɪç]; on the right, to the right rechts [ʀɛçts]

right-hand rechte(r, s) [ˈʀɛçtə (-tɐ, -təs)]

rigid fest [fɛst]

ring (up) telefonieren [teləfoˈniːʀən/-ˈniɐn]

ripe reif [ʀaɪf]

river der Fluss [dɐ flʊs]

road die Straße [di ˈʃtʀaːsə]

road map die Straßenkarte [di ˈʃtʀaːsnkaːtə]

roasted gebraten [gəˈbʀaːtn̩]

rock der Fels [dɐ fɛls]

roller skates die Rollschuhe *m pl* [di ˈʀɔlʃuːə]

rolls die Brötchen *n pl* [di bʀøːtçn̩]

roof das Dach [das dax]

room das Zimmer [das ˈtsɪmɐ], der Saal [dɐ zaːl]; *(space)* der Raum [dɐ ʀaʊm]

rope das Seil [das zaɪl]

rosemary der Rosmarin [dɐ ˈʀoːsmaʀiːn]

rotten faul [faʊl], verdorben [fɐˈdɔɐbm̩]

round *(drinks, sport)* die Runde

[di ˈʀʊndə]; *(adj)* rund [ʀʊnt]
round trip die Rundfahrt
[di ˈʀʊntfaːt]
route die Route [di ˈʀuːtə]; *(road)*
die Strecke [di ˈʃtʀɛkə]
row *(vb)* rudern [ˈʀuːdɐn]
rowing boat das Ruderboot [das
ˈʀuːdeboːt]
rubber boots die Gummistiefel *m*
pl [di ˈɡʊmiʃtiːfl]
rubber dinghy das Schlauchboot
[das ˈʃlaʊxboːt]
rubber ring der Schwimmring
[de ˈʃvɪmʀɪŋ]
rubbish der Müll [de mʏl], der
Abfall [de ˈʔapfal]
rucksack der Rucksack [de ˈʀʊkzak]
ruin die Ruine [di ʀuˈʔiːnə]
rule die Vorschrift [di ˈfoɐ̯ʃʀɪft]
run rennen [ʀɛnn], laufen [laʊfn];
(nose) tropfen [tʀɔpfn]; *(bus etc.)*
verkehren [fɛˈkeːʀən/-ˈkeːn]
rupture der Leistenbruch
[de ˈlaɪstnbʀʊx]

S

sad traurig [ˈtʀaʊʀɪç]
safari park der Safaripark
[de zaˈfaːʀipaːk]
safe der Safe [de sɛɪf/seːf]; *(adj)*
sicher [ˈzɪçɐ]
saffron der Safran [de ˈzafʀaːn]
sage der Salbei [de ˈzalbaɪ]
sail dasSegel [das ˈzeːgl]; *(vb)* segeln
[ˈzeːgln]
sailing boat das Segelboot [das
ˈzeːglboːt]
sailing cruise der Segeltörn
[de ˈzeːgltœɐn]
salad der Salat [de zaˈlaːt]
salad bar das Salatbüfett [das
zaˈlaːtbyˈfeː]
salami die Salami [di zaˈlaːmi]
sale der Verkauf [de feˈkaʊf];

(clearance) sale der Ausverkauf
[de ˈʔaʊsfekaʊf]
salt das Salz [das zalts]
same gleich [glaɪç]; the same derselbe [deˈzɛlbə], dieselbe [diˈzɛlbə],
dasselbe [dasˈzɛlbə]
sand pit der Sandkasten
[de ˈzantkastn]
sandals die Sandalen *f pl*
[di zanˈdaːln]
sand-castle die Sandburg
[di ˈzantbuɐk]
sanitary towels die Damenbinden *f pl* [di ˈdaːmmbɪndn]
satisfied befriedigt [bəˈfʀiːdɪçt],
zufrieden [tsʊˈfʀiːdn]
Saturday *(southern Germany)*
Samstag [ˈzamstaːk], *(northern
Germany)*
Sonnabend [ˈzɔnaːbmt]
sauce die Soße [di ˈzoːsə]
saucer die Untertasse
[di ˈʔʊntetasə]
sauna die Sauna [di ˈzaʊna]
sausage die Wurst [di vʊɐst], das
Würstchen [das ˈvʊɐstxən]
say sagen [ˈzaːgn]
scar die Narbe [di ˈnaːbə]
scarcely kaum [kaʊm]
scarf *(decorative)* das Halstuch [das
ˈhalstuːx]; *(for warmth)* der Schal
[de ʃaːl]
scenery die Landschaft [di ˈlantʃaft]
scent das Parfüm [das paˈfyːm]
school die Schule [di ˈʃuːlə]
sciatica der Ischias [de ˈʔɪʃias]
Scotland Schottland [ˈʃɔtlant]
Scottish schottisch [ˈʃɔtɪʃ]
scream *(vb)* schreien [ˈʃʀaɪn]
screw die Schraube [di ˈʃʀaʊbə]
sculptor der Bildhauer/die Bild-
hauerin [de ˈbɪlthaʊe/di
ˈbɪlthaʊeʀɪn]
sculpture die Skulptur
[di skʊlpˈtuɐ]
sea die See [di ˈzeː], das Meer [das
meɐ]

seagull die Möwe [di 'møːvə]

seasick seekrank ['zeːkraŋk]

seaside resort der Badeort [də 'baːdəʔɔet]

season die Saison [di zɛ'zɔŋ], die Jahreszeit [di 'jaːrəstsaɪt]; *(vb)* würzen [vvɛtsn]

seasoning das Gewürz [das gə'vvɛts]

seat der Sitz [də zɪts], der Sitzplatz [də 'zɪtsplats]

seat belt der Sicherheitsgurt [də 'zɪçɐhaɪtsgʊet]

seat reservation die Platzreservierung [di 'platsʁezɛˌviːʁʊŋ]

secluded einsam ['ʔaɪnzaːm]

second die Sekunde [di zeˈkʊndə]; *(adj)* zweite(r, s) ['tsvaɪtə (-tə/-təs)]; second(ly) zweitens [tsvaɪtns]

second-hand shop der Trödelladen [də 'tʁøːdllaːdn]

security *(safety)* die Sicherheit [di 'zɪçɐhaɪt]; *(guarantee)* die Kaution [di kaʊ'tsjoːn], die Bürgschaft [di 'bʏɐkʃaft]

security charge die Sicherheitsgebühr [di 'zɪçɐhaɪtsgəˌbyɐ]

security control die Sicherheitskontrolle [di 'zɪçɐhaɪtskɔnˌtʁɔlə]

sedative das Beruhigungsmittel [das bə'ʁʊɪgʊŋsmɪtl]

see sehen ['zeːn]

seldom selten [zɛltn]

self-service die Selbstbedienung [di 'zɛlps(t)bədiːnʊŋ]

self-timer der Selbstauslöser [də 'zɛlpstaʊsløːzɐ]

sell verkaufen [fɐ'kaʊfn]

send senden ['zɛndn], schicken [ʃɪkŋ]; send for abholen lassen ['ʔaphoːln lasn]; send on nachsenden ['naːxzɛndn]

sender der Absender/die Absenderin [də 'ʔapzɛndɐ/di 'ʔapzɛndəʁɪn]

sentence der Satz [də zats]

September September [zɛp'tɛmbɐ]

serious ernst ['ʔɛɐnst]; *(illness)* schwer [ʃveɐ]

serve servieren [zɛ'viːʁən/-'viɐn], bedienen [bə'diːnn], dienen [diːnn]

service der Dienst [də diːnst], die Bedienung [di bə'diːnʊŋ]

service charge die Bearbeitungsgebühr [di bə'ʔaːbaɪtʊŋsgəˌbyɐ]

serviette die Serviette [di zɛ'vjɛtə]

set *(vb)* setzen [zɛtsn], hinstellen ['hɪnʃtɛln], aufstellen['ʔaʊfʃtɛln]; *(TV)* der (Fernseh)Apparat [də ('fɛenze) ʔapaˌʁaːt]

set meal das Menü [das me'nyː]

severe *(wound, accident)* schwer [ʃveɐ]; *(judgement, winter)* streng [ʃtʁɛŋ]

severely handicapped person der/die Schwerbehinderte [də/di 'ʃveɐbəhɪndɐtə]

sexual harassment die sexuelle Belästigung [di sɛksu'ɛlə bə'lɛstɪgʊŋ]

shade der Schatten [də ʃatn]; *(colour)* der Ton [də toːn]

shadow der Schatten [də ʃatn]

shampoo das Schampoo [das 'ʃampo/'ʃampu]

shape die Form [di fɔɐm]

shaver der Rasierapparat [də ʁa'ziɐʔapaˌʁaːt]

shaving brush der Rasierpinsel [də ʁa'ziɐpɪnzl]

shaving foam der Rasierschaum [də ʁa'ziɐʃaʊm]

she sie [ziː]

shin das Schienbein [das 'ʃiːnbaɪn]

shirt das Hemd [das hɛmt]

shoe der Schuh [də ʃuː]

shoe brush die Schuhbürste [di 'ʃuːbʏɐstə]

shoe cream die Schuhcreme [di 'ʃuːkʁeːm]

shoe shop das Schuhgeschäft [das 'ʃuːgəʃɛft]

shoemaker's der Schuhmacher [də 'ʃuːmaxɐ]

shop das Geschäft [das gə'ʃɛft], der Laden [dɐ 'laːdn]; **shop window** das Schaufenster [das 'ʃaufɛnstɐ]; **go shopping** einkaufen ['ʔaɪnkaʊfn]

shore das Ufer [das 'ʔuːfɐ]

short kurz [kʊɐts]; **at short notice** kurzfristig ['kʊɐtsfʁɪstɪç]

short film der Kurzfilm [dɐ kʊɐtsfɪlm]

short-circuit der Kurzschluss [dɐ 'kʊɐtsʃlʊs]

short-cut die Abkürzung [di ʔapkʏɐtsʊŋ]

shorts die kurze Hose [di 'kʊɐtsə 'hoːzə]

shoulder die Schulter [di 'ʃʊltɐ]

shoulder bag die Umhängetasche [di ʔʊmhɛŋəˌtaʃə]

shout *(vb)* schreien ['ʃʁaɪn]

show *(vb)* zeigen ['tsaɪgn], vorzeigen ['foɐtsaɪgn]; *(exhibition)* die Ausstellung [di ʔaʊʃtɛlʊŋ]; *(entertainment)* die Revue [di ʁe'vyː], die Show [di ʃoː]

shower die Dusche [di 'duːʃə]; *(rain)* der Regenschauer [dɐ 'ʁeːgnʃaʊɐ]

shower gel das Duschgel [das 'duːʃgeːl]

shower seat der Duschsitz [dɐ 'duːʃzɪts]

shrimps die Krabben *f pl* [di kʁabm]

shut *(adj)* zu [zu(ː)]; *(vb)* schließen [ʃliːsn], zumachen ['tsuːmaxn]

shutter *(camera)* der Auslöser [dɐ 'ʔaʊsløːzɐ]

shuttlecock der Federball [dɐ 'feːdɐbal]

shy schüchtern ['ʃʏçtɐn]

sick krank [kʁaŋk]

side die Seite [di 'zaɪtə]

sidelights das Standlicht [das 'ʃtantlɪçt]

sights die Sehenswürdigkeiten *f pl* [di 'zeːnsvʏɐdɪçkaɪtn]

sightseeing tour of the town/city die Stadtrundfahrt [di 'ʃtatʁʊntfaːt]

sign das Schild [das ʃɪlt], das Zeichen [das 'tsaɪçn]; *(directions)* der Wegweiser [dɐ 've:kvaɪzɐ]; *(vb)* unterschreiben [ʔʊnte'ʃʁaɪbm]

sign language die Zeichensprache [di 'tsaɪçnʃpʁaːxə]

signature die Unterschrift [di 'ʔʊntɐʃʁɪft]

silence *(quiet)* die Ruhe [di 'ʁuə], *(personal)* das Schweigen [das ʃvaɪgn]

silent ruhig [ʁuːɪç]

silk die Seide [di 'zaɪdə]

silk painting die Seidenmalerei [di 'zaɪdnmaːləˌʁaɪ]

silly blöd(e) [bløːt/'bløːdə]

silver das Silber [das 'zɪlbɐ]

similar ähnlich ['ʔɛːnlɪç]

simple einfach ['ʔaɪnfax]

simultaneously gleichzeitig ['glaɪçtsaɪtɪç]

since *(time)* seit [zaɪt]; *(as)* da [daː], weil [vaɪl]

sincere herzlich ['hɛɐtslɪç]

sing singen [zɪŋŋ]

singer der Sänger/die Sängerin [dɐ 'zɛŋɐ/di 'zɛŋəʁɪn]

single ledig ['leːdɪç]

singles das Einzel [das 'ʔaɪntsəl]

sink das Geschirrspülbecken [das gə'ʃɪʁspyːlbɛkn]

sinusitis die Stirnhöhlenentzündung [di 'ʃtɪʁnhøːlnʔɛnˌtsʏndʊŋ]

sister die Schwester [di 'ʃvɛstɐ]

sister-in-law die Schwägerin [di 'ʃvɛːgəʁɪn]

sit sitzen [zɪtsn]

situation die Lage [di 'laːgə]

size die Größe [di 'gʁøːsə]; *(paper)* das Format [das fɔ'maːt]

skateboard das Skateboard [das 'skɛɪtbɔɐt]; *(vb)* Skateboard fahren ['skɛɪtbɔɐt 'faːʁən]

ski der Ski [dɐ ʃiː]; *(vb)* Ski fahren

['ʃi: 'fa:(ʀə)n]

ski bindings die Skibindungen *f pl*
[di 'ʃi:bɪndʊŋŋ]

ski boots die Skistiefel *m pl*
[di 'ʃi:ʃti:fl]

ski goggles die Skibrille
[di 'ʃi:bʀɪlə]

ski instructor der Skilehrer/
die Skilehrerin [dɐ 'ʃi:le:ʀɐ/
di 'ʃi:le:ʀəʀɪn]

ski poles die Skistöcke *m pl*
[di 'ʃi:'ʃtœkə]

skiing das Skifahren [das
'ʃi:fa:(ʀə)n]

skiing course der Skikurs
[dɐ 'ʃi:kʊɐs]

skin die Haut [di haʊt]

skirt der Rock [dɐ ʀɔk]

sky der Himmel [dɐ hɪml]

sledge der Schlitten [dɐ ʃlɪtn]

sleep der Schlaf [dɐ ʃla:f]; *(vb)*
schlafen [ʃla:fn]

sleeping pills die Schlaftabletten *f*
pl [di 'ʃla:fta,blɛtn]

sleeplessness die Schlaflosigkeit
[di 'ʃla:flozɪçkaɪt]

sleeve der Ärmel [dɐ ˀɛɐml]

slender schlank [ʃlaŋk], dünn
[dʏn]

slice die Scheibe [di 'ʃaɪbə]

slight leicht [laɪçt]

slim dünn [dʏn], schmal [ʃma:l],
schlank [ʃlaŋk]; *(vb)* abnehmen
[ˀapne:mm]

slow(ly) langsam ['laŋza:m]

small klein [klaɪn]

small packet das Päckchen [das
pɛkçn]

smell der Geruch [dɐ gəˈʀu(:)x];
(vb) riechen [ʀi:çn]

smoke der Rauch [dɐ ʀaʊx]; *(vb)*
rauchen [ʀaʊxn]

smoked geräuchert [gəˈʀɔɪçet]

smoked ham roher Schinken
[ʀoːɐ ʃɪŋkŋ]

smoker der Raucher/die Raucherin
[dɐ 'ʀaʊxɐ/di 'ʀaʊxəʀɪn]

smoking compartment das
Raucherabteil [das 'ʀaʊxɐˀap,taɪl]

smuggle schmuggeln [ʃmʊgln]

snack der Imbiss [dɐ ˀɪmbɪs]

snake die Schlange [di 'ʃlaŋə]

snapshot der Schnappschuss
[dɐ 'ʃnapʃʊs]

snore schnarchen [ʃna:çn]

snorkel der Schnorchel [dɐ ʃnɔɐçl];
go snorkelling schnorcheln
[ʃnɔɐçln]

snow der Schnee [dɐ ʃne:]

so *(adv)* so [zo:]; *(conj)* also [ˀalzo:]

soaked nass [nas]

soap die Seife [di 'zaɪfə]

sober nüchtern ['nʏçten]

socket die Steckdose [di 'ʃtɛkdo:zə]

socks die Socken *f pl* [di 'zɔkŋ]

soft weich [vaɪç]

solarium das Solarium [das
zoˈla:ʀɪʊm]

sole die Sohle [di 'zo:lə]; *(fish)* die
Seezunge [di 'ze:tsʊŋə]

solid fest [fɛst], hart [ha:t]

soloist der Solist/die Solistin
[dɐ zoˈlɪst/di zoˈlɪstɪn]

some einige ['ˀaɪnɪgə]

somebody jemand ['je:mant]

something etwas ['ˀɛtvas]

sometimes manchmal
['mançma:l]

son der Sohn [dɐ zo:n]

song das Lied [das li:t]

soon bald [balt]

sore throat die Halsschmerzen *m*
pl [di 'halʃmɛetsn]

sort die Sorte [di 'zɔɐtə], die Art
[di ˀa:t]

sound der Klang [dɐ klaŋ], der Ton
[dɐ to:n]

soup die Suppe [di 'zʊpə]

soup plate der Suppenteller
[dɐ 'zʊpmtɛlɐ]

sour sauer ['zaʊɐ]

sour cream die saure Sahne
[di zaʊʀə 'za:nə]

source die Quelle [di 'kvɛlə]

south der Süden [de zy:dn];
  south of südlich von ['zy:tlıç fɔn]
souvenir das Souvenir [das
  zʊvə'niɐ]
souvenir shop der Souvenirladen
  [de zʊvə'niɐla:dn]
space der Raum [de ʀaʊm]
spare tyre der Ersatzreifen
  [de ʔe'zatsʀaɪfn]
spark plug die Zündkerze
  [di 'tsʏntkɛɐtsə]
speak sprechen [ʃpʀɛçn]
speaker der Lautsprecher
  [de 'laʊtʃpʀɛçɐ]
special speziell [ʃpɛ'tsjɛl], Sonder-
  ['zɔndɐ-]
special (of the day) das Tagesmenü [das 'ta:gəsme,ny:]
special issue stamp die Sondermarke [di 'zɔndɐma:kə]
specialist der Facharzt/
  die Fachärztin [de 'faxa:tst/
  di 'fax ʔɛɐtstɪn]
speciality die Spezialität
  [di ʃpetsjali'tɛ:t]
spectator der Zuschauer/
  die Zuschauerin [de 'tsu:ʃaʊɐ/
  di 'tsu:ʃaʊəʀɪn]
speed die Geschwindigkeit
  [di gə'ʃvɪndɪçkaɪt]
speedometer der Tacho(meter)
  [de ,taxo('me:tɐ)]
spell buchstabieren
  [buxʃta'bi:ʀən/-'bien]
spend ausgeben [ʔ'aʊsge:bm];
  (time) verbringen [fe'bʀɪŋŋ];
  spend the night übernachten
  [ʔybɐ'naxtn]
spice das Gewürz [das gə'vʏɐts]
spinach der Spinat [de ʃpɪ'na:t]
spine die Wirbelsäule
  [di 'vɪɐblzɔɪlə]
splendid herrlich ['hɛɐlɪç]; (fig)
  glänzend [glɛntsnt]
splint die Schiene [di 'ʃi:nə]
spoiled verdorben [fe'dɔɐbm]
spoon der Löffel [de lœfl]

sport der Sport [de ʃpɔɐt]
sports ground der Sportplatz
  [de 'ʃpɔɐtplats]
sports shop das Sportgeschäft [das
  'ʃpɔɐtgəʃɛft]
spot die Stelle [di 'ʃtɛlə]
sprained verstaucht [fe'ʃtaʊxt]
spring der Frühling [de 'fʀy:lɪŋ]
squid der Tintenfisch [de 'tɪntnfɪʃ]
stadium das Stadion [das 'ʃta:djɔn]
stain der Fleck [de flɛk]
staircase die Treppe [di 'tʀɛpə]
stairs die Treppen f pl [di tʀɛpm]
stalls das Parkett [das pa'kɛt]
stamp der Stempel [de ʃtɛmpl];
  (postage) die (Brief)Marke
  [di ('bʀi:f-) ,ma:kə]
stamp machine der Briefmarkenautomat [de 'bʀi:fma:kn ʔaʊto,ma:t]
stand stehen [ʃte:n]; (bear) ertragen [ʔe'tʀa:gn]
star der Stern [de ʃtɛɐn]
start der Anfang; (vb) anfangen
start (from) abfahren (von)
  [ʔapfa:n (fɔn)]
starter (engine part) der Anlasser
  [de ʔ'anlasɐ]; (food) die Vorspeise
  [di 'foɐʃpaɪzə]
startle erschrecken [ʔe'ʃʀɛkŋ]
state (country) der Staat [de ʃta:t];
  (condition) der Zustand [de
  'tsu:ʃtant]; (vb) feststellen
  ['fɛ(st)ʃtɛln], aussagen [ʔ'aʊsza:gn]
statement die Aussage
  [di ʔ'aʊsza:gə]
station der Bahnhof [de 'ba:nho:f]
stationer's das Schreibwarengeschäft [das 'ʃʀaɪpva:ʀəngəʃɛft]
statue die Statue [di 'ʃta:tuə]
stay der Aufenthalt [de ʔ'aʊfntalt];
  (vb) sich aufhalten [zɪç ʔ'aʊfhaltn],
  wohnen [vo:nn], bleiben [blaɪbm],
  übernachten [ʔybɐ'naxtn]
steal stehlen [ʃte:ln]
steamed gedämpft [gə'dɛmpft],
  gedünstet [gə'dʏnstət]
steep steil [ʃtaɪl]

steeple der Kirchturm
[dɐ ˈkɪʁçtʊɐm]

step die Stufe [di ˈʃtuːfə]

steps die Treppe [di ˈtʁɛpə]

steward/stewardess der
Steward/die Stewardess
[dɐ ˈstjuaːt/di: ˈstjuadɛs]

stick der Stock [dɐ ʃtɔk]

still *(quiet)* still [ʃtɪl]; *(mineral
water)* ohne Kohlensäure [ˈʔoːnə
ˈkoːl(ə)nzɔɪʁə]; *(adv)* noch [nɔx]

still life das Stillleben [das
ˈʃtɪleːbm̩]

sting der Stich [dɐ ʃtɪç]; *(vb)*
stechen [ʃtɛçn̩]

stink stinken [ʃtɪŋkn̩]

stitch (up) nähen [nɛːn]

stock der Vorrat [dɐ ˈfoːʁaːt]

stockings die Strümpfe *m pl*
[di ˈʃtʁʏmpfə]

stomach der Bauch [dɐ baʊx],
der Magen [dɐ maːgn̩]

stomach-ache die Magenschmerzen *m pl* [di ˈmaːgn̩ʃmɛɐtsn̩]

stone der Stein [dɐ ʃtaɪn]

stony steinig [ˈʃtaɪnɪç]

stop *(train)* der Aufenthalt
[dɐ ˈʔaʊfn̩talt]; *(bus)* die Haltestelle
[di ˈhaltəʃtɛlə]; *(vb, stop doing sth.)*
aufhören [ˈʔaʊfhøːʁən]; *(car)* anhalten
[ˈʔanhaltn̩], *(person)* stehen bleiben
[ˈʃteːnblaɪbm̩], *(break off)* abbrechen [ˈʔapbʁɛçn̩], *(bus, train)*
halten [haltn̩]; stop! halt! [halt]

stopover die Zwischenlandung
[di ˈtsvɪʃn̩ˌlandʊŋ]

store *(shop)* das Geschäft [das
gəˈʃɛft], der Laden [dɐ ˈlaːdn̩];
(supply) der Vorrat [dɐ ˈfoːʁaːt]

storm der Sturm [dɐ ʃtʊɐm]

story die Geschichte [di gəˈʃɪçtə]

stove der Herd [dɐ heɐt]

straight gerade [g(ə)ˈʁaːdə];
straight across/through quer
durch [kveɐ dʊɐç]

straight on/straight ahead
geradeaus [gʁaːdəˈʔaʊs]

strange eigen [ˈʔaɪgn̩], fremd
[fʁɛmt]

stranger der/die Fremde [dɐ/
di ˈfʁɛmdə]

straw der Strohhalm
[dɐ ˈʃtʁoːhalm]

strawberries die Erdbeeren *f pl*
[di ˈʔeɐtbeːʁən]

street die Straße [di ˈʃtʁaːsə]

streetcar die Straßenbahn
[di ˈʃtʁaːsnbaːn]

strenuous anstrengend [ˈʔanʃtʁɛŋnt]

stroke der Schlaganfall
[dɐ ˈʃlaːkanfal]

stroll der Bummel [dɐ bʊml],
der Spaziergang [dɐ ʃpaˈtsiːegaŋ];
(vb) spazieren gehen
[ʃpaˈtsiːʁəngeːn/-ˈtsiːen-]

strong stark [ʃtaːk], kräftig
[ˈkʁɛftɪç]

studio couch die Schlafcouch
[di ˈʃlaːfkaʊtʃ]

study *(vb)* studieren [ʃtʊˈdiːʁən/
-ˈdiːn]

stuffed gefüllt [gəˈfʏlt]

stupid dumm [dʊm], blöd(e)
[bløːt/ ˈbløːdə]

style der Stil [dɐ stiːl (ʃtiːl)]

subtitles der Untertitel
[dɐ ˈʔuntɐtiːtl̩]

suburb die Vorstadt [di ˈfoɐʃtat],
der Vorort [dɐ ˈfoɐʔɔɐt]

subway die Unterführung [di
ˈʔuntɐˈfyːʁʊŋ]; *(US)* die U-Bahn
[di ˈʔuːbaːn]

success der Erfolg [dɐ ʔɛˈfɔlk]

suddenly plötzlich [ˈplœtslɪç]

sufficient genug [gəˈnuːk]

sugar der Zucker [dɐ ˈtsʊkɐ]

suggestion der Vorschlag
[dɐ ˈfoɐʃlaːk]

suit *(for men)* der Anzug [dɐ
ˈʔantsuːk]; *(for women)* das Kostüm
[das kɔsˈtyːm]; *(vb)* passen [pasn̩]

suitable for the disabled behindertengerecht [bəˈhɪndɐtn̩gəˌʁɛçt]

suitcase der Koffer [dɐ ˈkɔfɐ]

sum die Summe [di 'zʊmə]
summer der Sommer [dɐ 'zɔmɐ]
summit station die Bergstation
[di 'bɛɐkʃtaˌtsjoːn]
sun die Sonne [di 'zɔnə]
sun cream die Sonnencreme
[di 'zɔnnkrɛːm]
sun hat der Sonnenhut
[dɐ 'zɔnnhuːt]
sunbathing area die Liegewiese
[di 'liːgəviːzə]
sunburn der Sonnenbrand
[dɐ 'zɔnnbrant]
Sunday Sonntag ['zɔntaːk]
sunny sonnig ['zɔnɪç]
sunroof das Schiebedach [das
'ʃiːbədax]
sunstroke der Sonnenstich
[dɐ 'zɔnnʃtɪç]
suntan lotion die Sonnenmilch
[di 'zɔnnmɪlç]
suntan oil das Sonnenöl [das
'zɔnnˀøːl]
supermarket der Supermarkt
[dɐ 'zuːpemaːkt]
suppository das Zäpfchen [das
'tsɛpfçn]
sure sicher ['zɪçɐ]
surf (vb) surfen ['sœːfn]
surfboard das Surfbrett [das
'sœːfbrɛt]
surgeon der Chirurg/die Chirurgin
[dɐ çi'rʊɐk/di çi'rʊɐgɪn]
surgery (hours) die Sprechstunde
[di 'ʃprɛçʃtʊndə]; (operation) die
Operation [di ˀɔpəra'tsjoːn]
surprised, be ~ (at) sich wundern (über) [zɪç 'vʊndɐn ˌˀyː(ɐ)bɐ]
surroundings die Umgebung
[di ˀʊm'geːbʊŋ]
sweat (vb) schwitzen ['ʃvɪtsn]
sweater der Pullover [dɐ pʊ'loːvɐ]
sweet der Nachtisch [dɐ 'naːxtɪʃ];
(adj) süß [zyːs]
sweet shop das Süßwarengeschäft
[das 'zyːsvaːrəngəʃɛft]
sweetener der Süßstoff

[dɐ 'zyːʃtɔf]
sweets die Süßigkeiten f pl
[di 'zyːsiçkaɪtn]
swelling die Schwellung
[di 'ʃvɛlʊŋ]
swim (vb) baden [baːdn], schwimmen [ʃvɪmm]
swimmer der Schwimmer/
die Schwimmerin [dɐ 'ʃvɪmɐ/
di 'ʃvɪmərɪn]
swimming lessons der
Schwimmkurs [dɐ 'ʃvɪmkʊɐs]
swimming pool (public) das
Schwimmbad [das 'ʃvɪmbaːt];
(private) der Swimmingpool
[dɐ 'svɪmɪŋpuːl]
swimming trunks die Badehose
[di 'baːdəhoːzə]
swimsuit der Badeanzug
[dɐ 'baːdəˀantsuːk]
swindle der Betrug [dɐ bə'truːk]
Swiss (man/woman) der
Schweizer/die Schweizerin
[dɐ 'ʃvaɪtsɐ/di 'ʃvaɪtsərɪn]
Swiss francs Schweizer Franken
m pl [ʃvaɪtsɐ 'frankn]
switch der Schalter [dɐ 'ʃaltɐ]
Switzerland die Schweiz
[di ʃvaɪts]
swollen geschwollen [gə'ʃvɔln]
swordfish der Schwertfisch
[dɐ 'ʃveɐtfɪʃ]
symbol das Wahrzeichen [das
'vaːtsaɪçn]
symphony concert das Sinfoniekonzert [das zɪmfo'niːkɔnˌtsɛɐt]

T

table der Tisch [dɐ tɪʃ]
table tennis das Tischtennis [das
'tɪʃtɛnɪs]
tablecloth das Tischtuch [das
'tɪʃtuːx]
tablet die Tablette [di ta'blɛtə]

tail light das Rücklicht [das ˈʀʏklɪçt]

tailor der Schneider/die Schneiderin [deɐ ˈʃnaɪdɐ/di ˈʃnaɪdəʀɪn]

take nehmen [neːmm]; *(time)* brauchen [bʀaʊxn]; **take part (in)** teilnehmen (an) [ˈtaɪlneːmm (ʔan)]; **take place** stattfinden [ˈʃtatfɪndn]

taken *(seat)* besetzt [bəˈzɛtst]

take-off der Abflug [deɐ ˈʔapfluːk]

talk das Gespräch [das gəˈʃpʀɛːç]; *(vb)* reden [ʀeːdn], sich unterhalten [zɪç ʔʊntɐˈhaltn]

tall groß [gʀoːs]

tampons die Tampons *m pl* [di ˈtampɔŋs]

tap der Wasserhahn [deɐ ˈvasɐhaːn]

taste der Geschmack [deɐ gəˈʃmak]; *(try food)* versuchen [fɐˈzuːxn]

tasty lecker [ˈlɛkɐ]

taxi driver der Taxifahrer/die Taxifahrerin [deɐ ˈtaksifaːʀɐ/di ˈtaksifaːʀəʀɪn]

taxi rank/stand der Taxistand [deɐ ˈtaksiʃtant]

tea der Tee [deɐ teː]

tea bag der Teebeutel [deɐ ˈteːbɔɪtl]

tea towel das Geschirrtuch [das gəˈʃɪʀtuːx]

teach unterrichten [ʔʊntɐˈʀɪçtn], lehren [ˈleːʀən/leɐn]

team die Mannschaft [di ˈmanʃaft]

teaspoon der Teelöffel [deɐ ˈteːlœfl]

teat der Sauger [deɐ ˈzaʊgɐ]

telegraphic transfer die telegrafische Überweisung [di teləˈgʀaːfɪʃə ʔyːbɐˈvaɪzʊŋ]

telephone das Telefon [das ˈteːləfoːn]

telephone directory das Telefonbuch [das teləˈfoːnbuːx]

telephoto lens das Teleobjektiv [das ˈteːleʔɔbjɛktiːf]

television lounge der Fernsehraum [deɐ ˈfɛɐnzeːʀaʊm]

telex das Telex [das ˈteːlɛks]

tell erzählen [ʔeˈtsɛːln], ausrichten

[ˈʔaʊsʀɪçtn], sagen [zaːgŋ]

temperature die Temperatur [di ˌtɛmpəʀaˈtuɐ]; *(fever)* das Fieber [das ˈfiːbɐ]

temple der Tempel [deɐ tɛmpl]

temporary vorläufig [ˈfoɐlɔɪfɪç], vorübergehend [foˈʀyːbɐgeːnt], provisorisch [pʀoviˈzoːʀɪʃ]

tender zärtlich [ˈtsɛɐtlɪç]; *(soft)* zart [tsaːt]

tennis das Tennis [das ˈtɛnɪs]

tennis racquet der Tennisschläger [deɐ ˈtɛnɪʃlɛːgɐ]

tent das Zelt [das tsɛlt]

terminal das Terminal [das ˈtəːmɪnəl]

terminus die Endstation [di ˈʔɛntʃtatsjoːn]

terrace die Terrasse [di teˈʀasə]

terracotta die Terrakotta [di tɛʀaˈkɔta]

terrible fürchterlich [ˈfʏçtɐlɪç], schrecklich [ˈʃʀɛklɪç]

tetanus der Tetanus [deɐ ˈtɛtanʊs]

than als [ʔals]

thank danken [ˈdaŋkŋ], **thank you** danke schön [ˈdaŋkə ʃøːn]

that diese(r, s) [ˈdiːzə/ˈdiːze/ˈdiːzəs]; jene(r, s) [ˈjeːnə/ˈjeːne/jeːnəs]; *(conj)* dass [das]

theatre das Theater [das teˈʔaːtɐ]

theft der Diebstahl [deɐ ˈdiːpʃtaːl]

then dann [dan], *(in the past)* damals [ˈdaːma(ː)ls]

there da [daː], dort [dɔɐt], dorthin [ˈdɔɐthɪn]

therefore daher [ˈdaːheɐ], deshalb [ˈdɛshalp]

thermometer das Fieberthermometer [das ˈfiːbɐtɛɐmoˌmeːtɐ]

these diese [ˈdiːzə]

they sie [ziː]

thick dick [dɪk]; *(crowd, fog etc.)* dicht [dɪçt]

thief der Dieb/die Diebin [deɐ diːp/di ˈdiːbɪn]

thin dünn [dʏn]; mager [ˈmaːgɐ],

schmal [ʃmaːl]; *(sparse)* spärlich ['ʃpɛːɐlɪç], dürftig ['dʏftɪç]

thing das Ding [das dɪŋ], die Sache [di 'zaxə]

think denken ['dɛŋkn̩, meinen [maɪnn̩]; think (of) denken (an) ['dɛŋkn̩ ʔan]

third dritte(r, s) ['drɪtə (-tɐ, -təs)]

this diese(r, s) ['diːzə/'diːzɐ/'diːzəs]

this morning/this evening heute Morgen/heute Abend [hɔɪtə 'mɔɐgn̩/hɔɪtə ʔaːbmt]

those diese ['diːzə]; jene ['jeːnə]

thriller der Kriminalroman [dɐ krɪmiˈnaːlʀomaːn], der Thriller [dɐ 'θʀɪlɐ]

throat der Hals [dɐ hals]; die Kehle [di keːlə]

throat lozenges die Halstabletten *f pl* [di 'halstaˌblɛtn̩]

through durch [dʊɐç]

Thursday Donnerstag ['dɔnɐstaːk]

thus so [zoː], also ['ʔalzoː]

thyme der Thymian [dɐ 'tyːmiaːn]

ticket die Karte [di 'kaːtə]

ticket machine der Fahrkartenautomat [dɐ 'faːkaːtn̩ʔaʊtoˌmaːt]

ticket office die Kasse [di 'kasə]; *(transport)* der Fahrkartenschalter [dɐ 'faːkaːtn̩ʃaltɐ]

tie die Krawatte [di kraˈvatə]

tight *(clothes)* eng [ʔɛŋ]

tights die Strumpfhose [di 'ʃtrʊmpfhoːzə]

till bis [bɪs]

time die Zeit [di tsaɪt]; *(occasion)* das Mal [das maːl]; in time *(adv)* rechtzeitig ['rɛçtsaɪtɪç]; on time pünktlich ['pʏŋktlɪç]

time of arrival die Ankunftszeit [di ʔankʊnftsˌtsaɪt]

timetable der Fahrplan [dɐ 'faːplaːn]

tin die Büchse [di 'bʏksə], die Dose [di 'doːzə]

tin foil die Alufolie [di ʔaluˈfoːljə]

tin opener der Dosenöffner [dɐ 'doːzn̩ˌʔœfnɐ]

tincture of iodine die Jodtinktur [di 'joːtɪŋktuɐ]

tint *(vb)* tönen [tøːnn̩]

tip *(information)* der Tipp [dɐ tɪp]; *(gratuity)* das Trinkgeld [das 'trɪŋkgɛlt]

tire der Reifen [dɐ 'raɪfn̩]

tired müde ['myːdə]

to zu [zu(ː)], nach [naːx]; *(time)* bis [bɪs]

toast der Toast [dɐ toːst]

toaster der Toaster [dɐ 'toːstɐ]

tobacco der Tabak [dɐ 'tabak]

tobacconist's/tobacco shop der Tabakladen [dɐ 'tabakˌlaːdn̩]

toboggan der Schlitten [dɐ ʃlɪtn̩]

today heute ['hɔɪtə]

toe die Zehe [di 'tseːə]

together zusammen [tsʊˈzamm̩]; gemeinsam [gəˈmaɪnzaˑm]

toilet die Toilette [di toˈlɛtə]

toilet for the disabled die Behindertentoilette [di bəˈhɪndɐtn̩toˌlɛtə]

toilet paper das Toilettenpapier [das toˈlɛtn̩paˌpiɐ]

tomatoes die Tomaten *f pl* [di toˈmaːtn̩]

tomb das Grab [das graːp]

tomorrow morgen ['mɔɐgn̩]; tomorrow morning/tomorrow evening morgen früh/morgen Abend [mɔɐgn̩ 'fryː/mɔɐgn̩ ʔaːbmt]; the day after tomorrow übermorgen ['ʔyːbɐmɔɐgn̩]

tone der Ton [dɐ toːn]

tongue die Zunge ['tsʊŋə]

tonight heute Nacht [hɔɪt(ə) 'naxt]

tonsilitis die Mandelentzündung [di 'mandl̩ʔɛntsʏndʊŋ]

tonsils die Mandeln *f pl* [di 'mandl̩n]

too auch ['ʔaʊx]; *(with adj)* zu [zu(ː)]; too much zu viel [tsʊˈfiːl]; zu sehr [tsʊ zeɐ]

tools das Werkzeug [das 'vɛektsɔɪk]

tooth der Zahn [dɐ tsaːn]

toothache die Zahnschmerzen *m pl* [di 'tsaːnʃmɛɐtsn]

toothbrush die Zahnbürste [di 'tsaːnbʏɐstə]

toothpaste die Zahnpasta [di 'tsaːnpasta]

toothpick das Zahnstocher [dɐ 'tsaːnʃtɔxɐ]

top station die Bergstation [di 'bɛɐkʃtaˌtsjoːn]

torn ligament der Bänderriss [dɐ 'bɛndɐʀɪs]

touch *(vb)* berühren [bə'ʀyːʀən/ -'ʀyɐn]

tough *(not tender)* zäh [tsɛː]

tour die Tour [di tuɐ], die Rundfahrt [di 'ʀʊntfaːt]; *(of museum, palace)* die Besichtigung [di bə'zɪçtɪgʊŋ]

tourist der Tourist/die Touristin [dɐ tu'ʀɪst/di tu'ʀɪstɪn]; der/die Reisende [dɐ/di 'ʀaɪzndə]; **tourist information office** das Verkehrsbüro [das fɐ'keɐsbyˌʀoː]

tow (away) abschleppen ['ʔapʃlɛpm]

towel das Handtuch [das 'han(t)tuːx]

tower der Turm [dɐ tʊɐm]

town die Stadt [di ʃtat]

town centre die Innenstadt [di 'ʔɪnnʃtat]

town hall das Rathaus [das 'ʀaːthaʊs]

town walls die Stadtmauern *f pl* [di 'ʃtatmaʊɐn]

towrope das Abschleppseil [das 'ʔapʃlɛpzaɪl]

toy shop das Spielwarengeschäft [das 'ʃpiːlvaːʀəngə'ʃɛft]

toys die Spielsachen *f pl* [di 'ʃpiːlzaːxn]

traffic der Verkehr [dɐ fɐ'keɐ]

traffic jam der Stau [dɐ ʃtaʊ]

traffic light die Ampel [di 'ʔampl]

tragedy die Tragödie [di tʀa'gøːdiə]

train der Zug [dɐ tsuːk]

training die Ausbildung [di 'ʔaʊsbɪldʊŋ]

tram die Straßenbahn [di 'ʃtʀaːsnbaːn]

tranquilliser das Beruhigungsmittel [das bə'ʀʊɪgʊŋsmɪtl]

transfer die Überweisung [di 'ʔybɐ'vaɪzʊŋ]

translate übersetzen ['ʔybɐ'zɛtsn]

transmission *(engine)* das Getriebe [das gə'tʀiːbə]

travel reisen [ʀaɪzn]

travel agency das Reisebüro [das 'ʀaɪzəbyˌʀoː]

traveller's cheque der Reisescheck [dɐ 'ʀaɪzəʃɛk]

travelling bag die Reisetasche [di 'ʀaɪzətaʃə]

treat *(injury)* behandeln [bə'handln]

tree der Baum [dɐ baʊm]

trekking bike das Trekkingrad [das 'tʀɛkɪŋʀaːt]

trial *(court)* die (Straf)Verhandlung [di (ʃtʀaːf)fɐˌhandlʊŋ]

trip die Tour [di tuɐ], die Fahrt [di faːt], die Reise [di 'ʀaɪzə], der Ausflug [dɐ 'ʔaʊsfluːk]

tripod das Stativ [das ʃta'tiːf]

trousers die Hose [di 'hoːzə]

true wahr [vaː]

trunk *(case)* der Schrankkoffer [dɐ 'ʃʀaŋkˌkɔfɐ]; *(US)* der Kofferraum [dɐ 'kɔfɐʀaʊm]

try *(vb)* versuchen [fɐ'zuːxn]; **try hard** sich bemühen [zɪç bə'myːn]

Tuesday Dienstag ['diːnstaːk]

tumbler das Wasserglas [das 'vasɐglaːs]

tumour die Geschwulst [di gə'ʃvʊlst]

tuna der Thunfisch [dɐ 'tuːnfɪʃ]

tunnel der Tunnel [dɐ tʊnl]

turn back umkehren ['ʔʊmkeːʀən/-keɐn]

turquoise türkisfarben
[tʏɐˈkiːsfaːbm]
twice zweimal [ˈtsvaɪmaːl]; doppelt
[dɔplt]
typhoid der Typhus [dɐ ˈtyːfʊs]
typical typisch [ˈtyːpɪʃ]
tyre der Reifen [dɐ ˈʀaɪfn]

U

ugly hässlich [ˈhɛslɪç]
ulcer das Geschwür [das gəˈʃvyɐ]
umbrella der Schirm [dɐ ʃɪɐm]
unbearable unerträglich
[ˈʊnɐˌtʀɛːklɪç]
unconscious bewusstlos
[bəˈvʊstloːs]
under unter [ˈʊntɐ]
underground die U-Bahn
[di ˈʔuːbaːn]
understand verstehen [fɐˈʃteːn]
underwear die Unterwäsche
[di ˈʊntɐvɛʃə]
unemployed arbeitslos
[ˈʔaːbaɪtsloːs]
unfit ungeeignet [ˈʔʊngəʔaɪknət]
unfortunately leider [ˈlaɪdɐ],
unglücklicherweise
[ˌʔʊnglʏklɪçɐˈvaɪzə]
unimportant unwichtig
[ˈʔʊnvɪçtɪç]
university die Universität
[di ʔunivɛɐziˈtɛːt]
unpleasant unangenehm
[ˈʔʊnangəneːm], *(news)* unerfreulich [ˈʔʊnɐfʀɔɪlɪç]
unsuited ungeeignet
[ˈʔʊngəʔaɪknət]
until bis [bɪs]
unusual ungewöhnlich
[ˈʔʊngəvøːnlɪç]
up aufwärts [ˈʔaʊfvɛɐts], nach oben
[nax ˈʔoːbm], oben [ˈʔoːbm]
urgent dringend [dʀɪŋŋt], eilig
[ˈʔaɪlɪç]

urine der Urin [dɐ ʔuˈʀiːn]
us uns [ˈʔʊns]
use die Verwendung [di fɐˈvɛndʊŋ],
der Gebrauch [dɐ gəˈbʀaʊx], die
Anwendung [di ˈʔanvɛndʊŋ]; *(vb)*
anwenden [ˈʔanvɛndn], verwenden
[fɐˈvɛndn], gebrauchen [gəˈbʀaʊx],
benutzen [bəˈnʊtsn]; **be used to
s. th.** etwas gewöhnt sein [ˌʔɛtvas
gəˈvøːnt zaɪn]
usual gewohnt [gəˈvoːnt], gewöhnlich [gəˈvøːnlɪç], üblich [ˈʔyːplɪç]
usually normalerweise
[nɔˈmaːlɐvaɪzə]

V

vacation die Ferien [di ˈfeːʀiən
(ˈfeɐjən)], der Urlaub [dɐ ˈʔuɐlaʊp]
vaccination die Impfung
[di ˈʔɪmpfʊŋ]
vaccination card der Impfpass
[dɐ ˈʔɪm(p)fpas]
valid gültig [ˈgʏltɪç]
valley das Tal [das taːl]
valuables die Wertsachen
[di ˈveɐtzaxn]
vantage point der Aussichtspunkt
[dɐ ˈʔaʊsɪçtspʊŋt]
variety theatre das Varietee [das
vaʀiəˈteː]
vase die Vase [di ˈvaːzə]
vault(s) das Gewölbe [das
gəˈvœlbə]
veal das Kalbfleisch [ˈkalpflaɪʃ]
vegetables das Gemüse [das
gəˈmyːzə]
vegetarian der Vegetarier/
die Vegetarierin [dɐ vegəˈtaːʀiɐ/
di vegəˈtaːʀiəʀɪn]; *(adj)* vegetarisch
[vegəˈtaːʀɪʃ]
vending machine der Automat
[dɐ ʔautoˈmaːt]
very sehr [zeɐ]
vest das Unterhemd [das

'ʊntɛhɛmt]; *(US)* die Weste
[di 'vɛstə]

video camera die Videokamera
[di 'vi:deoˌkaməRa]

video cassette die Videokassette
[di 'vi:deokaˌsɛtə]

video film der Videofilm
[dɐ 'vi:deofɪlm]

video recorder der Videorekorder
[dɐ 'vi:deoReˌkɔɐdɐ]

view die Sicht [di zɪçt], die Aussicht [di 'ʔaʊszɪçt], der Blick
[dɐ blɪk]; *(opinion)* die Ansicht [di
'ʔanzɪçt], die Meinung [di 'maɪnʊŋ]

viewer der(Fernseh)Zuschauer/
die (Fernseh)Zuschauerin
[dɐ ('fɛɐnze)ˌtsu:ʃaʊɐ/
di ('fɛɐnze)ˌtsu:ʃaʊɐRɪn]

viewfinder der Sucher [dɐ 'zu:xɐ]

village das Dorf [das dɔɐf]

vinegar der Essig [dɐ 'ʔɛsɪç]

vineyard der Weinberg
[dɐ 'vaɪnbɛɐk]

virus das Virus [das 'vi:Rʊs]

visa das Visum [das 'vi:zʊm]

visit der Besuch [dɐ bə'zu:x]; *(vb)*
besuchen [bə'zu:xn], *(sights)*
besichtigen [bə'zɪçtɪgn]

visiting hours die Besuchszeit
[di bə'zu:xstsaɪt]

volleyball der Volleyball
[dɐ 'vɔlɪbal]

voltage die Stromspannung
[di 'ʃtRo:mˌʃpanʊŋ]

vote die Stimme [di 'ʃtɪmə]; *(vb)*
wählen ['vɛ:ln]

voucher der Gutschein
[dɐ 'gu:tʃaɪn]

voyage die Seereise [di 'ze:Raɪzə],
die Seefahrt [di 'ze:fa:t]

vulgar ordinär ['ʔɔdi'nɛ:ɐ]

waistcoat die Weste [di 'vɛstə]

wait (for) warten (auf) [va:tn
('ʔaʊf)], erwarten [ʔe'va:tn]

waiter/waitress der Kellner/die
Kellnerin [dɐ 'kɛlnɐ/di 'kɛlnɐRɪn]

waiting room das Wartezimmer
[das 'va:tətsɪmɐ], der Wartesaal
[dɐ 'va:təza:l]

wake wecken [vɛkŋ]; **wake up**
aufwachen ['ʔaʊfvaxn]

Wales Wales [wɛɪls (vɛɪls)]

walk der Spaziergang
[dɐ ʃpa'tsiɐgaŋ]; *(vb)* gehen [ge:n],
laufen [laʊfn]; **go for a walk** spazieren gehen [ʃpa'tsi:Rən ge:n],
einen Spaziergang machen [('ʔaɪn)n
ʃpa'tsiɐgaŋ maxn]

wall *(external)* die Mauer
[di 'maʊɐ]; *(internal)* die Wand
[di vant]

wallet die Brieftasche [di 'bRi:ftaʃə]

want wollen [vɔln]

ward die Station [di ʃta'tsjo:n]

warm warm [va:m]; *(regards)* herzlich ['hɛɐtslɪç]; *(vb)* wärmen
[vɛɐmn]

warning triangle das Warndreieck [das 'va:ndRaɪɛk]

wash *(vb)* waschen [vaʃn]

washbasin das Waschbecken [das
'vaʃbɛkŋ]

washing-up brush die Spülbürste
[di 'ʃpy:lbʏstə]

washroom der Waschraum
[dɐ 'vaʃRaʊm]

wasp die Wespe [di 'vɛspə]

watch die (Armband)Uhr
[di ('ʔa:mbant)ʔuɐ]; *(vb)* zuschauen
['tsu:ʃaʊn], *(observe)* beobachten
[bə'ʔo:baxtn]

watchmaker's der Uhrmacher
[dɐ 'ʔuɐmaxɐ]

water das Wasser [das 'vasɐ]

water canister der Wasserkanister
[dɐ 'vasɐkanˌɪstɐ]

water-colour (picture) das
Aquarell [das ʔakva'Rɛl]

water consumption der Wasserverbrauch [dɐ 'vasɐfɐbʀaʊx]

waterfall der Wasserfall
[dɐ 'vasɐfal]

water ski der Wasserski
[dɐ 'vasɐʃiː]; go water skiing Wasserski fahren ['vasɐʃi: 'faːʀən]

water wings die Schwimmflügel
m pl [di 'ʃvɪmflyːgl]

way *(manner)* die Weise [di 'vaɪzə];
(path) der Weg [dɐ veːk]

way in der Eingang [dɐ 'ʔaɪngan];
way out der Ausgang [dɐ 'ʔaʊsgan]

we wir [viɐ/vɐ]

weak schwach [ʃvax]

wear tragen [tʀaːgn]

weather forecast die Wettervorhersage [di 'vɛtɐfoˌheːza:gə]

wedding die Hochzeit
[di 'hɔxtsaɪt]

Wednesday Mittwoch ['mɪtvɔx]

week die Woche [di 'vɔxə]; weekly wöchentlich ['vœçntlɪç]

on weekdays wochentags
['vɔxnta:ks], werktags ['vɛɐkta:ks];

at the weekend am Wochenende
[ʔam 'vɔxn'ɛndə]

weekend rate die Wochenendpauschale [di 'vɔxn'ɛntpaʊʃa:lə]

weight das Gewicht [das gə'vɪçt]

weight training das Krafttraining
[das 'kʀaftʀɛːnɪn]

welcome *(adj, interj)* willkommen
[vɪl'kɔmm]; *(vb)* empfangen
[ʔɛmp'faŋŋ], begrüßen [bə'gʀyːsn]

well der Brunnen [dɐ bʀʊnn], *(oil)*
die (Öl)Quelle [di ('ʔøːl)'kvɛlə];
(healthy) gesund [gə'zʊnt], wohl
[voːl]; *(adv)* gut [guːt]

well-done durchgebraten
['dʊɐçgəbʀaːtn]

well-known bekannt [bə'kant]

wellingtons die Gummistiefel *m
pl* [di 'gʊmiʃti:fl]

Welsh walisisch [va'li:zɪʃ]

Welshman/Welshwoman der
Waliser/die Waliserin [dɐ va'li:zɐ/
di va'li:zəʀɪn]

west der Westen [dɐ vɛstn]

western der Western [dɐ 'vɛstɐn]

wet nass [nas]

wetsuit der Neoprenanzug
[dɐ neo'pʀeːnˌʔantsuːk]

what was [vas]

wheel das Rad [das ʀaːt]

wheelchair der Rollstuhl
[dɐ 'ʀɔlʃtuːl]

wheelchair cabin die Rollstuhlkabine [di 'ʀɔlʃtuːlkaˌbi:nə]

wheelchair user der Rollstuhl-
fahrer/die Rollstuhlfahrerin [dɐ
'ʀɔlʃtuːlˌfa:ʀɐ/di 'ʀɔlʃtuːlˌfa:ʀəʀɪn]

whether ob [ʔɔp]

while *(conj)* während ['vɛːʀənt
(veɐnt)]

whipping cream die Schlagsahne
['ʃlaːkza:nə]

white weiß [vaɪs]

white bread das Weißbrot [das
'vaɪsbʀoːt]

white wine Weißwein ['vaɪsvaɪn]

whole ganz [gants]

whooping-cough der Keuchhusten [dɐ 'kɔɪçhuːstn]

wide breit [bʀaɪt]; weit [vaɪt]

widow/widower der Witwer
[dɐ 'vɪtvɐ]/die Witwe [di 'vɪtvə]

width die Breite [di 'bʀaɪtə]

wife die Ehefrau [di 'ʔe:əfʀaʊ]

wild(ly) wild [vɪlt]

win *(vb)* gewinnen [gə'vɪnn]

wind der Wind [dɐ vɪnt]; *(med.)*
die Blähungen *f pl* [di 'blɛːʊŋŋ]

wind-force die Windstärke
[di 'vɪntʃtɛɐkə]

window das Fenster [das 'fɛnstɐ]

window seat der Fensterplatz
[dɐ 'fɛnstɐplats]

windscreen/windshield die
Windschutzscheibe [di 'vɪntʃʊtʃaɪbə]

windscreen wiper der Scheibenwischer [dɐ 'ʃaɪbmvɪʃɐ]

windsurfing das Windsurfen [das
'vɪntsœɐfn]

wine der Wein [dɐ vaɪn]

wine merchant's die Weinhandlung [di 'vaınhantlʊŋ]

wineglass das Weinglas [das 'vaıngla:s]

wing· der Flügel [də fly:gl]

winter der Winter [də 'vıntɐ]

winter tyre der Winterreifen [də 'vıntɐraıfn]

wisdom tooth der Weisheitszahn [də 'vaıshaıtsa:n]

wish for wünschen [vʏnʃn]

with mit [mıt]

without ohne [ʔo:nə]

woman die Frau [di fraʊ]

wonderful wunderbar ['vʊndeba:], toll [tɔl]

wood das Holz [das hɔlts]

wood-carving die Schnitzerei [di ʃnɪtsə'raı]

woodcut der Holzschnitt [də 'hɔltʃnɪt]

woods der Wald [də valt]

wool die Wolle [di 'vɔlə]

word das Wort [das vɔɐt]

work die Arbeit [di ʔa:baıt]; (vb) arbeiten [ʔa:baıtn], (function) funktionieren [fʊŋktsjo'ni:rən/-'niən]

world die Welt [di vɛlt]

worm der Wurm [də vʊɐm]

worry die Sorge [di 'zɔɐgə]; (vb) sich beunruhigen [zıç bə'ʔʊnrʊıgn]; be worried about sich sorgen um [zıç 'zɔɐgn ʔʊm]

worthless wertlos ['veɐtlo:s]

wound die Wunde [di 'vʊndə]

wrap einpacken [ʔaınpakŋ], verpacken [fɐ'pakŋ]

wrapping die Verpackung [di fɐ'pakʊŋ]

wristwatch die Armbanduhr [di ʔa:mbant̩ʔuɐ]

write schreiben [ʃraıbm]; write down aufschreiben [ʔaʊfʃraıbm]

in writing schriftlich ['ʃrıftlıç]

writing pad der Block [də blɔk]

writing paper das Briefpapier [das 'bri:fpapiɐ]

wrong falsch [falʃ]; be wrong sich täuschen [zıç 'tɔıʃn], Unrecht haben [ʔʊnrɛçt ha:bm]

X-ray die Röntgenaufnahme [di 'rœnçn̩ʔaʊfna:mə]; (vb) röntgen ['rœnçn̩]

Y

yard der Hof [də ho:f]; (US) der Garten [də ga:tn]

year das Jahr [das ja:]

yellow gelb [gɛlp]

yesterday gestern ['gɛstɐn]; the day before yesterday vorgestern ['fɔɐgɛstɐn]

yet (adv) noch [nɔx]; (conj) doch [dɔx]

yoga das Yoga [das 'jo:ga]

yoghurt der Joghurt [də 'jo:gʊɐt]

you du [du:], dich [dıç], dir [diɐ]; ihr [ʔiɐ], euch [ʔɔıç]; Sie [zi:], Ihnen [ʔi:nn]

young jung [jʊŋ]

your dein [daın], euer [ʔɔıɐ], Ihr [ʔiɐ]

Z

zoo der Zoo [də tso:]